PRAISE FOR *THE GHOST FOREST*

"*The Ghost Forest* is *the* book I've long wished someone would write, and Greg King has done it luminously well. He tells the epic story of the destruction of 96 percent of the primeval redwoods in California—including the criminal and bankrupt horrors of 'liquidation logging' done in the 1980s and 90s by corporate raider Charles Hurwitz and the Maxxam Corporation. And he tells the story of activists and protesting tree climbers (including himself) who put their lives on the line to save the Headwaters Forest Reserve, a jewel of the redwood realm."

—Richard Preston, author of *The Wild Trees* and *The Hot Zone*

"The farther I traveled into *The Ghost Forest* the more convinced I became I was reading an epic. It is encyclopedic in historical knowledge and detail, deeply felt in its love of redwood country, and fierce in its passion for saving the last remnants of old growth forest from rapacious and unconstrained capitalism."

—Charles Frazier, author of *Cold Mountain* and *The Trackers*

"*Ghost Forest* is a haunting requiem for one of Earth's magnificent forests. Human survival has rested on our ability to recognize opportunity by exploiting the planet's abundance. Once armed with fossil fuels and machines, we have felled entire ecosystems to serve our limitless demands. King's feelings of awe, humility, and love before giant redwoods are needed to slake our drawdown of the rest of nature."

—David Suzuki, OBE, international climate activist and author of *Tree: A Life Story*

"King is an American hero. And he has written a heroic book—a book befitting the California redwoods, which are the tallest, the oldest, and arguably the most magnificent creatures on the planet. *The Ghost Forest* is a stunning work: beautifully written, exquisitely researched, compelling, funny, angry, poetic, cynical, idealistic, and always fascinating. King's important reinterpretation of the history of the Save-the-Redwoods League reads like a detective novel. We are all in King's debt for having the courage to tell his story, and to tell it so beautifully."

—Jonathan Spiro, author of *Defending the Master Race*

"In this combination of memoir and investigative report, King, veteran of the Northern California timber wars, evokes the spirit of the long-gone fog shrouded giants that fell to axe and saw. He paints a picture both inspiring and disturbing of the heroic forest defenders, the intractable timber beasts, and the nefarious opportunists that played the two sides against each other for their own profit. He takes us on one final journey across the sacred ground where the great booming forests once stood and are now lost forever."

—Will Russell, professor of environmental studies, San Jose State University

"This book is the story of one man's fight to save the planet's tallest trees. As a young man, King risked everything to stop logging companies from hacking down the last big California redwoods. *The Ghost Forest* brilliantly recounts his odyssey to make sense of the millennial mystery and modern history of the great forest. It's an unforgettable story, and one more necessary than ever with the future of the earth itself under threat."

—Orin Starn, professor of history, Duke University, and author of *Ishi's Brain*

"*The Ghost Forest* is a tale both infuriating and inspiring. It covers the destruction of California's redwood forests, told from a perspective that could not be more up close and personal. From its gripping opening scene of activist vs logger, to its unfolding story of the magnificent trees themselves, the book rushes with the energy of a river in spring. All of us who care about the future of human existence on the planet, and who want to understand the ways in which that future can be compromised, need to read this story."

—Bruce Cockburn, international music star, author of *Rumours of Glory*

"Writing about redwoods is hard because of the ancient forest's unimaginable grandeur, in space and time, and because of the sickening violence and waste of its almost complete destruction in less than two centuries. Greg King has written about it exceptionally well, and with good cause. Having grown up in the "Redwood Empire," he has spent much of his life exploring the forest, on the ground and in libraries. He knows the tangled politics of forest destruction and protection in great detail from personal participation and observation. He has risked his life more than once to find and help save significant "last stands" like the Headwaters Forest. And he writes about it all with poetic fervor, scientific precision, political wisdom, and a droll, self-deprecating sense of humor that brings the adventuresome days of Earth First! and tree-sits to life with a clarity that is in wonderfully refreshing contrast to the muddle of mass media coverage."

—David Rains Wallace, author of *The Klamath Knot*

"The Ghost Forest is long overdue. The book is a page-turner, a calibrated adventure of the highest sort. At last we have a comprehensive accounting of the entire ancient redwood ecosystem that once stood, who cut it down, and who stepped up to save these fabulous trees—a story necessarily written by the most committed of redwood defenders. I have followed Greg King's work since 1987, just after he left a successful career as a journalist to lead an audacious fight for the last redwoods. Yet it is this journalist's eye for detail, and for the complex history of redwood logging and protection, that makes *The Ghost Forest* such an important contributor to the canon of American conservation."

—Yvon Chouinard, founder, Patagonia, Inc.

"The Ghost Forest captures the adventure and dangers of early redwood exploration and the evolution of a modern preservationist from an insider's perspective. Here Greg King explores threatened historic redwood groves which had never been seen before, and brings to life untold stories of the fight to preserve these last forests."

—Erv Peterson, Professor Emeritus, Environmental Studies, Sonoma State University

THE GHOST
FOREST

THE GHOST FOREST

Racists, Radicals, and Real Estate
in the California Redwoods

GREG KING

PUBLICAFFAIRS

New York

PublicAffairs
Hachette Book Group
1290 Avenue of the Americas, New York, NY 10104
www.publicaffairsbooks.com
@Public_Affairs

Printed in the United States of America

First Edition: June 2023

Published by PublicAffairs, an imprint of Perseus Books, LLC, a subsidiary of Hachette
Book Group, Inc. The PublicAffairs name and logo is a trademark of the Hachette
Book Group.

The Hachette Speakers Bureau provides a wide range of authors for speaking events. To
find out more, go to www.hachettespeakersbureau.com or call (866) 376-6591.

PublicAffairs books may be purchased in bulk for business, educational, or promotional
use. For information, please contact your local bookseller or Hachette Book Group Special
Markets Department at special.markets@hbgusa.com.

The publisher is not responsible for websites (or their content) that are not owned by the
publisher.

"The Earth Falls Down," from *The Complete Poems* by Anne Sexton. Copyright © 1981 by
Linda Gray Sexton and Loring Conant, Jr., executors of the will of Anne Sexton. Used by
permission of HarperCollins Publishers.

Print book interior design by Amy Quinn.

Library of Congress Control Number: 2023931381

ISBNs: 9781541768673 (hardcover), 9781541768666 (ebook)

LSC-C

Printing 1, 2023

For my parents

Something will have gone out of us as a people if we ever let the remaining wilderness be destroyed; if we permit the last virgin forests to be turned into comic books and plastic cigarette cases; if we drive the few remaining members of the wild species into zoos or to extinction; if we pollute the last clear air and dirty the last clean streams and push our paved roads through the last of the silence, so that never again will Americans be free in their own country from the noise, the exhausts, the stinks of human and automotive waste. And so that never again can we have the chance to see ourselves single, separate, vertical and individual in the world, part of the environment of trees and rocks and soil, brother to the other animals, part of the natural world and competent to belong in it.

—Wallace Stegner

For Man is God
and man is eating the earth up
like a candy bar
and not one of them can be left alone with the ocean
for it is known he will gulp it all down.
The stars (possibly) are safe.

—Anne Sexton

CONTENTS

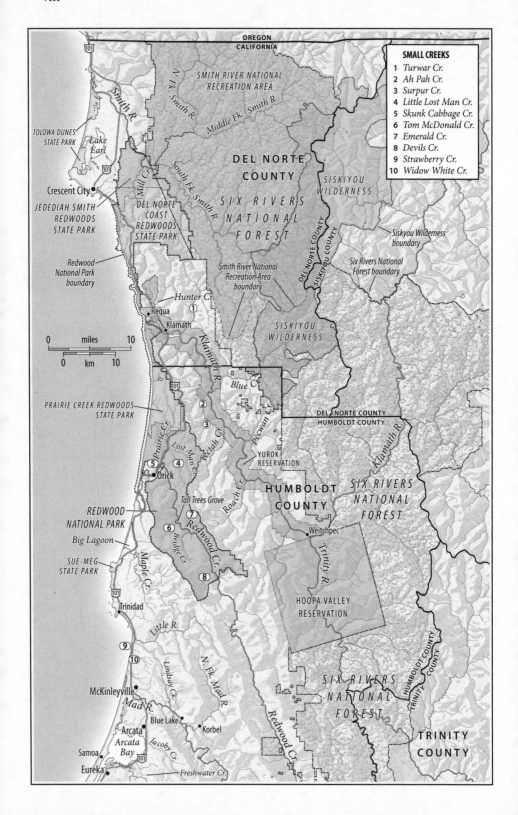

OREGON
CALIFORNIA

SMITH RIVER NATIONAL
RECREATION AREA

N. Fk. Smith R.

Middle Fk. Smith R.

TOLOWA DUNES
STATE PARK

Lake
Earl

DEL NORTE
COUNTY

SIX RIVERS
NATIONAL
FOREST

SISKIYOU
WILDERNESS

Crescent City

Mill Cr.

South Fk. Smith R.

JEDEDIAH SMITH
REDWOODS
STATE PARK

DEL NORTE
COAST
REDWOODS
STATE PARK

Smith River National
Recreation Area
boundary

DEL NORTE COUNTY

SISKIYOU COUNTY

Siskiyou Wilderness
boundary

Six Rivers National
Forest boundary

Redwood
National Park
boundary

Hunter Cr.

Requa ①

Klamath

SISKIYOU
WILDERNESS

Klamath R.

miles

km

Blue Cr.

PRAIRIE CREEK REDWOODS
STATE PARK

②

③

Prairie Cr.

Lost Man Cr.

Redel Cr.

Pecwan Cr.

DEL NORTE COUNTY
HUMBOLDT COUNTY

YUROK
RESERVATION

⑤

④

Orick

Tall Trees Grove

⑦

Roach Cr.

Klamath R.

HUMBOLDT
COUNTY

SIX RIVERS
NATIONAL
FOREST

REDWOOD
NATIONAL PARK

Big Lagoon

SUE-MEG
STATE PARK

⑥

⑧

Bridge Cr.

Redwood Cr.

Weitchpec

Trinity R.

HOOPA VALLEY
RESERVATION

Trinidad

Maple Cr.

Little R.

⑨

⑩

Lindsay Cr.

N. Fk. Mad R.

McKinleyville

Mad R.

Blue Lake

Korbel

SIX RIVERS
NATIONAL
FOREST

Redwood Cr.

HUMBOLDT COUNTY

TRINITY COUNTY

Arcata

Arcata
Bay

Jacoby Cr.

Samoa

Eureka

Freshwater Cr.

TRINITY
COUNTY

SMALL CREEKS

1 Turwar Cr.
2 Ah Pah Cr.
3 Surpur Cr.
4 Little Lost Man Cr.
5 Skunk Cabbage Cr.
6 Tom McDonald Cr.
7 Emerald Cr.
8 Devils Cr.
9 Strawberry Cr.
10 Widow White Cr.

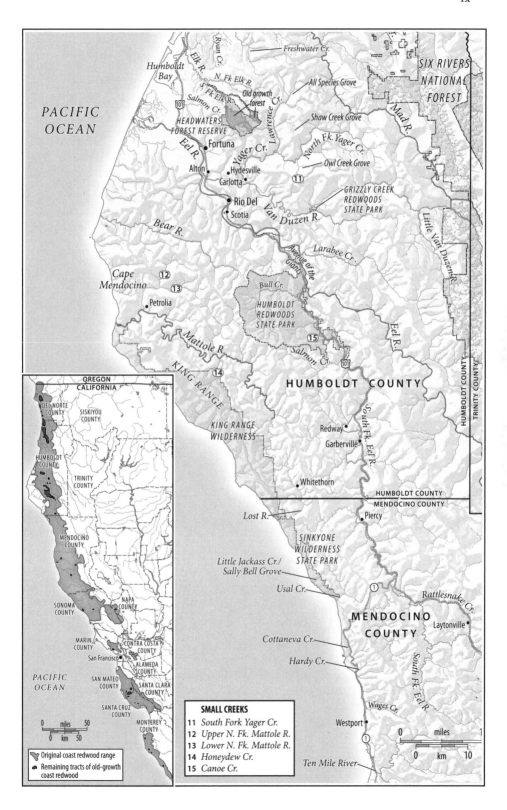

PACIFIC OCEAN

SIX RIVERS NATIONAL FOREST

Humboldt Bay

Freshwater Cr.

Elk R.
Ryan Cr.
N. Fk Elk R.
All Species Grove
Mad R.
S. Fk Elk R.
Old growth forest
Salmon Cr.
Lawrence Cr.
Shaw Creek Grove
HEADWATERS FOREST RESERVE
Eel R.
Fortuna
Yager Cr.
North Fk. Yager Cr.
Alton
Hydesville
Owl Creek Grove
Carlotta
⑪
Rio Del
Scotia
Van Duzen R.
GRIZZLY CREEK REDWOODS STATE PARK
Little Van Duzen R.

Bear R.
Larabee Cr.
Avenue of the Giants
Cape Mendocino
⑫
⑬
Bull Cr.
Eel R.
Petrolia
HUMBOLDT REDWOODS STATE PARK
Mattole R.
⑮
Salmon Cr.
KING RANGE
⑭
101

HUMBOLDT COUNTY
HUMBOLDT COUNTY
TRINITY COUNTY

KING RANGE WILDERNESS
Redway
Garberville
South Fk. Eel R.
Whitethorn

HUMBOLDT COUNTY
MENDOCINO COUNTY

Lost R.
Piercy
SINKYONE WILDERNESS STATE PARK
Little Jackass Cr./ Sally Bell Grove
Usal Cr.
Rattlesnake Cr.
①
MENDOCINO COUNTY
Laytonville
Cottaneva Cr.
Hardy Cr.
South Fk. Eel R.
Wages Cr.
Westport
①
Ten Mile River
0 miles 1
0 km 10

OREGON
CALIFORNIA

DEL NORTE COUNTY
SISKIYOU COUNTY
HUMBOLDT COUNTY
TRINITY COUNTY
MENDOCINO COUNTY
SONOMA COUNTY
NAPA COUNTY
MARIN COUNTY
CONTRA COSTA COUNTY
San Francisco
ALAMEDA COUNTY
SAN MATEO COUNTY
SANTA CLARA COUNTY
SANTA CRUZ COUNTY
MONTEREY COUNTY
PACIFIC OCEAN

0 miles 50
0 km 50

🌲 Original coast redwood range
🐚 Remaining tracts of old-growth coast redwood

SMALL CREEKS
11 *South Fork Yager Cr.*
12 *Upper N. Fk. Mattole R.*
13 *Lower N. Fk. Mattole R.*
14 *Honeydew Cr.*
15 *Canoe Cr.*

PROLOGUE

I SPENT THE SUMMER OF 1990 "HIDING OUT" AT MY PARENTS' MODEST home in western Sonoma County. At twenty-nine years old I'd landed back at the family abode after my two closest colleagues had been violently attacked and almost killed for attempting to protect redwood forests. I had a target on my back. So, hunkered in a nook on the back deck, thwacking an ancient Smith Corona like Jack Nicholson in *The Shining*, I began to write the first drafts of the story that would become part of this book. The process was cathartic, the prose near gibberish.

Over the ensuing years I picked up the thread a few times, only to shelve it. These iterations focused on the political and often physical struggle, during the 1980s and 1990s, to protect redwood habitats, in particular the three-thousand-acre Headwaters Forest, in Humboldt County, then the largest virgin redwood grove remaining in private ownership. In 1985 Headwaters Forest and thousands of acres of surrounding redwood lands were bought up for liquidation by a Houston company after a junk-bond-fueled corporate takeover. The epic struggle to save Headwaters Forest would generate headlines throughout the world. It was a big story. The version of the story I wrote, though, seemed somehow untethered. The anchor, it turned out, was history.

Beneath the surface of the fight to save Headwaters Forest emerged a much broader struggle. Headwaters was by no means a footnote. But what occurred there, and throughout the California Northwest during the last two decades of the twentieth century, is only really explicable if set in the context of western development since the 1850s. This book presents this history in its entirety, for the first time, and in doing so dissolves the many tropes and fallacies that have shrouded and obscured the true history of redwood logging and preservation efforts.

During the early 2000s I began the process of uncovering redwood history by gathering the stories of aging activists who had spent years in the trenches of the previous redwood battle—the movement to create a Redwood National Park during the 1960s and 1970s. Then, by a happy coincidence, during the 2010s archivists at the University of California (UC), Berkeley's Bancroft Library began organizing and curating a particularly revealing trove of hundreds of thousands of pages of primary documents. The Bancroft papers had been generated by an organization launched in 1917, when three prominent "men of science" met with titans of American commerce at an exclusive Sonoma County retreat and created a new organization that would dedicate itself, on paper, to "saving the redwoods." The collection unveiled an authentic yet unreported history of redwood liquidation.

At Bancroft I copied nearly ten thousand pages of the newly curated archive. These papers, alongside hundreds of other sources, demonstrate how and why American industry, even in the face of virulent public outrage, was able to clear-cut all but 4 percent of the original two-million-acre redwood ecosystem in what amounts to an ecological instant. After years of connecting dots, as with pointillism, a picture formed of a corporate shell game that stands out as one of the most tragic cons in American history.

A puzzling though prominent thread that ran through the Bancroft archive was the crossover between the leadership of this new organization and that of an emerging field called eugenics—or "scientific racism"—a pseudoscience rooted in a venomous strain of white supremacy that would eventually inform the Holocaust. This finding seemed important, and I have explored it here in detail.

To make sense of these interconnected but at times distinctive threads, I have broken this book into five primary sections.

Part One, "Stumps," explores the ancient redwoods of the lower Russian River, a western snake of a stream in my homeland of Sonoma County. The river's banks once grew crowded with some of the greatest collections of trees to have ever stood on planet Earth. This entire forest, more than one hundred thousand acres, had been eliminated well before my grandfather was born alongside the Russian River in 1903. Part One concludes during the mid-1980s, when my career as a reporter led me far deeper into the redwood story than I had ever expected to go.

Part Two, "Empire," tramps back in time, to the mid-nineteenth century, when the redwood belt north of Sonoma County remained wholly intact and in the public domain. Within a few decades, nearly all of these forestlands would be privatized, primarily through illegal acquisition and consolidation of US land grants. The notorious timber thefts gave corporations total control and ownership of nearly the entire redwood timber inventory, which in turn fed metastasizing levels of industrial growth in the West and throughout much of the country.

Part Three, "A League of Their Own," opens during World War I, when American capitalists were preparing to take hold of a greater stake in world markets that would inevitably follow the conflict then devastating Europe. The men of industry looked to the 1.2 million acres of redwood then still standing in California's northwesternmost counties—Mendocino, Humboldt, and Del Norte—as an irreplaceable building block of empire, alongside finance, water, petroleum, electricity, land, ore, and labor. Yet, at the same time, public efforts dedicated to protecting these primordial treasures were likewise growing in numbers and sophistication. A counteroffensive would be needed to usurp these movements and thereby ensure an unfettered flow of redwood products for industrial uses. The leading champion of this counteroffensive would emerge and grow in San Francisco alongside the offices of redwood producers and industrial redwood consumers. This champion created the nation's first and most successful example of a phenomenon that today we call "greenwashing," leaving a massive paper trail that would keep me in thrall for years.

Part Four, "The Empire Strikes Back," returns to the struggle to save Headwaters Forest and other redwood habitats from a warlike devastation that was perpetrated by major corporations and facilitated by the state. The rending of precious habitat would be mirrored by attacks against Americans who would dare attempt to save our last ancient redwoods. These attacks would be overlooked and enabled by those charged with protecting Americans from violence and upholding our constitutional right of dissent.

Part Five, "Home," follows a tornado and reminds us again that Dorothy was right.

In this book I present the most comprehensive account yet available of one of the world's greatest natural phenomena—the unique redwood belt—and the multigenerational efforts to exploit virtually the entire redwood biome in service of the manufacture of American empire.

Part One

STUMPS

This long connection of a family with one spot, as its place of birth and burial, creates a kindred between the human being and the locality, quite independent of any charm in the scenery or moral circumstances that surround him. It is not love, but instinct.

—*Nathaniel Hawthorne*

Wilderness begins in your own backyard.

—*Edgar Wayburn*

1

FOR MY FIFTH BIRTHDAY WE WOULD JOURNEY TO THE KINGDOM OF giant stumps. They stood just down the hill, and downriver from us, about a half mile away at the Clar Ranch, in my hometown of Guerneville. Why my parents chose the Clar Ranch for this particular birthday, on June 19, 1966, is a detail lost to time. We weren't particularly close to the Clars, though our families had been friends and acquaintances since 1877, when Ivon Clar landed in western Sonoma County from Santa Barbara, four years after my ancestors arrived from Canada. I do remember being excited to see the stumps.

In 1966 my birthday fell on Father's Day, so we celebrated both. My mom, Jessie, wore light pants and a floral blouse. She spun her ink-black hair into the beehive fashion of the day, then darted across our angular ranch house, tending to my little sister, Laura, not yet two years old, while gathering games and food. Mom stuffed party favors into paper bags she'd colored and inscribed with the names of each child. Anna, my older sister by eighteen months, stood in the living room, hands on hips, ostensibly in charge.

My dad, Tom, stacked firewood, then stepped inside to prep for the party. Dad was only thirty-two years old, but his impeccable banker's hair was already silver, a gift of the Irish. When Dad finished outside, he shed his "grubbies" and donned the summer uniform: white shorts, crewneck, and tennies. He popped the front trunk of our black 1960 Volkswagen Beetle, filled it with party goods, plopped Laura ignominiously into the "back of the backseat," and zipped us down the short, steep pitch of Birkhofer Hill to low-lying Drake Road.

Like most things in Guerneville, the Clar Ranch wasn't far away—a few hundred yards west on Drake Road to State Highway 116, then a quick jaunt southward, and we were there. Before it belonged to the Clar family, the land, like nearly every stitch of dirt along the lower Russian River, had held magnificent groves of ancient redwoods. In their grandeur the redwoods, individually and as a distinctly singular forest, had stood boldly as one of nature's greatest displays of breadth and three-dimensionality. Before Guerneville was Guerneville, great trees had glutted the landscape like candles on an octogenarian's cake.

Ivon Clar had purchased his ranch around 1890, after it was logged. To earn a living, he'd spent long days splitting thousands of shingles from the remaining stumps. For some reason Clar left several impressive examples of the former forest near his farmhouse. In 1966, and today, these edifices remained solid. To a five-year-old the stumps were magical spirits from a mythical kingdom. Amid the massive leavings, a dozen "river rat" progeny, mostly towheads, climbed, encircled, and hid behind the stumps. Other than this misty image, only one other memory stands out from that day: the moment that my friend Herbie, as we stood with the other kids atop what seemed an impossibly high stump, pushed me off.

I see the stump from which Herbie ejected my urchin self as standing ten feet above the ground, twenty feet across—room enough for twice as many children, or even a small cabin. The top was spongy and layered with viridescent mosses. My flight from the stump remains dreamlike, ceaseless, my hands rope burned from a hanging redwood branch that drooped from a nearby second-growth tree and slowed my descent.

Sonoma County's redwoods were among the widest and the tallest trees ever to have stood on earth. Many were wider than twenty feet. At one time Guerneville was known as "Stumptown," until the villagers, in 1870, changed the name in honor of the man who owned the largest redwood mill in the region. But the stumps remained ubiquitous, and the town simply grew up around them. Occasionally buildings and even roads were built atop the stumps. During the 1970s, workers installing Guerneville's first sewage system learned the hard way about the buried stumps when their trenchers ran into them. The stumps were as solid as the day they were cut, and the price of laying pipe doubled.

No doubt many visitors puzzled over the name "Stumptown," for nary a stump nor even a tree stood downtown after the mid-twentieth century. Before white settlers first occupied the lower Russian River, around 1860, the redwood forests were forever deep, cool, and moist, running along wide river flats for nearly thirty miles to the coast. The forest coated slopes and dominated streams that almost never saw sun. Forty years later, the great trees were gone. A forest without peer had been erased without pause. By the mid-1960s, tourists would again see green hillsides surrounding the town, but these were second-growth redwoods, as well as Douglas fir and hardwoods.

Today we know nearly nothing about the Guerneville redwoods or about similar though distinctive primordial realms that collectively made up the original coast redwood ecosystem. The natural redwood range covers an area of about 2 million acres. The forest follows a narrow band along California's coastal mountains for 450 miles, from Big Sur to a point 20 miles north of the Oregon border, never growing more than 30 miles inland.

Thanks largely to an accident of economics, a few small remnant groves of ancient redwood still stand, comprising almost eighty thousand acres, or about 4 percent of the original ecosystem. The redwood forest is a world fantastically alive. John Steinbeck called redwoods "a stunning memory of what the world was like once long ago."

Redwoods began evolving two hundred million years ago, at the beginning of the early Jurassic period, arriving just after the dinosaurs. They survived the breakup of the supercontinent Pangaea and continental drift, and they managed to withstand, escape, and evolve within raging climatological shifts. Sixty-six million years ago, when the Chicxulub meteor wiped out the dinosaurs and 75 percent of all life on Earth, redwoods prevailed and then thrived. To withstand ongoing reorganizations of climate, redwoods migrated. Today redwood fossils are found throughout the Northern Hemisphere. Tourists in the eastern foothills of the Rocky Mountains might visit a small group of large fossilized redwood stumps, at eighty-two hundred feet elevation, at the Florissant Fossil Beds National Monument in Colorado. The stumps are thirty-four million years old.

Eventually the redwood family split into three genera. Coast redwood, the "ever-living" *Sequoia sempervirens*, remains the only species of the *Sequoia* genus. Several small islands of the coast redwood's cousin, the giant sequoia (*Sequoiadendron giganteum*), still stand in the Sierra Nevada mountains and are major tourist attractions due to their otherworldly sizes. The redwood's true ancestor, the dawn redwood, or *Metasequoia glyptostroboides*, was long believed extinct until a small pocket of the trees was rediscovered in south-central

China in the 1940s. Once the coast redwoods settled along a tiny sliver of coastline in North America, they withstood cataclysmic earthquakes, epochal floods, raging wildfires, and hurricane winds—and prospered.

Nearly all of the ancient redwood inventory that stands today is found principally in five state parks (Jedediah Smith Redwoods, Del Norte Coast Redwoods, Prairie Creek Redwoods, Humboldt Redwoods, and Big Basin), Redwood National Park, and the federally managed Headwaters Forest Reserve. All except Big Basin, near Santa Cruz, are in Humboldt and Del Norte counties. No grove larger than 500 acres stands between the southernmost park, Big Basin, and the next one north, Humboldt Redwoods, a distance of three hundred miles. Perhaps most extraordinary about this grim statistic is that today in Mendocino County—where once 640,000 acres of ancient redwood grew in an unbroken band eighty-five miles long—fewer than 1,000 acres of the original forest remain.

The scattered archipelago of remaining ancient redwood islands provides sensational aesthetics and critical habitat—endangered marbled murrelets, for instance, would today be far closer to extinction were these redwood groves not available to them—but they are vestiges all the same. They stand as tiny remnants that remain vulnerable to "edge effect" from heavy and widespread industrial logging that continues to surround them. Climate change is already threatening the groves, as terrain dries and fog diminishes. In 2020, two of the preserved groves, Big Basin in Santa Cruz and Armstrong Woods in Guerneville, burned throughout, though not catastrophically at Armstrong Woods. The results are not in at Big Basin, which largely burned to a crisp, though, incredibly, most of the redwoods survived. Redwoods are generally fire resistant, thanks to thick bark and lack of resin. Yet even this hearty tree can withstand only so much scorching.

A walk through an ancient redwood grove remains a moving, even life-changing journey. It's not just the size of the extraordinary trees but their collectivity and dominance that awe the wayfarer. It's the absolute, even mystical quiet of place, under which an impossibly high canopy extinguishes sky and presents a prehistoric remnant of a twilight millions of years old. The breadth and history of the great forests are palpable, tidings from another dimension.

From an ecological perspective, the ancient redwoods that remain today stand as living artifacts, almost museum pieces, whose long-term survival is not a given. Tramping these worlds, the end of the redwood rope is quickly reached. The groves give us an idea of the original redwood ecosystem in the way a child's face reminds us of her grandparents. For the most part we can only guess at what was lost. Like our human ancestors, the true spirit of the ancient redwoods reaches us primarily as specter, or perhaps rumor.

The redwoods were in the wrong place at the wrong time. Redwood lumber was too fine, useful, and available to be saved from the grasp of industry. The rise of the United States, and especially of the western states, to world economic and military dominance was paved, sometimes literally, with the life of the redwood forest. Old-growth redwood produced mostly "clear" lumber products, meaning it was largely free of knots and straight grained. The wood was strong yet light, beautiful. No lumber was more versatile. Redwood lumber resists rot and pest infestations, and it can last for centuries. Timbers used by the Russian military to build Fort Ross, on the Sonoma Coast in 1812, today remain sound.

The northern redwood belt, which ranges from Sonoma County to the Oregon border, produced spectacular volumes of high-grade lumber. Most redwoods stood under twenty feet across, but some were much larger and reached widths of thirty feet. (My *house* is thirty feet wide.) One tree might have a diameter of twenty feet and stand near a twelve-footer, not far from a sixteen, with a smattering of babies (four to six feet) just to offer scale. And that's just one family. A stone's toss will reach another such clump. The scale of growth was far out of proportion to anything humans have ever known anywhere else on earth.

Redwoods grow so tall that a person standing in the middle of the forest rarely sees the treetops. Lack of light below the canopy renders lower branches superfluous, so the first branch might be 150 feet, sometimes more than 200 feet, above the ground. The trees are ancient. A nineteenth-century history compiled by Santa Rosa attorney Thomas Jefferson Butts claims that a redwood cut down along the Russian River, sometime in the 1870s, was thirty-three hundred years old.

Butts lived in Guerneville at the time. During the second half of the nineteenth century, Guerneville ranked second only to Eureka, in Humboldt County, as a supplier of redwood products. After counting the rings of this tree, Butts reported that the redwood was seventeen feet in diameter "when Christ was upon the earth." Its diameter was only twenty-three feet two thousand years later, meaning that the tree had put on just one inch of width every thirty years.

An 1895 edition of the trade journal *Pacific Coast Wood and Iron* carried an essay in which Butts claims that the old redwood was also "the largest tree that ever grew in Sonoma County, so far as is known. . . . It was chopped down by a man by the name of [William] English, and was manufactured into shingles of which it made upwards of 600,000." The key phrase here may be "so far as is known." Butts explains that very little witnessing for future generations occurred among the men who cut down these trees.

Three years later Butts ran his essay in the 1898 edition of Reynolds & Proctor's *Atlas of Sonoma County*. Here the author either corrects or embellishes the earlier piece. In the *Atlas* version, the great Russian River redwood would have yielded 150,000 board feet of lumber and earned English $3,000. (It took English two years to chop his 600,000 shingles, and he became prosperous in the process.) The exact number is unimportant, though I'm inclined to believe the larger figure. For instance, in 1876 a travel writer for the *Cincinnati Gazette* toured the West and somehow found his way to Guerneville. In what amounted to a footnote, the reporter noted that "one tree, and I helped to measure it, will cut 240,000 feet of inch boards, nearly all clear lumber." We have no idea where this astonishing tree stood or who cut and milled it.

Such a figure boggles the mind. During the latter half of the nineteenth century, the best of the East's remaining great pine forests produced 30,000 board feet *per acre*. Yet a single redwood that clocked 240,000 board feet, while not necessarily common, was certainly a regular discovery.

In his 1952 study, *100 Years of the Redwood Lumber Industry*, historian H. Brett Melendy notes, "The maximum volume known for [a single] coast redwood is 361,366 board feet, sufficient lumber for twenty-two five-room bungalows." Yet even this extraordinary figure requires updating. A redwood discovered in 2014, and still standing in one of the northern parks, may hold more than four hundred thousand board feet of lumber volume. Somehow Melendy missed the Lindsay Creek tree, which grew along a riparian flat just above the Mad River, in Humboldt County. According to an elderly logger, interviewed in 1971, the Lindsay Creek tree, at 390 feet tall and 34 feet in diameter at the base, contained a science-fictional tally of more than one million board feet of lumber. It was the largest known single-stem tree ever to have stood on planet Earth. Today the Lindsay Creek stump remains in place, still sound.

The "Church of One Tree," built in 1873, rose entirely from lumber milled out of one of history's well-referenced redwoods. This great conifer stood 275 feet tall and was 18 feet in diameter, according to historical records. It grew on the Guerneville "Big Bottom," an ancient river oxbow that drained when a natural levee breached some seven thousand years ago. Once dry, the south-facing plain held dozens of feet of silty soil that gathered airborne redwood seeds and grew a forest that, measured in volume and sheer physical grandeur, was equaled by just two other sites in the world, both of them in Humboldt County. When the levee broke it left a high, straight riverbank that, once logged, is where Guerneville pioneers built their town.

No tree grows taller than the coast redwood. The tallest measured tree found on the Big Bottom—and here I emphasize *measured*, for very few redwoods actually were—was affectionately known to locals as the "Monarch of the Forest." This grand spire topped out at 367.7 feet—62 feet taller than the Statue of Liberty. (In 1963, the National Geographic Society would announce discovery of the "world's tallest tree," on Redwood Creek in Humboldt County, which measured 367.8 feet.) Sometime in the 1870s, loggers felled the Monarch of the Forest along Fife Creek, near the present-day Guerneville Safeway, where I worked as a teenager.

There is little doubt that trees taller than the Monarch once stood on the Big Bottom and at less prominent sites along the lower Russian River and elsewhere in the redwood range that were witnessed only by timber workers. Some Russian River redwoods may have reached or exceeded 400 feet. In 1889, the *Humboldt Times* noted a redwood on Elk River that loggers claimed was 424 feet tall when they brought it down in 1886.

2

W HEN HE LIVED IN GUERNEVILLE DURING THE 1870S, THOMAS JEF-
ferson Butts worked as a logger and studied law. He reported on many
big trees, several of which he helped fell, including one near Guerneville that
was "22 feet in diameter, and was perfectly round and without blemish. The
bark on this tree was 14 inches thick, and in 1869 a ring of bark 4 feet long
was stripped from this tree and taken to New York" to be put on display.
In the redwood forest, even the dead trees—called snags—are spectacular.
Butts wrote of "the dead stub of a once mighty tree" that grew alongside the
Russian River. "This stub, long before the advent of civilized man into the
country, was broken off about 200 feet from the ground and was 10 feet in
diameter at the break. It was hollowed out like a huge flue or chimney. The
writer and another party felled this stub about fifteen years ago and manufactured from it over $900 worth of shakes and other products."

Butts found his trees primarily in an area that would soon be called Russian River Station—a place that no longer exists, but I know where it is.

During the late nineteenth century, the Northwestern Pacific Railroad
ran from Sausalito through western Marin and Sonoma counties until
reaching the Russian River five miles downstream of Guerneville, near the
small town of Monte Rio. Russian River Station primarily served the redwood timber industry, but even as early as the 1870s, Bay Area tourists made
the long journey by train to swim in the sparkling Russian River and see the
majestic, and doomed, ancient redwoods that stood along its banks. As it
happens, Russian River Station also stood at the heart of an eleven-hundred-
acre expanse of redwood forestland that was owned by my ancestors.

The low-lying and easily accessed groves on the property were logged
in the 1870s and 1880s, before my great-great-uncle Thomas King and his
partner, John Starrett, purchased the land around 1890. Yet the hillsides and

small tributaries remained coated in great redwoods. King and Starrett built their mill at Russian River Station. Lumber produced by the partners traveled swiftly along sleek rails to a burgeoning Bay Area and beyond.

Both King and Starrett were inveterate timbermen. The longtime friends hailed from large Canadian families that had spent the previous two generations clearing the Canadian wilderness outpost of Spencerville, Ontario, of its great pine and oak forests. Thomas King's grandfather, also Thomas, an English loyalist, had emigrated from Castleblayney, Ireland, to Canada in 1823 to take title to a 190-acre British Crown land grant, which the government awarded to settlers who would provide lumber for warships and merchant vessels.

The Thomas King who immigrated to Sonoma County in 1873 was one of four King brothers who, in the chain-migration pattern of the day, uprooted for the new land of American promise. Six siblings would remain in Canada. Thomas, William, and James King arrived in Sonoma County together that year, and a younger brother, my great-grandfather David, joined them in 1887. They were following their uncle John King, the son of Thomas and Margaret. During the late 1860s John King had settled in Westport, north of Fort Bragg in Mendocino County, to log the redwoods there.

On my wall hangs a black-and-white photo of the four King brothers. In late May 1915, they posed for Monte Rio photographer J. B. Rhea. The aging men stand shoulder to shoulder in front of redwood branches blurred by breeze. Rhea was photographing a King-Starrett family reunion, "the first time in 47 years that the Starrett family had gathered together, and 25 years since the King family had been together," reported the Petaluma *Daily Morning Courier*. More than fifty relatives attended. In the photo the King men are grizzled, grim faces pocked and etched. No one is smiling. Brow lines break like ocean surf to full heads of hair. They're lean in Sunday-best suits, ties, and collared white dress shirts.

Only David King does not wear a vest. A dress coat, rarely worn and too large, hangs off his rounded shoulders. It may have belonged to someone else. David's tie is oddly striped, poorly knotted, and doesn't reach his navel. He is the shortest, youngest, and evidently the least prosperous, the only King brother who failed to amass a small fortune.

David and his wife, Annie, did own land along the Russian River, in Monte Rio. They called it "King's Grove" and offered "boating, fishing and swimming," along with "tents and camping space to let by the day, week or month." They bought the land, four riverfront lots cleared of redwoods, in 1907, for $150. My grandfather, Tom King, and his siblings, John and Lorabelle, were all born in David and Lora's small redwood home across the dirt highway. My father was born there, too, in 1934.

James, to David's right in the photo, is the tallest of the brothers, standing about six feet. He wears a walrus mustache and pince-nez. He'd traveled for the event from his large dairy and poultry ranch in western Petaluma, in southern Sonoma County. He'd wanted nothing to do with the unwieldy redwoods.

On the right side of the photo is William King. He stands dapper, implacable in a tailored suit with a fine, stiff white collar. A gold watch chain loops from his vest and disappears under a pocket square. He glances away from the camera, as if distracted, or bored. Of the four brothers, William, or "Billie" to his friends and political cronies, was most successful. For many years William King served as Sonoma County deputy assessor, then as county supervisor. He was smart, smooth, and popular. He'd amassed nearly two thousand acres of prime ranch and timber land in the hills of Cazadero. The land is still called the King Ranch, though by now it's subdivided into "ranchettes" and vineyards. You get there by driving the labyrinthine King Ridge Road.

Austin Creek, which runs through the middle of "town," defines the Cazadero territory. It's a large stream, clear with deep pools, popular with swimmers and vacationers and the few year-round residents who call it home. The westernmost stands of the Russian River's redwoods grow on Austin Creek, and today a few examples of the river's original redwood forest still hug the flats of this fine stream. The trees were initially preserved by members of the prestigious Bohemian Club, of San Francisco, who began hosting their annual summer retreat underneath Austin Creek's redwoods in the 1880s. A decade later the Bohemians would move their camp upriver to create their now famous Bohemian Grove, eventually amassing twenty-seven hundred acres of redwood forestland, including two hundred acres purchased from Thomas King and John Starrett.

In the photo, between James and William, stands Thomas, the lumberman. Of the four cheerless faces, his is the bleakest. King and Starrett owned prime riverfront property that was surprisingly close to the Clar bunkhouse on Mays Canyon—though if you drove from one to the other, you'd never know it, because the lower Russian River curves in on itself like a snake. The drive is seven miles; a flight would be two miles. Once King and Starrett had exhausted their timber supply, around 1901, the partners set out to develop their two miles of Russian River frontage and the lush flatlands of Dutch Bill Creek, the lowermost mile of which they owned as well. They grew hops and built a hotel, sued and were sued. Competition was fierce in the growing West County. After selling land to the Bohemian Club, King, in 1915, sold his remaining interest to Starrett for a mortgage of $25,000. Starrett developed the land along the river into what now constitutes most of the town of Monte Rio.

3

I WAS TEN YEARS OLD WHEN I FIRST MET C. RAYMOND "BUSTER" CLAR. The encounter was, as often happened in Guerneville, by chance. Early one summer day in 1971, Dad announced that he was headed to the hills above town to chainsaw some downed oak and madrone for our winter firewood stash. Did I want to come along? The question was rhetorical. I loved these excursions. Dad didn't throw footballs or ride bikes. Tramping the land and cutting firewood was how we had fun together. First stop was two miles north, at my grandparents' small ranch, to borrow Grandpa's truck to haul the wood. Then it was up to the seventy-five-acre parcel—which we called "the property"—that my parents owned in the hills above Guerneville.

Even within the handsome low coastal mountains that surround Guerneville, our land stood out for its borderless fit into a larger natural area that was, and remains, Sonoma County's wildest outback. The parcel's western boundary adjoined Armstrong Woods, an 800-acre state reserve, half of which stood as the largest intact ancient redwood grove remaining in Sonoma County. (Before logging, 150,000 acres of virgin redwood forest grew in Sonoma County.) Armstrong Woods was adjacent to the 6,000-acre Austin Creek State Recreation Area, which itself abutted tens of thousands of acres of ranchlands that ran northward to Mendocino County and westward to the coast. My dad and grandfather and great-grandfather and their assorted siblings and spouses spent their lives traversing this rugged, almost unpopulated countryside, just as my sisters and I and our cousins would do when we came along.

I savored firewood days with Dad, laboring within the natural human framework of self-reliance. (Thoreau: "Every man looks at his woodpile with a kind of affection." Dad, and his dad, at the woodpile: "Every piece has a place it fits.") When the work was done, we'd plop onto the warm slant of a

14

sweeping meadow, under a great live oak on a high knoll one thousand feet above the valley. Branches the size of small trees grew overhead in mighty bends and reached back to the earth in front of us, arcing along the ground for a while before jutting back skyward. These oaks stood always inviolate— Dad never cut a standing tree.

Lounging against the oak's rough bark, we'd breathe the lea's perfumed air and cool tidings from the coast, and Dad repeated the landmarks: Guerneville proper and the canyon-hidden draw of the wide Russian River three miles in the evergreen south. Then, at two miles, Guerneville Elementary School, where I attended kindergarten through eighth grade, and where once stood one of the region's largest remaining stumps until the principal had it removed, around 1970, because the older kids smoked and necked behind it. Near the school rose the low protuberance of Lone Mountain, around which wrapped the wide ancient river oxbow of the Big Bottom. On the northwestern flank of Lone Mountain was my grandparents' ranch, our next destination.

Grandma and Grandpa—Annie and Tom King—occupied one of the more picturesque of the old-school properties that still dotted Guerneville's hidden niches. Surrounding the land and its long driveway were rustic picket fences constructed of eighty-year-old, hand-hewn redwood grape stakes. We noted the sign whose punctuation we always hoped was in error ("The King's Lone Mountain Ranch") and eased past two dozen Gravenstein apple trees, planted here and throughout Sonoma County in 1919 and 1920, when the Volstead Act, better known as Prohibition, banned production of all alcoholic beverages except hard cider. We left the truck laden with firewood and went in.

My grandparents' house was tucked into a hillside below second-growth redwoods. Visitors always entered through the back door, first fording the pantry, then reaching the kitchen. Everything happened in the kitchen. The front door was almost never used, except to venture outside with highballs and Cokes onto a long redwood deck that overlooked the Big Bottom and hundreds of acres of chardonnay grapes farmed by Korbel Champagne Cellars.

Lone Mountain Ranch was originally Grandma Anne's land. She was born there in 1903, and she died there in 2000. During the late nineteenth century, Grandma's father, Albert P. Laughlin, for whom the valley is named, hired on as a drover and herded cattle from Missouri to Sonoma County. At the end of his third drive, Albert collected his pay and stayed in

Sonoma County. He looked around for a while, then settled in Guerneville. In 1883 Albert Laughlin purchased 160 acres of cutover land on the Big Bottom. There, among house-sized stumps, Albert grazed his Holsteins.

Dad rapped briefly on the windowed pantry door, and we went right in. On most firewood days we'd spend a half hour in the kitchen to chat and listen to my grandparents' stories of life and characters on the Russian River of yore. I'd grab a Coke from the fridge, and Grandma would occupy her seat by the door to the hallway, while Grandpa spun yarns and chipped ice at the wet bar for bourbons and water. Today, though, was different. When we arrived, Grandma and Grandpa had a visitor, Buster Clar.

He was long and lean like a country preacher with the wizened face of a rural poet who liked to work outside. He wore a modest but trim button-up shirt and, no matter the heat of the day, a cotton sweater. Neatly combed graying hair retreated from his forehead and well above what I saw were large ears. Browline glasses with chrome highlights made his eyes look big, adding a professorial air. He stood solidly, almost formally, with his hand on a Naugahyde kitchen chair. Behind him stretched Grandma Anne's glass display case lined with thin, gleaming pottery, spun by her friend Marguerite Wildenhain, the noted Bauhaus artist whose home and Pond Farm Pottery were adjacent to Armstrong Woods. (The state has since annexed the property.) The Wildenhain cups, saucers, and bowls were just about the only "fancy" items owned by my practical grandparents, save their collection of Western-themed liquor bottles (gunfighters, race cars, schooners) that occupied high shelves built around the perimeter of the kitchen. An unlocked cabinet held a dozen of my grandfather's hunting rifles, all of them loaded. When Dad and I entered the kitchen, there sat the man who in Guerneville would always be known by his childhood name.

"Buster's writing a book," Grandpa told me, by way of presentation. Grandpa, a gracious man, included me as an equal. Dad needed no introduction; he'd known the Clars all his life. Both of my grandparents had known Buster since 1903, the year they all were born just a few miles apart on the Russian River. The old-timers spoke as familiar friends, no matter that they hadn't seen each other much over the fifty years since they all traveled by train to Santa Rosa High School.

Raymond Clar lived in Sacramento, as he had for decades, working as a forester and historian for the state of California. His brother, George, was the Guerneville postmaster and my grandmother's boss. George still lived on the family ranch where Herbie had ejected me from the stump.

Raymond Clar's archives are now held at the University of California, Berkeley's Bancroft Library. He set a high bar for original forestry research. He wrote *A Brief History of the California Division of Forestry* (1957), the historically important *California Government and Forestry: From Spanish Days Until the Creation of the Department of Natural Resources in 1927* (1959), and his last book for the state, now more pertinent than ever, *Evolution of California's Wildland Fire Protection System* (1969). (For many years the state's official program to address forest fires was called the "Clar Plan.")

Writers were so out of league with anyone I could imagine knowing that it was as if Grandpa had introduced me to an astronaut. I asked Buster Clar what his book was about. His thin mouth broke into a warm smile, and he answered me briskly.

"Guerneville," he said. Buster was there to pick my grandparents' brains about the "old days" for his forthcoming history, *Out of the River Mist*, which, upon publication in 1973, instantly became a regional treasure. Clar first published an exclusive run of four hundred copies for local folks who'd provided interviews and documents. Today I have my parents' signed copy, number 176.

On this day Clar was interested in the Big Bottom and my grandmother's history of the ranch where she still lived. He suggested we step out onto the deck.

Clar gazed quietly at the two-dimensional flat expanse that extended north and west for a half mile in each direction until the valley rose into the steep slopes of Pool Ridge and into a narrow canyon called Forgotten Valley. The large flat occupied the northwestern quadrant of the great river oxbow now drained seven thousand years. All of us on the deck that day were aware that a stupendous redwood grove had once occupied the valley. But on this day Clar made another claim, one that, to my impressionable ears, had the effect of parting the denatured grape field as if it were a theater curtain to reveal a three-dimensional specter, the vision of which remains with me today. Of all the remarkable redwood groves that had stood along the lower

Russian River, said Clar, pointing from the deck to the vineyard, "Right here was the greatest forest that ever stood."

In *Out of the River Mist*, Clar wrote,

One particular ox-bow flowed north, probably into the floor of present Armstrong Grove, and then turned south, leaving Lone mountain as a virtual island. Eventually, the river in flood state cut through the top of the ox-bow U, and the river assumed its present course. As a professional forester, and as one who insists upon exposing historical facts with as much accuracy as human activities and observations may be reported, I dare to make this bold statement. I believe that on the Guerneville Big Bottom there once grew the most voluminous and the tallest body of living vegetable matter ever to have grown upon this earth at any place and at any time.

Later in the book Clar explains that in 1886 John Washington Bagley, an early Guerneville pioneer who in 1865 had built the first sawmill on the Big Bottom, reported to the California State Board of Forestry that "the trees from one measured acre on the Big Bottom produced 1,431,530 board feet of redwood lumber. Only about one-fourth of the tree was utilized under the crude milling methods of the time." That one acre, containing perhaps six million board feet of lumber, was owned by William Henry Willits on his Big Bottom claim, the stump land later populated by Albert Laughlin's cows and the desertified vineyard I saw every time I visited my grandparents. The world's most magnificent forest had been reduced to bubbly.

For a while we stood on the deck without talking. No doubt one of the grown-ups broke the silence by saying, "Back then they didn't know what they were doing," a hollow refrain I'd heard many times in defense of our ancestors. Thing is, they knew exactly what they were doing. The destruction of the forest happened in real time; the math was simple, the visuals clear. In 1875 a writer for the *Sonoma Democrat* examined the county's redwood production, estimated "increased yearly demand," and concluded, "The demands of commerce [will] strip our redwoods within fifteen years." He was off by ten years, but the gist was accurate.

By 1880 the counties of Sonoma, Mendocino, and Humboldt were collectively producing well over two hundred million board feet of redwood lumber annually, an extraordinary volume. Even at the time, total exhaustion of the forest was given. The end came first to Guerneville. By the time Herbie pushed me off that stump, any aged Guerneville native could recount the day on February 7, 1901, when Bagley ceremoniously ran the very last redwood log through the town's very last lumber mill. The moment marked the end of one of the most rapid, forceful, and—given the unprecedented sizes and ages of the trees and fragile, irreplaceable habitat they produced—tragic outbreaks of deforestation in human history. Bagley had also run the first log through the mill thirty-five years before.

The closing of Guerneville's last mill was a countywide event, held on a Saturday. Spectators traveled from Santa Rosa, Petaluma, and even the Bay Area to witness the mark of time. "The idea was a neat one," the *Santa Rosa Press Democrat* reported the next day, "and a large crowd of spectators gathered to witness the performance of the work." The story continued,

> In the crowd witnessing the sawing of the last log were men who, while they had not the distinction belonging to Mr. Bagley of having run the saw through the first log, were present when he performed the task. These pioneers told a story of the day of long ago anew on Saturday afternoon and it was heard with deep interest. Down in their hearts these old-timers hated to see the saw make that last cut. It recalled the time when the mill was first built. Little by little, as the saw ran its way through the log the recollections of the thirty-five years came home to them. Once in a while one of the old men would point with his finger to the open stretch of country or to the hillsides for miles around which had been robbed of the mighty redwood giants during the tenure of activity in the milling days that ended with Mr. Bagley's sawing of the last log. Others recounted the millions upon millions of feet of lumber that had been turned out by the mill and as to its value. It was a time of reflection all round.

Like many government functionaries, Buster Clar believed that his presence in Sacramento could have a leavening effect on harmful timber practices. He was wrong, as he eventually came to understand. In 1969, just after he retired, Clar wrote to his brother, Clarence, "The loggers were only half the thieves—the remainder—and most responsible were: 1. the legislators at federal and state level who refused to meet the issue squarely; and 2. the profit-makers who shaped the government."

4

I GREW UP VERSED IN THE LORE OF THE GREAT REDWOODS THAT ONCE stood in Guerneville, and I absorbed the grandeur of the ancient forest during countless forays through Armstrong Woods. The redwoods became so much a part of my spirit that I chose a college, the University of California, Santa Cruz, in part for its proximity to the many redwood parks of Santa Cruz County.

Late in the summer of 1985, after I graduated college, I returned to Guerneville, as if connected by a rubber band. I took a job at the town's gutsy weekly newspaper, the *Paper* (today the *Bohemian*). I rented a house whose backyard overlooked a small redwood grove along the Russian River halfway between Guerneville and Monte Rio. As soon as I'd paid my rent and deposit, I hiked out the back door into the woods. I discovered an unused fire lane that ended at a well-maintained dirt road that, in one direction, headed uphill to a low ridge and, in the other direction, led downhill to a seventy-five-acre alluvial flat covered in large second-growth redwood trees. Very soon I would learn that this tract, called the Silver Estate, held the largest remaining flat grove of redwoods on the banks of the Russian River. It was also the southernmost extent of the old Clar Ranch.

The south-facing forest soothed me and drew me in. On warm days I reveled in the cool shade of the maturing redwoods. Easy ocean breezes commonly hissed through the canopy. A rough path, overgrown with ferns and mosses, wended through the flat to the river. In places the redwoods were five feet in diameter and stood two hundred feet or taller. The few stumps not milled by Ivon Clar were enormous and, like the one from which I descended on my fifth birthday, stood ten feet off the ground. The butts of the stumps were pocked with rectangular holes the size of bricks, where the loggers had fixed scaffolding to chop the trees, by hand, above the butt swell.

The forest was moist even on the driest days. Hearty sprays of bay laurel indicated a high water table. I felt lucky to have discovered the place, and I spent a lot of time tramping the small grove.

One day while wandering, I found a new stretch of woods near the center of the Silver Estate. As I stepped over and around the splayed branches of a large fallen tanoak tree, the corner of my eye caught something about fifty feet distant. Instantly I knew what it was. Individual old-growth redwood trees tend to visually announce themselves even from afar. I scurried over to the now obvious bole, stunned by the enormity of this great redwood. How was this possible? Here was a tree of trees, with a diameter of at least twenty feet, straight as a rod and showing little taper. Even at the time I understood that it was the biggest tree standing in Sonoma County.

In one of his Guerneville remembrances, Butts wrote, "There were formerly a great many trees in the forests of this county which ranged in diameter from 15 to 20 feet. But of all the large trees that once adorned the groves of Sonoma County, I know of but one tree that still remains standing that has a diameter of 20 feet, and that tree is known as the 'Clar Tree,' and stands on the south bank of the Russian River, about one and a half miles below Guerneville."

The Clar Tree! Raymond Clar, when he was twenty years old, had measured the great conifer and found that it stood 336 feet above the ground. It was then, and today remains, the tallest tree in Sonoma County. It is also the widest and, at possibly two thousand years old, likely the oldest tree in the county. Neither Clar nor anyone else I eventually talked with had any idea why the nineteenth-century loggers had left this one tree.

One day not long after I found the Clar Tree, I returned to the riverside tract. I came up short at a new sight. In the interim someone had strewn the forest with long strips of pliable orange plastic, which I would later learn is called "flagging." Other flags were blue; some were striped. I didn't know what these strips meant, but I was pretty sure it wasn't good. Back at the newspaper office, a few calls took me to a forester with the California Department of Forestry (CDF; today called CalFire).

"That stand," the forester told me, "is owned by Louisiana-Pacific [LP] Corporation, and they're gonna log it."

In 1985, Louisiana-Pacific stood among the world's largest forest products companies. I asked myself, and others, why LP would target such a small, biologically important grove as Clar Flat, a paltry seventy-five acres, when the company owned nearly four hundred thousand acres of redwood land in Mendocino and Humboldt counties and hundreds of thousands of acres of additional forest across the country and around the world.

Yet Louisiana-Pacific wasn't just targeting tiny Clar Flat. Later I would learn that the company was planning to log the rest of its twenty thousand acres of timber in Sonoma County, then sell the land for development. The company felt an imperative to liquidate its Sonoma County holding because the county's changing demographics were skewing toward an upwardly mobile class of nascent elites who were not fond of logging in their neighborhoods. The lovely views from these stately homes often included redwoods held by LP. When the new residents hiked in the Fort Ross and Sonoma Coast state parks, images of LP's adjacent logging would be even more pronounced. But about the time I moved into my house above Clar Flat, no one knew that the forest was in mortal jeopardy. It would take a whistle-blower alerting a reporter to expose Louisiana-Pacific's liquidation scheme.

Nick Valentine was a portly man who so rarely lifted himself from a ragged antique chair set behind an old metal desk laminated in hillocks of paper that he looked as much an office fixture as the desk itself. If you asked central casting for a robustly bearded, antisocial but warm, cynical small-town newspaper editor addicted to Coke and Virginia Slims, a crack journalist with the perfect name who expertly managed a small staff on an even smaller budget, they'd send for Nick Valentine.

Nick was my new boss at the *Paper*. When we met in 1985, Nick was running the *Paper* out of an office in downtown Guerneville. I needed a job, and happily, when I walked into his office one day in late summer, Nick Valentine needed a reporter.

A few months into the job, I approached Nick with a photo that I'd just processed in the *Paper*'s tiny darkroom. In the self-portrait I was squatting in front of a clump of large second-growth redwoods on Clar Flat. Nick leaned back, and his tired chair squeaked. The leather arms and back were frayed, as if slashed by a cat. Peering over his graying, nicotine-stained beard, spiked with a smoldering cigarette, Nick studied the image. I told him that I'd been trespassing in the grove for weeks, and LP was going to log it. I wanted to run a story. I could tell he was excited because his eyes widened slightly and his beard briefly nodded.

There was no aspect of logging with which I was familiar; my ignorance of the industry was total. I knew only that a transnational corporation was proposing to log my beloved Clar Flat. That was enough to get me started. I studied the labyrinthine laws and regulations that guided logging in California, principally the 1973 Forest Practice Act. The act had reconstituted the state Board of Forestry's role as a rule-making authority and had created the California Department of Forestry to examine logging and enforce those rules on private timberlands. There is no end to the labyrinth, just interlocking circles of dry and often discordant statues and rules designed to ameliorate the public's concerns about destructive logging practices while in large part allowing them to continue. The Board of Forestry printed its rules in a handy one-hundred-page, pocket-sized guide. I still have mine, from 1985, with its bright blue cover. When I first got the book, I went crazy with a red pen, underlining what I would soon learn were called "weasel words." The most significant result, and overriding purpose, of the Forest Practice Act was to assure the public that *California has the toughest timber harvest laws in the country*—a refrain I would hear with rueful regularity.

The "rules" spun logic into pirouettes. Clear-cuts were now limited to 80 acres but could be increased to 120 acres with CDF approval, and they could be spaced with buffers just 300 feet wide. In a few years the buffer could also be logged. One mystifying justification for increasing the size of a clear-cut from 80 to 120 acres was to "reduce the overall detrimental effects of erosion."

Trees were to be felled away from streams "to the fullest extent possible." Operators of thirty-five-ton steel-treaded tractors were required to carve into delicate soils and underbrush "in such a manner as to minimize damage" to soils and water quality. Other weasel words included "minimize the effect," "exercise due diligence," "wherever possible," "feasible protection," "reasonable expectation," "due consideration," and, as always, "exceptions may be proposed and used when approved by the director" of CDF.

Rich Lehtinen, an inspector with the Sonoma County Planning Department, had inspected the logging site. He told me that LP officials "didn't like us being out there. They obviously weren't very happy that anyone from the county was interested." When I pressed him about the possible impacts to forest habitat along the Russian River, Lehtinen admitted, "There will be some impact. They're going to cut a lot of trees."

Nick Valentine used the quote for the headline of my first logging story in the *Paper*. "They're Going to Cut a Lot of Trees" ran on November 21, 1985, and with that I was plunged headlong into the contentious and convoluted world of California timber politics. Once the story began spreading to other media outlets, locally and in the Bay Area, officials at CDF and Louisiana-Pacific received hundreds of complaints.

One reader of the article was Sharon Duggan, an environmental attorney who worked in Sebastopol, a small city fifteen miles southeast of Guerneville. Duggan's affability camouflaged a doggedness. For the past three years, she had been working with activists in Mendocino and Humboldt counties to halt the logging of a small virgin redwood grove that stood 150 miles north on the Mendocino coast. The activists had named the forest Sally Bell Grove, in honor of one of the last surviving Sinkyone Indians who had lived in the region. Sally Bell Grove held the last ancient redwoods for miles in all directions.

In December 1985, shortly after CDF approved LP's plan to log Clar Flat, I began regularly consulting with Duggan. She expertly dissected the morass of language and paperwork that constituted California's forest practice laws. Early in 1986, a local group formed to fight LP's logging in Sonoma County, and they hired Duggan to represent them.

At her Sebastopol office Duggan was warm and forthcoming, but when she recounted the timber industry's many violations of state laws that had occurred since passage of the Forest Practice Act and the state's ready approval of illegal timber harvest plans (THPs), an almost visible cast of incredulity limned her words.

I'd brought with me all of the paperwork I'd copied from CDF's Clar Flat logging file. Duggan thumbed the material, shaking her head and chuckling sardonically.

"This looks like the same plan," said Duggan, comparing the Clar Flat THP to another, nearly identical THP from 1982. "I can't believe they didn't notify more neighbors."

The forest practice rules required timber companies to contact owners of all properties found within three hundred feet of a proposed logging site. In 1982, LP foresters had contacted twenty-five neighbors. In 1985 they contracted three.

I told Duggan I was also worried about the Clar Tree. Louisiana-Pacific foresters had assured me that they would leave the tree standing. Nonetheless, it was worth nearly $100,000 as finished lumber. To my astonishment, Duggan said that no local, state, or federal statute obligated LP to preserve one of the world's widest, oldest, and tallest trees.

After we spoke Duggan decided to check for herself the distance between neighboring properties and Clar Flat. It was an unusual action for an attorney. But Duggan was an unusual attorney. She contacted a local tree surgeon, Darrell Sukovitzen—who would soon be teaching activists how to climb redwood trees—and together, tugging a three-hundred-foot rope, they piloted a rowboat from the riverside homes at Northwood to Clar Flat. They determined that LP had neglected to notify dozens of homeowners of the planned logging, as required by law. When I brought the omission to the attention of Greg Checkal, the LP forester who had designed the THP, he agreed he'd made a mistake.

Duggan was incensed by the "mistake," but she held CDF just as responsible as LP.

"I want to know why a state agency like CDF . . . could forget that these people were entitled to notice," Duggan told me. "To me that is an incredible abuse of discretion on the part of CDF."

Duggan told me that such abuses by the agency were the rule rather than the exception. Even when it came to the cutting of Sally Bell Grove, the last virgin redwood island on California's Lost Coast, CDF had violated state law by allowing Georgia-Pacific (GP) to liquidate the stand. Duggan and the Environmental Protection Information Center (EPIC), a small nonprofit group in Garberville, Humboldt County, and the International Indian Treaty Council had sued CDF and GP over the logging. Plaintiffs won their case in a California appellate court, setting a precedent that confirmed that logging in California was regulated not just by the Forest Practice Act but by the much stronger California Environmental Quality Act (CEQA). For decades the decision would reverberate through the superheated world of California timber politics, where I would find myself stirring the pot.

In early 1986, while Duggan litigated and I reported on timber dramas, Houston-based Maxxam Corporation was completing its hostile buyout of the Pacific Lumber Company in Humboldt County. By then Pacific Lumber (PL) was the world's largest—and indeed the last remaining—producer of old-growth redwood products. Maxxam was a mid-level conglomerate led by Texas native Charles Hurwitz, who specialized in buying "undervalued" firms and liquidating their assets. Pacific Lumber was the venerable Humboldt County timber operation that everyone at the time understood owned the last sizable holdings of ancient redwood still standing outside parks.

The Maxxam takeover marked the endgame of logging in the ancient redwoods. By now 95 percent of the entire old-growth redwood biome had been eliminated. At the time, and for whatever reason, I believed that logging California's old-growth redwoods was illegal. Over the coming years many people I spoke with told me they believed the same thing. The timber industry and state officials had a different perspective.

Maxxam paid just $872 million for all of Pacific Lumber, a company with assets reportedly worth five times that amount and which held a long-term debt of just $24 million. Maxxam accomplished the deal by securing $754 million in high-yield, high-risk, high-interest "junk bonds," popular at the time among smallish fish attempting to become big ones. To ensure success, the company's financial wizards employed the sleight-of-hand economic services of not one but three soon-to-be convicted financial felons: Ivan Boesky, Boyd Jeffries, and—at the notorious junk-bond firm of Drexel Burnham Lambert—Michael Milken.

As we spoke in her office, Sharon Duggan asked if I was at all familiar with the "northern redwoods."

Only as a tourist, I said.

She thought about that for a while and asked, "Do you know where the Pacific Lumber redwoods are located?"

I told her I did not.

"Have you been to Sally Bell Grove?"

I had not.

"Hmmmm," she said, before telling me she had to get back to work.

As an attorney, Duggan could not encourage me to trespass. Yet her family had roots in Humboldt County, where her father was an insurance agent, and she cared deeply for her homeland. I was a young reporter still learning the art of the understatement, so I was fortunate that I hadn't missed her point. When I returned to my desk at the *Paper*, I made some calls up north. I reached Richard Gienger, an activist with EPIC and the Sinkyone Council and a leading voice for protecting the Lost Coast.

"Sure, come on up," he said. "I'll show you around."

5

I N EARLY MARCH 1986, I TOOK A ROAD TRIP. IT WAS, AS THEY SAY, THE beginning of the rest of my life. Along the way I stopped at a lovely redwood home built into the sprawling prairies of Navarro Ridge, overlooking the Mendocino coast. Here resided Gail Lucas, chair of the Sierra Club's State Forest Practices Task Force, and her partner, Jim Sears. At that moment Lucas was tussling with the State Board of Forestry over its proposal to allow timber companies to clear-cut areas larger than 120 acres if they provided "clear and convincing evidence" that no harm would be done to the ecosystem—a baffling if not impossible-to-meet stipulation.

Lucas's home was surrounded by Louisiana-Pacific's three hundred thousand acres of second-growth redwood forest in Mendocino County. I got a few quotes for a story, but most intriguing was when Jim Sears, who published the *North Coast News*, a weekly paper in nearby Fort Bragg, mentioned that the paper "might be looking for an editor."

My next encounter was with Richard Gienger. I wrestled my beleaguered 1973 Toyota Celica down the sinuous, deserted arc of Navarro Ridge until the narrow lane dead-ended at California's Highway 1. Northward along the coast, I forded the tiny settlements of Little River, Mendocino, Caspar, and finally the small city of Fort Bragg, population five thousand. Then northward again through Cleone, Inglenook, Newport, and finally to Westport, home of my ancestors.

John King was the uncle of my great-grandfather David King. John King settled along Wages Creek, just north of Westport, sometime in the 1860s. He logged redwoods and kept a small ranch. The land was still wild. White settlers were little known north of John King's ranch. Family lore has it that, not long after John King built his ranch house on Wages Creek, a government surveyor traveled across the rugged, largely uncharted coastal hills to ascertain the northern terrain. He rested and dined for a few days at the King home, the last outpost of white civilization encountered by the surveyor for at least the next week. From the King ranch the surveyor continued north into the Lost Coast, which is anchored by a small, dramatic mountain range that rises four thousand feet straight out of the Pacific Ocean. Perhaps recalling his last soft bed, the surveyor named these mountains the King Range.

Seven miles north of Westport, at the once redwood-rich Hardy Creek, Highway 1 knifed inland. The route would not straighten for fifty miles; nor would I again see the coast, at least not while driving. Hardy Creek was an extremely steep stream with no flat land. The watershed marked the southern reach of the Lost Coast, twelve miles south of Sally Bell Grove. It's a place where residents understand that an entire half of their planetary existence is dominated by an endless sizzle of blue-gray slate, an oceanic infinity that ecologist Carl Safina calls "a place of tide and tantrum" that every year "gets hammered and reshaped like molten bronze."

A few miles after turning inland, I noticed, to my left, a dirt lane that did not appear drivable. This was the southern terminus of Usal Road. I stayed on the pavement. Here began eighty miles of driving across a wide geographic loop to reach the Gienger home, which was just fifteen air miles from Hardy Creek.

The road wended upward until I crossed a ridge and descended to an old steel-truss bridge that spanned the South Fork Eel River, just before Highway 1 ended at US Highway 101. Up the federal highway, at the former mill town of Piercy, I passed an odd establishment slathered across a wide flat on one of the river's bends: the Bridgewood Motel, now no longer a roadhouse but a provider of low-rent housing. With the Bridgewood to my left, a sign appeared: "Humboldt County."

I exited the freeway at the small, bustling town of Garberville. Two miles on a back road, following the South Fork Eel River, brought me to an even smaller village called Redway. Signs pointed to the King Range National Conservation Area. Driving was a workout.

Miles up the road I was in an outpost called Whitethorn. An old church stood by the road, pocked by a neon cross blazing the words "Jesus Saves." The Whitethorn Valley once boasted five lumber mills to process the thousands of acres of redwood and Douglas fir that surrounded the former boomtown. The region was also the site of a tannin industry. Tannin was derived from the bark of tanoak trees, whose acorns had fed the Native peoples of the region for millennia. A great tanoak is a sight, as stout a tree as you'll find. They can rise more than one hundred feet overhead in broad canopies of evergreen, with trunks four to five feet across. Many of the Mattole's tanoaks were very old, possibly older than three hundred years. The near-universal destruction of California's old tanoak trees is a story yet untold. Today, tanoaks that were growing prior to the arrival of white settlers are rarer than ancient redwoods.

I rolled southwesterly until pavement gave way to gravel, and I was back in Mendocino County. A scattering of old-growth redwoods, left for reasons unknown, lined the small river. Here the Mattole ran softly over fine pebbles, an easy flow that once served great migrations of spawning Coho salmon, a species now nearly extinct in California. The Mattole is an odd river in the redwood range. The only redwoods that grew naturally in the watershed were found in the headwaters, which lie just three air miles from the Pacific. From there the undammed river runs northeasterly, then wraps around the eastern flank of the King Range before the waters fan and slow through the wide meadowed flats near the river's mouth, sixty-two miles from where it started. Along the way the river takes in seventy-four tributaries, large and small, and runs parallel to, and west of, the South Fork Eel River. The Mattole River is the beating heart of California's Lost Coast.

I followed the Mattole headwaters nearly to their terminus and came to a high point, where I found a driveway at the sign marker Gienger had given me. I killed the engine and sat for several minutes, my view obliterated by an intense rainstorm. I had arrived in one of the rainiest locales in the Americas.

On foot I tramped along a trail, convinced that no one could possibly live here and that I would eventually be found soaked and dead from hypothermia because the light was now clearly on the wane and I would get lost and that would be it. I pressed on. A quarter mile in, a dim orange glow caught my eye: candlelight. I followed it to a tiny cabin. This was an occupied abode, but it seemed impossible that it was Gienger's, because he lived with his wife, Noni, and their three children. I knocked nonetheless.

"Mr. King! Come in!"

Richard Gienger was stout with a wide face and long, straight hair. A thick Pancho Villa mustache ran below his chin. His low voice was raspy, friendly. He'd been living on this land for nearly a decade, an East Coast transplant. By his mannerisms and speech, I'd stereotyped him as a former truck driver or brick setter. Yet he'd fled westward after earning a degree in architecture from the University of Pennsylvania. I would find many richly crafted lives in these hills, stories of folks whose outer layers revealed very little about them, except their obvious reverence for working and protecting a piece of land. Everyone had dirt under their fingernails.

I met Noni and the young children in the one-room shack. I had no idea people lived like this. We ate delicious stew and homemade bread. I slept in a sort of glorified tent made of greenhouse plastic, kept up half the night by the deafening percussion of the rain.

"Might not be the best day to see Sally Bell Grove," Richard said the next morning. We stood near his cabin on a luxurious meadowed bluff during a break in the storm. Clouds gathered at altitude and presented a wide view of the roiling Pacific. The ocean was two miles away, but from an elevation of fourteen hundred feet it appeared touchable. I agreed, thanked Richard and his wonderful family for the hospitality, and promised to return.

On the drive home I stopped at a charming Garberville bookstore called Orange Cat Goes to Market. Browsing, I passed a case of detailed US Geological Survey topographic maps that covered nearly all of Humboldt County and northern Mendocino County. Near the maps, a small queue had formed at the store's pay phone, which was coveted by hill dwellers who lived an hour away on dirt roads. The proprietor was a friendly man named John McClellan—aging sweater, welcoming smile, soft-spoken, articulate. An orange cat lazed on the counter, next to a display copy of Rob Connell Clarke's seminal DIY handbook *Marijuana Botany*. I asked if he had topographic maps for lands owned by Pacific Lumber. He gave me a knowing glance.

"Well," he said, finger at temple, "I have most of Humboldt County." He opened and closed a series of wide, narrow drawers stuffed with poster-sized maps. He dragged out a selection, put the rest back, glanced over his glasses at a map key taped to the wall, and circled an area with his index finger.

"I think around here," he said.

I bought ten maps that together covered roughly six hundred square miles. McClellan smiled, "That ought to do it."

Two weeks later I returned. South of Garberville I again noticed the Bridgewood Motel, looking no less beleaguered on a nice day. Yet hundreds of beautiful homesteads surrounded the town. After World War II, timber companies and small holders began liquidating the great fir forests that once carpeted the hills in all directions, leveling nearly everything in two decades. Many landowners maintained profits by subdividing and selling the land, cheap, to all comers. Canny entrepreneurs, notably Bob McKee, scion of early Humboldt pioneers, subdivided the ranches and sold them to disaffected "back-to-the-landers"—hippies and antiwar radicals, urban refugees, market-culture misfits. The Woodstock generation had made its nascent homeland in the rugged hills of that fine land.

Clashes were inevitable. At first, many old-timers resented the newcomers. When cannabis cash started resurrecting local businesses, things quieted for a while. Then people started turning up sick all over the newly occupied former forestlands. They soon learned that seven major California timber companies—and the federal government—were "treating" nearby clear-cut terrain with all manner of toxic herbicides, chief among them a combination of 2,4-D and 2,4,5-T otherwise known as Agent Orange. The companies wanted to destroy "weed trees," such as oak and madrone, that might compete with lucrative monocultures of conifers grown for the pulp market. The conifers themselves often grew from seeds that were first treated with rodenticide and tumbled in aluminum paint to keep birds from eating them. Predictably, the birds ate the seeds anyway and died. Then came the helicopters, piloted by Vietnam vets who first scattered the seeds, then returned with Agent Orange.

Herbicide spraying was often indiscriminate. Frequently the newcomers'—and many old-timers'—water supplies, gardens, pets, and even homes and children "accidentally" got doused.

In Vietnam, the taint of which many back-to-the-landers were attempting to escape, the US military had sprayed more than eleven million gallons of undiluted Agent Orange to defoliate eight million acres of virgin rainforest so that US servicemen shooting from helicopters, strafing from jets, and bombing from B-52s could better pick out targets. Agent Orange contains dioxin, the most toxic chemical in existence. Its use in Vietnam caused widespread cancer and birth defects among the local population and sickened US troops as well.

Perhaps not coincidentally, timber companies started buying Agent Orange in quantity shortly after the US government began phasing out its use in Vietnam, in 1971.

The Environmental Protection Information Center launched in 1977 when newcomers and some old-timers organized to ban aerial herbicide applications in Mendocino, Humboldt, and Del Norte counties. In July 1977, Garberville physician Irving Tessler reported to a state investigations committee that "young, strong, healthy people" living near spray areas were experiencing numerous and serious physical disorders, including liver damage. Humboldt County agricultural commissioner John Hart told the committee that the herbicides were "as safe as table salt." In August, the seven companies, facing down a lawsuit, declared a "voluntary moratorium" on aerial spraying, which stuck.

On this second northward journey, I was trying to find Garberville's chainsaw repair shop, behind which, in a tight gravel parking lot, sprawled the EPIC office. There I got out and leaned against the car for a while until an unresolved coil of a man shot out of the office, instantly noticed me, and beelined my way. He was slim and wore ratty jeans and inadequate shoes. A tired plaid shirt hung off his frame and, oddly, was tucked in. From his head exploded a knot of inky curls, which fairly bobbed under the pressure of short, impatient steps and was complemented by a kinky black beard. This was Darryl Cherney.

"Hey," he said, "how you doing?" He was affable, intense. I told him I was doing fine, that I'd just arrived from Sonoma County, and that I was looking for Sally Bell Grove.

Darryl thought about that for an instant. He drew a short breath and said, in a kindly voice, "Oh, well that's perfect, because we're *going* to Sally Bell Grove." He looked behind me at the Celica. "Can we take your car?"

Darryl explained that a large cadre of locals was, on that very day, caravanning to Georgia-Pacific property to plant redwood seedlings in the cutover landscape of Little Jackass Creek, just above Sally Bell Grove. He was afraid his vehicle wouldn't make it. He pointed to a van parked nearby, which Darryl had driven from his native Manhattan the year before, seeking a new homeland. By now, Darryl was managing the Bridgewood Motel.

Darryl told me that the tree planting was "an action" timed to coincide with the spring equinox. After planting trees, the group would camp at the small beach bisected by the end run of Little Jackass Creek, just below the remaining ancient redwood forest. I had no idea we were upon the equinox. I wasn't even sure what the equinox was. That night I would also learn, for the first time, how to find the North Star. In many ways, my timing was exquisite.

6

FOUR OF US CRAMMED INTO MY CAR, CAMP GEAR IN THE TRUNK AND ON laps. Darryl rode shotgun. We traced the same route I'd followed two weeks before, but this time, when we got to Four Corners, we launched onto Usal Road. The rutted dirt track ran fifteen hundred feet above the Pacific Ocean. Georgia-Pacific owned nearly fifty thousand acres on these near-cliffs and throughout the region. (Fourteen years earlier, Louisiana-Pacific had been carved out of Georgia-Pacific in an antitrust action.) By 1983, GP had been logging the Usal tract for two decades, but now it was nearly out of trees. Sally Bell Grove was the last seventy-five-acre plug of ancient redwood still standing on private land along the Lost Coast. The forest clung to the bottom of Little Jackass Creek, a five-hundred-acre clamshell watershed that GP had otherwise clear-cut over the past couple of years. The logging had caused severe landslides despite, or because of, the empty regulatory exhortations of the California Department of Forestry. Topsoil melted like candle wax into the creek. Inside tiny Sally Bell Grove, five small subwatersheds coalesced. Removing Sally Bell Grove would cause the watershed to blow out completely.

In the car, much of our conversation centered on Maxxam and Pacific Lumber and the last of the redwoods. I told Darryl that I'd been investigating Pacific Lumber's 1986 timber harvest plans at CDF headquarters in Santa Rosa. Until 1985 Pacific Lumber had spent four decades selectively logging its ancient redwood groves. Under Maxxam, the company was becoming a clear-cutting overachiever. "And it's pretty much all old growth," I told Darryl.

One of our passengers recalled the day that local activists stormed Sally Bell Grove, in October 1983, to shut down Georgia-Pacific's logging. The locals got help from a nascent environmental group called Earth First! One of the founders, Mike Roselle, helped plan the action.

Georgia-Pacific had anticipated the demonstration by financing dozens of Mendocino County sheriff's officers to defend the cut. The cops emboldened loggers, who now cut trees even at the risk of their falling on protesters. One tree landed on a local woman named Mem Hill, who was lucky to survive with just a broken arm. A center of the action was at the very bottom of the grove, at the end of a descending ridge that overlooked a confluence of three streams and held a stunning redwood, twelve feet in diameter, that activists called the Medicine Tree. "Most of us felt that this tree was the heart of the grove," Roselle later wrote in the *Earth First! Journal*. The loggers targeted the great redwood, slicing into it until a local activist named Lon Mulvaney draped his body across the logger's arms, inches from the saw. The logger stopped cutting, and shortly thereafter a runner arrived with a court order to stop the logging. Twelve protesters were arrested, but Sally Bell Grove was still standing.

We pulled off near a smattering of cars and parked on a wide flat of mud. The recently denuded landscape appeared as if plowed by a drunken farmer. We donned packs. Mine was freighted with two Nikon cameras, three lenses, and an eight-pound Bogen tripod—my burden, and blessing, for the next several years. We found a happy clutch of tree planters gathered along the path. Each planter carried a hoedad, an axe-like tool with a curved wooden handle and a flat blade that resembled the beak of a duckbill. They worked swiftly, swooping the hoedad into the mud, carefully placing the redwood tree root into the hole, then pushing the hole closed with a toe. The group planted thousands of trees.

The skid trail dropped suddenly to the north, forming a near free fall for almost a mile until we'd lost a thousand feet of elevation and found ourselves standing on the most charming stretch of sand I'd ever seen. The wide bowl of Little Jackass watershed rose sharply on all sides, as if we stood cupped in someone's hands. The expanse of beach covered no more than five acres. Surf pounded muffled explosions. Scents of evergreen and brine merged at the beach. The broad hiss of fanning white seas poured into coarse sands and sizzled like frying bacon. Sea lions bellowed in the near distance. In the southern sky, the sunshine blinked under a large brown bird. "Golden eagle," said one of my passengers.

A woman named Ayisha offered me a tour of Sally Bell Grove. Ayisha lived at an "intentional community" in Mendocino County called Annwfn (pronounced ANN-woofin).

We made our way along the creek zone, first through screens of grasses and shrubs, willow and alder. Conifers next, namely Sitka spruce, which will accommodate salt air, and Douglas fir. Several rare plants occupy the Sinkyone—Mendocino coast paintbrush, redwood lily, California pinefoot, maple-leaved checkerbloom, leafy reed grass—but I wouldn't have known them. I'd been dropped into a foreign country.

Huffing upslope, we spotted the first redwoods. These were of average size, but the trees grew bigger as we moved uphill. We encountered several giants, some sprouting bulbous buttresses or knotty burls the size of cars. The tops of many of the lower trees had blown off, leaving great branches spiking outward like umbrella ribs. We forded a small tributary that entered Little Jackass Creek to our right, then continued up the creek until we paused to marvel at three streams coalescing almost in the same place. Here we ascended into a nearly pure stand of ancient redwood, where we found the Medicine Tree.

The downhill side of the wide redwood hung over a steep drop. On this side we found a great scar where the logger had penetrated the ancient conifer with his chainsaw. The scar ran around much of the tree—he had attempted to girdle it. On the uphill side we saw that a large triangular wedge had been cut, removed from the tree, and then put back. Someone had slathered the scars with mud. We sat with the Medicine Tree for a while, then moved along.

Hiking a seventy-five-acre redwood grove is a short journey. I wanted to reach the top of the Little Jackass watershed, but Ayisha needed to get back to camp. I carried on alone, only to quickly understand why Ayisha had begged off. I moved through the forest until an encroaching brightness gave me pause. Moving along, I found several old-growth redwoods that had been sawed off at the base. It was here that GP had been logging. Maneuvering around the fallen trees, I reached a place so severely different from the forest that for an instant I was confused.

The clear-cut was a desolate ruin. I continued uphill as best I could, straight up, diagonal, side-hill, back down. I came to a large redwood stump and climbed aboard. Looking back the way I'd come, I saw that Sally Bell Grove formed a rectangle of trees, like a zipper, down the center of Little Jackass watershed. Expanding outward from both sides of the zipper were near vertical slopes sprouting not a single standing tree. The forest, once a living relic of an ancient past, had been razed.

I continued looping in a northwesterly arc, aiming to rejoin Sally Bell Grove near the middle of the zipper, but I was blocked by an immense landslide. The entire slope had failed, from the top of the ridge at fourteen hundred feet elevation, for a quarter mile, straight into one of the tributaries of Little Jackass Creek. Laying across the slide was a redwood that had stood taller than two hundred feet and was eight feet wide at the base. I crawled up a slash pile at the butt end of the tree, ascended the bole, and walked to the middle of the tree. I stood twenty feet above the deeply incised slide. Mud and debris loosed by the slide had dumped into the creek and created a dam at least ten feet thick.

My knees gave slightly, and I began to sob. The carnage was a shock, the tears a surprise. For reasons still a mystery to me, it was the first and last time I would cry at the sight of a clear-cut.

I wrote in my journal, "I wonder how much the Sally Bell trip will have eventually changed my life. I am inspired, charged, revolted by it all so much that I *know* its impact will be substantial."

I didn't know the half of it.

Back in Sonoma County, I continued reporting on Louisiana-Pacific's logging. Yet I kept one foot farther north. I was too aware that Maxxam was now liquidating the very last ancient redwoods—more than a hundred Sally Bell Groves. At the office, a sympathetic Department of Forestry official had called me to warn that Louisiana-Pacific was planning to log all of its twenty-thousand-acre Sonoma County redwood inventory and then sell the land to developers. My story ran with the headline "Cutting More to Get Out?" By the time the THPs were approved, in CDF's predictable rubber-stamp fashion, a citizens group had formed to litigate the logging.

On April 6, 1986, I took myself on a tour of Sonoma County backroads to get a look at one of the proposed logging sites, on Kolmer Gulch, near Fort Ross State Park. My plan was to park along an isolated county road and hike all day. But as soon as I stepped out of the car, one of LP's loggers pulled his soldierly diesel pickup behind me, emerged slowly like John Wayne off a horse, and said, "What are you doing here, Greg?"

My life didn't exactly flash before my eyes, but I well understood that this guy could kill me. He stood over six feet tall and was solid like granite. My dad knew his family. He came with a well-deserved reputation for violence.

"Oh," I said, "just looking at Kolmer Gulch."

"Yeah?" he seethed. He turned his bulging head slowly toward the forest in question, then slowly back and straight into my eyes. "Well, we might just bury you there." I was dumbstruck. We stood there longer than forever. Finally, he said, "Get out of here."

7

THE BATTLE FOR THE LAST ANCIENT REDWOODS ACCELERATED ON JULY 1, 1986. That day, Maxxam issued a prospectus that promised a doubling of Pacific Lumber's rate of cut in the ancient forests to pay off the debt the company had incurred with the takeover of PL. The prospectus was a gut punch: "The Company is exploring various alternatives for generating additional cash flow, including increased lumber production and enhanced marketing efforts. Management has already taken steps to substantially increase the timber harvest, the volume of sales of unprocessed logs, and lumber production and may consider selling portions of its timberlands." The company had also changed logging methods from selection to clear-cutting, meaning that now PL would be logging more than three times the volume of the previous year.

In public, the company would claim a "sustainable" increase in cut, justified because the old Pacific Lumber had been "underproducing." Shortly after Maxxam issued the prospectus, a PL spokeswoman told the *San Francisco Examiner*, "Redwoods are renewable resources. They are not something that will be wiped out in 10 to 20 to 30 years." Hewing to the playbook, the company's PR department issued a statement that said Pacific Lumber "conducts its harvest operations in strict compliance with all the regulations of the California Forest Practices Act, which is the most restrictive forest practice law in the country."

In November, Maxxam sold its downtown San Francisco office tower, at 500 Washington Street, for $31 million to a Tokyo real estate developer. Maxxam also sold PL's welding company for another $360 million and even raided the workers' $90 million pension fund. According to the *New York Times*, Maxxam kept $50 million of the pension fund and invested $37 million of it in high-risk annuities "purchased from the Executive Life Insurance

Company of Los Angeles, which has provided annuities to employees at several companies taken over with Drexel Burnham financing." The paper noted that "a large proportion of [Executive Life's] assets are in high-risk securities, among them a significant share of the [junk] bonds issued for Maxxam's takeover of Pacific Lumber." In 1990, after servicing a slate of quasi-legal and outright fraudulent corporate takeovers, Drexel Burnham Lambert declared bankruptcy. The following year, Executive Life, heavily invested in Drexel's junk bonds, also declared bankruptcy, taking with it the pensions of thousands of retirees.

None of the windfall from the Pacific Lumber fire sale went into paying down the company's newfound debt. Instead, Maxxam purchased Kaiser Aluminum, another venerable northwestern company, and eventually gutted that firm into bankruptcy as well.

Standing in relief against Maxxam's liquidation plan was the capitulation thereto by state officials, elected and appointed. In the summer of 1986, I'd attended a meeting of the California State Board of Forestry in Sacramento. During a break I hailed one of the board members as he strolled down an aisle. He stood out on the board because he was stout, with the taut face of a working man. He wore a Stetson cowboy hat and said very little. I asked the man why the state didn't step in and stop Maxxam's rapid clear-cutting, especially when such logging couldn't stand up to the spirit and intention of the combined California Forest Practice Act and the California Environmental Quality Act. In an appellate court ruling against Georgia-Pacific, the Environmental Protection Information Center had set a state precedent that determined that CEQA's powerful prohibition against environmental harm applied to logging.

The board member looked surprised. As if reading from a script, he claimed, "California has enacted the toughest forest practice laws in the country. There might have been some bad logging in the past, but today timber companies are responsible, good public citizens."

But, I said, those "good public citizens" couldn't include Charles Hurwitz, the man now liquidating the last of the world's ancient redwoods to pay off junk bonds and make himself rich. Couldn't the state step in and halt Maxxam's logging?

"Why would you want to do that?" he asked, incredulous. "An old-growth forest is a biological desert, anyway."

I stood there and blinked. "A what?"

"A biological desert. It's decadent, overmature, it's stopped growing. By clearing away the old, dead trees you make room for vigorous young trees that grow faster, they're more vibrant, more productive. Today there are more redwoods growing in Humboldt County than ever before." Then he walked away.

A man drew up behind me. He was slender and somewhat older than I was. He introduced himself as a California Assembly aide, and I realized we'd spoken on the phone. He'd been listening in.

"You know who that was?" the aide asked me.

"I was just about to go read his nameplate."

"Joseph Russ the Fourth."

"The fourth what?"

"The fourth. He's the patriarch of Humboldt County's most powerful family, some of Humboldt's first white arrivals. Quite a family. They own a lot of land up there. Duke put him on the board to carry water for Maxxam."

"Duke" was California's Republican governor George Deukmejian, a great friend of timber. In January 1986, in the earliest weeks of Maxxam's tenure in Humboldt County, Deukmejian had appointed Russ to the Board of Forestry.

Russ was the great-grandson of Humboldt County's first Joseph Russ, a pioneer who'd arrived on the North Coast as a young man in the early 1850s. During the 1880s, Russ the First was a principal organizer of one of the most notorious land-fraud schemes ever perpetrated against the US government. In a single, brazen con, two hundred square miles of prime ancient redwood forest were stolen from the public domain and turned over to timber companies and investors.

In 1986, the Russ family still owned fifty thousand acres in Humboldt County, among the largest noncorporate private holdings in the county, which they logged and ranched. Joseph Russ was an intelligent man; yet despite his nonsensical thinking—the breathtaking conceit, if not redundancy, of "biological desert"—I have no doubt he believed what he said.

Russ was not alone among those in Sacramento offering base justifications for eliminating the last of the ancient redwoods. On September 5, 1986, when I asked State Senator Barry Keene, a Democrat, if it would be possible to legislate a moratorium on logging old-growth redwood, he answered,

"What for? What good are they then? The old growth has basically stopped growing, and if you don't cut them then they just stand there, not doing anyone any good. The [redwood] parks are underutilized now."

In mid-July I visited Darryl Cherney at the Bridgewood Motel. After we greeted, Darryl grabbed a newspaper, the *Earth First! Journal*, which he'd picked up over the July Fourth weekend at the movement's annual Round River Rendezvous, held that year alongside the North Fork of the Lost River in the Challis National Forest, Idaho. I'd never seen the paper. Darryl jerked a freshly opened beer to and from his mouth, and the foam spewed like a volcano, a trademark.

"You see this?" he asked, clutching the tabloid. "These people are *pissed*!" Earth First! advocated "direct action" at the point of environmental destruction. The movement was loosely based on Edward Abbey's 1975 novel *The Monkey Wrench Gang*, a tragicomic tale of four disparate misanthropes who sabotage machinery and set out to destroy Glen Canyon Dam, on the Colorado River in Arizona. As the "real" Monkey Wrench Gang, Earth First! had announced itself to the world in 1981 by running a triangular three-hundred-foot length of black plastic down the face of the actual Glen Canyon Dam, "cracking" the seven-hundred-foot concrete edifice. At a gathering near the dam, Ed Abbey himself delivered the keynote address:

The industrialization, urbanization, and militarization of the American West continues. More dams are proposed, more coal burning and nuclear power plants are projected . . . more river diversion projects, more strip-mining of her mountains, more clear-cutting of her forests, the misuse of water, the abuse of the land. All for the sake of short-term profit, all to keep the industrial-military empire going and growing, until it finally reaches the point where it must self-destruct, and destroy itself. . . . Oppose the destruction of our homeland by these alien forces from Houston, Tokyo, Manhattan, Washington, D.C., and the Pentagon.

In 1985, Earth First! cofounder Dave Foreman, a former Washington, DC, lobbyist for the Wilderness Society, published *Ecodefense: A Field Guide to Monkeywrenching*. Ed Abbey wrote the foreword. The how-to handbook describes and illustrates methods and equipment needed for all manner of property destruction. As if to assuage an appalled public, Foreman later said,

"We are a movement, not an organization. If we ever took ourselves seriously, we might be dangerous."

Darryl echoed the sentiment. "There are no leaders," he said. "You just
call yourself Earth First!" That sounded good to me. But I told Darryl I
couldn't "join" because I was against property destruction.

"We can do whatever we want," said Darryl. "There are no rules."

The South Fork Eel River wrapped around the Bridgewood compound
and plowed into a steep wall of erosive streambank, creating a swimming
hole twenty feet deep. After nightfall, under a blazing full moon, we swam
in the tepid waters—too warm for fish, just right for humans—and discussed
Maxxam's liquidation of Pacific Lumber's redwoods. I told Darryl that I'd
been digging through Pacific Lumber's timber harvest plans at the California Department of Forestry. The THPs rarely identified the type of forest to
be cut—old growth or second growth—but when I asked CDF officials, in
writing, how much of a specific timber harvest plan contained old-growth
forest, the reply was always the same: "The entire plan is old growth."

A recent THP stood out. Maxxam was proposing to clear-cut ninety-six
acres on Thompson Creek, a tributary of the main stem of the Eel River.
The stand was directly across the river from the famous Founders Grove, in
Humboldt Redwoods State Park. Normally state foresters found little worth
noting in a THP, even those in virgin redwood groves. This time the CDF
inspector had written, "This is the last piece of virgin timber in this area. The
timber stand is very impressive and 'park like' in appearance. . . . The plan
will become highly visible [to the public]."

Later I learned that Pacific Lumber management had saved this classic
ancient forest since the early twentieth century for use as a private picnic
area. The site to be logged held hundreds of gigantic redwoods, some of
them undoubtedly among the tallest trees in the world. Some were close
to twenty feet in diameter. The redwoods grew on a wide alluvial flat at the
confluence of Thompson Creek and the Eel River. For a CDF forester to
express any sort of concern about the proposed logging betrayed the unusual
grandeur of the stand.

John Hummel, a biologist with the California Department of Fish and
Game who was charged with reviewing timber harvest plans to determine
their impacts on wildlife, noted that an osprey nest occupied one of the tall
redwoods. Throughout the year, this one nest would be the only bird, plant,

or animal habitat of any biological importance noted by the agency when reviewing PL timber harvest plans. Hummel nonetheless wrote, "The Pacific Lumber Company foresters have done a commendable amount of work to ensure retention and protection of this important wildlife site. The clear-cut silvicultural method will result in a reasonably undisturbed and natural appearing condition by the second season." Hummel recommended that the tree hosting the osprey nest not be cut down until after nesting season.

"We're not going to get any help from the state," I told Darryl. We decided to call a meeting of regional activists, to be held at Annwfn in two months, on the weekend of September 6 and 7. Forty people showed up, among them Mokai, né Marc DePolo, a "nomadic activist" based in Humboldt County. Mokai embodied radical chic: dark hair in long, luxuriant curls, full beard, knitted cap, and an olive-drab German army jacket. Like Darryl, he played guitar and wrote songs. Mokai had been an activist since his late teens. He'd been busted for locking down at nuclear power plants in Southern California and for blockading logging in Oregon. He would soon anchor our direct actions in the redwoods.

The Annwfn group planned two actions. The first would occur just a few days later, at the Bureau of Land Management office in Ukiah, to protest the federal government's sale of publicly owned ancient forests to private corporations, which clear-cut the increasingly rare ecosystems. The next demonstration would be more consequential. We would gather on October 22 in front of Pacific Lumber's headquarters in downtown San Francisco and call out Maxxam's planned liquidation of the last ancient redwoods.

8

WE TIMED THE SAN FRANCISCO ACTION TO COINCIDE WITH EARTH
First!'s 1986 California Rendezvous on October 18 and 19 at Big
Basin State Park, near Santa Cruz. Big Basin was California's first state
park, established in 1902 to protect fifteen hundred acres of ancient redwood forest. Dave Foreman, the Earth First! cofounder, was scheduled to
speak at the gathering, so I contacted him about addressing our San Francisco "demo." He quickly agreed. Next I phoned David Brower at his newly
formed organization, Earth Island Institute. Brower was an early Sierra
Club executive director who led fights against dams and in favor of creating
a Redwood National Park and other large habitat reserves during the second
half of the twentieth century.

"Sure, I'd love to be there," Brower told me.

I worked at the *Paper* through the third week of October 1986, then
headed down to Santa Cruz, where more than three hundred people had
already gathered at Big Basin.

During the rally, Dave Foreman gave the keynote. He wore a tight, black
Earth First! T-shirt, emblazoned with the command "DEFEND THE
WILDERNESS," the words framing a monkey wrench. Foreman's mus-
cular frame and full beard mirrored his brawny oration. He looked like the
mule packer he once was. Pacing the stage, smacking his hands together,
arms swirling and fisting his points, Foreman could not be ignored.

"The rainforest has been going on constantly, replenishing itself, being
immortal for a hundred million years," said Foreman. "Until us." He poked
himself in the chest. "Until Burger King. Until the World Bank. Until giant
dams. Until chainsaws. . . . We are destroying Eden today. It is on our souls.
It is in our hands to stop it. Are we going to do it? Or are we going to sit on

our fat, comfortable butts in front of our TV sets? It's up to us. It is our generation. It is our time on Earth."

After the Rendezvous, on Wednesday, October 22, 1986, two hundred boisterous souls gathered along Washington Avenue for a lunchtime rally in downtown San Francisco, in front of the Pacific Lumber office tower. "We need corporate responsibility," said David Brower, who advocated "environmental impact statements on business takeovers." Dave Foreman complained that "one man, Charles Hurwitz, is going to destroy the largest remaining block of redwoods out of sheer arrogance. Only we people can stop him." Foreman let out a wolf howl, and the crowd joined, startling passing executives.

On Monday, November 10, 1986, Jim Sears, publisher of the *North Coast News*, asked me to interview for the job of editor at his Mendocino County weekly. A week later I was in his office, accepting the job. I was twenty-five years old. Sears made it clear that I would need to give up activism. I knew it was coming, but I couldn't relinquish a career path I'd set for myself when I was eighteen.

After leaving Sears I traveled north to the tiny timber town of Carlotta, on the Van Duzen River in Humboldt County. A photographer named David Cross had told me that he and Mokai were scheduled to hike onto Pacific Lumber lands to view the ancient redwoods. No one outside Pacific Lumber, as far as he knew, had done this—except, it turned out, the man who would guide them. Would I care to join?

Our guide would be Chuck Powell, who lived in Carlotta with his wife, Sharon Green, and their two young children. He ran a small janitorial service that cleaned business offices in Fortuna, a timber town plunked alongside the Eel River ten miles downstream of Pacific Lumber's company-owned town Scotia. Pacific Lumber kept a log deck (where sectioned redwoods are stacked prior to trucking them to the mill) at the mouth of Yager Creek, a major tributary to the Van Duzen, which itself is a large tributary to the lower Eel River. The Fisher log deck covered forty acres and accommodated thousands of old-growth redwood logs, some of them ten to fifteen feet wide, stacked to heights of fifty feet. From here PL shipped logs to Scotia, to be processed in the world's largest lumber mill. Throughout 1986 Chuck and Sharon had seen a substantial uptick in the number of logging trucks that passed their house.

David Cross, Mokai, and I slept on the floor of a small utility shack. The next morning we piled into Chuck's van and navigated a county dirt road near his house that ran up the north side of the Van Duzen watershed and onto a ridge that separated the river from Yager Creek. Along the way, young second-growth redwoods lined the road, cloaking us in a false dusk. At some point we crossed onto Pacific Lumber land, but I didn't realize it until the small trees gave way to big ones. The redwoods were old growth, but it was not a virgin forest. This was a "residual grove." Before the Maxxam takeover, Pacific Lumber selectively logged its virgin tracts, leaving half of the trees standing.

Chuck pulled over, and we got out. Below us two loggers worked a redwood tree. The day was cloudy, and the men wore muted colors, so what stood out was their shiny new metal hardhats. One of them wielded what was obviously an extremely powerful chainsaw. Below the loggers a bulldozer carved a trench, or "layout," two hundred feet long in front of the redwood to cushion its fall. Every tree got its own layout. Suddenly the saw stopped, and the men darted away. Nothing happened for a few seconds, then the tree eased forward as if nudged by a slight wind. But it didn't swing back. Instead, the tree kept coming, descending in liquid slow-motion with a staccato of jarring cracks. Suddenly the butt end popped from the stump and jumped slightly into the air, then one hundred tons of cellulose hit the earth with the boom of a mortar.

We continued up the road about a mile, and Chuck parked the rig. We hoofed through dense foliage under a vibrant canopy of residual redwood forest. Along the way, Chuck tied flagging so we could find our way back, a mistake we would never repeat.

A half-mile tramp led us onto a recently gouged dirt path, a skid trail. The skid trail led another quarter mile to a recently bulldozed lane, a haul road. We hiked the haul road for a while, then skittered onto a wide landing that had been carved into the steep slope, to temporarily hold logs. The edge of the landing overlooked South Fork Yager Creek, where the stream dropped more than a thousand feet of elevation in under one mile. Blankets of mist rose continuously from hundreds of feet below. When the mists parted like a celestial curtain, a great wall of greenery came slowly into focus. Then the forest materialized like a ghost.

A spectacular wall of old-growth redwoods coated a near vertical slope of the incised creek channel. The mists continued to part, and the life of this place now fully emerged. The great conifers loped across several hills as far as we could see. We had entered the remnant of a planetary force now almost gone. Growing up I had frequently explored all of the protected ancient redwood parks. I had never seen, or especially felt, a *wild* redwood grove. It was as if I'd been reunited with a family member long given up for dead. Later we would call this stand Owl Creek Grove, for a small stream that ran through the middle of the forest.

Mokai stood to my right. He'd apparently been saying something, but I hadn't heard him. As I came around, he eyed me with a wry look and chuckled. If anyone understood it was Mokai.

"Incredible isn't it?"

"I can't take the job."

"What?"

Tramping back to Chuck's van, we stopped short against a trio of grim faces. The loggers had radioed headquarters. These men had found Chuck's van and easily followed the flags. One of the guys was short, lean, tightly wound, maybe fifty years old. He stood flanked on either side by a pair of human refrigerators. Shorty did all the talking. He told us we were on private land. "You're trespassing; you could go to jail." Chuck may have talked to him—I don't remember. I recall that when Shorty said, "Don't come back," no one answered.

As we drove off, Chuck said, "That was Bob Stephens, PL's chief forester." Apparently Robert Stephens had been after Pacific Lumber for years to cut more timber. He designed all of Maxxam's timber harvest plans, including the clear-cut of giant trees at the mouth of Thompson Creek, where Stephens himself had occasionally picnicked.

Once home in Sonoma County, I called Jim Sears to decline the editor's job. I told him about the trip to the forest, that my trajectory had been instantly derailed. He sounded mystified, as if I'd refused lottery winnings.

I grabbed my stash of maps from the Orange Cat and folded each one into five-by-seven-inch rectangles, quadrant name up, and put them into a clear plastic bag. I drove to an army surplus store in Santa Rosa and bought an olive-drab military pack with several side pockets. It would hold fifty pounds and had a lined pocket for maps. The pack sat high and squat on the human frame and was made for crashing through brush without getting hung up. I also purchased an olive-drab shirt and hiking pants, a thick, green wool overshirt, a lightweight camouflage tarp, a compass, and a headlamp. Next stop was a photo supply store, where I bought a dozen rolls of color slide film and another dozen of black-and-white. I told my landlord I'd be moving in a month. I had no idea where I would end up—just that it would be somewhere in Humboldt County. I had almost no money. I felt great.

9

O N December 3, 1986, our nascent Earth First! group brought the protest directly to Pacific Lumber's company-owned town of Scotia. The town and mill occupied more than two miles of riverbank along US Highway 101, twenty-five miles south of Eureka. Thousands of old-growth logs bobbed like slaughtered whales in a forty-acre pond, waiting to be put through the world's largest saws. Running south from the mill buildings were endless stacks of redwood lumber that followed the highway for a mile. The village of Scotia itself—a couple hundred homes overlooking the mill— lay dwarfed by industrial mass.

Darryl Cherney and a college student named Larry Evans had designed the Scotia protest as a "save the loggers" rally. They created brochures ostensibly published by the "Save the Loggers League," with the premise that, mathematically, Maxxam's liquidation would destroy the company in about twenty years, leaving timber families in the lurch, which is exactly what happened.

Mike Roselle attended the rally and spoke for the national Earth First! group. Two dozen residents of Southern Humboldt County, many of them members of the Acorn Alliance antinuclear group, helped fill out the crowd. After a few speeches we marched through the town, something no resident had seen in Scotia's entire 117-year history. A dozen local, county, and state cops stood idly by, as there were no incidents, and several timber workers hovered on the outskirts, more curious than upset.

In his Ben Davis work clothes, suspenders, and big black boots, Larry Evans looked like a quintessential logger. He stood six feet, two inches, wore a thick beard, and weighed between 220 and 240 pounds, depending on what he was doing that week. He'd grown up among union organizers in the hardscrabble Southern California labor city of San Pedro. Now he

was a forestry student at Humboldt State University (HSU). Every summer we lost Larry to his job managing trail crews in the Sierra Nevada
mountains.

"I just gotta bust rock, man," Larry told me one day, explaining his absence. "If I don't bust rock, I go crazy."

I met Nina Williams, an HSU student and a director of the College Center for Alternative Technology, and her friend Danielle Philippa, a brave and
enigmatic nomad who'd escaped the life of a young punk rocker in the Bay
Area. The professorial Todd Swarthout was there, along with brash, brazen
Kurt Newman. These activists were forming an ad hoc northern core group,
in the seat of Humboldt County power, to take on Maxxam. During the
Redwood National Park struggle of the 1960s and 1970s, HSU students had
provided an important local source of authority in favor of creating a Redwood National Park at Redwood Creek, thirty miles north of Arcata. (One
of those students, Steve Madrone, is now a Humboldt County supervisor.)
This new generation would do similar work.

After the Scotia "demo," two dozen of us caravanned north to Arcata
for Mexican food and pitchers of beer at a capacious downtown restaurant called Casa de que Pasa (House of What's Happening). An infectious tribal camaraderie bubbled up. After dinner most of us ambled north
through town to a bright-red, turn-of-the-century Craftsman home, where
we met in a circle to discuss future plans. Then the party just kept rolling.
New folks showed up. Mickey Dulas, who lived in town with her young
son, Dylan, arrived. Mickey would soon throw herself full-time into the
campaign. I also met Bill Devall, the "deep ecology" guru who taught sociology at Humboldt State University. Bill had been an intellectual force
ever since the Redwood National Park campaign. In 1985 Devall and
George Sessions published their seminal book *Deep Ecology: Living as if
Nature Mattered*, which argues, "We need to cultivate an ecological consciousness. . . . This process involves becoming more aware of the actuality
of rocks, wolves, trees, and rivers—the cultivation of the insight that everything is connected."

As the evening morphed to an anarchy of cross talk, catching up,
checking maps, comparing notes, singing songs, and general mayhem,
people roamed around, jabbering and gripping beers. After several hours
the crowd had hardly dissipated. If anything, the fervor was growing. At

one point I turned to a person standing next to me and asked, "Hey, whose house is this?"

"It's Lynn Ryan's. She's a local nurse and heads up the North Group of the Sierra Club."

"Oh," I said, looking around. "Which one is she?"

"She's not here."

Lynn was working a twelve-hour shift in the maternity ward at Arcata's Mad River Hospital. When she wasn't working, Lynn made the arduous journeys to Sacramento, prepared comments, and provided the intellectual and logistical glue for North Coast environmental campaigns. She viewed her beautiful old home less as "her" place and more as a resource for activists. That night several of us camped out in her front room, back rooms, and backyard—yet I wouldn't meet Lynn Ryan until morning, when she stepped over me to get to the kitchen.

On January 1, 1987, I wrote "An Open Letter Regarding the Pacific Lumber Company's Accelerated Timber Harvest Schedule." I sent the letter to fifty recipients, including Charles Hurwitz at Maxxam and officials at the Pacific Lumber Company. Also cc'd were two dozen media outlets; state officials at the California Department of Forestry, Board of Forestry, and Department of Fish and Game; all pertinent elected representatives; conservation organizations such as Save the Redwoods League, Greenpeace, the Wilderness Society, and Friends of the Earth; and Dave Foreman and Mike Roselle. The letter promised, "A protracted, heated battle over PALCO's virgin timber will continue for as long as the company logs it." (PALCO and PL were interchangeable acronyms for the company.) I proposed creation of "an agreement that would not only save all of PALCO's remaining old-growth forests, but also would supply MAXXAM with a reasonable purchase price. . . . [T]his prospect . . . is far more attractive than the years of litigation, protests, legislative debate, civil disobedience, and overall bitter conflict that will inevitably result from a policy of noncooperation."

The letter would have gone nowhere had not George Snyder, a reporter for the *San Francisco Chronicle*, used it as a hook to run a story on the last redwood roundup.

"North Coast environmentalists are gearing up for a long war against a Humboldt County lumber company that plans to cut what could be fully one-quarter of the virgin redwood trees left in the world," Snyder reported. "Greg King . . . opened this newest logging war last week by sending out dozens of letters."

Snyder quoted comments by CDF's Ross Johnson and PL's public relations manager Dave Galitz.

"We know we're going to be getting a lot of heat this year over old-growth cutting," Johnson told Snyder. "To a forester, old-growth trees don't produce. People who manage forests in an industrial sense want trees that are growing in order to produce a continuing crop, so they cut the old trees. It's real hard to tell somebody, though, that they've got the last of the old-growth trees and can't cut them anymore."

Galitz told Snyder, "We've been here for 118 years and we could be here for another 100. . . . We have 200,000 acres of timber. You can only clear-cut up to 80 acres, and then you've got to leave a buffer. There will be room for wildlife."

On January 6, Galitz called to see if I would meet with him and Pacific Lumber executive vice president John Campbell at PL headquarters in Scotia, on Monday, January 12. "I'll be there," I told him.

Galitz and Campbell hosted me in a roomy second-story conference room. The walls were paneled in lustrous old-growth redwood boards, not a single knot to be seen. John Campbell stood tall and paunchy, like Oliver Hardy, though clearly he had once been a man of some brawn. Filling in as Campbell's Stan Laurel was Dave Galitz, who said little during the meeting.

There would be no dealmaking, no attempt to rescue PL's ancient redwoods from the saws, said Campbell, because—wait for it—the old growth was "decadent, overmature. You have to cut the old trees to make room for a vigorous new forest. What you're proposing is that we shut down our entire operation and put a thousand people out of work. Is that what you want? To put us out of business and ruin the lives of these people?" (Later, in a court deposition, Robert Stephens, the PL forester, would take "decadent" one step further by referring to virgin redwood groves as "stagnant.")

"You know as well as I do that Maxxam's going to log PL's forests for twenty years and then get out of Humboldt County," I said. "The math is simple. A fifth grader could do it." I involuntarily shot a look at Galitz, and he flinched.

As if on cue, Campbell said, "You know what happens when you cut down a redwood?" I suffered a slight twinge of PTSD, remembering that, just before he threatened to kill me, the Sonoma County logger had asked that exact question, word for word, then answered it himself. "It grows back!"

"You're going to tell me it grows back," I said to Campbell.

"Precisely!" He assumed an air of victory.

Campbell invited me over to a picture window that overlooked the town of Scotia and the Highway 101 freeway. Rising eastward from the freeway was a hillside loaded with redwood forest. Campbell said, "You see that forest over there? It's second-growth redwood. The old trees were cut eighty years ago. Now it's a forest again. Redwood likes to be cut."

"It's not old growth," I said. "Habitat's totally different. Less than 5 percent of the original ancient redwood forest still stands. Don't you think industry has had enough?"

The next week, in Eureka, I purchased a single share of Maxxam stock. I still have it. A few days later I bought a round-trip flight to Los Angeles. In March, Maxxam would host a shareholder meeting, and I intended to be there.

10

WHEN DAVE GALITZ TOLD THE *CHRONICLE* THAT PACIFIC LUMBER had been in operation for 118 years and that, even under Maxxam, another century of logging was possible, he invoked a past that no longer existed. Back in 1869, when Pacific Lumber was founded, the northern ancient redwood belt remained almost entirely intact. When Galitz, John Campbell, and I spoke, it was almost gone. Ignoring history was among the timber industry's greatest failings, however intentional.

The story of how the Pacific Lumber Company came into being and acquired its first redwood inventory is little known. That said, some of the individuals involved in creating the company and their financial interests—especially in mining, banking, and railroads—consistently pop up in parallel narratives.

The first name in the narrative is that of William Ralston. The Ohioan made his fortune early in life by financing the gold and silver mining industry of the Comstock Lode. He'd arrived in California for the gold rush, late, in 1854, but by 1859 he was invested in, and a director of, most of Nevada's most successful bonanza mines. In 1864 Ralston and fellow mining financier Darius Ogden Mills founded the Bank of California, which quickly became the state's most powerful financial institution.

Ralston and Mills packed the directorship of their bank with what "became known as Ralston's Ring, or simply, The Bank Crowd," men who constituted "the West's wealthiest capitalists during the Civil War period," historian Gray Brechin writes in *Reclaiming San Francisco: History, Politics, Culture*. Like Mills, who was once California's richest man, Ralston was a savvy investor who "converted his Comstock capital into coastal transport, insurance, telegraph lines, currency speculation, woolen and silk mills, canal companies, hydraulic mines, political and judicial bribery, Alaskan furs, gas works, refineries, and hazardous real estate schemes," writes Brechin.

Add to that list redwoods.

Ralston was among the first regents of the nascent University of California, founded in 1868. He was also the university's treasurer. Ralston was well placed to wrench from the public domain more than ten thousand acres of redwood forest that grew along the Eel River and place it in the hands of the timber industry. In his 2014 book *Both Sides of the Bluff,* Humboldt County historian Jerry Rohde provides details:

> One evening late in 1868, when Ralston was at the height of his power, [he met with] Henry A. Wetherbee, a mill owner from the Mendocino Coast, and his long-time friend and adviser Frederick F. Low, who had recently finished a term as California's governor. Low was now looking for something to do in the private sector, and Wetherbee knew of a sector that was very private indeed—a tract of redwood timber along the Eel River that he and his partner, A. W. MacPherson, had their eyes on. . . . Early in 1869 Wetherbee's partner MacPherson purchased 10,794 acres of timberland on the Eel River from the Regents of the University of California. He reportedly did so on behalf of Samuel F. Butterworth, former U.S. District Attorney for Mississippi and current manager of the vastly rich quicksilver mine at New Almaden [San Jose]. Conveniently, Butterworth at that moment happened to be a regent himself. So was Ralston, while Low had served on the board the previous year during his term as governor. The sale was made under the Morrill Land Grant Act of 1862, which gave federal lands to certain states, each of which in turn was to sell the property and use the proceeds to endow "a college of agriculture and mechanical arts." . . . By then, MacPherson, along with Wetherbee and three others, were trustees of The Pacific Lumber Company, which was formed in February 1869.

For many years the owners of Pacific Lumber did very little logging or milling, for the simple reason that the company's forests, no matter how valuable, stood twenty miles from the closest possible shipping point along the south end of Humboldt Bay. Buckboards wouldn't cut it. A railroad was essential, but it could only be built after blasting an expensive tunnel through Table Bluff, which separated the Eel River from Humboldt Bay.

The Panic of 1873 also delayed development of Pacific Lumber. The economic crash devastated the nation's fragile financial webs. On the morning of August 26, 1875, a run began on the Bank of California. The company vault emptied before 3 p.m., at which point the bank closed its doors. At the time, Ralston owed the bank $5 million—about $150 million today—and his many other investments were in free fall. Mills and the other bank directors forced Ralston's resignation and compelled him to turn over all his remaining assets to director William Sharon, whom Brechin describes as a "piranha [who] devoured mines, mills, business associates, transportation, forests, and Virginia City's water works. . . . He directed the profits back to his partners in The Bank Crowd." Ralston then went "swimming" in San Francisco Bay, where he drowned.

One of the Ralston assets that did not end up in Sharon's hands was his one-fifth stake in the Pacific Lumber Company, which he'd acquired as a self-dealing UC regent. Not long before his final swim, Ralston signed over this asset to John Paxton and Allen Curtis, who, like Ralston, owned a bank, based in Austin, Nevada, that financed and profited from gold and silver mining in the state. The record is not clear as to why Ralston signed over this particular asset to Paxton and Curtis. But there is no mystery as to what they did with it.

In 1882, after completion of the tunnel through Table Bluff, a new railroad extended south from the Van Duzen River toward PL's redwood holdings. Pacific Lumber, now led by Allen Curtis, came to life and announced plans to build a mill at the present site of Scotia. South of the mill the company would log its untouched redwood inventory, a cherry-picked expanse of densely clustered conifers that coated both sides of the wide Eel River for nearly twenty miles, right up to and including much of lower Bull Creek, where Rockefeller Forest, the heart of Humboldt Redwoods State Park, now protects the world's largest remaining alluvial flat of ancient redwoods. Today little is known about most of the forest that stood between Scotia and Bull Creek, which would be liquidated over the coming decades, except that it was unbroken, diverse, primordial, and extraordinary. Northward the company would connect with the new rail line and ship lumber to the docks at Hookton Channel, on the southeastern rim of Humboldt Bay. John Paxton and Allen Curtis personally surveyed the company's railroad right-of-way.

Lumber shipments from Hookton Channel began early the next year, reaching San Francisco as well as ports throughout the United States and the world. Sawyers and mule teams spread southward along the river, turning in such heavy cuts that Pacific Lumber, overnight, ranked as the world's largest producer of redwood lumber, shipping twenty million board feet in 1888.

It would take several years to deplete the dense forest that surrounded Scotia. Yet the true motherlode began to reveal itself three miles farther south, or upriver, where, at the future settlement of Stafford, the river canyon opened into an unbroken flat that graced the Eel's riverbanks for eleven miles. Here stood the lumberman's prize, the single greatest expanse of forest ever known. Six thousand acres of pure redwood banked both sides of the river. Here and there small meadows dotted the alluvial flat, accenting the paradisical domain. Surrounding hills rose from one hundred to almost three thousand feet elevation and harbored tens of thousands of acres of contiguous ancient forest. Along the way several large tributaries also opened into broad flats of ancient conifers, some of them more than three thousand years old and nearing, or exceeding, four hundred feet tall.

Through this mystic world the Eel River ran slow and deep, a living memory of time itself. The flat sometimes switched banks, but it was continuous. Sunshine rarely reached the stream, as the trees along the river were uniformly the tallest in the world, and in any case the big river was regularly engulfed in hanging blankets of summer fog and winter storms. At its upriver terminus, beyond which the coastal mountains again pressed steeply against the stream, the flat expanded into a single arboreal crescendo of one thousand acres that engulfed the confluence of a major Eel River tributary, Larabee Creek. From here the flat, though narrower, ran four miles up Larabee Creek itself. The Bull Creek flat stood another five miles farther south.

Rockefeller Forest, while spectacular, is but an echo of the stand that grew downstream. No forest in the world could adequately compare with the great redwood flat of the Eel River, where many individual acres provided Pacific Lumber with one million, and in places more than three million, board feet of lumber. Today, no words can describe this supreme example of redwood growth, owing especially to the fact that almost no one saw it, save the surveyors and loggers who destroyed it.

11

IN MID-JANUARY 1987, I JOINED THE NORTHERN HUMBOLDT COUNTY Earth First! group, in Arcata, to begin mapping Pacific Lumber's remaining old-growth forest islands. A set of 1980 aerial photos showed the whereabouts of PL's virgin groves. We'd take turns traveling to the California Department of Forestry office in Fortuna to obtain copies of the site maps included in every Pacific Lumber timber harvest plan. We subtracted the THP boundaries from the virgin groves shown on the aerial photos to get what turned out to be an accurate picture of the remaining untouched forest. We traced this data onto our topographic hiking maps.

That month I also compiled a long list of Pacific Lumber's timber harvest plan applications filed with CDF in 1986, every one of which the agency approved with breathtaking haste, as if the very last of the world's ancient redwoods constituted so much corn. That year CDF approved fifty-two PL timber harvest plan applications, for a total of 10,855 acres, more than double PL's acreage of the previous year. Of this expanse, 9,589 acres contained old-growth forest, virgin and residual. Every standing old-growth tree—hundreds of thousands total—would be cut. Most of the THPs allowed logging to occur even during the North Coast's extremely wet winter months—a disastrous mode of operating.

By now California courts had codified the California Environmental Quality Act requirement that the California Department of Forestry take into consideration the "significant, cumulative, adverse environmental effects" of a THP when considered alongside "past, present, or reasonably foreseeable future" THPs in the plan area. Against this mandate, CDF's subsequent claims, made in official justifications for approving Pacific Lumber's logging plans, would appear far-fetched, beyond the scope of rationality. But they served their purpose, which was to get the cut out.

A CDF forester wrote that Maxxam's clear-cutting of 125 acres of virgin redwood on the South Fork Yager Creek, just upstream of Owl Creek Grove, was allowable under CEQA because

> tractor logging and new road construction will contribute to surface soil erosion, but it is unlikely to be significant at this time. Mass soil movement may happen but to say that it will be significant is to [sic] early. New road construction and tractor logging may somewhat decrease water quality but only for a short time period. It cannot be judged at this time if it will be significant. This stand of old-growth timber has direct access to the public, however it cannot be judged at this time if aesthetics would be significantly impacted. No endangered species were noted during the inspection. Old-growth timber has been noted to shelter all types of plants and animals. Unless one observes these species it cannot be judged if any significant impact would occur.

A nearby THP proposed clear-cutting 143 acres of virgin redwood on Owl Creek itself. Here Robert Stephens cleverly evaded the state's meager limits on the size of clear-cuts by providing a buffer between two separate clear-cuts that together measured 143 acres. The "buffer" was a massive landslide. The inspecting CDF forester wrote, "The two units, separated by the slide, do not exceed the clear-cut limit."

Department of Forestry officials specialized in throwing wildlife under the bulldozer. Incredibly, they often argued that habitat destruction benefitted wildlife.

"A general short-term improvement for wildlife habitat is seen from this plan," CDF wrote of a 294-acre old-growth redwood logging plan on Chadd Creek, adjacent to Humboldt Redwoods State Park. Likewise, a "possible minor improvement to wildlife habitat" would result from an 88-acre clear-cut of old growth on Corner Creek, and "wildlife habitat may be improved" after 309 acres of old-growth clear-cutting on Larabee Creek. On Strongs Creek, where Pacific Lumber would clear 760 acres of old-growth redwood, "some deer habitat will be improved."

West of Scotia, the Bear River shared a ridge with the North Fork Mattole River. Here stood a five-thousand-acre expanse of virgin Douglas fir forest broken by luxuriant prairies. In California's coastal mountain ranges, a large stand of uncut fir is rarer than old-growth redwood. As an initial foray toward liquidating the entire Mattole-Bear River stand, Robert Stephens proposed a sixty-five-acre clear-cut of virgin forest on Bear River. CDF wrote, "Wildlife habitat may generally improve in the short run after logging. Generally speaking old-growth timber will support some rare, threatened, or endangered species. However, none were observed during the inspection."

I printed several hundred copies of the THP information and mailed them to every post office box in Scotia, along with a letter requesting that PL employees resist Maxxam's liquidation. I got only one response, but it was notable. On March 18, 1987, Pacific Lumber placed a three-quarter-page ad in two Humboldt County newspapers, including the daily *Eureka Times-Standard*, that featured a letter written in February by Robert Stephens. Stephens had also mailed his letter to all post office boxes in Scotia. His letter served largely to call attention to our work. Stephens claimed, "Greg King . . . is dedicated to bringing about a total halt to all cutting of old growth trees." Stephens acknowledged the acreage figures I'd provided and, without refuting them, wrote, "Greg has no accurate knowledge of the true composition of the timber stands involved. He has listed statements and comments out of text [*sic*]."

Our mapping project continued through February. That month we located one of Pacific Lumber's virgin redwood islands just before the company, at the end of February, applied to clear-cut seventy-four acres of it. Later we would call this stand All Species Grove, but for now it stood simply as lines on a map. The forest appeared to be just over one thousand acres. Most shocking was that nearly half the THP acreage would consist of three miles of new roads, to be carved throughout the larger forest.

On Friday, March 8, Pacific Lumber and CDF conducted an on-site "preharvest inspection" of the area to be logged. The crew included a CDF forester, a biologist with the state Department of Fish and Game, a geologist with the state Division of Mines and Geology, and several Pacific Lumber representatives—including the mute refrigerators who had flanked Robert Stephens when he discovered our group four months before. As the world would soon learn in court, the refrigerators were on hand to keep order in the charnel house of redwood liquidation.

The forester for CDF was Roscoe Rowney. When I read the inspection report, the name stopped me short. Louisiana-Pacific's top forester and spokesman in the redwoods was Chris Rowney. I'd spoken with him several times while investigating the company's operations in Sonoma County. The Rowney brothers made an impressively destructive team.

In his preharvest inspection report, Roscoe Rowney claimed that the group had spent sixteen hours tramping the virgin redwood forest to be roaded and clear-cut. Addressing cumulative impacts, Rowney wrote, "It cannot be denied that a forty-seven-acre block of old-growth habitat will be lost, but that is not to say that wildlife cannot continue. There is still a large old-growth tract adjoining the block. The relatively small area will recover as a new forest takes over."

Yet, on the same page, Rowney notes, "The second project in this THP is the construction of approximately 2.5 miles of haul roads which will give access to most of the remaining stand." Apparently Rowney was in the dark as to what might be hauled on those haul roads.

Rowney concluded, "There do not appear to be any special wildlife considerations associated with this unit. No evidence of use by birds of special concern was noted."

By this time the rare habitat qualities preserved by the world's remaining ancient redwood groves were well known. Old-growth-dependent wildlife, such as the tailed frog, Olympic salamander, spotted owl, and marbled murrelet, among many other species, were on the edge of extinction. Degraded water quality from clear-cut operations was undermining California's last viable stocks of wild salmon and steelhead. Had state foresters been doing their jobs, they would have invoked several state and federal laws established to protect habitat and many other public trust values, even if the land was privately owned. In my view, then and now, state officials who uniformly, and out of whole cloth, invented grade-school justifications that allowed a corporation to illegally destroy the last of a precious, primeval forest ecosystem were as responsible as timber company officials for violating those laws. The courts would eventually agree.

Though they didn't know it, officials from Pacific Lumber and CDF were not alone in the forest on March 8. That morning, before first light, Danielle Philippa plowed her rattling Volkswagen microbus through the doglegs of

Kneeland Road, above Humboldt Bay, and dropped off Mokai, Nina Williams, Kurt Newman, and me near All Species Grove for an inspection of our own. We scampered down an unused ranch road and crossed a small stream, then followed a failing skid trail nearly a mile west until we were stopped short, at the property line, by a wall of titanic trees.

We were unprepared for what we'd find in All Species Grove. The initial short slog uphill peaked at a high, rounded, heavily forested knoll at sixteen hundred feet elevation. Even here many of the redwoods were very large, with diameters of eight, ten, even twelve feet, many of them clustered together in distinctive families. A dominance of tall redwoods had allowed dainty shade-loving plants to thrive along the forest floor. Hiking was easy across evergreen carpets of oxalis and salal and veils of sword ferns.

We continued west down a brief slope until the landscape eased into an improbable flat of consistently large redwoods. We were still above fifteen hundred feet elevation; yet the flat was expansive, covering about forty acres, which was unusual at such altitudes in the redwoods. To our right, a small, unnamed stream drew us forward. The stream ran for just one mile before joining the much larger Lawrence Creek, a major tributary of Yager Creek. Several yew trees stood high overhead with great arcing branches, their needles looking much like those of redwood. Some of the yews were three feet in diameter, meaning they were ancient. In many places the shiny red bark of the yews had been scored by bears.

Here stood a world unto itself, a seemingly forgotten Eden. Wide paths of viridescent mosses and deer ferns lined both stream banks. When we stepped near the stream, our boots sank a few inches into the moss, leaving imprints that did not resolve but rather etched the soft ground and slowly filled with water.

We moved uphill. Mokai sighed. "Just think what a bulldozer will do to this place," he said.

Of nearly three miles of road designed by PL's surveyors, one would slice across the land where we now stood, an understanding made clear by a long row of orange flagging that followed the small stream until the ribbons passed out of sight to the southwest. When we crossed the creek, we found another row of flagging that also disappeared into the distance, through troops of great redwoods.

We reached a place along the flat where the redwoods grew inside a natural bowl protected by ridges. The trees grew very tall and wide and tapered little in their extreme ascendancy. Broad canopies spewed gnarled branches the size of small trees. On most of the redwoods the first branches grew very high off the ground. Two of the biggest trees stood directly across the creek from each other. One was 13 feet in diameter, the other 10. Their first branches were 150 feet above the forest floor.

As the group scattered, I stood staring between the two trees, gazing into what I would later describe as a portal. The little creek ran in a gentle but consistent arc to the northwest. A broad curve of forest bent with it, and the tall trees formed an arboreal corridor, deep green and hundreds of feet high, wending in a perfect arc and leading toward what appeared to be the Jurassic. This order of antiquity, of scale, was so transfixing that for a moment time dissolved. Great conifers and the delicate plants they nurtured had gathered as a living tableau of primordial life so ancient, so inherently divine that, whereas I could feel the life of the forest coursing through me, never have I found words to adequately describe it.

The most compelling question, one that would be repeated by everyone I guided into these groves, was *How could anyone cut this down?*

On the way home we traveled mostly in silence. The forest was thrilling; yet its fate appeared grim. My notes from that day are overwrought. I referred to Maxxam's plans for All Species Grove as *"murder.* This is wanton slaughter. No consideration, no feeling, just reckless mindless destruction. What fools, what insane people could perpetrate such madness?"

A few days after we returned from All Species Grove, the Arcata group finished mapping. We'd located seven primary groves comprising eight thousand acres of virgin forest. No more ancient redwood remained outside parks. Most compelling was what we were calling "the big grove." The forest island took in the headwaters of Salmon Creek and Little South Fork Elk River, two small streams separated by a low ridge.

Just a half mile east of the big grove stood a one-thousand-acre island in an area called Elk Head Springs, which ran along the upper banks of the South Fork Elk River. Together the two stands held the last remaining ancient redwoods in the Humboldt Bay watershed and formed the most important forest habitat between Humboldt Redwoods State Park and Red-wood National Park, a distance of fifty miles.

All Species Grove stood four miles east of the big grove. From here, six miles south, was Owl Creek Grove. Three smaller stands rounded out the inventory. And that was it, the very last of the virgin redwoods.

Between and contiguous to these tiny yet ecologically important red-wood islands stood forty thousand acres of residual old-growth redwood forest. Another sixteen thousand acres of PL's residual forest stood on Bear Creek, adjacent to Humboldt Redwoods State Park, twenty miles to the south. Pacific Lumber's combined sixty-four thousand acres of old-growth redwood—virgin and residual—represented almost half the world's entire remaining inventory of the big trees, inside and outside parks. The con-tiguous forty-eight-thousand-acre block was more than twice the size of the second-largest old-growth redwood expanse, in Humboldt Redwoods State Park.

12

O N SUNDAY, MARCH 15, DANIELLE PHILIPPA AGAIN PILOTED HER VW microbus toward All Species Grove. On this day I would hike alone, starting in All Species Grove and making my way west to the big grove. I did not arrange for a pickup. I told Danielle I would trek to the freeway and hitch back to Arcata.

At dawn I crossed Booths Run Creek and scurried into All Species Grove. The luscious flat and the two big redwoods again brought me up short. I followed orange road flagging for a half mile through the otherwise trackless forest until I reached the rush of Lawrence Creek. Across the creek I emerged from the forest into a catastrophe of giant stumps and new road construction. Maxxam was now blazing roads into the southwestern section of All Species Grove, only no one knew it was happening. There were no approved roads or timber harvest plans in this area. Like nearly everything Maxxam did in the redwoods, this road was rogue. There was no question that Maxxam was coming for All Species Grove.

I walked into the slate of an overcast day, the pale sky a doleful vault over fields of churned mud. The perfume of the forest had given way to scents of diesel and earth. Streams of silt and debris flowed down slopes, along roads, and directly into the major salmon spawning reach of Lawrence Creek. Mud gripped my boots, often to the ankles.

I stopped at an overused four-way intersection. The roads were now thirty feet wide, enough room for two fully loaded logging trucks to pass in either direction. The swampy track skirted the steep inner gorge of Fish Creek, traversed a low gap at fourteen hundred feet elevation, and descended into the South Fork Elk River watershed. Along the way, blackened piles pocked the landscape, many of them still spewing smoke from recent slash burns.

In the far distance a wall of tall trees indicated the uppermost reach of South Fork Elk River. I crossed the small stream just as a fine mist began coating my face. I ducked into the forest and immersed myself in its quickening darkness, inside the one-thousand-acre stand at Elk Head Springs. I had trudged nonstop for twelve hours, yet only now, among the redwoods and Douglas fir, tanoak, huckleberry, and ferns, could I relax.

I bivouacked on a wide, fallen redwood that was unusually flat on top. A patter of rain fell onto my tarp, and a slight breeze hissed across the canopy. The next morning I continued west and stumbled into a montage of rocks, water, and great trees. Elk Head Springs was an unexpected find. Everywhere water seeped from the ground. Boulders and large rocks littered the forest floor, which was carpeted in neon mosses and dainty ferns. I hiked for two hours before noting a scattering of stumps. Decades before, when an adjacent timber company had logged its redwoods, it had also poached dozens, if not hundreds, of the biggest trees from Pacific Lumber property.

I exited PL land and entered the other company's forty-year-old clear-cut, half a mile wide and tangled with dense brush and tiny, suppressed second-growth trees. After an insane two-hour struggle against this woven wall of flora, I again entered a virgin forest. Small tanoak and red alders twined with huckleberry and salal beneath arrow-straight conifers. Beautiful blood currants were just beginning to bloom, their pink and white flowers a delight; yet they only tightened the knit. The forest was gorgeous. But I was in trouble.

The rains had ceased, but the brush remained slick underfoot and well-nigh impenetrable unless you hurled yourself through. After an hour I'd achieved perhaps four hundred yards. I was aiming for Little South Fork Elk River. My map showed dozens of tiny streams feeding Little South Fork as well as the larger South Fork, from whence I'd come, and Salmon Creek, which ran in an arc from south to west. After another hour I headed down a steep inner draw. But was it the right one? The feeder streams flowed in all directions, helter-skelter across the landscape. This was before GPS—I had no way of knowing exactly where I was. For a while I'd follow a feeder stream downhill, lose my nerve, head back up, and find another, then another, until I was completely turned around in a warren of tiny, brush-choked tributaries. This went on for hours.

Then I smelled churned earth. Fifteen minutes later I emerged from the foliage onto a freshly carved skid trail. No trees had been cut to carve this road. It was an exploration lane, sliced just weeks before to allow Robert Stephens and his foresters access to the big grove to measure it out for logging. I followed the lane southward. After nearly a mile, the infinite quiet dissolved into an unspeakable roar of chainsaws and D8 bulldozers. I'd found a large clear-cut of virgin redwood at the headwaters of Salmon Creek. Two full logging crews—four fellers, two bulldozers—were attacking this stand. I climbed a newly denuded hillock and watched the men cut trees. Skittering back to the edge of the old growth, I napped until they were gone.

When the loggers quit, I tramped on caked mud down and across Salmon Creek into the devastation of an old-growth redwood clear-cut. The depth of my remorse grew with each step. I noticed everywhere on the road, and scattered throughout adjacent slopes, hundreds and eventually thousands of desiccated yellow-spotted millipedes. I'd seen a few of these delightful creatures crawling around inside the forest, where they would capture my gaze for minutes on end. In this wasteland the tiny arthropods had no chance of survival. Their carcasses were everywhere.

From the clear-cut I hiked ten miles along Pacific Lumber's main haul road toward Yager Creek. At nightfall I reached a lit guard shack with someone in it. I skirted to the right, invisible in the darkness. I had found the company's Fisher log deck, where the last of the ancient redwoods lay in horizontal stacks four stories high. In the dark I walked a county lane one mile to State Highway 36, then another mile to the tiny town of Hydesville. I called a friend, and she retrieved me. The car felt dreadfully foreign.

One week after this hiking odyssey, Darryl Cherney connected me with friends who lived in North Hollywood, where I would encamp to prepare for the annual Maxxam shareholders' meeting at the Miramar Sheraton Hotel in Santa Monica. I trimmed my hair and beard and donned the business suit that my mother had bought me for college graduation. At the Miramar I was chatting with protesters when none other than Charles Hurwitz himself appeared on the concrete steps twenty feet away. He was trim and wore an expensive dark suit. A man accompanied him.

"Mr. Hurwitz!" I shouted. "Mr. Hurwitz! I'm Greg King." Aside from this weird pronouncement of self-identification, I hardly knew what to say.

His presence was shocking. He seemed uninterested, but I knew he wasn't, or he wouldn't have come out. "Mr. Hurwitz, you know, people in Humboldt County will really suffer because of the cutting," I said. He walked away.

A man stopped me at the door to the meeting room. "You're not on our list," he said, "but with this"—he was holding my one share of Maxxam stock—"you can go inside. But you can't say anything."

Through a door I could see a microphone standing in the aisle of the meeting room.

"But everyone else can speak?" I asked.

"That's right."

I took a seat next to the microphone. The room was smaller than I thought it would be and plain. Perhaps this was a reflection of Hurwitz's austerity. He eschewed gilded mansions and corporate jets (he reportedly flew commercial) and drove his own car from a luxury Houston condo to his twentieth-floor business suite. He worked all day and into the night. Two secretaries worked in relay to cover his long hours.

In the meeting room, Hurwitz sat at a table in the middle of a row of six people. Ezra Levin, an attorney who had served Hurwitz's interests since 1973, sat next to him and led the meeting. Levin was a director of Maxxam. He was also a partner in the Manhattan law firm of Kramer Levin Nessen Kamin & Frankel. As a fixer, he was instrumental in swinging Maxxam's takeover of Pacific Lumber.

Levin's gobbledygook escaped me until he asked shareholders if they had any questions. Just step up to the mike. Seeing no one rise, I did.

"In Humboldt County the last of the ancient redwoods are being clear-cut to pay a junk-bond debt incurred by this company." Instantly two goons were at my side. I insisted on addressing the shareholders. I said that I represented the redwood forest that this company was now liquidating.

"*You* do not dictate the agenda," said Levin. "The *corporation* sets the agenda. Please sit down."

"Sir, I traveled seven hundred miles to—"

One of the goons grabbed the mike and turned it away from me. I sat down.

The board actually took votes on agenda items. The meeting ended, and again I took to the mike.

"Your redwood liquidation will devastate the people and the ecology of Humboldt County," I said. "We will not let this go unchecked. Your operation may not turn out to be as profitable as you may think." Rarely have I been as wrong as I was on that last point.

Gravely, Levin looked behind me and drew his index finger across his throat. Was that for me or the mike? The mike went dead. I was alive. I yelled, "If anyone wants to talk, I'll be here, just find me." One woman did. She was nice looking, maybe forty years old, and had a sweet smile. "We're with you all the way," she said.

I walked up front. Hurwitz was talking with a reporter, who was scribbling feverishly. Hurwitz was telling the reporter that "nothing has changed at Pacific Lumber" since the takeover. He'd omitted junk bonds, financial felons, shady attorneys, asset sell-offs, and liquidation logging—lies ladled like dross directly into the cameras. I offered the reporter a correction.

"Everything has changed. They've tripled the cut. Maxxam will log for twenty years and get out." I said to Hurwitz, "People in Humboldt County are afraid the economy will come crashing in on them."

"We're aware of the situation, and we're watching it," Hurwitz said, somehow cryptically. Then he walked away.

Back in Southern Humboldt County, I visited with Cecelia Lanman, a leader of the Environmental Protection Information Center's legal efforts. Cecelia was a veteran of the herbicide war and the court battles to save Sally Bell Grove. Cecelia was pretty and soft spoken. A casual observer might peg her as a housewife, content to make lunches and get the kids off to school. She was certainly a great mom, but once the kids were at school, she changed demeanor. Around Southern Humboldt County Cecelia was known as "the velvet hammer." During a public meeting with officials from Georgia-Pacific, to discuss logging at Sally Bell Grove, Cecelia, stung by the routine lies bandied by corporate officials, turned to Jere Melo, the company's chief forester, who had designed the destruction of the Sinkyone, and in her calm housewife voice said, "You are slime, Jere Melo. Pure slime."

By June, Cecelia, along with Robert Sutherland—aka the Man Who Walks in the Woods—and a team of attorneys led by Sharon Duggan and

Jay Moller, would be suing Maxxam and the California Department of Forestry over redwood logging.

In Garberville I gathered gear and headed north. On the backseat of the Celica I carried an important set of tools: rub-on letters, an IBM Selectric typewriter, a paper-waxing machine, and rolls of thin black tape for making lines. In Arcata, our publications group was working to produce a tabloid, *Old Growth in Crisis*. We pounded out the tabloid until April 4, when Mike Roselle arrived in Arcata to help lead a group of thirty people in "nonviolence training." We would learn how to be arrested and practice the thrusting of self into potentially hostile situations: "We will not run. We will not carry weapons or drugs. We will not speak disrespectfully. If struck, we will not strike back."

On Sunday, April 5, Kurt Newman guided Ilana DeBare, a reporter for the *Los Angeles Times*, into All Species Grove. DeBare's "Old Redwoods, Traditions Felled in Race for Profits" ran on April 20, 1987, on the front page, just after *Businessweek* ran "A Takeover Artist Who's Turning Redwoods into Quick Cash." The articles marked the beginning of a long era of national and international media coverage of Maxxam's logging.

From April 6 through 9, the Arcata core group produced *Old Growth in Crisis*. Numerous locals dropped by to cook meals and help with pasteup. Bob Cremins, a noted illustrator, and Kathy Escott helped us create the all-important maps of Pacific Lumber's remaining old-growth redwood islands. The maps would allow the public and policy makers, as well as litigators at EPIC, to ascertain for the first time the size and location of Pacific Lumber's remaining ancient forests. While writing, I knew we needed something better than "the big grove" to identify the three-thousand-acre stand at Salmon Creek and Little South Fork Elk River. I opted to use the name I'd scribbled in my notes from my hike in March: "Headwater Forest." Someone, probably Larry Evans, added an *s*. The world's largest unprotected ancient redwood grove now had a name.

Old Growth in Crisis was at the printer by Friday, April 10. The following week we distributed ten thousand copies to every local, state, and federal elected official, including judges, to environmental groups, and to a lengthy mailing list. The paper shouted headlines like "Maxxam: State Supported Terrorists," "CDF/Maxxam Devastate Last Virgin Redwoods," and "CDF: Big Timber's Rubber Stamp."

Six months later, in EPIC's first court victory against Maxxam, a superior court judge would rule that CDF had "rubber-stamped" Pacific Lumber's illegal timber harvest plans. We couldn't have been happier.

After distributing the tabloid, eight of us piled into Danielle's van and hauled up to Takilma, a tiny hippie outpost set alongside the beautiful Illinois River in southwestern Oregon. We would lend our human numbers to the locals' ongoing opposition to Ronald Reagan–era logging of publicly owned ancient forests in the North Kalmiopsis wildland. The administration was planning one hundred thousand acres of clear-cut logging in one of the world's largest remaining islands of temperate rainforest.

A young woman named Mary Beth Nearing prepped us for the action. Prior to our arrival, Mokai said, "You're going to love MB." I did. One of nine children born to a Christian family out of Eugene, Oregon, Mary Beth tended to dress like a nineteenth-century rural parishioner: high collars, thick, full-length skirts, short brown hair neatly tied back. She spoke calmly but authoritatively—she'd already been arrested a few times for blockading logging in the North Kalmiopsis, starting in 1983, when Dave Foreman and Mike Roselle showed up to help guide an activist revolution in the woods.

The eight Californians blockaded a road and were arrested, marking the beginning of an activist labor exchange between the two regions. In July, we would return to Oregon to help haul gear for a tree-sit.

On April 24, I wrote to my parents from Takilma. They still lived in our old Guerneville home. They worried about me, and the letter couldn't have helped. I told them all about the action, getting arrested, and being hauled off in a police van that had been confiscated from a cocaine dealer. "The movement to preserve our wild places is very strong here and is growing quickly," I wrote. "It should be down your way in a few months." (It wasn't.) Later I learned that my parents had learned of my Oregon arrest the day after it happened from an article in the *San Francisco Chronicle*.

13

O
N MONDAY, APRIL 27, MAXXAM AND ROBERT STEPHENS TOSSED A
Molotov. They submitted to the California Department of Forestry
two timber harvest plan applications that proposed clear-cutting 274 acres
from the heart of Headwaters Forest. It was a tactic first used during the
Redwood National Park struggles of the 1960s, to render a "parklike" forest
less attractive as a preserve. One of the THPs would cut virgin redwoods
from the fragile streambank of Little South Fork Elk River all the way to
the ridgeline; the other would do the same on Salmon Creek.

On May 2, Nina Williams, Mokai, and I made the second activist hike to
Headwaters Forest to review the THP sites. We reached the first orange flag
a half mile into the woods, and it led directly into the trackless old growth
slated for logging.

"They're just going to assassinate this place," Mokai seethed.

The local CDF forester in Fortuna who would review Maxxam's new
logging plans, Stephen Davis, saw nothing amiss in the ecological dismantling of Headwaters Forest. A few days after our hike, Davis had
whipped through CDF's new "Cumulative Impacts Checklist" for the
THP, contained at the end of the review document, as if he were renewing
a driver's license. A "review team meeting," attended by personnel from
various state agencies, would follow. A checklist question asked whether
the clear-cutting would cause "significant adverse cumulative environmental effects . . . to fish or wildlife or their habitat." Davis answered, "No.
Minimal impacts will occur to these values; some wildlife may benefit."

I'd already attended a dozen review team meetings for Pacific Lumber
logging plans. Robert Stephens always attended, flanked by the refrigerators, and CDF always approved the plans. There had been no exceptions in
1986 or so far in 1987.

Yet, for whatever reason, when the THPs for Headwaters Forest reached the review stage on May 7 at CDF, no one from Pacific Lumber showed up. The company had just turned in the most barbaric and consequential THPs of the Maxxam era, but Stephens and John Campbell had apparently decided to sit back and let CDF officials do their dirty work.

Cecelia Lanman and I attended the meeting. If you're CDF and Cecelia attends your meeting, you know you're in trouble. We sat near each other at an oblong table; Stephen Davis sat directly across from us. John Hummel, from state Fish and Game, sat to his right. I pulled out a cassette recorder, turned it on, and placed it on the table in front of Davis. He was a tall, languid man who looked like he might fall asleep. I did my best to wake him up. Reading over Davis's cumulative impacts checklist, I asked him, in the language of the California Environmental Quality Act, if clear-cutting nearly 10 percent of the world's largest remaining unprotected grove of ancient redwoods wouldn't significantly, cumulatively, and adversely impact the rare, threatened, and endangered species that depended on the grove for survival.

"I don't think so," said Davis.

I looked up. "You don't think so?" I asked.

"No."

"What makes you not think so. Once the old-growth habitat is gone, how will the wildlife species that depend on that habitat survive?"

"What habitat are you speaking of?"

"The old-growth-forest habitat."

"Who?"

"*This*"—I pounded my fingers into a THP map that was on the table— "this old-growth-forest habitat."

Davis said, "I don't think there's a cumulative effect on those."

"You don't think so? You don't think that by eliminating old growth in general, old-growth-dependent species will also be eliminated?"

"There's plenty of habitat out there."

I turned to John Hummel. I'd reviewed all seventy or so of PL's timber harvest plans since the Maxxam takeover, and Hummel hadn't written a single negative word about any of them. Here I expected the same sort of response. Yet, for whatever reason, no doubt owing at least in part to the absence of Robert Stephens and his cooling units, Hummel found himself suffering a come-to-Jesus moment. I asked Hummel if he agreed with Stephens's assessment. Wouldn't these THPs eventually extinguish old-growth-dependent species in the Headwaters Forest area, species protected by state and federal statutes?

"Yes," said Hummel. Several chairs shifted. Hummel continued,

> This is an ecological concept that was understood many, many years ago. The population is going to decrease. You'll lose it. There's no question about that. . . . "Minimal impact will occur to these values" is rather an inadequate statement. "Wildlife may benefit." That's rather weak and undirected. . . . Once you reduce that stand down to ground level whatever the population and diversity of species that existed there before are not going to be there. . . . The species that are dependent [on] and related to, keenly associated with old-growth stands are going to be absent.

The two-hour meeting ended with CDF review team chairman Dave Drennan recommending that the Maxxam clear-cuts be approved. It was as if Hummel had said nothing at all. The law wasn't even a speed bump. Check a box and cut all the redwoods you want.

On May 11, I used the Selectric and rub-on lettering to create the first copy of what I called the *Humboldt News Service*. Headline: "Fish & Game Says Pacific Lumber/CDF Eliminating Wildlife." I quoted Hummel at length. One month later, as expected, CDF approved the plans. The Environmental Protection Information Center immediately sued in Humboldt County Superior Court.

In their robust offense, attorneys Sharon Duggan, Jay Moller, and Thomas Lippe entered the *Humboldt News Service* as evidence in the case and subpoenaed John Hummel. In September, Hummel took the witness stand and there faced grilling by Maxxam attorney Jared Carter. Carter was a notorious legal mercenary who represented the worst of California's rogue timber firms, including Georgia-Pacific in the Sally Bell Grove case. Carter had served as undersecretary of the Interior Department under Richard Nixon, where he worked to allow private development of federal shale oil reserves and to remove obstacles to building the trans-Alaska oil pipeline. Carter would lose several important timber cases. No matter. In 1999, to facilitate

Maxxam's endgame in the redwoods, Carter joined Pacific Lumber as executive vice president and general counsel.

Carter asked Hummel if he had told CDF officials that Maxxam's logging would harm wildlife. Yes, Hummel replied, he'd said it. Carter asked why Hummel had never spoken up before. Hummel told the court that he and other state representatives felt "intimidated" not just by Pacific Lumber foresters but by CDF officials—and not only in their offices but in the field, where Hummel had feared for his personal safety. Later, a CDF official critical of Maxxam's logging began carrying a sidearm while inspecting timber harvest plans.

In November, Judge Frank Petersen ruled in favor of EPIC. Petersen wrote, "It appears that CDF rubber-stamped the timber harvest plans as presented to them by Pacific Lumber Co. and their foresters."

Amid the frenzy of meeting, publishing, hiking, and being arrested, Humboldt's Earth First!ers organized what we called a National Day of Direct Action against Maxxam, slated for Monday, May 18. Darryl Cherney anchored outreach from his bunker at the Bridgewood, arranging for an Earth First! presence in Houston, Los Angeles, and Marin County and on Wall Street. I remained in Arcata to organize a tree-sit and a blockade at the Yager Creek log deck—the same redwood cemetery I'd forded during my solo hike two months before.

My friend Darrell Sukovitzen, the Sonoma County arborist, arrived a few days early to teach us how to climb redwood trees with spurs on our boots and a lanyard around the tree—like those guys climbing power poles, only these poles would be ten feet across. We would put five tree-sitters high into redwoods at the ongoing clear-cut on the edge of All Species Grove. On Sunday, May 17, twenty people hauled climbing gear, food, water, sleeping bags and pads, and five three-by-six-foot plywood platforms two miles into the clear-cut. This was to be the first redwood tree-sit, a forest-defense tactic pioneered in southwestern Oregon two years before.

Mary Beth Nearing arrived two days before the action to help direct. The idea was to put tree-sitters into the canopies of five giant redwoods in the middle of the active timber harvest plan and connect them with ropes to inhibit logging. By the time a pair of Pacific Lumber maintenance workers wandered into the logging site early on Sunday morning, only three climbers, Sukovitzen, Kurt Newman, and Larry Evans, had made any progress ascending the huge trees. When the maintenance crew ordered them down, they simply kept climbing. Larry and Sukovitzen made it to a hundred feet—they hadn't yet reached the first branches—and Kurt tied his platform off at forty feet. Everyone else scattered and hid alongside Kneeland Road, to be picked up later.

After three hours of standing in spurs, Sukovitzen descended. At nightfall Kurt Newman, possessing no gear and wearing just a T-shirt, joined him. Larry descended after an excruciating day stranded in his spurs. Later I asked him how he could withstand such suffering.

"It's only pain, man," he said.

The discovery and arrest of the three tree-sitters fueled a fervor the next day. Between ten and twenty protesters showed up at each of the satellite demonstrations in Manhattan, Houston, and Los Angeles. In Marin, fifteen demonstrators glued large stumps in front of the doors of the Pacific Lumber sales office, blocking entry for the day. Five protesters were arrested.

At the log deck on May 18, more than one hundred people gathered to blockade log trucks carting Maxxam's booty to the mill. Normally a truck would leave every fifteen minutes. Now they idled. A dozen sheriff's deputies flanked the boisterous crowd, which grew larger every few minutes. People chanted slogans and flew banners. An airplane circled overhead. In his front-page article for the June 21 edition of the national *Earth First! Journal*, Mokai described the unfolding scene.

> The Humboldt County sheriffs are deployed inside the gate. Suddenly three women leap the barrier, carrying a banner, and head toward the stack of impossibly large logs. The sheriffs sprint to intercept them before the banner can be read. . . . The cops hit in a flying wedge. Karen Pickett, Berkeley eco-activist, is straight-armed face first against the logs. Sinkyone Warrior Agnes Mansfield is forced to her knees as the sheriff twists her arm behind her back, dislocating her shoulder. Aster [aka Danielle] Philippa, Arcata Earth First! coordinator, squirms in her captor's grip, struggling to spread the banner until a cop pins it under his boot. Other women take advantage of the confusion to climb to the top of the stack [of logs]. The women dance from log to log, garlands in their hair, as cops pursue them.

The sheriff's deputies seemed mostly intent on preventing an unfurling of the banner. I said to one of the cops, "Looks like you guys are just working for Maxxam."

"They pay taxes," he said. "You don't."

Following the blockade, seven of us returned to All Species Grove to retrieve the climbing gear our crew had stashed when the cops arrived. Most of the equipment had been donated. When we got it back, I didn't like the look of it. We would entrust our lives to these tired ropes and assorted pieces of metal. I wanted new gear.

I also wanted to refine our woods actions. We could no longer simply wander into a logging site, thinking we could take it over. At our next meeting the Arcata core group agreed that from here out we would climb at night, and whenever feasible we would hike at night. An exception would be All Species Grove, which was reached through a neighbor's land that was not patrolled.

After the meeting I contacted Paul Tebbel, the grants coordinator for the Patagonia clothing company. Celebrated mountaineer Yvon Chouinard and his wife, Malinda, had founded Patagonia during the early 1970s with a commitment to "tithing" a percentage of profits to environmental causes. Yvon had also founded Chouinard Equipment, which sold the world's finest mountaineering supplies. I asked Tebbel if Chouinard could donate ropes, carabiners, harnesses, and other gear.

"Well," he said. "I'll ask." For the next several years, Chouinard Equipment sent our group troves of climbing gear, and Patagonia provided grant funding—the largesse personally approved by Yvon and Malinda Chouinard. The Chouinards set a high bar for corporate giving. At this writing, they still do. In 2022 the Chouinards—Yvon, Malinda, and their children, Fletcher and Claire—turned Patagonia into a purpose corporation and donated the firm to a new nonprofit organization called the Holdfast Collective. At the time, Patagonia was valued at more than $3 billion. The family gave away their company to "ensure that all of its profits—some $100 million a year—are used to combat climate change and protect undeveloped land around the globe," the New York Times reported. That week I spoke with Malinda Chouinard about the family's donation of the company, and we reflected on the Maxxam era. She said, "This period you write about is the exact reason we gave away Patagonia."

14

A T THE START OF SUMMER, A COLLEGE STUDENT SUBLET ME HER ROOM in a house on Fickle Hill, one mile above Arcata. Her two remaining roomies were in for a surprise. The house stood adjacent to the Arcata Community Forest, a one-thousand-acre second-growth redwood reserve where the city practiced light-touch selective logging. A couple of the redwoods behind my house were large enough for would-be tree climbers to practice with spurs and lanyards. Before he went off to the Sierra to "bust rock," Larry Evans beefed up our one-inch Manila lanyards by threading a quarter-inch steel cable through the middle. In his redwood tree the month before, Larry realized how vulnerable he was, attached by just the Manila rope, to the single swing of an axe.

In one of the trees Kurt Newman secured a fixed rope, which dangled all summer in my backyard and accommodated several trainees whom Kurt would teach to climb. I was his first student. Using one of the new lanyards, spurs on his boots, and a tree-climbing harness, Kurt shot 40 feet up the tree. Uncoiling behind him was a 170-foot length of new Chouinard nine-millimeter static climb line. Kurt also carried a doubled, 20-foot length of one-inch tubular webbing. The webbing was constructed of a strong nylon weave that held up to two thousand pounds. He wrapped the webbing around the tree, just above the first branch, and looped it through itself—the "girth hitch." From the end of the loop, he attached a carabiner that "locked" when the user screwed a small clamp over the gate to prevent it from opening. He slipped a looped end of the climb line into the carabiner. I was next.

Kurt demonstrated how to tie a series of seemingly magical knots and how to climb a fixed rope using mechanical ascenders. The Jumar brand was the Kleenex of mechanical ascenders (the verb is *to jumar*), and we now owned several pairs. One end of a Jumar wrapped around the rope and was held there, under weight, by a set of small, spiky teeth. The toothed piece moved on a cam, and the angle of the teeth allowed climbers to slide the Jumar up the rope, then put weight on it. A good climber can ascend a hundred feet in a few minutes.

"It's a puzzle," Kurt said. "A simple one, but all the pieces have to connect just right or you'll probably die." He chuckled.

Kurt shimmied ten feet up the rope and bounced around as a test. In that short climb Kurt's arms appeared to double in size, and his chest shot out from his T-shirt. See Kurt Newman on the street and he looks like your average bookworm. On a rope, he's Captain America.

At the top of the tree, Kurt tied a prusik knot around the rope, attached it to one of his safeties, then rappelled back to earth.

"Your turn," he said.

By now we were hiking almost constantly. The task at hand was to familiarize ourselves with the forests where we would undoubtedly find ourselves, getting in the way of logging. A former longtime Pacific Lumber employee, who had quit in disgust shortly after the Maxxam takeover, informed us that since May 18, Maxxam had beefed up its security crew. They were easy to spot. The security pickups were painted a unique orange with green hoods. Security chief Carl Anderson carted his tenuous ego in a special all-white truck.

In early June, Robert Stephens continued his blunt attack on the best remaining redwood groves. With Maxxam's plans for Headwaters Forest now frozen by the Environmental Protection Information Center's lawsuit, Stephens targeted All Species Grove with a 263-acre "modified select cut" that proposed cutting virtually every tree out of the heart of the grove. The numinous redwood flat appeared to be doomed. The cutting would leave a gaping hole in the 1,000-acre habitat island, with two small remaining islands of old growth standing more than half a mile apart. By now, the clear-cut on the eastern edge of All Species Grove, and the forest itself, was the go-to location for tours of what was immediately at stake.

In my "official" comments to the California Department of Forestry regarding the All Species Grove timber harvest plan, I made sure to hit on any points that could be useful in court—in a lawsuit, plaintiffs were allowed to address only those issues that had been introduced into the record during the review period—but I also packed a bit of extra powder into the charge. I understood that EPIC was economically sapped and administratively challenged by its ongoing lawsuit to save Headwaters Forest. It was unlikely that the tiny organization could also litigate against this THP, and the national "green" groups continued to ignore the crisis. All we had left were our words and our bodies. Words came first. I noted that, again, the timber harvest plan claimed that the destructive logging would "provide for a much more diverse habitat for wildlife and bird species." I countered,

> As Fish and Game wildlife biologist John Hummel recently pointed out at a previous review team meeting for a PALCO THP, MAXXAM's logging will not provide a more diversified wildlife habitat, but in fact will eliminate wildlife dependent on old-growth forests. PALCO's statement here, coming on the heels of Hummel's public revelations, is nothing short of a lie. This plan must be denied, if only for the dishonesty displayed here by Robert Stephens. . . . As Hummel pointed out, eliminating old-growth forests will not increase wildlife habitat and carrying capacity, nor will wildlife diversification be "increased." This blatant untruth is included in PALCO's THPs to better facilitate resource extraction and profit maximization at the expense of wildlife that apparently is afforded no relief by CDF. This plan must be denied.

The plan was not denied. Nor was another crushing THP, which proposed logging 385 acres from the north side of 1,000-acre Elk Head Springs Grove. Addressing this THP, I told CDF officials that the previous month I had sighted marbled murrelets in Headwaters Forest. The rare avian species "must be protected by your agency," I wrote. Earlier I'd trained in Prairie Creek Redwoods State Park with murrelet expert Tom Sander, who pointed out the sharp *keer! keer!* of the murrelets' calls. At dusk, we saw the tiny birds racing through the old-growth redwood canopy. The murrelets zipped so quickly that if Sander hadn't been there, I might not have known what I'd seen. In California the murrelets nest only in old-growth trees. Their numbers were, and remain, dangerously low. Murrelets find a wide, mossy branch, where they lay a single egg. They bring their chicks food from the ocean, where the murrelets spend most of their lives. In a few years the murrelets themselves would be named as plaintiffs against Maxxam.

As an incision through bureaucratic gibberish, I wrote, "That CDF consistently ignores [the law] by approving illegal THPs is a slap in the face of all Californians, all Americans. . . . These lengthy, obfuscating official responses, combined with CDF's continuous rubber-stamp approvals of illegal, environmentally disastrous THPs, are illustrative of the magnitude of collusion between Big Timber and CDF."

I wrote my All Species Grove comments on June 18, the day after I returned from the logging site with Paul Nussbaum, a reporter from the venerable *Philadelphia Inquirer*. When Nussbaum called the previous week to see about hiking in the threatened redwoods, the news junky in me kicked in.

"Great," I said, "but it's trespassing."

"Not a problem," said Nussbaum.

Reaching All Species Grove was not a difficult slog. Still, when Nussbaum showed up at my house in a pressed shirt, khakis, and loafers, I began to worry. I asked if he'd brought a camera, and Nussbaum said no. Would the paper be sending a photographer? Negative. "I don't think I'll need one," he said. I told Nussbaum I'd be right back. I ducked into my room, grabbed a second Nikon and loaded it with black-and-white film, and stuffed it into my pack. Then we were off.

We clambered through Maxxam's disaster zone until we stood at a big, bright orange stump and gazed downhill at dozens of great trees that had been cut in just the past few days and left for the hauling crews. Standing some fifty feet behind us was the stunning wall of old-growth forest, the one thousand acres of All Species Grove that remained. Nussbaum was quiet for a while before he spoke.

"Wow," he said. I handed him the camera. He shot the entire roll of film. Then we explored the great flat of ancient trees inside All Species Grove. Standing amid ferns that grew to eye level, peering through the vortex of the two big redwoods that had drawn me in a few months before, Nussbaum said, "I can't believe anyone would cut this down."

On June 29, 1987, Nussbaum's story and photo ran on page one of the *Inquirer* under the headline "Corporate Takeover Turns Forest into a Battlefield." A week later, on July 6, *Newsweek* ran a report titled "Razing the Giant Redwoods: A Houston Investor Takes on a National Treasure." I'd brought

Newsweek reporter Pam Abramson to the All Species Grove clear-cut—like everyone else, she was appalled.

The next media star to arrive was Ray Brady, the Emmy-winning financial reporter for *CBS Evening News with Dan Rather*. I met Brady the same day that *Newsweek* ran its piece. He came with producer Barbara Pierce and a two-person camera crew. We all trudged to the clear-cut at All Species Grove. As we reached the high point of the cut, near the "wall" of old growth, I noticed a white object traversing a stretch of meadow in the distance. I knew that from here we could see vehicles traveling on Kneeland Road. I also knew that the white thing was almost certainly Carl Anderson's truck.

Fifteen minutes later, while Brady and Pierce were directing shots, everyone froze at the report of four blasts coming from not very far away, to the north.

"What was that?" Brady asked.

"Shotgun," I said. "We don't usually hear that sort of thing around here."

A few minutes later I saw the white truck headed back the way it had come on Kneeland Road. The truck stopped where we could see it. A glint of glass. Binoculars. Everyone noticed.

"Probably PL's security guy," I said. I asked the cameraman to zoom in on the truck. As he turned the lens eastward, we all flinched at the report of four more shotgun blasts.

Brady was pissed. He defiantly strode to a big stump, climbed aboard, and told the crew to film him there. When he got back to town, he filed a complaint against Anderson and Pacific Lumber with the Humboldt County Sheriff's Department. Then he filed a five-minute magazine piece that anchored the end of Dan Rather's CBS News show and pilloried Charles Hurwitz and Maxxam.

15

O N JULY 27, 1987, CHUCK POWELL AND I HIRED A SMALL PLANE AND flew over Pacific Lumber's forestlands. We found at least ten active logging sites, many of which, we knew, were being hammered by logging crews—fellers, buckers, choker setters, and tractors—twice the size of normal crews. From the air, the crawling yellow tractors, the straight lines of ancient forest abutting brand-new clear-cuts, and the desolation dotted by smoldering slash piles looked like warfare.

One crew was working steadily in a northeasterly direction, from the edge of All Species Grove toward the great flat at All Species Creek. The California Department of Forestry had approved the 263-acre timber harvest plan on the very day it was legally allowed to do so, after taking public comment, which counted for nothing. At the beginning of the following week, CDF approved the clear-cut at Elk Head Springs. We were witnessing the results of a collusive and tightly choreographed rampage across some of the planet's finest remaining examples of primordial life. With a macro view of Maxxam's business plan unfolding beneath us in a geometry of terrestrial ruin, it occurred to me that a species so blindly destructive would eventually devour itself along with everything else.

At midnight on Sunday, August 9, Kurt Newman and I departed for a four-day reconnaissance of Headwaters Forest and Elk Head Springs. We had no idea how to save these places, but we had to do something. A driver dropped Kurt and me at a gate, seven miles from the edge of Headwaters Forest. We grabbed full packs, jumped the gate, and sprinted up the first one hundred yards of dirt road. The night was crisp and clear, the full moon a gift, as the days had chosen us, not the other way around, and we dared not use flashlights.

I'd come to relish night hiking. In this and many ways, forest activism awakens the senses. Traipse across miles of moonless nights on labyrinthine logging roads, with fifty pounds on your back and an injunction on your head (Kurt already had one; mine was coming), on roads patrolled by armed, territorial security squads, and your senses do push-ups. Climb a thirteen-foot-diameter tree in the middle of the night and you're running a marathon. Do it enough and the trees start talking to you.

On dark roads your senses learn how to find landmarks without your eyes, how to feel when a vehicle is approaching. At the slightest sound, your ears seem to double in size. The scent of petroleum might indicate tractors parked a quarter mile up the hill. If we spoke while hiking, we whispered.

You realize that a moonless, motionless dark is not simply black. The stars are your friends. In open country you can see a companion's face. Where the road bisects dense woods, you don't see anything in front of you—not the track, not the person inches away. You learn to feel the road with your feet, to understand that a distinct pitch to one side might end in a thirty-foot drop. A road through trees cuts a path into the night sky. To see where you're going, look up.

Memory is key. Know where you are. Hike often. Understand that the long, arcing curve in the road that appears after the big snag that stands against the sky like Thor—muscled arms of wood, spidery dead branches dangling—crests at a major crossroads, but you don't want one of these lanes. You're after the skid trail that veers off at two o'clock, between the main roads—your private entrance to the forest primeval.

Always, no matter the time, there was risk of encountering a vehicle. It was not unusual to dodge a truck at 3 a.m. We would dive off the road, even if we couldn't make out the landing. I still have scars.

We all wore watches. Drop times were not as important to nail as pickups. You couldn't miss those. Pickup drivers would wait maybe five minutes. You couldn't just hang out in your car in front of a logging gate. This was especially true as our actions became notorious. Neighbors grew wary. They started keeping dogs outside on runs. In Humboldt County you assume that everyone is armed. So if you didn't reach your pickup at, say, exactly midnight, your driver was going to leave for an hour or so. If you missed the second one, you would be sleeping out again. After a couple of years of being

acutely tuned in to the clock, I could often tell you the time within five minutes, even if I hadn't seen a watch all day. I still can. My family calls me the
"time and temperature man."

We arrived at the clear-cut of the desiccated millipedes at 4:30 a.m., achieved
a high berm near the wall of old growth, and safely sacked out for a few
hours. We ate rice crackers and cheese and beef jerky, drank a liter of water
each, and moved into the old growth on the skid trail I'd found five months
before. Flagging indicated that we'd entered THP 87-240, which the Environmental Protection Information Center now had tied up in court.

We soon found the Elk Head Springs THP. The South Fork Elk River
was tiny; yet, I noted, "the water here flowed as if August did not exist, and it was pure. We drank much." From here we zigzagged up and
down throughout the weird, wonderful world of Elk Head Springs: big
rocks pocking the earth, redwood spires jutting from dozens of small seeps
across the terrain, which everywhere was slippery. I wrote that we'd found
"a unique world, a natural wonder never to be duplicated. Until, of course,
it's clear-cut."

Road flagging wended throughout the large grove. Kurt would follow one
line of flags and I another; then we'd meet up and do it again. Some of the
roads were designed to cross unstable slopes with grades steeper than 65 percent, which feels almost vertical. After the first season these roads would fail
and discharge mountains of debris directly into South Fork Elk River.

Finally, after half a day of exploration, Kurt found a logging road that
ran alongside the South Fork Elk River, on the north side, directly across
from Pacific Lumber's property line and the magnificent "wall" of Elk Head
Springs Grove. This was not a Pacific Lumber road; it belonged to a different
timber company. We crossed the river, stood on the road, and looked back.
The trees grew very tall—it's likely that many reached heights of three hundred feet. From the road we had an unobstructed view of the grove, perfect
for photos. Here we could occupy the great conifers at the edge of an ongoing logging operation, and we could stage the action from a neighboring
property where ground crews could hide and photographers could get their
shots. We'd found an easy way to access Elk Head Springs on a road not
patrolled by Maxxam.

On August 27, fifteen activists, including four from Oregon, filled the floor of my living room, packing gear. Organizers created a half dozen independent piles containing ropes, webbing, carabiners, assorted hardware, sleeping bags and pads, tarps, food, and fifty one-liter plastic water bottles. The bottles had little loops at their bottom ends, allowing them to be strung together and dangled from a tree.

We would tote more than five hundred pounds to the action site. At first my two roommates looked on in awe, if not fear, until one of them joined in—a tall, lean college student who could haul sixty pounds at a solid clip. Heading up the Oregon group as the picture of calm resolve was Mary Beth Nearing. Together, MB and I would ascend and occupy the great redwoods of Elk Head Springs.

Just after midnight on Saturday, August 29, four vehicles dropped fifteen trekkers and packs at the end of Elk River Road. In silence we hopped the gate and simply walked. No one waited; no one talked. We would regroup a quarter mile up the road. The waxing moon had come and gone, so we navigated by starlight. The night air was perfectly cool. In my distress over witnessing a long summer of Maxxam's accelerated destruction, I found succor in the easy tune of thirty tramping feet. Our action would be symbolic, but at that point it was all we had.

At base camp everyone sacked out until dawn. At first light five of us crept across the river to scope the site. Logging and road building, even on Saturday, were ongoing just up from Elk River, about a quarter mile from base camp. Even from a distance the sound of two bulldozers roared. Above the din an agonized chainsaw ripped through a redwood, followed by dead air at the end of the cut, then a succession of pistol cracks that preceded the redwood's explosive crash to earth. This occurred every thirty minutes. Scattered across the scoured landscape were dozens of boles awaiting transport.

We scurried back to camp and waited for the loggers to leave, then returned to scout for trees. We chose two tall redwoods, close to the logging site, that stood along the wall of old growth near the river. Both trees were 8 feet in diameter at the base. They stood 50 feet apart. Four climbers—Kurt Newman, Mokai, and two Oregonians named Phil and Tim—each hauled 40-foot cable-core lanyards to the base of the trees. The trees were too big for a single climber to flip his rope all the way around it, so two people would spur-climb each redwood. Hanging onto the lanyard, the climber spurred

4 feet upward and hugged the tree, while the second climber, on the other side, lifted his partner's lanyard. Over several hours the climbers achieved heights of 130 feet. Using a pully system, they hauled up 3-by-6-foot plywood platforms. Six guy ropes secured each platform to an independent girth hitch that wrapped around the redwood. A second girth hitch held a fixed line. The climbers also secured a taut static rope between the two trees: the traverse, allowing Mary Beth and me to visit each other. Mary Beth and I hugged, then jugged upward.

The ascent came easily, and the platform was a welcome abode. We signaled our ground crew with a thumbs-up. We also tested our handheld CB radios, which seemed to work, and I made a call to Arcata on the radio phone, which also worked. The radio phone allowed us to call a dispatcher in Eureka, who would plug the call into whatever phone number you asked for. These would not be private conversations. One of the first calls I made was to Eric Brazil, a veteran reporter with the *San Francisco Examiner.*

"What would please me more than anything would be to have a few thousand people up here protesting the destruction of these magnificent redwoods," I told Brazil.

The loggers did not work on Sundays. The day would be dominated by the divine quiet of the forest. Before I took to the tree, Kurt Newman had talked to me about how to maneuver on the traverse line. The idea was to creep along slowly—otherwise, he said, the traverse would act as a zipline. That sounded good to me. I situated the pully, inspected the mechanism, and jumped off the platform.

The speed was shocking, exhilarating. A sumptuous carpet of green below the trees blurred past as I hurtled toward Mary Beth at twenty miles an hour. The line bowed, and I came up short on the gravity of the ascent. I was a few feet from MB's platform, and I climbed aboard. Our smiles were as wide as the world spread out below us. The ground crew quietly clapped; then all but two of them hoofed it back to town.

That night, Dan Rather's *CBS Evening News* ran Ray Brady's blast at Maxxam.

16

At dawn on Monday, August 31, the timber crew returned to Elk Head Springs. The loggers didn't notice us until their lunch break. From our trees Mary Beth and I had dangled fifty-foot banners ("THIS TREE HAS A JOB / HURWITZ OUT OF HUMBOLDT" and "FREE THE REDWOODS"), which attracted the workers' eyes. After a loud tramping of underbrush, two loggers in steel hardhats emerged from the greenery and craned their necks skyward. One of the men let out a long whoop, shot an index finger my way, and shouted, "You fuckers are *crazy!*" I couldn't argue with him.

A bulldozer carved a small platform into the hill above our perch. A two-tone Maxxam security pickup arrived, and we learned that we would now have a twenty-four-hour guard—a "babysitter," Mary Beth called him. To my endless chagrin, we would also have floodlights pointed at us all night, powered by an insanely loud generator. The next day Carl Anderson himself showed up, along with two sheriff's deputies. We later heard from someone in the company that Anderson was "personally offended" by our presence in "his" trees. We'd been all over "his" woods, and he knew it. The deputies walked to where we could see them and announced, "You are on private property. You are breaking the law, and you are under arrest. Come down now."

"No," I said, "we're not coming down. Charles Hurwitz is the one breaking the law, and he has abrogated his right to private property."

"We'll come down when Maxxam has stopped logging redwoods," said MB.

Anderson couldn't get to us, so he targeted our banners. He'd brought in Pacific Lumber's tree climber, Dan Collings, who approached the base of my tree. Mary Beth yelled, "He's climbing your tree!" "Climber Dan," as he became known, ripped down my banner and kept climbing—to get me or my gear, I wasn't sure which—so I descended twenty feet on my fixed line to prevent him from farther ascending. Dan climbed with a link chain, which allowed easy flipping around even the largest trees. There we were, thirty feet from each other, in a state of arboreal suspension and inevitable human impasse. We could have been brothers.

"Nifty outfit you've got there," I said. "A chain. Wish we'd thought of that."

"Yeah, it works," he said. "But remember, a chain is only as strong as its weakest link."

After four nights of raging generator noise, the forest lit up like a shopping mall, and the loggers blasting air horns at dawn, I traversed to Mary Beth's tree. "Let's get out of here," I said.

"You mean escape? We'll never make it."

"That's fine. We're under arrest anyway. We'll go down the dark sides of our trees. See what happens."

At 10 p.m. on Friday, September 4, we stuffed our backpacks with gear. While we were packing MB shouted over the din of the generator, "This is suicide!" It was almost a premonition. I watched MB lower her pack to the ground before descending. I had a better idea. I would wear my heavy pack. But as I made to step off the platform, the guy ropes had me locked in. The pack wouldn't fit through. A red Swiss Army knife hung around my neck. I drew out the big blade and sliced through one of the guy ropes. Instantly the platform lurched downward and shot me out into space, and into the flood-lights, like a wrecking ball. At the top of a ludicrous arc, with the open knife flailing wildly, two words came to mind.

"Uh oh."

I slammed face-first into the tree. By now I was nothing but instinct, gripping the rope with my gloved left hand. Involuntarily I shot downward into an abrupt five-foot free fall, but then came up short on the extra carabiner, forcing out a blaring, involuntary grunt. In this way I descended the great redwood in a series of excruciating lurches and unhuman squawks. "UNGH! UNGH! UNGH!" I wove in and out of the lights.

Then my beard caught in the eight-ring. It had been almost a year since I'd "gone Humboldt" and stopped shaving, so my beard was long, and it was now inexorably locked into the loop between rope and steel. My left hand was hot and having trouble holding my weight. There was no way I could ascend the rope to free the hair. It was either sit there all night, or . . .

I yanked my head hard to the right and shot downward. UNGH! When the rope caught, I held myself to recover and could feel the newly freed hairs as they drifted down and tickled my face. The lurching lasted an eternity until I awoke from a dream safely afloat a cool bed of salal and ferns. Footsteps approached. I was busted.

"Greg! Are you alright?" It was Duff and Soul, college students who'd signed on for a shift of our twenty-four-hour ground crew. They gathered our gear and squirreled us across the river, where we regrouped before hightailing out of the woods.

Mary Beth and I went joyfully on the lam. We spent a week with David Simpson and Jane Lapiner at their beautiful Mattole ranch. The couple were founders of the Diggers, an alternative community of artists, anarchists, and activists who took over parts of San Francisco during the 1960s. They were among the early "back-to-the-landers" who had settled on the California North Coast during the 1960s and 1970s. They put us up in a 1940s-era pickup truck, the back of which was burdened with a top-heavy, hand-built "genuine hippie truck-house," said David. Jane and David had lived in the wooden structure for a couple of years while they searched for a good place to settle.

Later MB and I hiked to a remote, rocky edifice that defines the primary ridgeline between the Eel and Mattole watersheds. We enjoyed an easy sojourn camped out in a cleft of the ridge, overlooking the whole of the Lost Coast and most of the Mattole Valley. I couldn't believe my luck, alone with Mary Beth Nearing in this glorious place. She was fierce of heart and as true as the needle on a compass. A few years later Mary Beth's aversion to the destruction of her western homeland caused her to roam north, to Alaska, where she's been ever since.

A few days later we sheltered in the embrace of a great madrone that stretched a hundred feet above our heads, its smooth, deep-red bark shedding papery layers, which littered the landscape. The heat conjured scents of earth and dry grasses, evergreens and distant ocean air. I turned to Mary Beth.

"Let's do it again," I said.

"Okay, let's," she said.

On Sunday, September 27, at 5 a.m., three drivers dropped a group of eight people and our gear alongside the county road outside All Species Grove. I wanted to occupy the middle of the stand, where logging crews, working from the southwest, probably wouldn't arrive for a year. The idea was to occupy the grove, hang a banner between two trees ("SAVE THE OLD GROWTH / EARTH FIRST!"), and then bring in media to show the world just what was at stake. It was to be the last stand for All Species Grove.

I knew the ideal trees: the ten-footer and the thirteen-footer, one on each side of All Species Creek, the portal to antiquity. Climbing occurred through Sunday. There was no need to climb at night, as we weren't near an active logging site. Mokai and Larry Evans climbed my tree, the thirteen-footer. Their climbing spurs were problematic. The spikes of Larry's spurs were too short for the spongy redwood bark. Several times during the six-hour climb, he'd "burn out" as the spurs gave way and slammed him into the tree. The ankle padding on Mokai's spurs was too thin. By the time he reached ground, his calves were bloody. Yet the climbers had been able to rig the redwoods at their first branches, 150 feet above the ground, and to string the banner and traverse line between the conifers, which were eighty feet apart.

Mary Beth and I ascended, and I zip-lined over to her tree. We shared food and spoke quietly. By the time I returned, an early afternoon breeze was meandering through the forest. No matter where my eyes took me, the forest stood steeped in seas of deep green that were pillared with ancient redwoods. After a while the horizon began moving. The entire landscape shifted slowly, back and forth, as a single entity. What sort of illusion was this? I came to understand that the breeze was swaying my tree, only the motion was imperceptible. To my eyes, the forest itself was moving.

The next morning an approaching helicopter blasted the reverie. A local TV reporter, Eric Silvern, had convinced NBC's *Today* show that he could get footage of the returning tree-sitters. Following Silvern was Joe Cempa, a photographer with United Press International, accompanied by a reporter. "What in the fuck happened out there?" the reporter asked, jutting a thumb toward the clear-cut. He looked around. "They're not going to cut *this* are they?"

I rigged the traverse and jumped off while Cempa shot photos. One of his shots—a dangling activist dwarfed by the banner but more so by the forest— ran in papers throughout the world. That night local TV aired Silvern's footage, which is how Pacific Lumber executives learned of our return.

At dawn the next morning, several sets of feet tramped the underbrush from the ridge near the clear-cut and plodded down the hill toward us. These were not our people. I counted twelve of them, moving deftly in a line. They stomped into and across All Species Creek, as if it weren't there. "Alright assholes," one of them yelled up at us. He was carrying a chainsaw whose bar was longer than I was. "We're cutting these trees right now whether you're in them or not. They'll be in Scotia in the morning." He fired up the saw. I got on the radio phone and called the Humboldt County Sheriff's Department. I told him we were in the trees and loggers were threatening to cut us down.

"Well," he said, "why did you call me?"

Next came the bulldozer. In ten minutes the big CAT cut a quarter-mile skid trail from the clear-cut to our trees. Trucks followed the tractor. More men emerged. The last truck to arrive was white. Carl Anderson got out, said nothing, and stared up at us. He was pissed. We'd burned his ass. He delivered the usual lecture.

"This is private property. You are trespassing. Come down now."

"Carl!" I shouted. "I can't believe you still have a job."

Out of the trucks came two generators and four banks of lights. One man, climber Dan Collings, donned a harness. As four of the loggers lay on the duff looking up at me, Collings ascended. I lowered fifty feet of rope and descended, preventing him from getting any higher. He was aiming for the banner, if not our gear.

"Dan, nice to see you again."

Collings was one hundred feet above the ground; yet even here the redwood was eight feet in diameter. It took him fifteen minutes to reach a height that our guys had achieved in four hours. He estimated that this single tree held at least fifty thousand board feet of lumber, more than an entire acre of the best pine forests of the East. For a while Collings grew quiet. He looked around the forest. When Collings climbed, it was always in an active logging site. He'd rig trees with cables for yarding systems. I wondered if he'd ever climbed in the heart of an undisturbed redwood forest. I heard him say, to no one in particular, "Nice tree."

For the next several days four loggers babysat us, two per tree. They took an immediate liking to Mary Beth, who spoke their language and, no matter that she was about the same age as our guards, came off as motherly. She dropped a length of paracord so the loggers could send her a sandwich and a Coke.

One of the more affable loggers seemed intrigued by the willingness of a man about his age, who looked much like he did, to risk his life and freedom to save trees that had obviously been put there for human uses. Even from this distance I could see he wore a "CAT Diesel Power" baseball cap, plaid shirt, and blue jeans. I'll call him Joe.

Joe wanted to know what caused us to take such risks. "I mean, even if you make it down alive, you'll never be able to get a job with an arrest record." I replied that we were in the trees as an act of civil disobedience, a form of protest protected by the US Constitution. We had every right to be there, I said—indeed, "a moral obligation."

"Well, maybe," said Joe, unconvinced. "But Maxxam owns this land. They have the legal right to cut it."

"They do own it, but the right to cut down these trees doesn't necessarily come with ownership. There are important public trust issues at stake. Maxxam doesn't own the water or wildlife that exists on this land. These things are owned by the people of California, of the United States, and a corporation is technically not allowed to harm them. We believe that logging these groves violates a bunch of laws. So who's the bigger criminal here?"

Joe thought about that for a short while. Then he straightened and, with index finger now jutting my way, shouted, "Yeah? Well how come *you're* the one going to jail? Ah ha ha ha ha!"

The logger was right. The wrong people would be sent to jail to answer for Maxxam's crimes. Yet we had these *laws*, right? Deep in the quiet of the canopy, the questions came with force. What about all that powerful legislation, "the toughest logging laws in the country," the white knight of the California Environmental Quality Act, the heralded Endangered Species Act, the securities statutes? Why weren't they invoked and enforced the very minute that Charles Hurwitz rode his junk bonds into town? Why was not a single major environmental group—including the only one dedicated solely to "saving the redwoods"—stepping up to stop Maxxam? I understood that, during the mid-nineteenth century, virtually the entire redwood biome had remained in the public domain, owned by taxpayers; yet by the end of the 1880s, nearly none of it did. How was this possible?

Many years would pass before I finally set myself to seeking definitive answers to these and other questions. When I finally began digging in earnest, I started by examining redwood procurement and logging during the nineteenth century. As I worked forward, a universe emerged. These were the worlds of interconnected finance and industry, of railroads and mines, of hydroelectric power and industrial agriculture, of metastasizing cities and international markets, of investment schemes and troves of "natural resources" in the American West that stood unprotected and would be rapidly consumed. I would learn that, by the turn of the twentieth century, the resource that most connected and supported these worlds, alongside water, oil, hydropower, land, ore, and labor, was redwood lumber.

At the same time, an increasingly mobile American public would begin visiting the redwoods in great numbers. They were shocked by the devastation, horrified by the rending of what many would call "God's temples." By then the nation's business leaders viewed redwood lumber as an irreplaceable resource, foundational to the continued growth of industry—to an expansion of infrastructure and wealth unprecedented in human history. Amid a growing clamor for redwood protection emerged a direct and long-lasting, though spurious, response—a movement dedicated not to saving the redwoods but to protecting them from preservation.

Across All Species Creek, coastal air sizzled through redwood needles. I could see Mary Beth snacking on some food. Below, our guards did too. They seemed to be enjoying the quiet as much as we were. As darkness fell, I began to drift off. For the first time since the timber crew arrived, I began to relax. Then a logger fired up the generators.

Part Two

EMPIRE

We are nearing the end of an ancient relationship between humans and forests, which may portend great suffering for our species. It happens in tidy offices like this, with all the appearance of order.
But make no mistake. It's a real war.

—*Jerry Martien*

Powerless against that which has been done, the will is an angry spectator of all things past.

—*Friedrich Nietzsche*

17

B EFORE WHITE SETTLERS BEGAN COMMERCIALLY LOGGING THE RED-
woods, around 1850, 536,000 acres of virgin *Sequoia sempervirens* grew
throughout Humboldt County's western watersheds. Mendocino County
had 640,000 acres, virtually all of it contiguous—the largest single block in
the redwood range. In Sonoma County stood 150,000 acres of redwood; in
Del Norte County, 130,000 acres. In this, the northern redwood belt, the
new arrivals laid claim to a motherlode of fiber, 1.46 million acres of timber
that would produce more clear lumber, and of higher quality, than 20 million acres of the best eastern pine forest.

State officials had been abetting commercial redwood logging almost
since the day California became the Union's thirty-first state, on September
9, 1850. When I walked into the California Department of Forestry and
Board of Forestry offices in the 1980s, I entered a lair of obfuscation and
prevarication in service of power that by then had deep roots. While the
conceit of the 1973 Forest Practice Act was to curb abusive logging practices
in California, its thrust was to follow state precedents that would allow such
practices to continue. In 1975, *Ecology Law Quarterly* reported that the 1973
act "is not a radical departure from prior law. . . . [T]he Act's overriding
purpose is production of timber."

"Prior law" included the California Forest Practice Act of 1945, which
provided regulations in much the way a high school booster club might regulate on-field play. The law read, "It is declared to be the policy of the State
of California to encourage and promote and require such development, use
and management of forests and forest lands as will maintain the continuous production of forest products." The law was not clear on just how the
state might "require" landowners to provide lumber, but "require" was just a
word. For the next forty years there would always be an "adequate supply" of

old-growth redwood and other species, particularly Douglas fir, whose rapid postwar liquidation fed suburban housing booms throughout California and the United States and around the world. There would also be an oversupply of words.

California passed its first logging statute in 1864. The act prohibited cutting trees on lands owned by the state. But, as a template for subsequent weasel words, the law did not apply if trees were cut for lumber, firewood, mining, agriculture, or tanning. Twenty-one years later, California founded its first Board of Forestry, in a bill signed on March 3, 1885, by Governor George Stoneman.

Stoneman was sanguine about deforestation. He formed the state's first Board of Forestry as a largely ornamental body. Stoneman's father was a prominent New York lumberman. His Board of Forestry would not so much regulate logging as cheer it on. The board was so ineffectual that the state disbanded it during the Panic of 1893, an economic depression that would last until 1897. The board's brief tenure coincided with the most notorious theft of public lands ever to occur in the United States, a public scandal in the redwoods of Humboldt County then roiling Washington, DC, and New York; yet the board neither made mention of the land fraud nor sought to curb it.

The Board of Forestry did leave behind some compelling literature. In early 1887 the board released a "biennial report" that examined timber production and trends over the previous two years. The report had the overall tenor of a prospectus. "The lumber resource concentrated in the redwood belt [is] the most important in the State," "quite equaling in productive power of merchantable lumber at least that of all the balance of the State combined." State writers made clear that "one must mainly look for material increase in the redwood cut."

The Board of Forestry reported the important fact that "as the redwood becomes scarcer . . . centralization of ownership into a few hands renders control of the market possible." Here board writers were not so much soothsayers as observers. When Americans first entered the northern redwoods in 1850, the entire ecosystem belonged to the federal government—that is, to the people of the United States. Yet privatization proceeded rapidly, followed by consolidation of ownership of redwood lands, mills, markets, investments, and supply chains, a process that never ceased. Today, fully half of the two-million-acre coast redwood biome is owned by just two companies.

The board reported that, in 1885, redwood producers had milled and shipped to domestic and international markets 254 million board feet of lumber, enough to build thirty thousand twelve-hundred-square-foot homes. It was a record figure, and an astonishing one given the unwieldy nature of felling, transporting, and milling the great trees. More astonishing was the rapid increase in redwood production. The 1885 figure was more than double the 1880 total of 120 million board feet, which itself was triple the 40 million board feet produced in 1870.

Early loggers employed Herculean means to cut and mill the enormous redwoods. Because the butt ends of the trees were so dense and heavy, they sank during stream transport and in mill ponds. For this reason, and to get above the wide "butt swell" that anchored the trees, loggers built scaffolding ten to twenty feet above ground and began cutting there. A large redwood, cut with axes and handsaws, might weigh five hundred tons and take a week to bring down. Once the tree was horizontal, sawyers yielding "misery whip" handsaws up to twenty feet long sliced the tall trees into lengths of sixteen to twenty-four feet. The largest boles were split with dynamite to allow the oversized sections to fit through mill saws.

In the northern counties, prior to arrival of the local railroads in the late 1870s and 1880s, workers piled most of the redwood logs into streambeds to await winter "freshets," which lifted and transported thousands of gargantuan battering rams toward their saws. Stream log transport was unbelievably destructive. Trees were stacked two hundred feet across a watershed, in a band a quarter mile long, poised to burst through "splash dams" that summer work crews had constructed from logging debris to hold winter rains. As the creeks and rivers rose, the logs eventually floated, moved forward, and blew out the dams. The crush of material scoured stream banks and channels with an abrasive force that gathered ever-greater loads of rock, soil, and logging slash. In towns miles away, people heard the roar and understood that the trees were coming. And they celebrated. Newspapers cheered, "The river is now full," "enabl[ing] the loggers . . . to drive a large portion of their logs to tide water," for in a dry year "our largest mills [are] obliged to shut down for want of logs."

It wasn't just the mills that got shut down. The North Coast's celebrated runs of anadromous salmon and steelhead typically gathered offshore, in fall, until signaled by early rains to begin their miraculous upstream migration to freshwater spawning grounds. But they'd be stymied by the splash dams, until the dams blew out; then the boles and rock and slash would pummel whole runs of fish to their doom.

18

As early as 1870, more than twenty-five thousand lumber-manufacturing companies, large and small, operated in the United States. At the time, "lumber interests ranked second in bulk and value in the products of the country," reported Harold H. Dunham, a professor of history at Denver University, in his 1941 book on land fraud, *Government Handout*. Nonetheless, said Dunham, "many companies were paying nothing for their supplies" because they were filing fraudulent land claims or simply stealing government-owned timber. (Often it was both.)

The problem, as seen by industry leaders, was that by the end of the 1870s, the carpet of trees coating the western United States remained in public hands. There were few legal provisions to log it. The difficulty was exacerbated by two phenomena: the obvious depletion of the softwood forests, mainly pine, of the East and the rapid growth and industrialization of the nation, especially in the West.

The virtually unbroken forest that grew from Washington into Northern California stood as the southern reach of the great Pacific Northwest temperate rainforest ecosystem: a three-thousand-mile band of conifers that stretched from San Francisco Bay to the Gulf of Alaska. It was the single largest temperate rainforest in the world. Industrialists targeted the western forest to provide an essential raw material. Institutional investors were eyeing the West's forests for short- and long-term financial gain. Following the 1878 federal passage of a new and distinctly violable legislative divestment of public lands, men who traded in money would become principal forces behind forest liquidation.

The 1878 Timber and Stone Act would forever solve the problem of public ownership of the country's finest remaining reserves of softwood forest, including some of the densest, most spectacular examples of the redwood ecosystem that ever stood. The bill's author, California senator Aaron Augustus Sargent, had previously distinguished himself as a champion of federal funding for monopolistic railroad companies, whose expansion in the West was inexorably tied to timber production. The primary, and predictable, outcome of the Timber and Stone Act was that millions of acres of "publicly owned timber passed into corporate ownership at a small fraction of its value," wrote Pulitzer Prize–winning historian Bernard DeVoto in 1953, almost all of it "by fraud."

News that President Rutherford B. Hayes had signed the Timber and Stone Act reached industrialists and the nation's financial sectors as if etched on golden tablets. Between 1858 and 1900, American consumption of wood products quadrupled. Lumber exports grew commensurately. During this era, "Humboldt was . . . one of the foremost lumber producing counties in the United States," writes Daniel A. Cornford in his 1987 book *Workers and Dissent in the Redwood Empire*. It would remain so for a century after passage of the Timber and Stone Act.

The act differed from previous federal land giveaways—the 1841 Preemption Act and the 1863 Homestead Act—and various state laws enacted to distribute lands in that it applied only to the states of California, Oregon, and Nevada and to Washington Territory. (Washington became a state in 1889.) All three acts allowed homesteaders to acquire 160 acres of federal land in exchange for a small charge (usually $1.25 to $2.50 per acre) and the requirement that claimants live on the land and make it "productive." At the time, little of the West's nearly unbroken carpet of forest was valued as low as $2.50 per acre. Given immediate returns on investment, the land was practically free.

All three land laws were similarly, and predictably, abused. In 1979, the *Journal of Economic History* reported that "from one-half to three-fourths of all Timber and Stone entries and one half to nine-tenths of the Preemption and Homestead claims were fraudulent." Timber theft was particularly comprehensive in the redwoods. University of Kansas economics professor John Ise, in his seminal 1920 book *The United States Forest Policy*, reported, "Millions of acres were taken up fraudulently under the Preemption law. Gangs of men were often employed to make entries, a certain fee being paid for each fraudulent entry. In the redwood district of California, large tracts of valuable timber lands were acquired under this act and under the Homestead

Act." The entries were fraudulent because the men who acquired them didn't homestead there, as required by the law, but instead immediately transferred title to a middleman, who compiled the entries for corporate consumption. The redwood theft, said Ise, was one of "the grossest frauds [ever to occur] under the public land laws."

In 1878, nearly all of the 1.4 million acres of ancient redwood that originally stood in Mendocino, Humboldt, and Del Norte counties remained intact, and 80 percent of it still belonged to the public. These government lands held the most potentially lucrative and useful timber inventory in world history. Historian H. Brett Melendy notes, "Fraudulent . . . purchases were typical of the entire region from Del Norte to Mendocino, [as] provisions for those caught were ridiculously low." It was as if the government had opened Fort Knox to sell gold at a fraction of its value. Owing to the sell-off of valuable forestland, "new companies in the redwood region began to appear," said Melendy. "These companies differed from the pioneer concerns in that the new firms held their timber primarily for speculation."

Nearly all of the redwood inventory made available to the public was worth far more than the government's asking price of $2.50 per acre, and the gross value to mills was up to $1,000 per acre. The board foot volume taken from one acre of redwood was ten to one hundred times that of any other forest type.

Investments in standing redwood instantly gained value that accrued predictably over time. Once transportation, such as rail lines, reached formerly inaccessible groves, the investments matured by an order of magnitude. For decades after passage of the Timber and Stone Act, corporate and institutional investors bought and sold redwood lands like corn futures.

There was no way to read the Timber and Stone Act except as a legal torch set to the great forests of the American West. Indeed, John Muir called the law the "dust and ashes act." In 1879 US Interior Secretary Carl Schurz, clearly shaken by the act's threat to the redwoods, called for the immediate removal of forty-six thousand acres of federal redwood forest from public entry. Schurz warned that the ancient redwoods "will entirely disappear unless steps be taken to preserve at least a portion of them." Overall, said Schurz, the act would "stimulate a wasteful consumption beyond actual needs and lead to wanton destruction. . . . [E]nforcement of the regulations will prove entirely inadequate, and as a final result, in a few years the mountainsides in those states and territories will be stripped bare." Schurz was ignored, and he was right.

Although the federal government made some token, well-publicized arrests for timber fraud (including of one sitting US senator, John Mitchell of Oregon), few high-level perpetrators ever saw the inside of a courtroom, much less a jail. Investors and timber bosses who most benefitted from what might be characterized as the greatest corporate crime spree in American history—national icons such as Frederick Weyerhaeuser, James Hill, Thomas B. Walker, C. A. Smith, A. B. Hammond, and, in Humboldt County, Joseph Russ, David Evans, Charles King, John Vance, and four brothers by the name of Hooper—took their plunder straight to the bank.

The most brazen and notorious fraud scheme perpetrated under the Timber and Stone Act was the singular theft, in one fell swoop, of at least 124,000 acres of one of the densest redwood inventories that ever stood. The perpetrators were Humboldt County and Bay Area timber barons, big-city financiers, and a Scottish investment syndicate with deep ties to Canadian and American timber markets. It was a flimflam so naked and comprehensive that it sparked public outrage and resulted in federal indictments, congressional inquiries, and national news coverage. The central office was the back room of Gorham Barnum's saloon in the bayside village of Eureka, Humboldt County. Everyone in town knew of the "secret" land fraud, in which hundreds of shopkeepers, laborers, farmers, and drunken sailors (called "entrymen" or "dummies") were chased down in the streets and offered $50 each to "enter" and thereby claim a redwood quarter section (160 acres) as allowed under the Timber and Stone Act. The claims were signed by the same six paid witnesses, then noted in newspapers, as required, and immediately signed over to middlemen, who compiled them for "sale" to timber baron David Evans, who turned them over to the Scots. Evans partnered with two of Humboldt County's leading land peddlers, Joseph Russ and Charles King, and the quartet of Hooper brothers, who ran their Humboldt redwood empire from the Bay Area.

The timbermen collaborated in the theft with James Walker of the San Francisco investment firm Falkner, Bell & Co. and Walker's partners in Scotland at the Scottish American Investment Company Ltd. The Scottish American Company, founded in 1872, was headed by Sir William John

Menzies, a wealthy corporate attorney in Edinburgh. The Europeans created an American advisory committee that included John Stewart Kennedy, the famous Scot who headed an American railroad and banking empire and was instrumental in forming the Scottish American Company.

The heart of the timber inventory purloined and kept by the Scottish syndicate and the Russ gang included nearly every acre of redwood in the Little River, Maple Creek, Redwood Creek, and Prairie Creek watersheds, as well as tributaries to the Klamath River. Overall, this unbroken stand of more than one hundred thousand acres averaged two hundred thousand board feet per acre, though many individual acres held one million board feet or more—astronomical inventories seen only in the redwoods.

The scheme devised by Humboldt's leading locals to pilfer the expansive forests that surrounded their homes was at once cartoonish, thuggish, and successful. Functionaries made payoffs up bureaucratic ladders and bribed visiting federal investigators. Goons beat potential witnesses and dragged them away. Someone supposedly put rat poison in the coffee of a federal agent, though the record here is unclear—it may have occurred in Washington Territory. A corrupt notary public, a county clerk, and the local land officer were in on the sham, signing and resigning deeds and documents with an Old West insouciance. A Eureka newspaper editor ran articles in support of the fraud and was later exposed as one of the dummies. Seasoned land scammers called shots from San Francisco, Wisconsin, New York, Washington, DC, Canada, and Scotland. The US secretary of the interior decried the deal, just before the *New York Times* reported that his brother was among the principal investors. The conspiracy involved hundreds of people; yet only Charles Beach, who had solicited dummies, was convicted, though he never went to jail.

Over the course of three years, the federal government did send four investigators to Humboldt County and indicted eleven people, including Russ, Evans, and King. Timber baron Vance was also indicted for illegally expanding his empire by coat-tailing on the Scots' network to gobble up thousands of acres of his own. The Hooper brothers, who made up a prominent San Francisco lumber family, were never indicted. All died very wealthy men with clean records.

A former Vance employee, David Cutten, was the deputy county clerk of Humboldt County to whom Evans handed the quotidian task of preparing, ahead of time, hundreds of blank deeds to facilitate the land fraud. For every deed he signed in Gorham Barnum's back room, Cutten received $5. Cutten's role was clear—his name was on hundreds of phony transactions—yet he was never indicted. The plot was so well organized that within minutes of a federally approved plat map arriving at the Eureka Land Office, identifying the redwood tracts that would be opened to public entry, dozens of men hired by the syndicate would arrive "with papers already prepared to apply for all the timberland in those townships," writes Marvin Shepherd in his 2015 book *A Scottish Syndicate in the Redwoods*.

In 1883, Wilson T. Smith, an investigator with the General Land Office, an arm of the Department of the Interior, in Washington, DC, stepped off a schooner at the redwood dock in Eureka, prepared to investigate the fraud. After refusing a $5,000 bribe from David Evans, Smith reported back to his superiors on the detailed and exhaustive redwood fraud scheme and on the bribe offer. The federal response was swift. Smith was immediately pulled off the case, then demoted, then fired.

Evans was a firm believer in his own impunity. From November 1882 to July 1883, he accepted 426 fraudulent deed transfers to his name—including 300 in a single day—for a total of 68,160 acres. Evans later circulated a second batch of 349 deeds, totaling 55,840 acres, for a grand total of 124,000 acres. This is a much greater sum than reported at the time, or since, and it represents only a small fraction of the redwood land grants fraudulently accumulated during the late nineteenth century in Mendocino, Humboldt, and Del Norte counties. Evans then signed over the majority of the acreage—though not all of it—to the Scottish syndicate.

In 1888, the General Land Office, under the "reform" presidency of Democrat Grover Cleveland, issued a final report on the Humboldt land swindles. The report found that the Russ cartel, Falkner, Bell & Co., and the Scottish American Investment Company had perpetrated the single largest theft of federal lands in the redwoods. The report noted, "David Cutten was employed by Russ & Co. to prepare the necessary deeds, [and] the money to pay the [dummies] was furnished by Russ & Co." Joseph Russ was an old hand at land scams. By the 1880s he had already spent nearly three decades compiling Humboldt County land grants and buying out other landowners to create a private fief of nearly two hundred thousand acres of ranch land and timber—one of the largest private holdings in California at the time.

The General Land Office noted that in September 1882 Russ's partners in the redwood scam, James Walker and Charles King, had sailed to Europe for meetings with the Scottish investors, who then created a shell organization, California Redwood Company Ltd., to take title to as much redwood land as the Humboldt trio and their partners in San Francisco could fraudulently accumulate. As if to confuse things, Russ, Evans, and King also created a California Redwood Company, this one followed by an American "Inc." rather than the British "Ltd." The American CRC facilitated the transfer of title to the Scottish CRC, though both companies held land, and on maps the stolen parcels were noted only as "California Redwood Co." Three years later, with the federal investigation ongoing, the Scots, in a shell game, created the Humboldt Redwood Company to take title to the purloined land. The directors of both companies were the same people.

In 1889 the Republican administration of Benjamin Harrison took power and immediately countenanced the timber theft by ignoring the transfer, in February that year, of 50,404 acres of fraudulently accumulated grant land from the Humboldt Redwood Company Ltd. to the American Lumber Company, another Scottish firm registered in Illinois. As with the previous land transfer, the directors of ALC and CRC were nearly identical. The transfer made the American Lumber Company Humboldt County's largest owner of virgin redwood forestland. It also complicated a federal effort, if it existed at all, to return the redwood acreage to the public domain. The second-largest redwood landholder that year was the New York–based Central Trust Company, with 46,595 acres. In 1889 the Scots leveraged the California Redwood Company land with Central Trust in exchange for a $300,000 mortgage.

During the late nineteenth century, trusts were unregulated financial institutions that could add opacity, banks of attorneys, and highly placed operatives to the creation of monopolies and land scams. A leading figure at the Central Trust Company was trustee John Stewart Kennedy. Kennedy specialized in connecting his close friends and associates with investment opportunities. These figures included J. P. Morgan, William Rockefeller (brother of John D. and cofounder of Standard Oil), and Darius Ogden Mills, the seminal gold rush banker. As soon as these redwoods entered the black hole of the Central Trust Company, at 40 Wall Street (site of today's Trump Building), there was little chance of the federal government ever getting them back.

In 1885 Russ, Evans, and two of the San Francisco Hooper brothers—
Charles Appleton "C. A." Hooper and George Hooper—created the Excelsior Redwood Company by extracting from the Scottish land fraud
twenty-three thousand acres of superb ancient redwood on Freshwater
Creek, a large feeder to Humboldt Bay. Excelsior was now the third-largest
timber holder in the county.

By 1888, these three companies—American Lumber, Central Trust,
and Excelsior—controlled two hundred square miles of the densest, most
valuable, and arguably the most beautiful and otherworldly forest that ever
stood, none of which was legitimately obtained.

19

THE CENTRAL TRUST HOLDING, BECAUSE IT WAS THE CLOSEST TO transportation, was the most immediately valuable of the redwood tracts stolen by the Russ cartel and the Scots. The forest stood just north of Humboldt Bay and, not coincidentally, included one of the greatest flats of ancient redwood that ever stood. It wasn't a riparian flat, such as those typically banking a river or creek, but an unusually large and spectacularly fecund marine terrace of ten thousand acres that rose out of the Pacific Ocean just north of Arcata and ran for ten miles past Trinidad to Big Lagoon, ranging from a half mile to almost two miles wide.

Because it was a coastal landscape, the terrace wasn't totally level. Instead, the land ebbed and flowed in wide, gentle waves, like a quilt tossed onto a bed. A few of the coastal streams that ran through the flat, such as Luffenholtz Creek, did drop precipitously into canyons, but otherwise the folds and streams of the beautiful landscape were dainty, gentle. The forest seemed to respire great veils of summer fog. Numerous springs and small creeks ran throughout the bench, which was spongy with blankets of viridescent mosses and centuries of duff. The world's tallest trees did not grow here, as coastal winds would have sheered the redwoods to the lowly height of, say, 250 feet. Still the stand would have been self-protecting, with the gathered conifers presenting a bloc that rendered the forest nearly impervious even to Pacific gales. No doubt many redwoods stood wider than 20 feet across. Growing among the dominant redwoods were Douglas fir, grand fir, hemlock, moss-covered maples, and the gnarled Pacific yew. Perhaps most impressive were the Sitka spruce. Humboldt County grew the largest spruce trees "in the world," according to a 1909 history by Humboldt County botanist Albert F. Etter. Some of Humboldt's Sitka spruce reached diameters of 10 to 15 feet and heights in excess of 300 feet. "Now we have not even a photograph to tell us of their former greatness," wrote Etter. (Today the world's tallest Sitka spruce tree stands at 317 feet and is located in one of the protected redwood parks.)

Bordering the northeastern flank of the redwood flat, over a low ridge, was Maple Creek, a watershed of thirty thousand acres that flowed northerly into the south end of Big Lagoon. Just over half of the Central Trust lands were in Maple Creek. The entire watershed, flats and hillsides alike, was covered in magnificent groves of redwoods.

The Central Trust lands were bordered to the south by a small but significant redwood grove that stood along Little River, which drains to the Pacific Ocean just south of Trinidad. Per square mile, Little River grew one of the densest forests that ever stood on earth, including the Crannell Giant, the second-largest tree ever measured. The Crannell Giant was 20 percent larger in volume than the current largest tree, the General Sherman giant sequoia in the Sierra Nevada. Although the redwood was "only" 308 feet tall, it was nearly 30 feet in diameter at its base and an extraordinary 15 feet wide at 200 feet above the ground. The volume of lumber in this single tree exceeded one million board feet, twenty to thirty times the yield of the best single *acre* of any other high-producing tree species on earth.

In 1882 David Evans and Charles King quietly conducted a little side business under the Timber and Stone Act. Using dummy entrymen, the pair fraudulently compiled twenty-two 160-acre federal land grants to create a 3,520-acre redwood holding on Little River. In a deal brokered by C. A. Hooper, the land then sold to the Canadian timber giant Bronson & Weston, which cofounded the Little River Redwood Company six years later. The *Humboldt Times* referred to this grove as "the finest timber in Humboldt County," a very high bar. In 1926, at the height of feverish public efforts to protect "representative" redwoods, the company finally reached the Crannell Giant. When they got there, they simply cut it down.

According to federal documents, before signing on to the redwood deal the Scottish investors employed the services of North Woods timberman Henry C. Putnam to "cruise" the lands in question to determine their worth as an investment. (A timber cruise is a measurement of the number of board feet of lumber estimated to exist in a standing forest.) Putnam deemed the forest more than worthy. In return, Putnam was allowed to buy 10 percent of the stock in the newly formed California Redwood Company. He also bought redwood land of his own.

Putnam was perfect for the job. In the 1860s, while working as a federal agent in a Wisconsin land office, Putnam fraudulently compiled land grants for Frederick Weyerhaeuser. He did the same for Cornell University, illegally gathering an astonishing nine hundred thousand acres of some of the best pinelands remaining on the upper Mississippi River to net the college, in 1868, a founding endowment of $5 million. It was the largest university endowment in the nation at the time. In that operation Putnam had partnered with Henry William Sage, an East Coast timber baron with large holdings in New York, Michigan, and Wisconsin. As one of Cornell's first trustees, Sage advocated, successfully, for the admission of women to the college. Nearly five decades later, Sage's youngest son, William H. Sage, would buy up major portions of the Scottish syndicate lands and other tracts in Humboldt and Mendocino counties to become the world's single largest holder of ancient redwood.

In Wisconsin, Putnam had partnered in forest acquisition with timber baron William F. Vilas. In January 1888, Vilas became the seventeenth US secretary of the interior, under President Grover Cleveland. The once heavily timbered Vilas County, Wisconsin, is named for him. Harold H. Dunham, in *Government Handout*, reports that in 1888, while federal investigations of redwood fraud remained ongoing, Secretary Vilas "was placed in an embarrassing position [because] Mr. Vilas' brother, Joseph, was an owner of a large timber tract in Humboldt County, California." Joseph Vilas owned the land with Henry Putnam.

When Putnam traveled to Humboldt County in 1882, Joseph Vilas came along. Quietly, the two men purchased, "from the same agents and reportedly secured in the same fraudulent manner," according to Dunham, 25,120 acres of redwood forest that stood adjacent to the lands obtained for the Scots. These "same agents" were Joseph Russ, David Evans, and Charles King. Vilas's Interior Department soon canceled the Putnam-Vilas entries and placed them back into the pot of land available for public entry.

Of all the Scottish fraud lands, Putnam's were furthest north and east. Transportation could not possibly reach these groves for decades, making them the least valuable of the Humboldt fraud lands at the time. Yet just ten years later they would again be illegally compiled and sold, by

American land-scam poster boy and Humboldt County native Stephen "S. A. D." Puter. This time there would be no outcry or investigation, as Puter successfully peddled the acreage to yet another North Woods timber baron, C. A. Smith of Minnesota.

Although the Scots-Russ conspiracy represents the largest of the redwood land scams, it was only one of many. The first successful theft of publicly owned redwood under the Timber and Stone Act occurred in 1882, when a Buffalo Syndicate quietly took title to twenty thousand acres of redwood along the banks of the Van Duzen River, the large, gentle tributary of the lower Eel River. The year was no coincidence. Not only had the Timber and Stone Act suddenly opened this once public carpet of virgin redwood to private entry, but in 1882 Russ, John Vance, William Carson, and other local timbermen and speculators had agreed to build the long-desired railroad from the ports of Humboldt Bay southward to the Van Duzen River. Planning and negotiations for the railroad began in 1879, just after passage of the act. It was at that point that the two-thousand-foot tunnel got carved through Table Bluff and a four-hundred-foot trestle was built to span the Van Duzen River. For these formidable tasks and for laying track, the timbermen employed mostly Chinese labor. Three years after the line was completed, all but one of the several hundred Chinese nationals who had worked under slave-like conditions in Humboldt County were herded onto steamers and "deported" to San Francisco.

The prominent Noyes brothers headed the Buffalo Syndicate. New York timber baron John Noyes was eager to acquire redwood lands, as he had run out of trees in his home state, near Buffalo, where he was known as the king of the lumber trade. His brother, Henry T. Noyes, was a New York congressman. Another brother was Charles Goodwin Noyes, the stocks editor for the *San Francisco Daily Chronicle* and an investor in the ore-rich Belcher mine of the Nevada Comstock Lode. The Nevada mining and banking firm of Paxton & Curtis, whose namesakes had founded the Pacific Lumber Company fourteen years earlier, also bought into the Buffalo Syndicate redwood acquisition, along with Millard Powers Fillmore, son of the president.

For Charles Goodwin Noyes, the Van Duzen redwood theft was a simultaneous swindle, as he had been among the principal San Francisco investors in the Scottish land scam, for which he was indicted in 1884. (The federal charges were quickly dropped.) Nonetheless, that year Noyes partnered with

San Francisco photographer Edgar Cherry to produce *Redwood and Lumbering in California Forests*, a lavish investment primer funded by members of the Scottish and Buffalo syndicates. The syndicates produced just six hundred copies of the book. Each contained twenty-four original, five-by-eight-inch albumen photographs, hand-processed by Cherry's technicians from glass negatives and presented on individual leaves framed by purple borders. The photos depicted logging sites, lumber, milling operations, and virgin redwood lands.

Redwood and Lumbering "was undertaken with a very distinct goal in mind: to promote redwood [and create] a strong and growing demand for redwood lumber," wrote Humboldt County historian Peter Palmquist, who created a facsimile of the book in 1983. "The book's intended audience included investors, and potential investors, most of whom had never set foot in a redwood forest, [as well as] lumber agents, bankers, and others in a position to influence the international lumber market."

Once the Van Duzen River land grants had been compiled and purchased, title to several thousand acres of the stolen redwoods that stood along a tributary to the river were placed with the Central Trust Company. The tributary was Yager Creek, which would anchor Pacific Lumber's redwood trade after World War II and host Earth First!ers in the 1980s.

In 1886, while the US Interior Department and the courts continued to investigate the Humboldt County land fraud, Joseph Russ died, at the age of sixty-one, of complications from a "bladder ailment," according to his family at the time. No other explanation was offered. He was one of the wealthiest and most powerful men in California. His funeral train was nearly two miles long. At the time, Russ was a sitting California assemblyman. Just before his death, a group of Bay Area Republicans had attempted to recruit him to run for governor in the 1888 election.

After the death of Joseph Russ, David Evans took control of the Excelsior mill, on Freshwater Creek. Evans allowed his facial hair to grow into the longest, proudest accomplishment beard known to Humboldt County, a graying flag that, in his waning years, reached his chest. He enjoyed posing for photos alongside his booty: specially chosen gargantuan redwood boles carved out of Freshwater Creek. In one image, Evans stands slightly slouched, posing with a dapper colleague between trainloads of logs leaving the timber camp for the mill. The logs are so large that each requires its own flatcar. These are the blue whales of the forest, newly discovered dinosaurs converted to cash.

Evans wears a black western suit and black derby; the other man, who is not identified, is also in a black getup but with a white hat. Conductors poke their heads out of trains, and men of finance stand off to one side in front of a whitewashed building, ready when needed. No women are present. In the distance stand two children, waifs in grim repose. They add a mournfulness to the funereal scene.

Evans went on to serve as president of the Eureka Chamber of Commerce, then became mayor of that city. (Similarly, in 2006, residents of Fortuna elected Pacific Lumber's John Campbell as mayor.) In 1902, just as America's expanding corporate interests were taking over troves of redwood timberland that had been illegally compiled on the North Coast, David Evans died a wealthy man. The table had been well set for new arrivals, who knew a fine meal when they saw one.

20

I N EARLY 1900, THE *HUMBOLDT STANDARD* PUBLISHED A RETROSPECTIVE editorial that lamented the Russ syndicate's land scam and warned of a bleak future for the region if outside corporate domination could not be curtailed. Although Zipporah Russ and her thirteen children still owned nearly two hundred square miles of the Humboldt County land base, the paper failed to mention Joseph Russ.

"The big syndicate scheme, which was to do so much for Eureka, proved disastrous to both laborers and businessmen," wrote the *Standard.*

> Eureka, in fact the whole county, suffered in consequence. None made any money save the speculative promoters who became wealthy, to wit: David Evans and C. H. King, commonly known as "Redwood" King. Everybody else suffered. . . . In the light of these facts, what have the common people to hope from any syndicate which may get control of our mills, railroads and timber lands hereafter? The larger the syndicate the more disastrous will be its effects. . . . Heaven defend us from the consequence of such combinations, especially if the men who control them live elsewhere and have not interest in the country save the money they can make out of its resources.

While essentially accurate, the editorial was oddly out of step with the times. The preceding two decades of acquisition and consolidation of redwood forests, lumber mills, and railroads that followed passage of the Timber and Stone Act had already, and quite clearly, cemented the inexorable control of the local industry by people who "live elsewhere and have not interest in the country save the money they can make out of its resources." By 1900 the available redwood inventory from Sonoma County south had been all but depleted; yet the northern three counties held more than one million acres of virgin redwood. Here stood the motherlode of all the world's timber inventories. The majority of this landscape was already well in the hands of outside corporate interests, including industrialists who counted on unlimited supplies of redwood lumber to undergird the growth of their industries.

Adding value to redwood inventories was the recovery of the American industrial machine after the Panic of 1893. The recovery came concurrently with the near exhaustion of the once seemingly boundless forests of the East Coast and North Woods, which had served the nation for generations. The extreme economic value of redwoods was further advanced by ongoing technological innovations that allowed for smoother movement and milling of the unwieldy trees and for transporting redwood lumber across the country and around the world. And everyone knew that a forest fire in the redwoods virtually never killed the trees. Redwoods were like precious metals: investments in the resource would continue to accrue value even if no mining occurred there. The *Humboldt Standard* editors could lament until they ran out of ink. It would make no difference.

E. Scott, secretary of the powerful San Francisco Chamber of Commerce, heralded the nascent century and its promised largesse with a New Year's Day proclamation in the *New York Times*.

"Our wharves are filled with merchandise and our docks with shipping," wrote Scott. "In fact, it is difficult for vessels to obtain places in order to load or discharge their cargoes. Our streets are crowded with drays and trucks. . . . Our business houses have been and are exceedingly busy. Retail trade is unusually good. . . . We seem to be on the threshold of having the most bountiful and prosperous year in our history." In large part, the wharves of San Francisco Bay were filled with redwood, as northern timber companies were recording record production.

On January 3, 1900, Frederick Weyerhaeuser greeted the new century with a $5.4 million purchase of nine hundred thousand acres of heavily forested grant land owned by the Northern Pacific Railroad in Washington State. "Empire Builder" James J. Hill, of the Northern Pacific, and financier J. P. Morgan had orchestrated the deal. It was the single largest forestland acquisition in American history, comprising a land base 15 percent larger than the combined footprints of today's Los Angeles, San Francisco, Chicago, and New York City. In 1864, Congress had passed legislation that chartered the Northern Pacific Railway Company and granted it nearly 40 million acres of land as a means of funding construction. The legislation included a provision, identical to that of the Timber and Stone Act, that restricted land sales to individuals in 160-acre allotments. Yet Weyerhaeuser and the Northern Pacific, like most big timber companies and railroads of the day, largely owed their great fortunes to institutionalized corruption and uniform government ineptitude, if not collusion. The companies simply ignored the land grant restriction, with no legal repercussions whatsoever. The brazen transaction would further fuel an already fiery run on the nation's remaining forestlands.

In the nineteenth and early twentieth centuries, there were seemingly no limits on the number and types of industries that relied on redwood products, and people were always finding new and sometimes surprising uses for the wood. In his 1952 study, H. Brett Melendy reported that, even as late as 1950, "redwood goes into a greater variety of uses than any other single species." Redwood framed homes, shingled roofs, and paneled gilded mansions—it was even used in foundations. After the 1906 earthquake and fire, San Francisco was built, for the second time, predominantly of redwood. A life might begin in a redwood crib and end in a redwood coffin.

All Western railroads consumed whole forests of redwood products. Redwood supported rail beds with hundreds of millions of ties and held trains on magnificent trestles, seemingly impossible geometric wonders that stood sometimes 600 feet long and 140 feet high. The life of a railroad tie made of redwood averaged twelve years, three times longer than those made of pine and twice as long as oak. By the early twentieth century some redwood ties were found to be sound even after fifty years of use. Throughout the United States, redwood was used in tanks along railroad tracks to water steam engines and to build railroad stations and gangways, piers, and freight and passenger cars.

Water was stored in half-million-gallon redwood tanks for cities and in individual storage tanks for homes and businesses. Often the tanks were fed by redwood stave pipes that ran for miles. Redwood pipes averaged thirty-six to seventy-two inches in diameter, but the largest pipes were thirteen feet wide, and they had myriad uses, including sewage outflow.

Industrial cooling towers were built of redwood. Early oil producers stored crude and other products in redwood tanks. Redwood silos dotted farms throughout the United States. Thick planks of redwood "paved" factory floors. As early as 1880, ninety thousand acres of grapes were staked with redwood, and seven million acres of farm and ranch land were enclosed with redwood fence posts. Underground gold, silver, and copper mines in Nevada, Arizona, and Montana absorbed millions of feet of redwood beams to support mine shafts. By the late nineteenth century, Europe was receiving regular shipments of redwood, and tropical countries imported millions of feet of redwood because it resisted rot. Australia was a major redwood importer because that wood alone resisted the country's voracious termites (then called "white ants").

In 1900, Humboldt County redwood lumber production exceeded two hundred million board feet. A few years later sales reached three hundred million feet. A small enclave of three counties—Humboldt, Mendocino, and, to a lesser extent, Del Norte—was now among the world's foremost producers of wood products. By 1903, the number of mills in Humboldt County had diminished from twenty-six to sixteen; yet the mills themselves grew in size and output. The number of people and companies controlling the redwood lumber industry was shrinking rapidly as sales and profits reached new heights.

At the end of 1900, the *Los Angeles Times* reported that "eastern capitalists" that year bought up more than one hundred thousand acres of Humboldt County redwood land, including tracts sold by the Scottish syndicate and its American partners. Melendy notes, "Not only were the Eastern timbermen of the Midwest and New England investing in the timber, but shortly they were to take over the lumber mills and form stock holding companies along the lines of the modern corporations of the East." Nonetheless, Melendy underreports the degree to which the frenzy of speculation was upending and forever transforming the redwood lumber industry.

In April 1900, a consortium of Humboldt County timber brokers formed Redwood Land and Investment Company (RLIC) to take advantage of the hot market and, in doing so, promoted even more redwood sales. The RLIC located and consolidated redwood land grant patents for sale to outside buyers. It was a natural outgrowth of the Russ cartel and served as a neocolonial agency that represented and hawked local riches for outside private gain—a dynamic that became embedded in the culture and would prevail in Humboldt County for decades, through the Maxxam takeover of Pacific Lumber, up to the present day.

One of the RLIC partners was David Cutten, who'd signed the fraudulent deeds for the Russ cartel and the Scots. In reporting on the creation of RLIC, the *Humboldt Times* noted, perhaps with a wink, that Cutten had "for years been engaged in the real estate business and clerical pursuits here." Another partner was J. E. Barnard, "the recognized timber expert of this county," who at the time worked as "superintendent of the California Redwood Company."

Consolidation of redwood lands was so rapid and extreme that by 1902 thirteen companies and individuals owned 294,000 acres, or 74 percent, of Humboldt County's uncut redwood forest inventory. Seven owners held an additional 24,000 acres, and a few dozen more owned 83,000 acres. Despite the extensive logging that had occurred along riparian flats and into small areas of adjacent hillsides, this forest, even at the dawn of the twentieth century, stood nearly unbroken.

Here then, at the turn of the twentieth century in Humboldt and Del Norte counties, stood nearly six hundred thousand acres of redwood forest in its contiguous, primeval state. At the time the United States had supposedly entered the "Progressive era," which sought social, political, and economic reforms centered on alleviating the corruption, graft, usury, and waste that defined the Gilded Age. Yet addiction to money, power, and empire, like alcoholism, is not easily forsworn.

The first decade of the 1900s was an excellent time to own a stake in the redwood rush. It was a terrible time for the redwood forest.

21

ODAY IN HUMBOLDT COUNTY, A POPULAR WALKING AND CYCLING destination is the Hammond Trail, a former stretch of railroad that runs for five miles through western McKinleyville, a town across the Mad River from Arcata. In places the old iron rails remain visible, and signs allude to the railroad's namesake, Andrew Benoni "A. B." Hammond, a timber baron whose Machiavellian MO, however quintessential, was noteworthy even in such a crowded field. A few additional scattered pieces of Hammond's old rail line are found just west of Arcata, in a now-protected ecosystem of wetlands and coastal dunes that make up the northwestern rim of Humboldt Bay.

One day, in 2009, I traipsed sand dunes above the bay and dropped onto a hardened path. There I noticed a squarish chunk of wood sticking slightly out of a mound of compacted sand. With minor excavation I was able to unearth the butt end of an old railroad tie. The tie had been in place at least since 1949, when the very last train chugged forty miles from one of Hammond's northern lumber camps to the firm's sprawling redwood sawmill in the company-owned town of Samoa, a few miles south of where I stood. I opened my pocketknife and sliced into the tie. The wood was firm and sound, fairly glowing in its original reddish-brown hue and with the lustrous sheen one gets from a fresh piece of old-growth redwood lumber. Unlike every other type of wood used for railroad ties, this one had not been dunked in a preservative such as creosote. It was as if the tree from which the tie was milled had been cut down just the day before. In redwood time, it had.

The trail led me to a slough, which was spiked with dozens of whole trees, or what used to be trees, protruding from the water. These were redwood poles sunk eighty years before to support a bridge for Hammond's trains. Incredibly, the poles remained mostly sound, though rot on top allowed huckleberry to sprout. Lurking in the far north was an old, narrow, steel truss bridge, built in 1941 for Hammond's trains. Today the bridge marks the south anchor of the trail bearing his name. Beyond the bridge, an unfolding of clustered ridges belied the hidden meanders of Little River, Maple Creek, and, in the far distance, Redwood Creek. Farther north, nearly fifty miles distant, was the former redwood kingdom of the Klamath River. Large swaths of this land were at one time owned and clear-cut by A. B. Hammond.

On September 1, 1900, Hammond confirmed the *Humboldt Standard*'s worst fears of just a few months before by purchasing the John Vance Mill and Lumber Company for $1 million. While the Vance timber holdings weren't the most extensive in the county—just under ten thousand acres, most of it obtained through fraudulently compiled land grants—the company's annual production of redwood lumber, drawn from some of the densest groves on earth, was higher than that of any other firm with the exception of Pacific Lumber. Vance products shipped to markets throughout the world, including Europe, Australia, Hawaii, the East Coast, Los Angeles, and the Bay Area. The *Blue Lake Advocate* called Hammond's purchase of the Vance operation "the beginning of the end."

Hammond's incursion into California both anticipated and promulgated a new, accelerated era of acquisition and liquidation of redwood holdings in northwestern California. No credible financier or observer of the American lumber industry could have been unaware that investors were sitting on more than one hundred thousand acres of prime redwood forestland in Humboldt County adjacent to Hammond's new company, ready for sale and not far from expanding rail lines. Another three hundred thousand acres of untouched redwood still stood in the county, most of it likewise held by speculators.

In their 1988 book *Steam in the Redwoods*, Humboldt County historians Lynwood Carranco and Henry Sorensen write, "In 1901 records were broken. Capitalists began to buy redwood holdings, and there was almost a lumber famine in the county as a result of the unprecedented building boom. Special trains had to be run daily on the railroad to supply the great number of vessels anchored" along Humboldt Bay. (Carranco was born in 1921 in Hammond's company-owned town of Samoa.)

Much of the Vance acreage purchased by Hammond was on Lindsay Creek, a tributary of the lower Mad River. It was here, in 1874, near the confluence of the Mad River and Lindsay Creek, that Vance had built his Big Bonanza redwood mill to process this unusually dense redwood inventory, much of which he'd acquired in deals brokered by Charles King.

In 2018 Mark Andre, a forester and the former natural resources director for the city of Arcata, challenged Raymond Clar's assertion that the Guerneville Big Bottom once held the greatest concentration of biomass ever to stand anywhere in the world. He told me, "If I had to guess the most primo micro site for growing the most volume per acre on earth, it would be Fieldbrook," the town that Vance had carved out of the redwoods along Lindsay Creek.

Several Lindsay Creek redwoods grew to girths that approached thirty feet, evidenced today by a few of the house-sized stumps that remain solid and are visited by the curious. Today the largest known Fieldbrook stump, that of the Lindsay Creek Tree, which I have measured, is thirty-two feet in diameter—meaning the redwood was thirty-four feet wide when it still had two feet of bark attached.

In August 1887, *Pacific Coast Wood and Iron* carried a report from Henry Putnam that stunned the timber world. A few years earlier, while cruising publicly owned redwood lands for the Scots and himself, Putnam had paid a visit to the Vance woods on Lindsay Creek. Even this most jaded of timbermen stood awestruck by what he described as "2,500,000 to 3,000,000 feet of redwood on several acres, and an average on the 12 acres which we measured of over 1,000,000 feet per acre." In other words, a section of forest one-tenth the area of a modern airport runway would provide enough lumber to build at least fifteen hundred three-bedroom homes.

Not only had Hammond acquired what were then the highest per-acre timber volumes in the world, but he also obtained "the largest redwood lumber mill in existence, a secondary mill, 3,900 acres of grazing and cutover land, an 18-mile-long railroad with five locomotives, two bay steamers, and four lumber schooners," according to Greg Gordon's 2014 biography of Hammond, *When Money Grew on Trees*. Hammond now had "everything [he] needed to launch a West Coast lumber empire."

North of Hammond's new acquisition stood nearly 250,000 acres of dense, contiguous redwood forest. A full 100,000 acres of this land was now held by the Scots' American Lumber Company and California Redwood

Company (the latter ensconced within the Central Trust Company). There is little likelihood that Hammond would have so boldly entered the redwood market unless he had already lined up acquisition of some of this standing inventory.

One month after buying the Vance operation, Hammond purchased out of the Central Trust holding eight thousand acres of pristine redwood forest northwest of Lindsay Creek, owned by the California Redwood Company. The $320,000 deal represented what the *San Francisco Chronicle* called a "projected invasion of that territory" by eastern investors and railroads. This was the great coastal flat that ran behind Trinidad from the Mad River to Big Lagoon. That same month Hammond added another forty-six hundred acres of contiguous redwood and nearly three thousand acres of cutover land that included the townsite of Trinidad, also from California Redwood and Central Trust. While buying up redwood lands, Hammond also founded a bank, the First National Bank of Eureka, to control local interests and gain a strategic foothold in the regional economy.

In April 1901, A. B. Hammond caused a stir in Humboldt County by arriving on the steamer *Pomona* with several investors. The *Humboldt Times* reported that Hammond's entourage included "J. Sloat Fassett, of Elmira New York, J. E. Henry and son of Lincoln, New Hampshire, W. F. N. Davis of the [timber] firm of Blodgett and Davis of Michigan and Henry T. Noyes Jr. of Rochester, New York. All are timbermen with the exception of Mr. Fassett, who is a capitalist and well known financier of the Empire State."

Hammond and timberman J. E. Henry were ideological brethren. Henry's principal operations were in New Hampshire, but he was running out of trees. Back home, Henry's foes called him Wood Butcher, Heartless Lumber King, Mutilator of Nature, and the Grand Duke of Lincoln. In his 1946 book *The Great White Hills of New Hampshire*, Ernest Poole noted, "To the widow of a man drowned in the river while loading logs, J.E. explained that since the man had not turned in his time that night, he would have to dock him that day's pay."

Henry had come to Humboldt County to view his newest holding, thirty-one thousand acres of a densely forested watershed called Maple Creek. He'd purchased the holding just a few months before, from the Scots' California Redwood Company, via the Central Trust Company. Every inch of Maple Creek was loaded with mammoth redwoods, save where the gentle stream fanned out at Big Lagoon, where a beautiful expanse of towering, water-loving big-leaf maples stood like arboreal courtiers. Out of the maple canopy stood spires of Sitka spruce.

Although Sloat Fassett was little known on the West Coast, to Hammond he was the most important of the new arrivals. Fassett was married to Jennie Crocker, of the famous Crocker family of railroad titans, politicians, developers, and financiers. Jennie's father was Edwin B. Crocker, an attorney who'd relocated from upstate New York to Sacramento in 1852. In 1863 California governor Leland Stanford appointed Edwin Crocker to the state supreme court. Stanford, along with Edwin's brother Charles Crocker, was one of the "Big Four" robber barons who owned the Southern Pacific Railroad, otherwise known as "the Octopus," as well as the Central Pacific Railroad, which had built the western half of the first transcontinental railroad. The Big Four had worked to elect Stanford as governor specifically to advance the cause of the Central Pacific Railroad.

In a way, Fassett accompanied the 1901 excursion as an avatar for the money and influence of the Crockers and others connected to the Southern Pacific. Among Hammond's many business boosters, none was more important to his rise than the nation's largest railroad. In 1900 Hammond and his family relocated to San Francisco, where, for the previous eleven years, he had spent months at a time forging relationships in the country's most important financial center outside New York. In San Francisco, Hammond located his company's main office in the city's new Merchants Exchange Building at 465 California Street, where the Southern Pacific Railroad occupied nine of the building's fifteen floors. Hammond's Bay Area connections would provide him with financing and political clout that was specific to the West.

In those days, San Francisco could feel provincial, except that it happened to be occupied by some of the nation's wealthiest individuals and largest, fastest-growing businesses. One of those individuals was William H. Crocker, son of Charles and cousin to Jennie. Hammond and William Crocker came from far different backgrounds—Hammond, the rough-hewn individualist with little formal education who'd scrapped his way to the top; Crocker, the inheritance prince who'd excelled at Yale and enjoyed top-seeded status in myriad Western industries—yet in time their interests would merge.

On September 22, 1901, a breathless report in the *Humboldt Times* revealed to the region's isolated readers just who was backing Hammond.

"The feature about the [Hammond] company that at once commends earnest attention is the magnitude of wealth represented by the directors and stockholders," wrote the unnamed *Times* reporter. "Men of gigantic fortunes, even as fortunes are reckoned nowadays, are financially interested in the company."

The *Times* list of Hammond investors included "the C. P. Huntington estate. . . . [T]he big Searles estate is represented by Mr. Hubbard, a director of the Central Pacific, and a millionaire himself. The estate of Marcus Daly, the late Montana millionaire, has an interest . . . as also has Mr. Claflin, the big New York millionaire." Gordon, in his book, adds Francis Leggett, "owner of New York's largest grocery firm," and notes that each investor contributed $600,000 to the enterprise. Hammond's incorporators were essentially Gilded Age racketeers who were betting on the stored value of Humboldt's redwood trove and Hammond's ability to liquidate it.

Like Leggett, Horace Brigham Claflin was a wealthy New Yorker. He owned the world's largest dry goods company and was a longtime Hammond investor. The name Searles was vague until you understood that in 1887 Edward Searles had married Mary Hopkins, widow of Mark Hopkins, one of the Big Four founders of the Central Pacific and Southern Pacific railroads and among the richest Americans. (Mark Hopkins was the son of married first cousins, and Mary Hopkins, née Sherwood, was likewise Hopkins's first cousin.) The Searles-Hopkins wedding was scandalous at the time in that the nearly indigent groom was twenty-two years younger than the royally affluent bride. Shortly after the wedding, Mary changed her will, cutting out her adopted son and leaving everything to Searles. She died four years later.

Thomas Hubbard was a Union Civil War hero who managed the investment portfolio of what was now the Searles estate, and he was a director and vice president of the Southern Pacific Railroad. Hubbard had also personally invested in the Hammond Lumber Company.

Marcus Daly was a mining engineer who'd arrived in Montana after exploiting the Nevada Comstock Lode. For nearly two decades, Hammond had provided Daly with lumber for his mines, industrial buildings, and shanties.

Of all the Hammond investors, it was undoubtedly Collis P. Huntington whom readers recognized as a transformative figure of American industrial might. He was the longest lived of the Big Four founders of the Central Pacific and Southern Pacific railroads and the only one who had fully dedicated his entire adult life to the task of building a global railroad and shipping empire. In the Gilded Age polygon of American industrial might, Huntington is found in all quadrants. Like Daly, Huntington would die just a few months after investing with Hammond in 1900.

The *New York Times* announced the death of Collis Huntington in a manner normally afforded a head of state, which in effect he was. The story appeared on the front page, two columns wide, from the top of the page to the bottom, and read like a novella. The jump page also ran top to bottom, only in three columns. At the time, the Southern Pacific Company was the world's largest transportation business, "with nearly ten thousand miles of rail line and more than sixteen thousand miles of steam-shipping routes," wrote historian Richard Orsi in his 2005 paean to the company, *Sunset Limited*. When ordering ties, staves for water tanks, and building materials for its western lines, the Southern Pacific almost always procured redwood. The railroads and steamships also generated lucrative freight rates by hauling millions of board feet of redwood annually.

Hammond's links to executives at the powerful Southern Pacific Railroad were elemental to his rise, and they were long-lasting. The company's tentacles connected the nation's newest satellites of economic might with troves of natural resources along a network of trunk and branch lines that ran from Portland, Oregon, south to the Bay Area, from there northeast to Salt Lake City and south to Los Angeles, from LA east again to Phoenix, Tucson, El Paso, San Antonio, and, finally, to shipping harbors in Houston and New Orleans. Huntington's personal vortex of power was his office at 9 Nassau Street in Manhattan, about fifty feet from the Central Trust building at 40 Wall Street.

"Wall Street could seem local," wrote Stanford University history professor Richard White in a 2003 essay examining US railroads in the Gilded

Age. "Wall Street was, in fact, a hybrid. A tightly knit world, it was also the nexus between local financial worlds and the emerging virtual world of financial information, which was both national and international." Redwood-rich Humboldt County, once a relative backwater, had by 1900 become a stitch in that tightly knit world. As the weave of finance, industry, and corruption grew tighter around the region, the rare and delicate ecosystems nurtured and harbored by these forests would collapse and disappear, largely replaced by what can only be described, in relative terms, as wasteland. Likewise, human communities would disperse and disappear as whole towns, such as Falk on the South Fork Elk River, Korbel on the Mad River, Crannell on the Little River, Newburg on Strongs Creek near Fortuna, and Camp Grant on the Eel River, among myriad others, disintegrated once the redwoods had been exhausted.

Hammond didn't limit himself to redwoods. In December 1900, he bought 14,500 acres of Oregon grant land from Southern Pacific, which owned nearly 20 percent of the standing forest in western Oregon. Like most of Hammond's major timber deals, this one was demonstrably illegal because the original federal land grant to the railroads required that the properties be sold in 160-acre allotments to individual buyers. No matter, within a year Hammond would purchase from the railroad another 50,000 acres of virgin forest in Oregon's Coast Range east of Portland, on the Trask and Tualatin Rivers, "the largest unbroken tract of timberland still remaining in first hands in this State," according to the *Portland Oregonian*. Hammond's empire grew by the day. The Southern Pacific, meanwhile, made bank by selling him the land and then hauling the lumber and by manipulating loans and securities markets associated with both ventures.

When he wasn't in New York, Collis Huntington was often in San Francisco, where he spent three months each year overseeing Southern Pacific's main office, which was otherwise managed by his nephew, Henry Huntington. Henry in large part worked as a fixer. Among his duties, Henry was charged with distributing his uncle's many bribes and with hiring private detectives to spy on the firm's enemies and even allies. Hammond frequently met with the Huntingtons in San Francisco. After the elder Huntington died, Hammond and Henry Huntington maintained a close business bond—Huntington remained a director of the Hammond Lumber Company until his death in 1927. Though Henry Huntington was also a railroad man—he developed the "Yellow Car" and "Red Car" urban streetcar systems for Los Angeles, which were eventually displaced by the automobile—he gained fame as a major developer, especially in Southern California, and as an art collector, bibliophile, and philanthropist. In 1920 Huntington and his wife, Arabella, built the Huntington Library in the wealthy Los Angeles suburb of San Marino, a city developed by Henry Huntington. (Henry married Arabella in 1913, well after the death of her first husband, Collis Huntington.) Today the Huntington Library is a treasured international research institution replete with rare texts and documents and visited by scholars of world and American history, including, ironically, Richard White, whose 2011 book *Railroaded* documents the destructive power and unnecessary profusion of nineteenth-century transcontinental railroads.

When Collis Huntington died, Hammond anticipated that he would continue to receive the backing of the fathomless Southern Pacific pots of money and political influence. Virtually from the moment he purchased the Vance operation, Hammond had been collaborating with Southern Pacific officials to develop a rail line, for exclusive or at least preferential use by the Hammond Lumber Company, from Humboldt County to either Oregon or the Bay Area, to harness what the *San Francisco Chronicle* characterized as "the immense and profitable traffic that is expected to flow from the development of Humboldt's immense timber resources." The southern line was a more likely prospect, as the state of California had chartered the Northwestern Pacific Railroad in 1898 to extend the railroad from Sonoma County to Eureka.

The first half of what would become the Northwestern Pacific, the California Northwestern Railroad, reached Willits, in northern Mendocino County, in 1902. The impact of the railroad's arrival was obvious. According to *Pacific Coast Wood and Iron*, annual lumber shipments from Mendocino County increased from under 100 million board feet in 1901 to 128 million board feet in 1904 and to 148 million board feet in 1905. The numbers also reflected a booming economy. In January 1903 the *Mendocino Coast Beacon* reported, "[Since the turn of the century] the demand for building material has increased tremendously, while prices have been exceptionally well maintained. . . . Never before in the history of San Francisco and of the other coast cities has there been such activity displayed in construction circles as at the present moment . . . while the lumber mills are rushed to their utmost filling the orders." Still, Humboldt County would have to wait another decade before the railroad arrived at its doorstep. From Willits the line would need to scale a seemingly endless cascade of steep, unstable coastal mountains to penetrate what is fondly known today as the "redwood curtain," which had kept Humboldt County largely apart from the world.

22

WHEN A. B. HAMMOND PURCHASED THE VANCE OPERATION, HE ALSO acquired two mill sites. One occupied a prime location at the foot of G Street, in Eureka, but the footprint was too small to accommodate his obsessive vision. The other site, across the bay on the north spit, in what would become the company-owned town of Samoa, housed the main Vance mill but still had ample room to sprawl. Flush with cash from investors and from the sale of the Blackfoot mill to Marcus Daly, Hammond added machinery and men to the mills and to the woods. In 1900 the Vance company had shipped twenty million board feet of lumber, an estimable sum. Within a few years Hammond had increased the company's milling capacity to ninety million feet annually.

Two hundred men at a time toiled in the deep woods now owned by Hammond. While Vance had kept two logging camps operating in the redwoods, Hammond ran six. It was normal for two axe-wielding "choppers" to work simultaneously to fell a redwood. Lefty choppers were in demand. Like many of their fathers and grandfathers, these men bucked the great trees with handsaws. By the late 1910s, however, misery whips would be largely replaced by heavy gas-powered drag saws, forerunners of chainsaws. The camp's well-paid sharpener constantly honed axes and saws.

A redwood bole might weigh fifty tons or more. Some preternatural specimens, when horizontal, stood four times taller than the loggers. To move these behemoths, a "yarding" crew employed steam-powered "bull donkey" cable systems to drag the logs across now-barren ground for up to two miles. An ear-splitting, five-hundred-horsepower, wood-fired steam engine powered two one-thousand-cubic-inch cylinders that cranked the cable drums. A four-man crew built the contraption in place upon a square foundation of redwood logs, each thirty-two feet long and seven feet in diameter, half sunken into the earth. Hammond's bull donkeys were "the largest ever made," according to a 1902 report in the *Humboldt Times*. They were also the loudest. Men went deaf toiling in what had previously been one of the world's quietest places.

To feed his mills, Hammond rapidly expanded the Vance company's rail network. Hammond had already built two major lines in Oregon, the Corvallis and Eastern, with 142 miles of track, and the Astoria and Columbia River, with 118 miles. Hammond's purchase of the Vance holding included the Eureka & Klamath River Railroad, which was chartered to reach that great river's redwood inventory fifty miles north and could extend another fifty miles to southwestern Oregon. Hammond immediately extended the existing Vance track twelve miles to the north, which brought the road farther up Lindsay Creek to breach the low ridge behind Fieldbrook to access the rich redwood groves of the upper Little River that Hammond had purchased in late 1900. Soon the line would cross Little River on a bridge more than one hundred feet above the water. By 1903 trains were rolling into the new Hammond redwood holding at the coastal flat that ran behind Trinidad to Big Lagoon. By then Hammond's Humboldt railroad was powered by 7 locomotives and included 2 passenger coaches with 4 more on the way, 25 flatcars for lumber, and 120 log cars.

Despite the northward charter of his railroad, Hammond was more interested in southern options. The most useful rail route would naturally be from Humboldt County to distribution yards in the Bay Area, where lines of commerce to all corners of California, the United States, and the world were well in place. Until such time, and well after the Northwestern Pacific became operative to Humboldt County in 1914, Hammond utilized what others called "Hammond's navy": the world's largest line of lumber steamships, including the first steel ships used for hauling wood products.

Hammond built many ships. He leased the Bendixsen shipyard, which was next door to the Hammond mill in Samoa, and built thirteen ships in ten years at the deep-water port just north of the mouth of Humboldt Bay. In 1902 Hammond contracted with the Huntingtons' Newport News shipyard to construct the largest lumber ship ever built there, an oil burner that accommodated 1.5 million board feet of cargo. The capacity quickly paid off. Less than two years later, Hammond would fill an order for 15 million board feet of redwood placed by the Ontario Power Company of Buffalo, New York, to construct a water flume and stave pipe that stretched more than a mile from Niagara Falls to a hydroelectric plant that provided Buffalo with electricity. The lumber was first shipped by sea to San Francisco, where it was loaded onto three hundred train cars for the long trek to New York. The *San Francisco Call* noted that it was "the largest individual [lumber] order that has ever been placed in California."

Hammond's shipping operation was so successful that, in 1910, he commissioned construction of the largest lumber carrier on the West Coast, the *Edgar H. Vance*, which was longer than a football field and could haul 2.5 million board feet of lumber. By then Hammond had become the first redwood lumber producer to log year-round, and the company was shipping redwood throughout the world, including to Europe, China, Australia, and South Africa. Hammond's largest ships would eventually accommodate 6 million board feet. The Hammond ships, nearly eighty in all, announced themselves with flags and smokestacks emblazoned with the company logo, a blue *H* set in a white diamond.

In addition to filling corporate lumber orders, Hammond sought a bigger share of redwood profits by building wholesale and retail lumber outlets throughout the West, including sixty-five retail yards in California alone. In 1903 Hammond leased from the Southern Pacific Company thirty-nine acres on Terminal Island in the San Pedro area of Los Angeles. Two years later he founded the National Lumber Company, capitalized at $1 million, and built a wholesale lumber yard at Terminal Island to facilitate domestic and international distribution. The yard's quarter-mile-long deep-water dock accommodated the company's oversized steamships, and it was accessed by rail. Later Hammond built another distribution yard, a twenty-eight-acre expanse at Alameda and 20th Streets in Los Angeles that had fifteen railroad feeder tracks—"the biggest retail lumber yard on earth," reported the *California Lumber Merchant*. Hammond had purchased the land from Henry Huntington.

This was Hammond's style: build quickly, build big, and crush the competition. There would be no slowing, not even for watersheds that were bleeding into the ocean under the strain of total deforestation or for the health and safety of timber workers, among whom injuries, deaths, and turnover were epidemic. Like his hero, Napoleon, Hammond would construct his personal empire from the ashes of everything he touched. As he vied to put competing redwood manufacturers out of business, his company also harnessed the most efficient and powerful industrial technologies ever known, improved and enlarged them, and prosecuted a complete and permanent ecological transformation of the delicate life of the ancient redwood forest.

After his three purchases in 1900, comprising almost twenty-five thousand acres of virgin redwood on Lindsay Creek, Little River, and the Trinidad coastal flat, Hammond went looking for more.

On May 14, 1902, he acquired 35,242 acres of what the *Humboldt Times* would call "the finest redwood land in Northern Humboldt." It was the single largest land purchase in California history. This was the Scots' Redwood Creek tract, held by the American Lumber Company. The property stood adjacent to the large, uncut holdings owned by C. A. Smith and J. E. Henry. The federal government had yet to patent title to the property, so it remained tainted by fraud. Hammond was undeterred. The price was an extraordinary $1 million, the same amount that Hammond had paid for the entire Vance operation just two years before. Hammond partnered in the purchase with the Michigan timber firm Merrill & Ring, which took a 50 percent stake in the land. Merrill & Ring had by now depleted its once vast North Woods timber holdings. Owner R. D. Merrill lived in San Francisco, a few blocks from Hammond in the exclusive Pacific Heights district.

The price of Hammond's new tract reflected swelling values of redwood timberland that had occurred since the turn of the century. In reporting the sale, the *San Francisco Chronicle* wrote, "This advance in the price of redwood timber is due largely to the fact that many fine tracts of timber have been bought up by Eastern timber experts."

Another reason for the high price is that this watershed wasn't called Redwood Creek for nothing. By 1902 Pacific Lumber had made such deep incursions into the Eel River that Redwood Creek was now second only to the Klamath River as home to the world's largest unbroken expanse of ancient redwood remaining in a single watershed. Sixty thousand acres of contiguous redwood forest, including some of the tallest trees in the world, coated Redwood Creek from bank to bank along nearly forty miles of stream. The trees were tightly spaced and of the highest quality. Hammond would log toward Redwood Creek for decades; yet, owing to the immensity of timber standing along the way, nearly all of Redwood Creek would remain pristine until after World War II.

The redwood market ran hot. Everyone wanted in, and prices rose commensurately. In 1908 yet another Michigan firm, Hill-Davis, a Weyerhaeuser subsidiary, paid nearly $1 million for Merrill & Ring's half interest in Hammond's Redwood Creek tract, double the price of just six years before. That year most major redwood companies would follow Hammond's lead and begin logging year-round. By this time Humboldt and Mendocino counties alone were milling more than four hundred million board feet of prime softwood lumber, in addition to producing millions of railroad ties, shingles, and shakes—a tally equal to 25 percent of the entire output of the state of Oregon.

Hammond kept buying. In 1903 he acquired more than ten thousand acres along the Van Duzen River, including the rich groves of tall redwoods standing on the wide isthmuses created by the sinuous stream. Hammond purchased the Van Duzen tract from Russell A. Alger, a principal in the Buffalo Syndicate's fraudulent redwood acquisitions and, at the time of the sale, a US senator.

Not long after buying the Buffalo Syndicate lands along the Van Duzen River, Hammond procured five thousand acres of redwood standing along the main stem of the Eel River. The land included a large flat, called Camp Grant, which banked the river just upstream from its confluence with the majestic South Fork Eel River. In 1863 the US military had constructed Camp Grant to capture and remove Native Americans to benefit white settlers. Some troops sought to protect Indians from roving bands of white vigilantes that during previous years had prosecuted several massacres of Native Americans. But troops killed Indians too. The camp was named for Ulysses S. Grant. In 1854 Grant had served at Fort Humboldt, a US military base in Eureka. Native peoples had fished at the Camp Grant site for millennia, as legendary runs of salmon, steelhead, and lamprey migrated up both forks of the Eel during most months of the year. By 1866 the Indians had been exterminated or relocated, and their fish would now be canned and exported to national and international markets.

Most of Hammond's new redwood inventory stood uphill from the flat at Camp Grant and was difficult to access. Hammond would certainly log this forest, but that's not why he'd bought it. With this transaction Hammond took title to five miles of Eel River frontage, through which the Northwestern Pacific Railroad would need to build its line from southern markets to Eureka. Hammond now owned a choke point in the line. He also owned the very site, Camp Grant, that would become a staging area for the railroad's construction, then a depot. He was a brutal and masterful player.

23

FOR FIFTY YEARS AFTER THE TURN OF THE TWENTIETH CENTURY, THE Hammond Lumber and Pacific Lumber companies vied for title of world's largest producer of redwood products. The lead regularly changed hands, but the contest was always close. After World War II, Pacific Lumber amended its forest practices to rely almost exclusively on selective logging in the unentered ancient redwood groves. The Hammond company would not follow suit. Until the Maxxam takeover, in late 1985, Pacific Lumber was, for forty years, the only redwood firm that logged in a way that might be described as patient. After the war the company generally leveled fewer than five thousand acres each year—some years the company cut fewer than two thousand acres—while leaving half of the old-growth trees standing once logging was completed.

In contrast, Hammond Lumber logged with an extremely heavy hand until 1956, twenty-two years after the death of A. B. Hammond and eleven years after the death of his son, Leonard. That year Hammond stockholders sold their shares to a rapidly expanding Oregon timber company, the Georgia-Pacific Corporation (GP), for $75 million. The *Sacramento Bee* called it "one of the largest financial transactions in the history of the lumber industry" and noted that the new name of the firm would be the Hammond-California Redwood Company. Georgia-Pacific attacked the woods with a vengeance equal to Hammond's. The difference was in GP's public relations department, which employed assuaging terms such as "tree farm" and "sustainable forestry" to mask the company's ruinous logging practices.

The Pacific Lumber operation had always been immense. For eight decades the Pacific Lumber board of directors would be dominated by the Murphy family, lumbermen originally from Maine. Simon Jones Murphy was "the aged patriarch of the Murphy family that had created a lumbering and mining empire stretching from Maine to the Great Lakes and on to the Southwest," Jerry Rohde writes in *Both Sides of the Bluff*. By the mid-1860s Simon Murphy was living in Detroit and leveling tens of thousands of acres of North Woods forest. In 1890 Murphy shifted his focus when he discovered oil near his winter haunt in Southern California. He quickly became Detroit's wealthiest resident. At the same time his son, Frank Murphy, operated in Arizona, where he owned the state's largest gold mine. He also owned the Santa Fe, Prescot & Phoenix Railway, which he sold to the Santa Fe Railway in 1901. The following year the Santa Fe backed Murphy's bid to take control of Pacific Lumber, which occurred in 1903.

Murphy also took over the Excelsior Lumber Company. Joseph Russ, David Evans, and the Hooper brothers had carved Excelsior out of the Scottish land scam, but now Evans and Russ were dead. The purchase came with seventeen thousand acres of redwood forestland. The Murphys now controlled the world's largest producer of lumber and forty-two thousand acres of virgin redwood.

Under Murphy, Pacific Lumber operations accelerated. In August 1905, Pacific Lumber reorganized and incorporated in Maine with a new board of directors and a new president, Selwyn Eddy, a timberman from Saginaw, Michigan. The new directors, headed by the Murphy clan, laded the company with a $900,000 loan from the Union Trust Company of Detroit, "the largest loan ever floated for a private interest in Michigan," reported the *Detroit Free Press*. By that time production at the Pacific Lumber mill had ramped up to five million board feet per month.

The Murphys were able capitalists. Only two other families—the Hoopers and the Hammonds—would be as responsible for as much redwood logging as the Murphys. After the death of Simon Murphy, writes Rohde,

other members of the Murphy family and their business associates then operated PL, hiring a succession of presidents until 1931, when Albert Stanwood Murphy, Simon's grandson, became the first Murphy to serve as PL's president. Albert Stanwood was elevated to the chairmanship of PL's board in 1961. His son, Stanwood Albert Murphy Sr., served as president from 1961 to 1971, when he took over as chairman of the board. He died the following year, at which time the Murphy dynasty ceased to rule PL.

Stanwood Albert Sr.'s son, Warren Murphy, served for many years as PL's manager of lumber operations. Another son, Stanwood Albert Murphy Jr., or "Woody," was a road crew supervisor. Both sons held stock in the company. One week after Maxxam bought out Pacific Lumber in 1985, the brothers and their sister, Suzanne Murphy, sued Maxxam for violating securities laws during the takeover. A federal judge, who'd been appointed by President Gerald Ford, immediately tossed the suit.

In October 1909, the so-called Humboldt Promotion Committee purchased, for $1,000, a four-page spread in the *San Francisco Chronicle*. The committee included L. F. Puter, a Eureka attorney, redwood timber broker, and brother of infamous land-fraud king S. A. D. Puter. Born in 1857 and raised in the Humboldt County logging town of Blue Lake, S. A. D. Puter illegally, and almost singlehandedly, amassed, consolidated, and sold nearly two hundred thousand acres of prime forestland in Oregon, as well as the thirty thousand acres of redwood he'd sold to C. A. Smith in Humboldt County.

The committee's four-page ad alerted readers to several business opportunities, including "IMMESURABLE FORESTS OF GIANT REDWOODS." On December 20 the *Eureka Herald* followed up with an eight-page "Railroad Edition" that reflected and fueled local fervor for the promised arrival of the Northwestern Pacific Railroad. With a banner headline announcing, "HUMBOLDT GREATEST REDWOOD COUNTY IN THE WORLD," the special section, clearly aimed at outside investors, sought to catalogue the local riches—principally redwood—available for the taking.

"Del Norte and Humboldt counties are especially the 'Home of the Redwood,'" announced the *Herald*. "In these counties the wonderful timber has apparently reached the acme of its development. . . . What Humboldt has already done with this vast resource without a railroad, marks a magnificent effort. What the resource will mean to Humboldt upon the completion of the railroad to this country is something which is left to the imaginative power of the reader." Probably few Humboldt residents at the time possessed the imaginative power necessary to foresee the ecological catastrophes that would follow completion of the railroad or the ongoing economic implosions wrought by the resulting redwood liquidation.

In pitching the more distant, and more important, readers, the *Herald* would leave little to the imagination.

"Redwood timber is as good as government bonds [and] its appeal to the investor is of the strongest," the *Herald* noted. The numbers set the hook. In 1905 Humboldt County had shipped a record 300 million board feet of redwood lumber, shakes, shingles, and railroad ties. In 1907 it shipped 374 million board feet, meaning that "the annual output of lumber from Humboldt will doubtless soon reach the half billion mark."

Finally, in a museum-quality contribution to the annals of tone-deaf newspaper prose, the *Herald* proclaimed, "RAILROAD! It is the one word in the English language which today sets the rich red blood a tingling through the veins of Humboldters as the name ABRAHAM LINCOLN startles the American negro and gladdens his heart. And it is on the same principle, too, for it is the RAILROAD which is to emancipate Humboldt county from the SLAVERY of ISOLATION just as LINCOLN freed the negroes from another form of slavery."

On September 22, 1914, after laying 107 miles of track primarily across the crumbling slopes of the main branch of the Eel River, the Santa Fe Railway and the Southern Pacific Railroad completed "one of the costliest pieces of railroad construction in the United States," according to a 1932 edition of the *Railway and Locomotive Historical Society Bulletin*. "Many tunnels, bridges and suspended construction of roadbed was required for this line." After the October 23 golden-spike ceremony, held at Cain Rock, along the Eel River in southeastern Humboldt County, a large party of revelers left by train to join a three-day celebration in Eureka. A landslide delayed their arrival and foreshadowed the entire history of this crumbling line.

The Northwestern Pacific trains did not supplant steamships for hauling lumber. During the second half of the nineteenth century, shipping lumber out of Humboldt Bay had well served the region's exporters, and ship transport would continue even after completion of the rail line. Rather, the railroad was intended to allow Humboldt's redwood production to grow, which it did, mightily, and for lumber to be delivered faster and more reliably. One of the first major rail shipments left Humboldt County in 1914, when an entire trainload of construction-grade redwood journeyed to the Salton Sea, near the Mexico border, to build the town of Niland, California.

The following year the *Los Angeles Times* reported, "The largest single order for lumber ever given in the San Fernando Valley was placed with the Hammond Lumber Company [for] construction of flumes to convey the Owens River water from the San Fernando reservoir to the Encino Rancho, a distance of six miles." Hammond shipped the lumber by train on twenty-two flatcars. The water was destined for use by the American Beet Sugar Company to grow fifteen thousand acres of beets. "Laterals," also made of redwood, "will distribute the water to intervening land, thus making the Owens River water available immediately to thousands of acres."

Although this particular water was leased to Los Angeles farmers, city officials and private speculators had secured the Owens River water in 1905 to feed their dream of building an urban West Coast empire that could challenge the supremacy of San Francisco. Two of those speculators were E. H. Harriman and Henry Huntington, economic allies of A. B. Hammond. Harriman was the "twentieth century's paramount railway tycoon [who formed] his own railroad empire out of the wrecks of the 1890s," writes Richard White. Harriman was president of the Union Pacific Railroad, which had built the eastern leg of the first transcontinental railroad. After the death of Collis Huntington, Harriman purchased a 50 percent share of the Southern Pacific Railroad.

24

Not coincidentally, the Northwestern Pacific Railroad opened for business just two months after completion of the Panama Canal, in August 1914. The canal would nearly halve the time and cost of shipping lumber from the West Coast to the eastern seaboard. This was just one year after the US government's investment of more than $1 million to build jetties to stabilize the tumultuous mouth of Humboldt Bay. The jetties would erode the mystery of what time, or even what day, a ship laded with redwood lumber might leave port.

Most Humboldt County residents understood the coming of the railroad as a revenue enhancer. Railroad historian Fred Stindt, in his 1964 remembrance *The Northwestern Pacific Railroad*, notes that Humboldt County "was a land almost entirely isolated from the state and the nation of which it was a part—it's mountains and valleys covered with the only remaining forest of redwood available for commercial exploitation." In addition to lumber, the railroad would also haul Humboldt County's many agricultural products to the Bay Area, and it would generate tourist dollars.

The tourists would please hoteliers but needle redwood producers. For the first time the lay public could easily view, in close proximity, the horrors of Humboldt's industrial redwood logging. The problem of tourism would worsen in 1918 with completion of the Redwood Highway from Sonoma County to Eureka. The nation's new class of motorists could now take themselves to the fabled land of magnificent trees whenever they had the itch to do so.

To the uninitiated, as well as the initiated, there was no denying the grim specter of a redwood clear-cut. Trains carted awestruck travelers along the majestic main stem of the Eel River, and automobiles brought them along the South Fork. Window views included diverse landscapes of towering Douglas fir and other conifers, ancient oak woodlands, wild rivers, and succulent prairies. Suddenly these breezy landscapes gave way to the deep, magnificent riverside groves of impossibly large redwoods, darkened fairy lands never previously imagined. Children squealed, but grownups quieted. Soon an unforgettable smokey scent foreshadowed an emerging glare of treeless, desiccated earth blackened by fire. Had a great war occurred here? Thousands of charred stumps, some as big as houses, and still-smoldering snags—some of them hundreds of feet tall—ravaged the virgin sensibilities of these new arrivals. Children cried; their parents fumed. When tourists returned home, they wrote letters of protest.

The Northwestern Pacific was the last major US line built by a transcontinental railroad. Whereas Hammond, Pacific Lumber, and other redwood producers would benefit from faster, more reliable transportation by rail and by sea, industrial consumers of redwood products formed a community equally dedicated to achieving transportation improvements. Virtually all businesses that were now experiencing exponential growth in the American West—including bedrock industries such as housing, agriculture, hydroelectric power, finance, and railroads—rose on a foundation of redwood products. As Richard White notes in *Railroaded*, the railroads were "only part of a second, much larger web of politicians, newspapermen, bankers, and businessmen." In some respects, this web relied just as much on redwood as it did on railroads.

It took White ten years to write *Railroaded*, which was a finalist for the Pulitzer Prize and draws in large part from the personal papers of nineteenth-century railroad men (including receipts from congressmen for bribes they'd received). The book deeply explores Gilded Age finance and industrial expansion, told through the lens of railroads as a transformational force. One particular aspect of White's book jumps out.

As White notes, one's "friends" in business were key to survival and expansion. Business executives operated in Venn diagrams of individuals and institutions who controlled finance, resources, transportation, labor, media, and public officials. Rarely was the public privy to the actual goings on in these spheres. This was a world of *inwardness*, writes White, "a nineteenth-century term to denote things whose meaning was not apparent on their surface, of legislation, newspaper stories, or administrative decisions."

While cooperation among business owners was often integral to financial growth, competition—often to the point of economic doom—could be an even more potent force. White notes that, within the opaque world of financial wars often waged by the unseen hands of corporate managers and financiers,

> *reformers*, too, became part of the networks that corporations created. Networks created *friends*, and while a reformer might be one railroad's enemy, he could as a result become another railroad's friend. . . . [R]eformers . . . could, in certain circumstances, prove useful. . . . [R]eform and corruption were often allies. . . . Political friendship was itself virtually always corrupt; friendship facilitated the movement of public goods to secure private favors, but *leagues* of friends also mobilized to prevent such transfers, sometimes for the public good and sometimes because they wished to have the spoils themselves.

The emphasis above is mine. Although White principally investigates the "inward" worlds of railroads, the model is applicable across the corporate spectrum—perhaps especially with regard to the tension between the redwood industry, the corporate demand for redwood products, and growing public outcry over redwood logging.

Over decades of immersion and study, I'd seen disturbing trends in the history of redwood logging and associated redwood protection efforts that occurred after the turn of the twentieth century. I'd found—though I didn't have a word for it yet—a deep *inwardness* at play within the byzantine relationships that drove and enriched North Coast redwood producers and allied industries, especially with regard to pacifying an outraged public. A significant underpinning of this particular inwardness was the scope and purpose of a *league* created by *friends* of redwood producers and, even more so, of the industries that relied on redwood products. These friends called themselves *reformers* intent on saving redwoods, but they were quite the opposite. They were insiders who would support redwood preservation, but only of token groves and always on their own terms. The insiders would serve the larger objective of protecting standing redwoods for investment and eventual inclusion within the maw of industrial expansion.

This new league sought to forestall the public's calls for redwood protection by subverting and subsuming those efforts. The league would be led by powerful and influential leaders of industry, politics, and finance, who would generate thousands of glowing newspaper stories about their ersatz efforts. They would submit or kill state and federal legislation according to their needs. As they gathered accolades and donations, they would also collect into a political eddy, and then drown, the unwitting support of tens of thousands of concerned people, from the United States and throughout the world, who demanded redwood protection.

In 1917 a cadre of these friends would gather at the exclusive Bohemian Grove, in Sonoma County, to create the first, the largest, and the longest-lasting example of an inward political and economic phenomenon that today we call "greenwashing"—that is, rhetorical support for environmental protection by an institution actually working on behalf of destructive corporations. Emerging from their redwood hideaway, these men carried with them the seeds of a new organization, which they would call Save the Redwoods League.

Part Three

A LEAGUE OF
THEIR OWN

*Facts are not secure in the hands of power.... [I]f the modern political lies
are so big that they require a complete rearrangement of the whole factual
texture—the making of another reality, as it were, into which they will fit
without seam, crack, or fissure, exactly as the facts fitted into their own original context—what prevents these new stories, images, and non-facts from
becoming an adequate substitute for reality and factuality?*

—*Hannah Arendt*

People wandering the streets with their heads shot off by money.

—*Denis Johnson*

25

On a warm September day in 2009, I drove eight hours south from my home in Humboldt County through most of California's coast redwood ecosystem. I was aiming for the wooded urban oasis of Portola Valley, an incorporated town that overlooks Silicon Valley. There I met, for the first time, famed environmental activist Martin Litton. At ninety-two years old, Litton was forty-four years my senior. Each of us, in our time, had been deeply involved in efforts to save the last large redwood ecosystems then standing: Redwood Creek, in what is now Redwood National Park, and Headwaters Forest.

Esther Litton, Martin's wife of seventy years, greeted me at the door. She was warm and diminutive in a floral blouse and practical slacks. In his rich baritone, Martin bellowed something from the back, then emerged. He was tall and robust, his face wrapped in a full silver beard. Litton stood regally straight and held the room like a ship's captain.

"Mr. King!" he announced, a big hand jutted my way. "How good it is to finally meet."

Litton was a legendary adventurer and environmentalist. In 1955 he became the 185th person to paddle the Colorado River through the Grand Canyon. In 2004, at the age of eighty-seven, he became the oldest person to do it, running the river solo, in a dory. Four years later he did it again.

By the time he made his first run of the Colorado, Litton and his friend, the "Archdruid" David Brower, Edgar and Peggy Wayburn, and other "young Turks" of the era had repurposed the Sierra Club from a small, regional collection of nature lovers into what would become the world's most powerful environmental organization. In 1960 the Club would launch the first and only authentic campaign to create a large, whole-watershed Redwood National Park. At the time, Litton was a director of the Sierra Club, and he doubled as the travel editor for *Sunset* magazine, a job he held from 1954 to 1968.

Because he was a pilot, Litton conducted much of his research by light airplane. In this fashion Litton saw a lot of the western United States, including proposed dam sites. Among many other victories, during the 1950s and 1960s the Sierra Club halted several major dam proposals. Two dams would have flooded the Grand Canyon reach of the Colorado River, and two more were destined to inundate Dinosaur National Monument. They failed to stop construction of Glen Canyon Dam. In a 1982 documentary about Earth First!'s "cracking" of the Glen Canyon Dam, Litton flew the film's cinematographer for aerial footage of 161,390-acre Lake Powell, the result of backing up the Colorado River for 186 miles through Arizona into Utah.

By 1960, Litton had flown several times over the northern redwood belt, and he had driven through it as well. That year he produced a cover story for *Sunset*, "The Redwood Country." Litton's photos included bleak images of a new freeway cutting through "protected" redwoods inHumboldt Redwoods State Park. The magazine received several letters from outraged readers, as did elected representatives. The story is widely credited with having catalyzed the modern Redwood National Park movement. In her 1983 book *The Fight to Save the Redwoods*, Susan Schrepfer referred to Litton as the "decisive influence in the redwood battle."

During his flights for *Sunset*, one landscape wouldn't leave Litton alone: an unusually large and intact carpet of emerald forest along Redwood Creek, in northern Humboldt County. Litton knew the parks and understood that this was not one. Yet the redwoods under his Cessna undulated for miles, tens of thousands of acres rising out of the Pacific and lolling serenely across coastal slopes and both sides of the stream to the ridgelines. Here was a large redwood watershed almost entirely unlogged, a precious remnant that was clearly the last of its kind in the world. It was the single largest virgin redwood forest remaining inside or outside parks.

Litton suggested a late lunch. I readily accepted, not understanding that he meant to drive us eight miles into the bustling city of Palo Alto. He was, after all, ninety-two. But there was something special he wanted to show me.

"There's one big redwood left," he said. "Where the town got its name."

Like Portola Valley, the flats of Palo Alto and the hills to the west once hummed with the life of spectacular mixed forests that included giant redwoods. During the late 1800s, the region served as a deep-water port for transporting redwood lumber. Now, in the flats not far from the bay, a few second-growth redwood trees, and apparently one big one, dotted the urban landscape.

The big tree was a disappointment. It stood in bleak repose against an unnatural landscape—stark, shortened, apparently dying from the top, a pair of railroad tracks covering its fragile roots. By now it really was just a *palo alto*, a "tall stick." Lunch was better. I don't remember my entrée, but I do recall we drank martinis. Litton efficiently downed his, then ordered another.

I asked Litton about the early Redwood National Park campaign.

"I guess you could say that I discovered Redwood Creek," he said. After spotting the "big grove" in 1959, Litton flew it a few more times over the ensuing months. "At that time it was generally untouched," said Litton. In 1961 the John F. Kennedy administration showed some interest in establishing a Redwood National Park, but its National Park Service lacked funds even for a survey of potential sites. In 1963 the National Geographic Society (NGS) granted the Park Service $64,000 to conduct a survey. In May that year Litton picked up the NGS team, which included Chet Brown and Paul Fritz, landscape architects with the National Park Service, and NGS senior naturalist and photographer Paul Zahl. He flew the trio over Redwood Creek. The team later hiked to a grove tucked into an oxbow at the heart of the enveloping forest, deep at the bottom of the watershed and surrounded for miles in all directions by ancient redwoods. Trying to convince Brown that their highest calling in that moment was to save Redwood Creek as a national park, Litton recalled that he smacked a nearby tree with his hand and said, "For God's sake, Chet, this could be the tallest tree in the world." That tree, he told me, "turned out to be taller than any other measured redwood."

Litton was right: four of the world's tallest trees known at that time, including the tallest, at 367.8 feet, stood within a stone's throw of each other on that flat—an understanding that a returning NGS team confirmed by triangulating their height. In July 1964, the discovery of what soon became known as the Tall Trees Grove made the cover of *National Geographic* and was given fifty-two pages inside the magazine.

Federal interest in a Redwood National Park, and the splashy coverage, energized the Sierra Club's ambition, simmering since 1956, to create a large, watershed-wide Redwood National Park. Paul Zahl was clear that his team hadn't just found the tallest tree, or even four of the tallest. They'd found a primordial kingdom of seemingly impossible grandeur that almost no one knew existed.

"I stopped in a small clearing and, pivoting slowly, counted the number of great trees visible from that single spot: 30 with trunks at least ten feet in diameter, some perhaps 14 or 16 feet," wrote Zahl. "Within just a few acres we counted more than a hundred giants ten feet or more in diameter—most of them at least 300 feet high." Later Zahl and the others floated in rafts fifteen miles downstream, to the town of Orick near the coast. Along the way they encountered "sheer walls of towering redwood [and] one of the thickest trunks I had seen anywhere in the valley—almost 20 feet. . . . [W]e drifted past line after line of redwood treasure. . . . This was certainly one of the few remaining redwood wildernesses, [offering] some of the most extraordinary scenery in the world."

After the magazine's coverage dropped on the nation like a clarion wake-up call, there could be no doubt that Redwood Creek ought to be preserved as a national park. But there was a hitch.

Litton took another sip, then said, almost under his breath, as if to himself, "It was so weird and strange that Save the Redwoods League would oppose getting a new national park" on Redwood Creek.

I was stunned. How could the world's foremost redwood preservation organization oppose the creation of a Redwood National Park that would preserve the largest remaining intact redwood watershed? The League didn't object to a national park per se, said Litton. It wanted to take one of the existing redwood state parks—seven-thousand-acre Jedediah Smith in Del Norte County—add a small amount of unprotected old-growth forest standing alongside Mill Creek and a severe expanse of adjacent cutover land, and make that into a Redwood National Park.

"We knew it wasn't adequate, it wasn't enough," said Litton. "We already had Jedediah Smith, it was already saved. It was just as well off as a state park as it would have been as a national park. What we needed was new territory that hadn't been saved, and where in fact the tallest tree in the world was found at that time."

Why, I asked Litton, would Save the Redwoods League argue against protecting ancient redwoods and the world's tallest trees and instead push for "protecting" a small, damaged area?

"Ignorance," he said. "They didn't know where the redwoods were."

Later I would learn that Litton was wrong. Since at least 1920, officials at Save the Redwoods League had known exactly where every remaining ancient redwood tree stood. As I scoured the League's archives at the University of California (UC), Berkeley's Bancroft Library, I found a definitive 1920 report by US forester Paul Redington that identified the location and stand characteristics of nearly two hundred thousand acres of contiguous virgin redwood forest, just in Humboldt County, that was worthy of preservation. The archive also contained associated documents, including dozens of maps, provided by timber companies and other sources, that delineated in real time, over decades, where logging had occurred and where virgin groves still stood in the northern redwood belt. Yet, even if League officials had for forty-five years somehow remained ignorant of the redwoods' whereabouts, by July 1964, when the likes of *National Geographic* announced one of the most extraordinary discoveries of the modern age, locating the big redwoods was now easily done.

As we left the restaurant, I sheepishly asked Litton if he'd like me, or Esther, to drive. "Oh no," he said, "I'm fine." I recalled an incident from thirty years before, when Litton flew his Cessna within one hundred feet of a passenger jet coming in for a landing at Oakland International Airport, causing the big plane to veer off course. Litton gunned the sedan across two lanes of rapidly approaching traffic and launched us straight into the center median. From the backseat Esther warbled, "Oh, Martin!" I gasped at the oncoming cars, which, miraculously, stopped. Litton jammed the car into reverse, spun the rear tires until the front end lurched off the curb, then meandered down the highway as if nothing had happened.

But something *had* happened. Until that moment I'd long considered Save the Redwoods League to be a weak, often incomprehensible organization but not one that would oppose an opportunity to save the last great redwood ecosystem still standing outside of parks. As Martin Litton blithely tootled along, I tried to reconcile the incongruity of an organization that called itself "Save the Redwoods" with the League's opposition to preserving Redwood Creek. That was the beginning of a years-long deep dive into the history of redwood logging and protection efforts, an immersion that included perusal of many thousands of pages of League archives and other material. I subsequently learned that the League's work to undermine creation of a Redwood National Park on Redwood Creek was not an aberration from, but a continuation of, its entire history to that point. The League's opposition to the park had been drawn from the organization's founding playbook, which had been established in 1917 and would be maintained until the mid-1990s.

26

On October 13, 2018, Save the Redwoods League hosted a lavish, sold-out gala, advertised as the "party of the century," at San Francisco's Union Square to celebrate the organization's centennial anniversary. More than seven hundred wealthy supporters gathered inside a custom big top. Guests dined on a gourmet dinner from McCalls Catering and wines by Charles Krug. Acclaimed Bay Area artist Stanlee Gatti crafted dozens of fern centerpieces that adorned long wooden tables, and for ambiance he'd pumped in CO_2 fog. The cost of a table sponsorship (dinner for ten) ranged from $10,000 to $100,000, a tithe befitting a downtown organization whose annual budget topped $40 million and whose CEO that year earned more than $300,000 in salary and other compensation. San Francisco socialite Charlotte Mailliard Shultz and her husband, former US secretary of state George Shultz, then ninety-seven, served as honorary cochairs of the event, which raised nearly $2 million.

During dinner the dapper crowd hushed for an impactful three-minute video narrated by actor Peter Coyote.

"Those dedicated to protecting the coast redwoods worked tirelessly to launch the world's only conservation group devoted to the permanent protection of redwoods throughout their natural range," Coyote reminded listeners. "As the League's founders developed the tools of land conservation, they sparked a cultural shift in the country."

The League commemorated the anniversary by releasing two books that catalogued the organization's full century of operation. One of them, *The Once and Future Forest*, is an oversized, coffee-table edition that cost $100. According to the *Santa Rosa Press Democrat*, the book "rises to the majesty of its subject with breathtaking photography . . . and essays by five major writers."

The League also published *Saving the Redwoods: The Movement to Rescue a Wonder of the Natural World*, a 600-page narrative by historian and California parks advocate Joseph H. Engbeck Jr. (Engbeck died in 2020, at the age of eighty-seven.) This book, which primarily traces League efforts to protect coast redwoods, as well as the giant sequoias in the Sierra Nevada, was self-published by the League, and it cost $50.

The League has earned steady plaudits and exaltations nearly from the day of the organization's founding. Finding negative critiques of the League at all, anywhere, is almost impossible; tributes are innumerable. Yet the real story of Save the Redwoods League is far more dynamic, fascinating, and contradictory than the organization will, or ever could, let on.

Throughout the twentieth century, the League created a voluminous paper trail that today includes hundreds of thousands of pages of organizational records and related material stored in 150 file boxes at UC Berkeley's Bancroft Library. As I immersed myself in these records, they led me on an almost surreal journey into the little-known history of the organization.

The records demonstrate that the League didn't simply defer to the redwood timber industry and to businesses that relied on redwood products. Instead, the League was created by the men who owned and controlled those firms. Many were second-generation scions of West Coast industrial pioneers whose interests included mining, logging and lumber milling, railroads, steel manufacturing, petroleum extraction and refinement, hydroelectric power, construction and community development, agriculture, dry goods, road building, government, and finance.

Industrial leaders of the early twentieth century also pioneered the arts of community and philanthropical false fronts to quell negative public opinion about the many social and ecological burdens that arose as a result of industrial expansion. They called their new business tool public relations. In addition to owning and controlling virtually all sources of transportation, resources, finance, and labor, these business leaders maintained undue influence in the courts, and they owned virtually all media outlets. They came to specialize in developing thickets of obfuscating and glorifying documentation, a model that today continues to produce manufactured impressions of corporate beneficence.

The business leaders also shared a common and accurate understanding that together they were constructing an economic federation with a power and scope unmatched in human history. Western resources were not just abundant; under modern methods of tapping, refining, and transporting goods, the rapidity with which these raw materials could be montetized was also unprecedented. Within such a system, it was imperative that the redwoods be saved not from the saws but from preservation.

27

IN THE EARLY SUMMER OF 1917, NEW YORK ATTORNEY MADISON GRANT filled a satchel with several copies of a new book and departed his downtown Manhattan office for a promising and long-awaited journey to California. Grant was headed to San Francisco to join two friends, John C. Merriam and Henry Fairfield Osborn, for an automobile journey to Sonoma County. There the trio would attend the annual two-week encampment of the Bohemian Club at its private retreat along the Russian River, after which they would emerge as the esteemed founders of Save the Redwoods League.

At Bohemian Grove, the trio would fraternize at any number of intimate camps secreted inside the one-thousand-acre redwood expanse. Bohemian Club members would swim and boat in the Russian River, wander the Grove's many trails, drink to excess, and—no matter the Grove's Shakespearean motto, "Weaving Spiders Come Not Here"—knit webs of financial and corporate collaboration.

According to Save the Redwoods League lore, Grant, Merriam, and Osborn had come to Bohemian Grove to discuss means of protecting the "last" ancient redwoods, particularly the fabled but unprotected groves that stood two hundred miles to the north, in Humboldt County. At the time, more than 60 percent, or 1.2 million acres, of the original ancient redwood biome still stood, almost all of it in Mendocino, Humboldt, and Del Norte counties. After the Bohemian encampment, the trio would leave for a long motor trip through Humboldt County, where the destruction of redwoods, particularly alongside the Eel River, would inspire their patrician hearts and highly evolved intellects. Outraged by what they found, the trio, in 1918, founded a new and potent organization dedicated to wresting the noble conifers from the horrors of deforestation.

Grant was just the man for the job. By the second decade of the new century, Madison Grant could count himself among the nation's leading conservationists. He'd spearheaded efforts to create bison preserves that forestalled extinction of the species, and he was instrumental in the eventual establishment of the Olympic, Everglades, and Denali national parks, as well as the Bronx Zoo. He was a longtime trustee and benefactor of the American Museum of Natural History and chairman of the New York Zoological Society. In his 2009 book *Defending the Master Race: Conservation, Eugenics, and the Legacy of Madison Grant*, Jonathan Spiro notes that "Grant helped rescue from the verge of extinction . . . the elephants of Africa, the koalas of Australia, the chinchillas of South America, the gorillas of the Congo, the giant tortoises of the Galapagos," and several other notable species.

Grant's ancestors were some of the earliest and most prominent Puritan settlers in New England (touchdown: 1624). In 1887, Grant graduated with honors from Yale University, after which he'd earned a law degree from Columbia. He would be chauffeured through the gates of Bohemian Grove as a beacon of economic and social affluence. In his expensive New York suit and silk tie, tapered stiletto mustache, and authoritative black fedora, Grant, then fifty-one, was fashionable, rakish, and obviously rich.

Grant was also welcomed as a modern torchbearer of racial superiority. By 1917, Grant was the walking embodiment of a purely racist ideology that had long directed and justified American expansion across the continent and which, at the dawning of the new century, was undergoing a facelift in the halls of science. That ideology now had a name—eugenics—and Grant was among its American progenitors. He would be well received at Bohemian Grove.

The book in Grant's satchel concerned itself not with conserving wildlife but with preserving the white race. Grant viewed his new tract, *The Passing of the Great Race*, as a magnum opus that would place him among the high thinkers of the "scientific racism" movement then gaining popularity in the United States and Europe. Eugenics warned against the growth of "inferior races," wrote Grant, which were populated by groups "now engaged in destroying the privilege of wealth." Grant reminded readers, "Mankind emerged from savagery and barbarism under the leadership of selected individuals [who] were able to use the brute strength of the unthinking herd as part of their own force and were able to direct at will the blind dynamic impulse of the slaves, peasants or lower classes." Grant assured readers of the benevolence of the system.

"From a material point of view, slaves are often more fortunate than free-men when treated with reasonable humanity," Grant wrote, using a turn of phrase echoed exactly one hundred years later by Fox News host Bill O'Reilly. Now that most slaves, Black as well as Indian, were relatively free in the United States and Europe, more dramatic measures would be needed to maintain the superiority of the white race. (Joseph Engbeck, in his history of the League, reported that Grant's book "established his reputation as an authority in anthropology" and was "favorably reviewed in *Science*, and in a wide array of other periodicals.")

"Mistaken regard for what are believed to be divine laws and a sentimen-tal belief in the sanctity of human life tend to prevent both the elimination of defective infants and the sterilization of such adults as are themselves of no value to the community," Grant wrote in a chilling passage. "The laws of nature require the obliteration of the unfit and human life is valuable only when it is of use to the community or race. . . . [D]efectives have been care-fully preserved by modern charity. . . . A great injury is done to the commu-nity by the perpetuation of worthless types." Such "human residuum," wrote Grant, should be "eliminated." Grant warned against "the long suppressed, conquered servile classes rising against the master race . . . the white race." To recover the "former control . . . and prestige" of the white race, wrote Grant, "will take several generations and perhaps wars."

Grant penned his book during the First World War, and his prose would inspire and inform perpetrators of the Second. Shortly after Adolf Hitler was appointed chancellor of Germany in 1933, the Führer wrote a personal letter to Madison Grant praising *The Passing of the Great Race*. "This book is my bible," wrote Hitler. Today Grant's tract has many fans among white supremacists in the United States and Europe. In 2011, a Norwegian white nationalist, Anders Breivik, released a fifteen-hundred-page manifesto titled "2083—A European Declaration of Independence," that draws significantly from the writings of Madison Grant. After releasing the manifesto, Breivik murdered seventy-seven mostly Muslim people on the Norwegian island of Utøya and in Oslo.

Another giant in the fields of race and charismatic megafauna that year was Grant's traveling mate and close friend, Henry Fairfield Osborn. By 1917 Osborn was a prominent paleontologist (he named *T. rex*) who'd founded the biology department at Columbia University and served as president of the American Museum of Natural History. His study of mammalian fossil records in Central America led Alfred Wegener, in 1912, to develop the now accepted theory of continental drift. Osborn, a nephew of J. P. Morgan and, like Grant, a leading eugenicist, also hailed from seventeenth-century Puritan stock. A chunky, ostentatious dilettante who had inherited a shipping and railroad fortune—his father, William Henry Osborn, founded the Illinois Central Railroad—Osborn robustly agreed with Grant's conclusion that open immigration laws were resulting in a "resurgence of inferior races" in the United States, as "defectives" with "unstable brains" were flooding a nation once exclusively controlled by the stronger, smarter, cleaner, whiter, and primarily Nordic descendants of northern Europe. "Racial hygiene" was the answer.

"As science has enlightened government in the prevention and spread of disease, it must also enlighten government in the prevention of the spread and multiplication of worthless members of society," Osborn wrote. His own publication in the genre, the popular *Men of the Old Stone Age*, preceded Grant's by two years and had informed much of Grant's work. In 1921, Osborn served as president of the Second International Congress of Eugenics, which ran for a week at the Museum of Natural History.

In 1934, shortly after the Nazis took power, Osborn traveled to Germany to accept an honorary doctorate from Johann Wolfgang von Goethe University in Frankfurt. Upon returning to the United States, Osborn reported that he was "greatly impressed by the . . . new conditions of the Hindenburg-Hitler regime." Historian Brian Regal notes that Osborn viewed the Nazis not as authoritarian sadists but as "a beaten Nordic people using their race plasm and scientific advancements to overcome great obstacles." In private letters, Osborn celebrated the "metempsychosis of Germany" as "one of the most extraordinary phenomena of modern times." Americans had the wrong idea about what was happening in the Third Reich, said Osborn, because "the American press is controlled by the Jews."

In his book, Engbeck ignores Osborn's leading role in establishing and promoting a pseudoscientific bludgeon that was shortly, if not predictably, wielded in service of genocide. Instead, he establishes the paleontologist's environmental cred by referring to him as "John Muir's old friend."

In San Francisco, Grant and Osborn stayed with another friend, John C. Merriam. Merriam was also an eminent paleontologist who was, and remains, a highly respected pioneer in paleontological circles. "His papers on the Tertiary echinoids of California remain perhaps his most significant contribution to invertebrate paleontology, for they laid the foundation on which important phylogenetic and stratigraphic studies were based by later investigators," wrote Chester Stock, Merriam's friend and former colleague, in 1951.

Merriam was just sixteen when he earned a bachelor's degree in science from the now defunct Lenox College, a Presbyterian institution in Iowa. He then moved with his family to Berkeley, where he studied at the University of California under Joseph Le Conte, the famed geologist and cofounder of the Sierra Club.

Merriam presented a sere and intimidating figure, and he rarely smiled. He had a high forehead and thin, dark hair combed in a slick above his angular face, lips commonly pursed, and a mustache that grew thickest under the nose. He was an able speaker and a brilliant scientist. Like Grant and Osborn, Merriam stood among the world's leading eugenicists, just as he was a leader in most of the fields he studied and practiced. In 1912 UC Berkeley's influential president Benjamin Ide Wheeler appointed Merriam chairman of the recently formed Department of Paleontology. Seven years later Merriam became chairman of the National Research Council, and in September 1920, just six months after accepting the dean of faculties position at Berkeley, he left the college to become president of the Washington, DC–based Carnegie Institution. Merriam joined Carnegie with a generous annual salary of $18,000 and "four months' time allotted to his own personal research activities," reported the *Los Angeles Times*. By the time Merriam took over at Carnegie, he was among the world's most famous scientists, and the institution was the world's preeminent scientific think tank dedicated to advanced studies in numerous emerging fields.

All three founders of Save the Redwoods League were early members of the Boone and Crockett Club, an exclusive clique of white supremacist big game hunters that included President Teddy Roosevelt and Charles Curtis, who later became US vice president under former California mining engineer Herbert Hoover. Grant and Roosevelt, both Manhattan natives of gilded lineage, had been friends for decades. (Roosevelt blurbed a later edition of *The Passing of the Great Race*.) Together the three colleagues attended the encampment at Bohemian Grove, where, among other weighty matters that year, club members discussed means by which American industry might capitalize on the world war. For instance, a hot topic in 1917 was a project then underway by the American Geographical Society, where Madison Grant served as councilor. In 1918, newspapers reported that the society had been working for nearly two years on "a map making program hitherto without precedent in this country." The maps would provide the administration of Woodrow Wilson, and especially the nation's business leaders, with detailed cartographic depictions of European terrain, borders, colonies, and national assets that could be seized and exploited by the United States following the war.

28

Madison Grant, John C. Merriam, and Henry Fairfield Osborn were genuinely dedicated to saving redwoods, though to different degrees and for different reasons. Merriam and Osborn, the scientists, recognized in redwoods characteristics of a "living fossil" that provided a scientific link to the planet's ancient history. In his 1930 book *The Living Past*, Merriam referred to coast redwoods as "surviving remnants of a splendid race that has been many millions of years in developing to its present majestic stature." In order to continue providing humanity with examples of these remnants, Merriam and Osborn sought protection of "representative areas" of redwood in small groves dotted alongside roads. Neither Merriam nor Osborn was particularly concerned that the majority of redwood trees might be logged for industrial uses. Rather, they believed in the "cooperative" approach established by Save the Redwoods League to setting aside "typical" groves of the coniferous specimens. Writing posthumously of Merriam, his friend and former Berkeley student Ralph W. Chaney, who would later become president of the League, summed up Merriam's belief that a few small samples of redwood should be set aside "to stimulate the imagination of the visitor who sees in Sequoias the oldest living things, who comes to recognize in them a kind of beauty associated only with antiquity."

Of the three Save the Redwoods League founders, only Madison Grant could accurately have been called an environmental activist. His work focused primarily on protecting big tracts of habitat to preserve apex species as examples of superior races. As one critic noted, Grant was not concerned with "little birds." Bison, grizzly, elk, elephants, redwoods, WASPs: these species should be preserved because that's what the laws of nature intended.

Nonetheless, even before the League incorporated as a nonprofit organization in 1920, the founders' beliefs about which redwoods, and how many, should be saved would be rendered superfluous by the industrialists who would actually create and take control of the organization. These men used and exalted their founders as sparkling figureheads who would consistently provide the organization with a patina of respectability, while behind the scenes the real work, on behalf of industry, went on. It helped that neither Osborn nor Merriam needed convincing that, when it came to identifying which tracts to preserve, small worked just as well as large. Grant would have to be more aggressively (or passive-aggressively) marginalized, but this would be easily done. Madison Grant lived in New York, and for the final sixteen years of his life, until he died in 1937, he would suffer from a crippling disease (probably infectious arthritis) that kept him largely bedridden. After 1921, Grant's trips to the West Coast were rare, and then they stopped altogether.

Merriam was genuinely dedicated to creation of public parklands, but only as a means of protecting natural features for purposes of human study and education. "He thought such sites could become part of a state's 'educational program' as a kind of open-air university," National Park Service historian Stephen R. Mark writes in his 2005 book on Merriam, *Preserving the Living Past*. "In his view, a national park should be a 'super-university of nature.' . . . [H]e saw parks as valuable primarily for how they inspired visitors." For this reason, Merriam, though he saw little need to preserve large landscapes, believed that those lands set aside should be protected from overzealous development (such as proposals for carnival attractions in Yosemite Valley) and unchecked trampling by tourists. Until 1920, Merriam had served as chairman of the League's nascent, five-member Executive Committee, but after taking the job at Carnegie, he assumed the presidency of the League, a titular post he held until his resignation in 1944, at the age of seventy-five.

In 1917, the same year that Grant, Osborn, and Merriam embarked on their fabled journey through the redwoods, the Carnegie Institution absorbed the Eugenics Record Office. Leading American eugenicist Charles Davenport had founded the Eugenics Record Office in 1910, in Cold Spring Harbor on Long Island, to collect and house data on the physical traits of American residents in order to develop solutions to population growth among inferior human beings. To fund his operation, Davenport had cultivated the sympathies of Mary Harriman, whose husband, railroad magnate

E. H. Harriman, had died the previous year. (E. H. Harriman would have appreciated the new venture.) Mary Harriman became the owner of the Eugenics Record Office's physical plant. When Carnegie and the Eugenics Record Office merged, Mary Harriman deeded to Carnegie all of the assets of the Eugenics Record Office, including the land and buildings, along with an extra $300,000 ($6 million today).

In his 2003 book about American eugenicists, *War Against the Weak*, Edwin Black writes that the Eugenics Record Office would also transfer "its collection of 51,851 pages of family documentation and index cards on 534,625 [American] individuals. Each card offered lines for forty personal traits." Under Merriam's leadership, the index cards would nearly double, to 930,000, by 1923. Black notes that the Nazis would employ exactly this sort of databasing, using IBM Hollerith tabulation machines and punch cards, during the 1930s and 1940s to identify and locate Jews, Roma, Communists, and other "defectives" throughout Europe. (Although IBM sold the tabulation machines, it maintained a monopoly on the necessary punch cards, which it sold to the Third Reich throughout the war.)

"In the early 1930s, when the Nazis were developing racial policies and struggling to find a scientific rationale for their vision of Aryan citizenship, they looked for practical models and endorsement from the American eugenics movement," writes Anthony M. Platt, emeritus professor of social work at California State University, Sacramento, in his 2006 book *Bloodlines: Recovering Hitler's Nuremberg Laws, from Patton's Trophy to Public Memorial.* "On the East Coast, they appreciated the work of the Eugenics Record Office (ERO) at Cold Spring Harbor."

Although he was a eugenicist and a scientist, Merriam nonetheless, and in his quiet way, thrilled to natural settings. In *The Living Past*, Merriam's poetic invocation of ancient time as embodied by a redwood forest is among the finest I've read. Merriam adapted this chapter from "Forest Windows," his noted 1928 essay published that year in *Scribner's Magazine*. In these tracts, Merriam sets a high bar for literary examination of the inscrutable yet undeniable presence of history in an ancient forest.

Woven through this picture [of an ancient redwood forest] is an element which eludes the imagery of art. The sense of time makes itself felt as it can but rarely be experienced. While, through contrasts of their seemingly fantastic architecture, ancient castles may tell us of other ages, living trees like these connect us as by hand-touch with all the centuries they have known. The time they represent is not merely an unrelated, severed past; it is something upon which the present rests, and from which living currents still seem to move. The mysterious influence of these groves arises not alone from magnitude, or from beauty of light filling deep spaces. It is as if in these trees the flow of years were held in eddies, and one could see together past and present. The element of time pervades the forest with an influence more subtle than light, but that to the mind is not less real.

29

Madison Grant and Henry Osborn made their daylong journey from San Francisco to Bohemian Grove in a chauffeured 1917 Packard Twin Six luxury convertible. John Merriam, hard at work at the university, would join them later. An auto ferry run by the Northwestern Pacific Railroad forded the knifing currents of the Golden Gate and deposited the travelers in the seaside village of Sausalito. From there the eighty-mile drive to western Sonoma County took four hours, north through San Rafael to Petaluma, then northwest into Sebastopol. Following dirt lanes to the agricultural town of Freestone, the big twelve-cylinder car traversed the former redwood wonderland of Occidental. From there the Packard edged downslope along a Russian River tributary, Dutch Bill Creek. Shortly before reaching the river, the men entered a patch of second-growth redwoods—the land once owned by my ancestors—then arced rightward into Bohemian Grove. Today the route from Freestone to Monte Rio is called the Bohemian Highway.

Grant, Osborn, and Merriam would stay as guests at the Bohemian camp called Pleasant Isle of Aves, a zone of influence commonly occupied by regents of the University of California. Here, goes the tale, Save the Redwoods League was born.

A collegiate camp in the redwoods, especially one associated with UC Berkeley, might today sound like the perfect place to launch a progressive organization dedicated to preserving similar trees to the north. Yet in 1917, every UC regent was a business titan. There were no exceptions. The regent's role was to mine the university for minds to man the many diversifying and interlocking levers of industry.

Among the eighteen UC regents of 1917 stood not a single academic, not even so much as a schoolteacher, to help guide education policies at the

West's premier academic institution. (See the appendix for a list of UC regents serving in 1917 and their affiliations.) Instead, we find something of a royal court of capital dedicated to directing one of the nation's most significant brain trusts toward exploring and manifesting ever more modern means of extracting and processing natural resources to benefit American industry. Students would explore the breadth and availability of resources, technology, and labor, domestically and worldwide, and the interconnected arts of extraction, transportation, processing, marketing, management, public relations, accounting, and banking. Their intellects and ambitions would be placed in service of the smooth and steady flow of concentrated profits to centralized beneficiaries.

"As Rome had once depended upon Greece for a ready supply of intellectuals, so would San Francisco's capitalists increasingly rely upon the academy at Berkeley to provide managers and engineers for their Pacific imperium," Gray Brechin writes in his 2006 book *Imperial San Francisco*. The benefits were mutual. "The fortunes of the University of California were tied from the beginning to those of San Francisco's financial district," writes Brechin.

Within this complex and interconnected economic milieu, redwood became an essential component of virtually every industry. No other foundational resource was more versatile, reliable, proximate, and available to fuel the predicted exponential growth of western commerce. Had redwood in 1917 suddenly been removed from industry's short list of essential resources, the calculus of exploiting and profiting from the region as a whole would have altered dramatically. The idea that three men could camp for a week with UC regents and hundreds of the nation's most powerful capitalists and there devise viable plans for saving redwoods is, on its face, farfetched.

Naturally, Berkeley president Benjamin Ide Wheeler was at Bohemian Grove. Wheeler had assumed the president's position in 1899 and served for twenty years. It behooved the powerful president to court industry leaders within the Grove's informal but potent setting. Wheeler was instrumental in directing the college's intellectual firmament toward support of industry, and he was skilled at generating funds. There was no better place to secure pledges than the Grove, over cocktails.

Under Wheeler's direction the college experienced rapid development and expansion of departmental studies focused on mining, petroleum extraction and refinement, hydroelectric power and transmission, pharmaceuticals, law, engineering, economics, genetics, medicine, botany, and agriculture, including irrigation and pesticide production. Berkeley's Forestry Department became the largest of its kind in the world. Benjamin Ide Wheeler had many confederates in the timber industry. One of his closest friends was William H. Sage, of the Sage Land and Improvement Company. Sage was the youngest son of East Coast timber baron Henry W. Sage. By 1917, the Sage company was on the cusp of becoming the world's largest owner of redwood forest land.

The college also offered programs at satellite campuses that would eventually become their own UCs. The university school of agricultural sciences at Davis would grow into an international leader in industrial agriculture. Under Wheeler, the Davis campus developed a satellite program in tropical agriculture at Riverside in service of Wheeler's commitment to exploiting what he called "our new colonial possessions." Millions of board feet of redwood, in the form of tanks for water and chemicals, stave pipes, housing, and railroad ties, would be consumed by rapidly expanding markets in corporate agriculture.

By 1917, the University of California had evolved into a singular intellectual underwriter for what UC Berkeley geography professor Richard Walker, in 2000, characterized as "a high rate of technical innovation" that was "crucial to an extraordinarily rapid rate of discovery and plunder of resources for over a century" in California. "The plunder is staggering," writes Walker, "yet often underrated even by California historians." Walker quotes Karl Marx, who as early as 1880 said, "California is very important . . . because nowhere else has the upheaval most shamelessly caused by capitalist centralization taken place with such speed."

If the Board of Regents, in such Shakespearean relief, included a priest (Charles Adolph Ramm of Saint Mary's Cathedral) to offer absolution from sin, it would also need a clever and cunning king, one born to the throne of western commerce. With his hands in virtually every western market, his inherited black book of social and economic power, and his seemingly innate ability to simultaneously charm the public and devour the public trust, you bucked this man at your peril. The name of this UC regent was William H. Crocker.

30

In *Railroaded*, Richard White observes, "The elimination of affection from corporate and political friendship in the Gilded Age was its genius." During the following Progressive era, the heirs to such friendships would build upon the genius of their forebears by crafting an *affectation* of affection. The faux affection took many forms—philanthropy, "providing jobs," choreographed displays of civic virtue, organizations dedicated to the "common good"—but the intent, often, was to create an opaque snow globe of good tidings while the unseen mechanics of the music box rang out a much different tune across the planet. Certainly the era resulted in some real reforms, such as the California Public Utilities Act, which ameliorated favoritism and rate gouging by railroads and power companies. Yet the act became law because corporate clients demanded rate stability. The consuming public remained largely powerless.

After the turn of the century, faux affection underwent a design phase and emerged in the form of a public relations industry that sought to mask the social and ecological suffering caused by rapid industrialization. Logged-over redwood tracts stood out among the suffering lands. To many observers, redwood logging after the turn of the century appeared as an assault against heaven itself. Yet many Bay Area business leaders were dependent on a steady supply of redwood products.

William H. Crocker was preeminent among industrialists who demanded unlimited and continuous access to troves of redwood lumber. The full extent of Crocker's vast holdings and control of industries was little known even to people who worked closely with him. He lived a consummate life of inward connections and economic preeminence. It was William Crocker, son of Big Four railroad baron Charles Crocker, who most possessed the gravitas, the socioeconomic tools, and the need to create and mold a perfectly disguised

Save the Redwoods League. Chiefly through surrogates, Crocker would dedicate himself to the task. He understood the imperative of convincing the public that a new and powerful organization had emerged, one whose managers had heard their cries and would incorporate them into meaningful programs designed specifically to save redwoods.

"There were few men . . . whose opinions carried more weight in formulating important community decisions," San Francisco writer David Warren Ryder wrote in his 1962 biography of Crocker, *Great Citizen*. "Indeed, for many years the answer to the question: 'How does W. H. stand on this?' very frequently determined the fate of the proposal." James Watson Gerard, a New York politician who served as US ambassador to Germany from 1913 to 1917 and was married to Mary Daly, daughter of copper king Marcus Daly, once said that William Crocker was "one of the fifty men who rule the nation."

He certainly ruled what Upton Sinclair, in his 1922 book *The Goose-Step: Study of American Education*, called San Francisco's "interlocking directorate" of corporate officials. Sinclair writes that in San Francisco

> we find one of the grand dukes of the plutocracy in charge—Mr. William H. Crocker, whose father looted the Southern Pacific railroads, covering all California. Mr. Crocker is a "social leader," and active head of the Republican political machine, which runs the government and is run by the finance of the state. We shall feel at home with Mr. Crocker, when we discover that he is a director of the Equitable Trust Company of New York, one of the five great banking institutions of the Money Trust, and that he sits on this board with Mr. Coudert, attorney for the plutocracy and trustee of Columbia University; also when we learn that he was a director of the Parkside Land Company, all of whose officers were indicted in the San Francisco graft scandal.

The company was actually called Parkside Realty. In 1905, a consortium headed by Crocker began amassing undeveloped real estate in western San Francisco, south of Golden Gate Park, until Parkside Realty owned a treasure trove of more than one hundred square blocks. Parkside was just one of at least two dozen major corporations controlled by Crocker that required large, predictable purchases of redwood products.

Creating an inward organization in San Francisco dedicated to crafting an outward expression of redwood protection in order to shield timber companies from public opposition could not have occurred without Crocker's approval. But Crocker did more than approve of the League. Although he was not one of the League's titular "founders"—Madison Grant, Henry Osborn, and John Merriam would always retain the honorific—he was among the League's founding group of "councilors" (who at first were called vice presidents), where he would serve, remaining largely, though not always, in the background, until he died in 1937. In general, League councilors were ornamental figures who held little actual power, as the organization's by-laws would invest virtually all authority in its Executive Committee and that body's powerful chairman's position. Through the years, however, some councilors served as potent influencers, and no one in the Bay Area during the early twentieth century was more influential than William H. Crocker.

Crocker was the type of headman who often preferred to speak and act through proxies, including even his wife, Ethel Crocker, née Sperry, heir to the West Coast flour fortune. The Save the Redwoods League's 1924 Annual Report listed "Mrs. William Crocker" as one of the organization's two "associate founders." In addition to Ethel, Crocker would employ as his avatar, both in business and at Save the Redwoods League, his wife's cousin, James "J. C." Sperry.

The other League associate founder in 1924 was Edward E. Ayer, the Chicago railroad magnate who had made a fortune supplying millions of ties and telegraph poles, most of them redwood, to railroad companies such as the Chicago and North Western, the Union Pacific, the Santa Fe, and the Mexican Central.

In 1882, when Crocker was just twenty-two years old and one year out of Yale, his father, Charles Crocker, purchased a controlling interest in the San Francisco–based Woolworth Bank and gave it to his son. They partnered in the venture with Ralph C. Woolworth, who two decades earlier had mentored with Darius Ogden Mills at the National Bank of D. O. Mills in Sacramento. ("Charles Crocker is the moneyed man," reported the *San Francisco Examiner*.) In 1893 Woolworth, like many partners and functionaries in the Crocker empire, died of a heart attack in his early fifties, after which William Crocker took control of the bank and reorganized it. Crocker was a director of the bank, as was his brother, Charles Jr. The new firm, which would eventually be called Crocker National Bank, opened with a ceremonious deposit of $500,000 in gold bullion.

After the death of Charles Crocker in 1888, his four surviving children—George, Harriet, Charles Jr., and William—established the Crocker Estate Company to take possession of and manage the many valuable holdings handed down by their father. Collectively the Crockers, like today's Waltons, represented one of the nation's wealthiest families. William Crocker's rise would be augmented in 1897 by the death of his forty-two-year-old brother, Charles Jr., then a vice president of the Southern Pacific Railroad. At the time of Charles's death, William Crocker was a director of the Pacific Improvement Company, the famous firm created by his father and the other Big Four railroad barons to hold, leverage, loan, and sell the boundless compass of assets accrued over decades by the Central Pacific and Southern Pacific railroads. Later William Crocker would become president of the company. Only a few holdings in the world could exceed the combined value of the Pacific Improvement Company and the Crocker Estate Company. Following the 1909 death of his only remaining male sibling, George Crocker, who had also served as vice president of the Southern Pacific, William Crocker took over the Crocker Estate Company as well.

By the time he entered the gates of Bohemian Grove, in 1917, William H. Crocker was president and majority shareholder of eleven major corporations and a director of two dozen others. He controlled municipal water systems, real estate throughout the country, electricity production and distribution (in particular hydroelectric power), steel production, irrigation, real estate development, telephone companies, railroads, ranch lands, coal and gravel extraction, oil wells and refineries, cement plants, life insurance, flour production, and the mining of numerous metals and minerals. Redwood lumber was an essential component in the growth of nearly all of these industries.

The fortunes of banks and financial institutions were therefore also tied to "getting out the cut" in the redwoods, just as they were directly invested in redwood lands, bonds, and mills. Crocker well understood this dynamic. In addition to owning Crocker National Bank and controlling other major financial institutions, in 1905 William Crocker purchased from the heirs of redwood timber baron John Vance a majority interest in the Humboldt

County Bank. The following year he bought all the Humboldt County Bank stock from three additional shareholders, who also sold him their interests in the Humboldt Savings Bank—investments Crocker would hold for decades. Few people in the world were as financially tied to standing redwood inventories and redwood lumber as was William H. Crocker.

By 1917 Crocker had been a member of the Bohemian Club for thirty-two years. He was among a handful of veteran Bohemians who had transformed the Club from a small collective dominated by actual bohemians to an elite business coterie largely denatured of them. At Bohemian Grove, Crocker controlled a camp called the Land of Happiness, a neat and attractive hideaway near the Grove entrance, tucked into its finest twenty-acre section of ancient redwood forest. That year there was no question who was king of Bohemian Grove.

I am well familiar with Crocker's camp and the forest that surrounds it. The southeastern boundary of the Louisiana-Pacific (LP) Silver Estate abutted Grove property. Often, when I ran through LP land, I'd keep going into the Grove and traverse its many miles of trails and dirt roads. Sometimes I'd circumnavigate the Grove's twenty-seven hundred acres, remaining on fire roads that wrapped like a crooked horseshoe around Smith Creek watershed. Other times, feeling more daring, I'd casually walk the dirt lane that ran along the low, almost imperceptible pass that separated the Russian River, on the north side of the Grove, from an unnamed tributary one mile south. Along the way I'd see some of Bohemian Grove's 120 camps, where two thousand men (and only men) annually frolicked for two weeks within the property's 100-acre grove of ancient redwoods. I enjoyed these forays, and though I never entered the Grove during an encampment or any other gathering, occasionally I'd see people either working or just strolling—often a couple, member and wife on a weekend visit. We'd wave, and all was well.

On the garden path the big trees stood as the last tiny speck of ancient forest of any type near the Russian River, which was once among the greatest of all redwood streams. That such a treasure is privately owned by the ideological descendants of those who'd leveled the rest of the redwoods is no small irony. Bohemian Grove isn't a pure stand—over decades many large trees were removed to accommodate structures—yet its ancient grandeur remains. Steep, forested slopes anchor both sides of the small flat in a coniferous canyon now riven with unpainted redwood cabins, large eating halls, hillside emplacements, and other buildings carved in here and there. The camp facilities were more rustic than I'd expected, yet oddly regal. A long piece of old-growth log had been hand-hewn into a beautiful bench with a high, pitted back. One big redwood had a wet bar snugged into a large hollow, called a "goose pen," at the base of a living tree.

As I ambled south toward the Grove entrance, I'd be sure to veer off before reaching the guard shack, instead slipping inside the twenty acres of old growth that housed Crocker's Land of Happiness. Along the way I'd pass the lovely pond and beautiful amphitheater where each year club members staged their opening ceremony—the "Cremation of Care"—a grandiose, macabre ritual that suggested a cultlike rite and concluded with a pyrotechnic display. Later some of the world's greatest talents would perform plays, operas, and symphonies, and "great minds" gave speeches. One noteworthy roster, in 1970, included Ernest L. Wilkinson, president of Brigham Young University; Melvin Laird, Richard Nixon's secretary of defense; Edward Cole, president of General Motors; and Henry Kissinger.

31

THERE IS LITTLE DOUBT THAT AT BOHEMIAN GROVE ON SUNDAY, AU-gust 5, 1917, the night after the annual play, William Crocker took a leisurely stroll from his Land of Happiness to the Pleasant Isle of Aves to join the other regents and business leaders for their meeting about the fate of the redwoods. The group was undoubtedly augmented by the many redwood company executives who normally attended the encampment, including the San Francisco–based leaders of the four largest redwood producers: A. B. Hammond; Pacific Lumber (PL) vice presidents Donald Macdonald and H. M. Robinson; C. R. Johnson of the Union Lumber Company in Mendocino County; and James Tyson, head of the Northern Redwood Lumber Company. The timing was crucial. Although the available stocks of redwood timber were now all but depleted in the southern range of the forest—Sonoma County to Santa Cruz—the northern redwood inventory remained largely intact. More than one million acres of virgin redwood still stood in Mendocino, Humboldt, and Del Norte counties. The stands were all cruised and measured and locked into private ownerships. The rapidity with which American industry was expanding and was expected to grow after the world war portended use of virtually every tree—if somehow the public could be assuaged of its growing calls for redwood protection.

Citizen activism during the previous two decades had demonstrated the strength of popular movements to protect redwoods. In 1902, a years-long grassroots campaign resulted in the state acquisition of ancient redwoods at Big Basin, in Santa Cruz County, which became California's first state park. Fifteen years later, in March 1917, a sustained effort by Sonoma County residents to save four hundred acres of ancient redwood at Armstrong Woods, in Guerneville, resulted in the Sonoma County Board of Supervisors approving an outlay of $70,000 to buy the grove. While Armstrong Woods was much smaller than Big Basin, the campaign had been highly charged, well funded, and tightly organized. In 1916 a citizens group had created an eight-page tabloid, with photos, articles, and maps, and paid to run it in several newspapers. Local residents, including my grandmother, Annie Laughlin King, then a teenager, and her parents lobbied the supervisors continuously.

The campaign for Armstrong Woods demonstrated the newly realized power, mobility, and willfulness of citizen action on behalf of ancient redwoods—a phenomenon not lost on Bohemians just four months later and five miles down the road. They understood that growing numbers of tourists to the northern counties would witness smoldering ruins where once grew sublime forests. And they would howl, collect in numbers, and insist that the redwoods be saved. Business leaders would need to protect the ability of their industries to grow and flourish. They understood the imperative of creating an organization dedicated to protecting redwoods from preservation.

Following the Sunday meeting at the Pleasant Isle of Aves, the trio of putative Save the Redwoods League founders made their fabled chauffeured drive from Monte Rio north along the Sonoma-Mendocino coast, following a rutted dirt lane that would eventually become California's Highway 1. At the time the route was the only means of "motoring" to Humboldt County. It was a long journey fraught with the pitfalls of a highly mobile landscape, and they would see few other cars along the way. Throughout Mendocino County the trio witnessed numerous redwood logging sites and mills, as well as the crazy quilt of redwood chutes that laced many of the rugged coves along the way. The chutes, some up to a mile long, allowed lumber to be loaded onto ships in a region with few natural harbors but a lot of redwood. Nonetheless, the travelers would later make little mention of Mendocino County.

North of the redwood boomtown of Fort Bragg, headquarters of the giant Union Lumber Company, the trio entered a thriving village called Westport. This was the town that served my ancestors, who lived on Wages Creek one mile north. Farther up the road they encountered a large redwood lumber operation at Hardy Creek, which John Hooper owned until his death in 1925, at the age of eighty-seven.

The men passed into and through the upper Mattole River, skirting the land where I would meet the Giengers seven decades later. Then they crossed a low ridge and entered the Eel River tributary of Redwood Creek. Fording numerous bends and ruts, they followed the stream to the South Fork Eel River at present-day Redway. Downstream of Redway, the travelers noticed that the redwoods were beginning to dominate the South Fork. They knew they were close to their goal, which on this day was to explore what Madison Grant later called "the superb woods of . . . incomparably grand . . . Bull Creek flats."

North of Bull Creek the group would follow the completed length of the Redwood Highway. Along the way the men passed several "split products" operations, where shakes, shingles, grape stakes, and railroad ties were still hand-hewn by small teams of two to four men who might spend months cleaving a single tree. They passed through Eureka and soon hit Arcata, where they boarded at the iconic Hotel Arcata, built two years before as a sportsman's retreat overlooking the lovely Arcata Plaza. The hotel and the plaza today remain at the heart of the small city.

While at the hotel, Grant, Henry Osborn, and John Merriam wrote letters to California governor William Stephens asking for his help to protect ancient redwoods. Grant, in particular, was appalled by the bleak images of logging that plagued his angry eyes along the road. Stephens had previously announced an imminent visit to Humboldt County as part of his ongoing campaign to support highway development; the traveling trio would alert him that the logging he would see along the way was not good. California road construction was directed by Stephens's state highway commissioner, Charles F. Stern, a native of Arcata. Incredibly, when Stern arranged for the state to purchase from timber companies a right-of-way through their redwood groves, he failed to acquire the trees then still standing in the right-of-way. In 1919 Madison Grant wrote, "We were shocked to learn that the California Highway Commission not only had failed to acquire a sufficient right of way to protect the timber along the route, but actually had contracted with the owners of the land for the removal of the timber." In another document Grant wrote, "Frank Stern was largely responsible for the mistake." Perhaps it was no mistake. Given the wedded interests of California industries and their regulators, it's just as likely that Stern was doing his friends a favor by paying timber companies with tax money to cut their own trees.

To build the Redwood Highway, Stern had secured labor from state prisons—an allowable use under a 1915 law passed by the state legislature and written by Stern himself. Construction was on time and within budget. Stephens was impressed enough that in 1918 he appointed Stern to the position of superintendent of banks, from which he would regulate the financial bedrock critical to achieve the conversion of ore, water, power, timber, and land into the quickly growing empire called California. At the time Stern was vice president of the First National Bank of Los Angeles. Within two years he would also join the earliest members of Save the Redwoods League's all-powerful, five-member Executive Committee, a formative posting that goes unmentioned by Joseph Engbeck.

In 1919 Madison Grant published a scathing essay on redwood logging in the bulletin of the New York Zoological Society, a leavened version of which ran the following year in *National Geographic*. Grant declared that destruction of the world's greatest forests provided "examples of human waste and greed [that] can scarcely be described."

"The forests are now threatened with annihilation," wrote Grant. "It will not last sixty years because the new and efficient methods of logging by machinery now generally introduced are not only more rapid, but make a clean sweep of every standing stick." In a surprisingly touching sentiment, Grant refers to the redwood as "a beautiful, cheerful and very brave tree."

Grant paid attention. He identified four main bodies of ancient redwood under immediate threat in Humboldt and Del Norte counties: "the groves along the south fork of the Eel River and the west bank of the main Eel, culminating in the Bull Creek Flat and the Dyerville Flat; the immense Redwood Creek grove; the Klamath River groves, and the Smith River groves in Del Norte County." Combined, these stands held more than a half million acres of ancient redwood, with more than three-quarters of the forest standing contiguously. Grant wanted to protect all of it. He added that, although the world's tallest tree was then thought to stand 340 feet, "it is probable that trees will be found which will exceed this maximum altitude. . . . One would anticipate the discovery of this *tallest tree on earth* either in Bull Creek Flat or along Redwood Creek." He was right on both counts. In 1931 surveyors announced the discovery of the "world's tallest tree," named the Founders

Tree for the three founders of Save the Redwoods League, which stood 364 feet at Dyerville Flat, across the South Fork Eel River from Bull Creek. (Subsequent measurements have shown that the Founders Tree actually stands at just under 350 feet.) Then, in 1963, Martin Litton and the National Geographic Society discovered the tall tree on Redwood Creek (367.8 feet), which lost its champion status in 2006 when "big-tree finders" located what is today considered to be the world's tallest tree, a 379.1-foot redwood also growing on Redwood Creek.

Grant was also right to insist that "any park in connection with the highway must take in the entire erosion valley of the south fork of the Eel from crest to crest." As Grant advocated for the protection of entire watersheds of intact redwood forest, his colleagues at the nascent Save the Redwoods League responded by moving to neutralize his efforts.

On August 2, 1919, seven men gathered in downtown San Francisco for a private meeting at the opulent Palace Hotel, which by now was controlled by William Crocker, prominent Bay Area industrialist Frank Drum, and Wellington Gregg Jr. Gregg was a favored Crocker lieutenant and protégé who represented Crocker's interests in oil production and served as vice president of Crocker National Bank. Attendees included Madison Grant, John Merriam, director of the US National Park Service Stephen T. Mather, University of California forestry professor Walter Mulford, future UC president Robert Gordon Sproul, San Francisco business empresario Joseph Donohoe "J. D." Grant, and Benjamin Ide Wheeler. It was on this day that Save the Redwoods League officially came to life.

The minutes of the meeting serve as an exercise in passive verbs. "The following were nominated" for foundational posts at the League: Franklin K. Lane, then serving as US secretary of the interior, for president, and Sproul for vice president. Ray Lyman Wilbur, president of Stanford University and future US secretary of the interior, was also nominated. An additional seventeen men "were nominated" to serve as vice presidents (soon to be called councilors), including, apparently for appearances, ornithologist Frank Daggett and the botanist Willis Jepson. Both Grants, Madison and J. D. (not related), were nominated, along with Crocker, Osborn, and Mather. Charles Stern was nominated, as was a little-known but increasingly powerful corporate attorney named Wigginton Creed.

The minutes note, "It was moved and seconded that Prof. J. C. Merriam be named as Chairman of the Executive Committee and that the other members of the Committee be named by him in conjunction with the Chairman." The League's next meeting, held at the Palace Hotel on August 20, was attended by just five people, whom Merriam had chosen to fill the seats of the League's all-powerful Executive Committee: Merriam, Stern, Wilbur, J. D. Grant, and Creed.

When I first read the minutes of the August 20 meeting, I was surprised that Madison Grant had not been included as a member of the Executive Committee. Nor would he ever sit on it. Grant was certainly willing, as his correspondence at the time and later would indicate. I was also intrigued by the seminal placement of this guy with the pulp-fiction name of Wigginton Creed and by the near-total omission of Creed from the League's official histories. Engbeck dedicates a single sentence to Creed, noting that he was a "San Francisco–based attorney [who helped] get the league incorporated as a nonprofit organization."

Wigginton Creed didn't just help the League "get . . . incorporated." He wrote the organization's bylaws and articles of incorporation. At the same time, as a founding member of the Executive Committee—also unmentioned by Engbeck—Creed became a creator and director of League policy and programs.

Only when I began digging into Creed's life did I understand just how important it was for the League to excise Creed from its founding history. By 1919, Wigginton Creed was a powerful corporate attorney who controlled major holdings in several large companies. And these weren't just any firms. Several of them were major consumers of redwood products, while others produced great volumes of redwood lumber and brokered redwood timberlands for corporate consumption. Few people in the world had more to lose under a robust movement for redwood preservation than did Wigginton Creed. Few people had more to gain by controlling such an organization.

32

In 1904, the *San Francisco Chronicle* covered the marriage of Wigginton Ellis Creed and Isabel Martha Hooper as a notable affair. While the groom, a young attorney, was up-and-coming in Bay Area society, it was Creed's bride who garnered press attention. Martha Hooper was the daughter of C. A. Hooper, of the Hooper redwood dynasty, perhaps the wealthiest and most active of all redwood lumber barons.

Raised in Oakland, Creed had attended public schools, then excelled at the University of California, where he was student body president. There he adopted the look of the new American executive: clean shaven, coiffure kept short and neatly parted in a slight wave. Soon he would don the masks of philanthropy and civic largesse that now tended to coat Progressive Age capitalism with a thin veneer of beneficence. Through three decades of adulthood, Creed was always photographed in what appeared to be the same wire-rim glasses. His hairline never receded, though his forehead remained high. Creed's gaze appeared sincere, if not perplexed—a tinge of boyish confusion that in later years would resolve to a scowl.

When Creed graduated from Berkeley, in 1898, he would still look much like a boy in his mid-teens. Out of college he accepted a job as principal of a grammar school in Fresno to earn money to put himself through law school.

"Then there occurred an incident such as I have often noticed has marked the careers of quite a number of young men who were destined to reach high place and power later in life," wrote B. C. Forbes in a lavish 1923 profile of Creed that appeared in the new magazine that bore his name. "President [Benjamin Ide] Wheeler of the University of California was asked by one of America's foremost citizens and capitalists of that day, D. O. Mills, to recommend a private secretary for him." Wheeler gave the nod to Creed. The new position "brought Mr. Creed into intimate touch with financial and business matters of great magnitude," wrote an understated Forbes. In New York, Creed would work with Darius Ogden Mills until mid-afternoon, then attend law classes. Creed likely learned more while mentoring with Mills, the master craftsman of leveraged connections and fiduciary black magic, than he did at law school.

Mills had been among the earliest and most powerful financial architects of San Francisco's rapid ascension as an international city-state. He'd founded his National Bank of D. O. Mills and Company in Sacramento in 1850 at the age of twenty-four. The Mills bank became a black hole for gold. Within a few years Mills settled his empire in the Bay Area. Half a century later Mills continued to run his bank and several other institutions, including the Bank of California, which had somehow recovered almost immediately after the crash of 1873. By 1900 the Bank of California and the Bank of D. O. Mills were tightly yoked by mutual investments.

Although he'd moved to New York in the early 1880s, Mills returned to California frequently to monitor his western concerns and meet with fellow dynasts. He enjoyed the perfect climate of Millbrae, on the San Francisco Peninsula, where he'd knock around the forty-two-room mansion he'd built in 1870 on a 150-acre estate. Mills died at Millbrae in 1910, at the age of eighty-four, just three months after the death of his close friend John Stewart Kennedy, of the Scottish American Company and Central Trust Company.

Creed was an excellent student. No doubt Mills, like Wheeler, saw in the ambitious young man an aptitude for business and an eagerness to please. He was also viewed as a potential leader among a new generation of capitalists to whom the art of public relations came naturally. Whitewashing the true intent and results of industrial expansion was becoming ever more important in the face of exploding labor unrest, public outrage over corrupt and usurious banks and utilities, the industrialization and centralization of once humble industries such as farming, widening gaps between the poor and the superrich, and widespread environmental damage. Speaking with Forbes, Creed was clear about the need of American business managers to continuously touch up the paint.

"We cannot shut our eyes to the fact that business has failed to tell its story fully enough or often enough," said Creed. "There is need of the story. Large numbers of our people lack understanding of . . . the mutuality of interest between the people and large business units, of the importance to society and the welfare of the people that business make money and add to the national wealth. . . . Business should, therefore, pay as much attention to its public relations as it does to its finance, operation, and distribution."

That same year, Creed wrote *Safeguarding the Future of Private Business*, published by Houghton Mifflin and the UC Board of Regents. Creed writes, "Business morality is higher today than it ever has been in the world's history." The veracity of the claim was on par with another made in the book, six years before the onset of the Great Depression: "In banking and in the public service industry, sound doctrines of regulation have been adopted." The writing style is suspiciously similar to that of Forbes.

When Creed finished law school, Mills "was anxious to place his young secretary in some attractive position in New York," wrote Forbes. But Creed demurred and returned west. He settled in Berkeley. At the age of twenty-three, Creed was admitted to the California Bar. He then joined the San Francisco law firm of Bay Area power broker Louis Titus, who made Creed a partner. Among Titus's many clients was San Francisco–based Hobbs, Wall & Co., then the largest redwood company operating in Del Norte County. The Hobbs, Wall holding of nearly twenty thousand acres included a stunning five-thousand-acre flat of ancient redwood that grew in a contiguous belt near Crescent City, all of which the company would log off.

Titus was also the head of the powerful Syndicate Water Company, an umbrella corporation that had bought up one-third of all water companies of the East Bay Area. The water company would well serve the Berkeley Development Company, of which Titus was president, and the North Berkeley Land Company, which he co-owned. Both companies owned large tracts of vacant land in the Berkeley Hills to be developed as luxury estates. Always in such matters, access to water was key. To transport and store water, redwood was key, as there was no better wood for building water tanks and stave pipes. Creed was a legal partner in the development ventures, and he was a quick study on water law. Creed would oversee the paperwork as the Syndicate Water Company consolidated with the Contra Costa Water Company—itself comprised of a dozen smaller water suppliers—and the Richmond Water Company to become a utility with the Orwellian name of the Peoples' Water Company. Creed guided the quicky growing water interests until 1916, when the Peoples' Water Company reorganized as the monopolistic East Bay Water Company, at which point Creed became the new company's first president and chief counsel.

For decades, these water companies and hundreds of others in the West consumed whole forests' worth of redwood products, fueling growth in the region at otherwise unattainable levels.

On July 12, 1914, C. A. Hooper, "the pioneer lumber king," died of heart failure at his "country home" in Los Medanos. He was seventy-one years old. The *San Francisco Chronicle* wrote, "A resume of the growth of California commercially would be incomplete indeed did one fail to mention the aid that the late Charles Appleton Hooper, of C. A. Hooper & Co., shipping and lumber, gave to the upbuilding of the State." This for a man who had completed just one year of high school.

At the time of his death, Hooper was a director of sixteen Bay Area companies and president of ten. His holdings were umbrellaed by C. A. Hooper & Co. and included the Big Lagoon Lumber Company, which continued to trade in redwood lands; Excelsior Investment Company, a land brokerage; the L. W. Blinn Lumber Company; the Russ Lumber & Mills Company; the Southern California Lumber Company; the Bostonia Fruit Growers and Packers Company; and the South Shore Land Company, which sold real estate in Alameda. It also included several firms he'd founded at Los Medanos, now called Pittsburg, in the East Bay: the Redwood Manufacturers Company (Remco), the four-thousand-acre Avon Ranch, the Diamond Brick Company, the Diamond Milling Company (which produced flour), and the Columbia Steel Company. Assets included valuable properties throughout the Bay Area, including downtown San Francisco, and in Southern California, as well as an untold tranche of cash and securities. It was a bountiful estate worth many millions.

Hooper had appointed his partner and attorney son-in-law, Wigginton Creed, as his executor. For ten years Creed had served as Hooper's legal arm in many new and existing developments, and he was intimately familiar with the books. When Hooper died, Creed assumed control of an empire built from and maintained by the life of the redwood forest.

33

L ATE IN 1906, AS REDWOOD LUMBER SALES BOOMED WITH THE REBUILD-
ing of San Francisco after the earthquake, C. A. Hooper reorganized
his redwood conglomerate. He'd founded C. A. Hooper & Co. almost immediately upon arrival in San Francisco, in 1865, but since then the landscape had changed. For one, his brother, George Hooper, had announced to
the family that he was retiring due to ill health.

The Hoopers were a tight-knit family, and they were quiet. Unlike many
leading capitalists at the time, they did not draw attention to themselves. In
2021, John Hooper, the great-grandson of lumberman John Hooper, told me
that the four Hooper brothers lived by three maxims:

1. "In times of prosperity, be moderate."
2. "Stay hidden; stay happy."
3. "Fools' names and fools' faces tend to appear in public places."

With George leaving the firm, C. A. Hooper sought new partners from
within the family. He'd never had sons, and of course daughters could not
conduct business. He would entrust his redwood empire to his new son-in-
law. In Wigginton Creed, Hooper now had a house attorney who could draw
up the new incorporation papers and oversee the legal end of redwood commerce. Creed became a director of the new company.

The reorganization served a second purpose. In December 1906, C. A.
Hooper & Co. founded the Big Lagoon Lumber Company, capitalized at
$1 million. The new firm then purchased from J. E. Henry the thirty thou-
sand acres on Maple Creek that Henry had acquired in 1901 from the Scots,
a deal brokered by C. A. Hooper. Not a stick had been logged. The forest had simply sat there, accruing equity and earning money through bond

sales secured by the standing timber. Hooper and his representatives had undoubtedly cruised this land many times since the 1860s, as it sat adjacent to the former Hooper holding in Trinidad. In early 1908, Hooper and Creed launched an impressive double play when they gathered a consortium of San Francisco and East Coast timber buyers to purchase the Maple Creek tract for $4 million, nearly $1 million more than C. A. Hooper & Co. had paid just over a year earlier. Here was Hooper's unmatched knowledge of redwood lands and select timber buyers weaving like strands of DNA with the legal skills of his new son-in-law to pull off one of the most spectacular and lucrative timber flips in US history.

The new owners would eventually form a syndicate of prominent timber dealers in New York, Pennsylvania, and Ottawa, Canada, which in 1912 founded the Lagoon Lumber Company. The consortium would also purchase the magnificent 3,520-acre expanse of gigantic redwoods on Little River, giving the owners a contiguous inventory of more than 35,000 acres of virgin redwood forest. Even at that time no logging had occurred in this stunning redwood wilderness, which was contiguous with A. B. Hammond's holding on Lindsay Creek and the upper reaches of Little River and with his 35,000 acres of unentered forest on Redwood Creek. Another 300,000 acres of untouched redwood stood to the east and north. By the time Save the Redwoods League formed in 1918, only a small edge of this land had been logged.

To C. A. Hooper, it wasn't enough to simply flip timberlands and own milling operations, shipping lines, and wholesale and retail lumber yards. There were many ways to exploit the "ever living" trees that kept on giving. In December 1892, C. A. Hooper proved his farsighted genius when he founded the Excelsior Wooden Pipe Company, named for, but independent of, the redwood operation he then owned on Freshwater Creek. The new company would take his lumber business to the next generation of finished products. While Excelsior produced goods such as tanks, silos, window sashes, and lumber, the company specialized in producing lumber for construction of miles-long wooden pipelines that would forever change the face of the American West.

Wooden pipes were not new. In 1915 Bernard Alfred Etcheverry, head of the Department of Irrigation at the University of California, examined the history and utility of wooden pipes in his textbook series *Irrigation Practice and Engineering.* In volume two, *Conveyance of Water,* Etcheverry wrote that bored logs had been used as pipes in Europe since at least the early seventeenth century and in the New World since the 1790s. "It is reported that these pipes were in use over 200 years in England, over 70 years in Portsmouth, and over 100 years in Philadelphia," wrote Etcheverry.

The stave pipe, Etcheverry noted, had been around only a short while. A stave pipe is made up of two principal components: specially milled lumber and steel hoops that bind the pipe along its length from one to two feet apart or as close as a few inches under heavy pressure. On one end of each hoop was a bolt, on the other a washer and nut. The staves ran from ten to twenty feet long, two to six inches wide, and up to three inches thick depending on the size of the pipe and the pressure it would need to endure. Each stave was notched with a male and a female end to allow them to fit snugly together and thereby create the continuous pipe.

The pipe's simple design, the ability to construct it in place over miles of rugged terrain, and the relative ease of transporting component parts into hinterlands made stave pipes the obvious choice for all manner of uses throughout the country. For builders of pipelines, however, the question of durability also came into play. Hooper knew that most woods were unreliable over time. Most woods except redwood.

Hooper incorporated the Excelsior Wooden Pipe Company with his brother George as a junior partner. He hired D. C. Henny, a Dutch engineer educated at the Polytechnic Institute of Delft, in Holland, to design the pipes to perfection. The Dutch knew water. Henny had worked on several water projects in the United States for a decade before Hooper hired him. Henny didn't come cheap, but his ability to reliably move water, one of the greatest of all engineering challenges, would make Hooper a fortune. Finally, Hooper hired his former coconspirator, Charles King, to represent the company as a sales agent. King set to garnering contracts, which flowed into the company almost instantly.

As the twentieth century approached, the growth of Southern California would in large part become anchored to Excelsior pipes. Less than four months after incorporating, the Excelsior Wooden Pipe Company built three miles of a twelve-mile sewer line for the city of Los Angeles. Municipal engineers from throughout the country watched the line's progress. The *Chicago Tribune* reported that the line's "capacity is for a city of 135,000, just double the present population of Los Angeles. A space is left for putting in a parallel siphon when needed. . . . Redwood was used as the best known wood for resisting decay." In 1894, an Excelsior pipe was used to drain the Arroyo de los Reyes, now the site of downtown Los Angeles. A short time later Excelsior built two miles of pipeline to feed Los Angeles with water from San Gabriel Canyon. Excelsior complemented many of the pipelines with redwood tanks, such as the one-hundred-thousand-gallon unit built for the West Los Angeles Water Company in 1898.

Farms and ranches laced their fields with Excelsior pipes. In 1898 Excelsior built a half-mile pipe from Santa Ana Canyon, in Southern California, to service the spreading citrus groves of Orange County. The pipe worked so well that Excelsior would continuously expand it, which allowed the region's fabled Valencia groves to cover twenty thousand acres by 1915. Farther north, Excelsior built more than a half mile of redwood pipe five feet in diameter, as well as many appurtenant pipes and numerous storage tanks, for the sprawling Spreckels beet sugar farms in the Salinas Valley, California.

The Crocker-Huffman Land and Water Company utilized miles of redwood stave pipe. After the death of Charles Crocker in 1888, the Crocker Estate Company bought out co-owner C. H. Huffman and took charge of Crocker-Huffman's kingly holding of fifty thousand acres in Merced County, California, including much of the city of Merced. William H. Crocker assumed the presidency of the firm, whose ownership came with prodigious water rights. The company's holdings included nearly one hundred square miles of prime agricultural land and another thirty square miles of rangeland in the Sierra foothills. Charles Crocker had long taken a personal interest in developing the property, and Will continued the work.

By 1914, according to a report by the *Merced County Sun*, Crocker-Huffman had tapped the Merced River and other water sources that flowed through the land. It built four hundred miles of canals and "4,500 structures including dams, flumes, cement chutes, siphons, culverts, drops and various other structures." "Other structures" included redwood stave pipes. "The majority of the structures which we visited on the main stem of the system are of concrete and redwood," reported the *Sun*. In 1920, Crocker-Huffman sold the irrigation system to the Merced Irrigation District, then began selling parcels piecemeal to small farmers. "To assist colonizers in purchasing the land the company established the First National Bank of Merced," David

Ryder reported in his biography of Crocker. "Also it built a water system to supply domestic water to the residents of Merced." That system utilized redwood tanks and redwood stave pipes. Crocker was also a major investor in California Delta Farms Inc., which reclaimed and planted forty thousand acres of former wetland in the lower San Joaquin River, watered through redwood stave pipes.

Excelsior sold its redwood pipes throughout the country. Some of the pipes were greater than twelve feet in diameter. In 1894 Excelsior built two miles of thirty-inch redwood stave pipe to water the city of Tacoma, Washington. The city of Charlotte, North Carolina, would lay more than a mile of Excelsior pipe as a domestic water supply. By early in the twentieth century, Colorado, New Mexico, Arizona, Utah, Montana, Oregon, Idaho, Washington, and California were quilted in redwood pipes. Many pipes served hydraulic mines. In 1908 Excelsior installed thirteen miles of redwood stave pipe in the Yukon to transport water to placer mines on Bonanza and Hunter Creeks. The pipeline was one component of the famous "Yukon ditch," which stitched seventy miles of flume, ditch, and redwood stave pipes for the purpose of gutting the gold-laden streams. In 1910 Excelsior installed a redwood stave pipe for the Homestake gold mine, in South Dakota; the pipe remained in continuous use for 107 years.

Hooper understood that cities and farms would always need water, usually more of it every year, and they would need sewage lines. Hooper's Excelsior pipe company would move the entire flow, in and then out. But new, possibly more lucrative markets for his pipes and tanks hovered within grasp. Hooper already had offices in downtown San Francisco, but just before the turn of the century, to better position his companies for the coming bonanza, he opened a New York office at 220 Broadway, two blocks from City Hall and six blocks from his friends at the Central Trust Company. The New York opening coincided with his next big venture, one that would eclipse every milestone that Charles Appleton Hooper had achieved thus far.

34

CALIFORNIA'S FABLED DIABLO RANGE RUNS 150 MILES FROM THE northeastern shores of San Francisco Bay south to Antelope Valley, sixty miles northwest of Bakersfield. To naturalists, the Diablo Range is the "spine of California," home to all manner of wildlife, including the world's highest concentration of golden eagles. Still the range is little known, even to the millions of people who now surround the diverse conglomeration of jagged ridges and varied habitats.

At the northern end of the range, 3,849-foot Mount Diablo overlooks flatlands now coated with interstates, dense human populations, and dozens of heavy industrial facilities that ring multiple aquatic landmarks: San Francisco Bay, San Pablo Bay, Grizzly Bay, and Suisun Bay to the west and north, and to the east, the San Joaquin–Sacramento River delta, the largest wetland ecosystem in California.

Before Americans began taking over California in 1846, the Mexican government had carved the Diablo Range into large ranchos that were given to loyalists mostly for production of cattle, lumber, and food crops. One of the properties, Rancho Los Medanos, covered 8,890 acres—or approximately two square leagues—that ranged from the San Joaquin–Sacramento confluence to the foothills of Mount Diablo. The rancho's borders formed an obtuse triangle, with the longest line fronting six miles of water, much of it deep enough, it turned out, to accommodate large commercial ships.

In 1872 a Kentucky railroad builder named L. L. Robinson came to own Rancho Los Medanos under dubious and complicated circumstances. He died in 1892, leaving eight thousand acres of the ranch to his sister, who was unable to pay the mortgage. Unfortunately for her, the mortgage was held by the Bank of California, which foreclosed in 1900. By then both the Southern Pacific and the Santa Fe railroads had trunk lines running through the rancho. The land itself would well accommodate the Bay Area's near instantaneous expansion of homes, farms, and especially industry.

The bank sale made headlines. The *San Francisco Chronicle* called the auction "one of the most important sales of outside property which has taken place in a long time." Even at the time of Robinson's death, eight years before the auction, the *Chronicle* valued the property at $1 million. Now, on September 22, 1900, with the economy booming after recovering from the Panic of 1893, the elite San Francisco real estate firm of Baldwin & Howell auctioned the rancho. The buyer was C. A. Hooper, who paid just $175,000.

How Hooper acquired Los Medanos for less than one-fifth its value has never been determined. Undoubtedly there was a payoff to Baldwin & Howell, a firm that also worked closely with Louis Titus and Wigginton Creed to develop the East Bay hills. Another important Baldwin & Howell partner was William H. Crocker, who worked with the real estate firm to develop Redwood City, a waterfront boomtown twenty miles south of San Francisco. In 1909 Baldwin & Howell allied with Crocker and other San Francisco luminaries to sabotage efforts to develop the Hetch Hetchy water system—an attempt to protect their investments in the Spring Valley Water Company, which for almost fifty years had enjoyed a near monopoly on water service from creeks in the lower peninsula to San Francisco taps.

C. A. Hooper wasted no time transforming Los Medanos into an industrial nucleus, which evolved so rapidly and forcefully that within two decades it would rank among the most polluted sites on the West Coast. A few years after Hooper purchased the rancho, the waterfront property would host three fish canneries, a brick factory, a dairy, a rubber plant, a shipyard, a steel plant, and an oil pumping facility.

Anchoring the industrial mélange was the Excelsior Pipe Company, which Hooper rapidly expanded along with his redwood wholesale and shipping operation. By 1903 Hooper was shipping up to fifty million board feet of lumber annually to East Coast markets. Orders for stave pipes and tanks, among Excelsior's other products, were pouring in, and not just for transport and storage of water and sewage. New, important industries that were taking hold in the West demanded redwood for stave pipes and tanks. Two of the ventures, hydropower and petroleum, promised a concentration of riches.

Hooper well understood the superiority of redwood over other lumber products, an understanding confirmed decades later in a 1921 edition of *Engineering World* magazine, published in Chicago. "During the last 30 years the demands for wood pipe of both the continuous-stave and machine-banded types, have greatly increased, and the business of wood-pipe manufacturers has expanded to meet those demands," wrote associate editor W. A. Scott. In addition to serving irrigation needs, the wooden stave pipe was a critical component of "water-power projects, the outfall sections of sewer systems, and those to conduct water for hydraulic sluicing and to make hydraulic fills." The article notes the superiority of redwood for stave pipes and cites several examples of redwood pipelines that had stood the test of time.

Among the most transformative uses of redwood stave pipe was the thirty-two-mile line laid from the Verde River, in Arizona, to Phoenix, which allowed the state capital to double its population during the 1920s to fifty thousand people. This line and several others examined by Scott were built by C. A. Hooper companies. Today Phoenix, a desert metropolis, is the fifth-largest city in the United States.

Redwood pipes and tanks had myriad uses. For decades, gold mining companies purchased thousands of redwood tanks to hold cyanide solutions— used to extract gold from ore—because redwood resisted the chemical's corrosive effects. In 1917 the *Mining and Oil Bulletin*, published in Los Angeles, reported that, in the northern Bay Area, the Hercules Powder Company had made "probably the largest single order for wood tanks ever placed, requiring about 3,500,000 feet of three-inch clear dry redwood" to construct 172 tanks with a total capacity of thirteen million gallons. The tanks would hold potash, made from kelp, to feed California's, and the nation's, rapidly expanding agricultural industries. Most of the tanks held fifty thousand to sixty thousand gallons, though six tanks were built to capacities of one hundred thousand gallons each, and ten tanks held four hundred thousand gallons each. Construction of the tanks took just four months, "a remarkable fact when considering the required amount of dry, clear redwood of special sizes," reported the *Bulletin*. The magazine heralded "the superiority of California redwood for this and similar work."

In Richmond, on San Francisco Bay, the Standard Oil Company littered the flats and hills with redwood tanks and pipes for storing and transporting oil and its products. The twenty-nine-hundred-acre compound is still used today by Chevron, which was spun off from Standard Oil in 1911 under the Sherman Antitrust Act. Until steel pipe could be economically manufactured in the 1920s, no material eclipsed the value of redwood for petroleum tanks and pipelines.

On May 16, 1917—two months before Save the Redwoods League's founders landed at Bohemian Grove—engineer J. F. Partridge presented to the American Society of Civil Engineers his paper, "Modern Practice in Wood Stave Pipe Design and Suggestions for Standard Specification." If any questions remained regarding the efficacy of redwood pipes, Partridge would settle them. Partridge analyzed several existing stave pipes that had been in use for at least two decades and concluded, "Redwood is the best known material for wood pipe, and its longevity is excelled only by cast iron. The acid or other peculiar constituent of this wood acts as a preservative or micro-organism destroyer, and protects and preserves it." Still, just any grade of redwood wouldn't do. It had to be the best.

"The staves shall be of clear, air-dried, California redwood, seasoned at least one year in the open air, and shall be free from knots," wrote Partridge. Such wood was most often found in the lowermost half of huge redwoods that grew in pure stands along riparian flats or on low hillsides in the northern redwood belt. By 1917, it was clear to western industrialists that these groves would need to be protected from preservation.

35

B Y 1900, C. A. HOOPER AND HIS BROTHERS HAD PRODUCED AND DIS-
tributed redwood lumber for nearly four decades. Hooper knew what he
had. He wasted no time building a planing mill and several redwood manufacturing plants alongside his six miles of waterfront at Los Medanos. Within
three years the total demand for Hooper's redwood products had grown so
swiftly that he took the unusual step of inviting a dozen redwood producers
to buy into a new firm he was forming, the Redwood Manufacturers Company, which became known as Remco. Hooper founded Remco to secure an
adequate flow of raw redwood into his booming manufacturing business and
to increase sales of redwood products to the East Coast and internationally.
Sales of all products accelerated, particularly redwood stave pipes.

C. A. Hooper & Company held the controlling interest in Remco, and
C. A. himself was president of the firm. Shortly after Remco was founded,
Pacific Coast Wood and Iron reported that the new facility would be "of great
benefit, not only to the mills directly interested, but to the whole redwood
trade." Remco purchased from C. A. Hooper & Co. the Excelsior manufacturing plants plus one hundred acres on the waterfront, which included
sixteen hundred feet of deep-water frontage. Expansion began immediately,
as demand for all redwood products was increasing. According to state forestry records, total redwood sales jumped from 360 million board feet in 1899
to 519 million feet in 1904 and 659 million feet in 1906. The Panic of 1907
shrunk redwood orders to 404 million feet, but within two years the figure
again reached nearly 600 million board feet.

Shortly after its founding, the Remco operation had on hand "for ship-
ment to the east at all times about 30,000,000 feet of redwood lumber,"
according to a 1907 history of Benjamin Snow, a Puritan pioneer whose descendants included the Hoopers. "This is the largest stock of redwood lumber

for eastern shipping carried anywhere." Remco maintained the world's largest single repository of shingles. In 1904 the *San Francisco Call* reported, "There are stacked fully 340,000,000 shingles in the company's yard." There was also a plant for constructing sashes and doors. Manufacturing buildings ranged from fifteen thousand to thirty thousand square feet. Several acres of the site were laden with hundreds of thousands of railroad ties, destined for domestic and international markets. Five parallel railroad tracks lined the deep-water wharf, which would eventually accommodate eight lumber ships simultaneously.

The Pacific Telephone and Telegraph Company, a large and rapidly expanding firm controlled by William Crocker and Bay Area industrialist Frank Drum, was also a voracious consumer of redwood provided by Hooper, Remco, and other firms, as telephone and telegraph companies erected millions of redwood poles throughout the West. Frank Drum was a director of Crocker National Bank, though he left the bank in 1916. Yet Crocker and Drum remained connected through several other firms, in particular Pacific Gas and Electric (PG&E), where Drum was president and Crocker served as a director. (Crocker had joined the firm as a founding director in 1905, and he would remain on the board until his death in 1937.)

Frank Drum's brother, corporate attorney John Drum, was also a director of PG&E. The Drum brothers were upper-tier owners of corporations and capital. Together they controlled large fortunes and several industries. In 1920 Frank Drum was a director of thirteen corporations, including four oil companies, three power companies, and two banks. John Drum was a director of twenty-one corporations. Virtually all of these firms relied heavily on redwood lumber. The power companies controlled by William Crocker and the Drum brothers were among the world's greatest consumers of redwood for poles, large power line towers, and especially hundreds of miles of stave pipes that provided hydropower to nearly all of California and fueled rapid growth in the American West.

By 1914, fourteen major power companies operated dozens of dams and power plants in California. Most of them drew water from the magnificent streams of the 450-mile Sierra Nevada mountain range and sent it to turbines in redwood stave pipes. Nearly all of the fourteen companies also owned several smaller power firms. Of the fourteen, PG&E was the largest, followed closely by the Pacific Light and Power Company, which had grown out of the San Gabriel Electric Company. That year Pacific Light and Power operated eight hydroelectric plants in the Sierra Nevada and provided power to nearly two million people between Los Angeles and Fresno. According to the company, the second-largest source of consumption of its electricity in 1914 was "motors [operated] for irrigation purposes." Irrigation water ran through redwood stave pipes.

So substantial were PG&E's demands for stave pipes that in 1910 the power company bought Remco. C. A. Hooper retained his investment in the firm and his position as president. In 1914 PG&E vice president John A. Britton told a gathering of the San Francisco Chamber of Commerce that "the strength and stability of California, and its progress, are measured largely by the number of its hydro-electric plants and the miles of its transmission lines; for, by electricity we can transmute the roar of the waterfall into the roar of the spinning wheel, we can change endless time into a hurried telephone call and we can displace an awful darkness by a spell of light."

By 1920 PG&E was operating twenty-four hydropower plants and ranked as the world's single largest consumer of redwood stave pipes. The company corked great rivers with ever larger dams and tethered the Sierra foothills with hundreds of miles of worming redwood tubes, most of which stood taller than the men who had constructed them. As water for power, irrigation, industry, and homes was critically important to the growth of the West, redwood was just as important for its ability to harness that water.

When C. A. Hooper died in 1914, Wigginton Creed was director of no company. By 1916 he was not only a director but president of nine companies, including the First National Bank of Contra Costa County and the redwood-consuming East Bay Water Company. The other seven companies were inherited Hooper concerns, including Big Lagoon Lumber Company and Excelsior Investment Company. Creed also took over as president of the prosperous and diversified C. A. Hooper & Co., which remained invested in Remco and other redwood enterprises. That year the *Timberman* reported, "The Redwood Manufacturers Co. are busy. The pipe factory is running on a double shift to keep up with its orders, while the tank and silo department is also enjoying a good trade. The company find a growing eastern trade. . . . President W. E. Creed of the C. A. Hooper Co., and also president of the

Columbia Steel Works, takes a very deep interest in the development of Pittsburg."

The double shift at Remco reflected rapid accelerations in all sectors of municipal and industrial growth, perhaps especially the movement of water. For instance, by 1913 the city of Los Angeles had completed the 233-mile Los Angeles aqueduct, which transported water from the Owens Valley to the growing southern metropolis. Once Owens water started flowing, the aqueduct sprouted hundreds, if not thousands, of giant redwood straws. When construction of the aqueduct began, in 1908, the city of Los Angeles erected along its proposed route thousands of redwood poles to hold "telephone and transmission line material" to provide communication along the way.

As president of the Tempe Land and Improvement Company, Creed oversaw much of the development of the Arizona city into a thriving suburb of Phoenix. The company owned most of the land base of Tempe and watered it through redwood stave pipes.

In assuming the presidency at Columbia Steel, Creed would lead the firm that he and Hooper had formed together in 1909 along with another Hooper son-in-law, Sumner Crosby. With Hooper's money the trio had purchased the steelworks, and the name, from the Columbia Steel Company, in Portland, Oregon, and moved it to Los Medanos, where they expanded the operation. In 1911 the *Stockton Evening Mail* reported that Columbia, after just one year of operation, was "the largest steel plant in this part of the world." The company produced castings for "machine shops, cement mills, smelting plants, gold mills, sawmills, logging camps and railroad shops."

In 1918, Wigginton Creed joined the University of California Board of Regents, an expected ascension. In 1919 Creed's fellow regents handed him his first big assignment, a tour of the East Coast to headhunt a replacement for UC president Benjamin Ide Wheeler, who had fallen out of favor with local patriots owing to his warm relationship with German kaiser Wilhelm II. (In 1911, Wheeler had nominated Wilhelm for a Nobel Peace Prize.) Creed's partner on the two-member search committee was regent James K. Moffitt, who remained in partnership with redwood lumber titan (and Creed's uncle-in-law) John Hooper at the First National Bank of San Francisco and its subsidiary the First Federal Trust Company. While Creed was in the

East, John Merriam appointed him as a founding director of Save the Redwoods League.

No matter his workload, Creed was an eager volunteer. The League's
Executive Committee held its second meeting on October 2, 1919, "as the
guests of Mr. Wigginton E. Creed at luncheon at the Pacific Union Club,"
according to the one-paragraph minutes of the apparently short meeting.

On July 28, 1920, Frank Drum resigned as president of PG&E, though
he remained a director, alongside William Crocker. On the way out, Drum
handpicked Wigginton Creed to succeed him in one of the most powerful
corporate posts in the country. At the time the *Oakland Tribune* reported, "It
is understood that $100,000,000 or $200,000,000 will be spent within the
next few years by the gas and electric company in developing gigantic power
plants to care for the immense San Francisco bay industrial expansion." Today such an investment would be worth between $2 billion and $4 billion. A
significant portion of the funding would pay for redwood products including
stave pipes, poles, buildings, and other infrastructure. The paper noted that
the founder of PG&E, UC regent John Britton, would be giving a dinner
for Creed the following week, at the Palace Hotel. In 1922, PG&E, under
Creed, would record profits of nearly $40 million, $1.5 million over the previous year.

Even as he prepared to take the helm at PG&E, Creed was hard at work
on another important matter. On August 17, 1920, the newly hired assistant secretary to Save the Redwoods League, an eager public relations ninja
named Newton B. Drury—a University of California graduate and champion debater who had served as secretary to UC president Wheeler—wrote
to Stephen Mather with some happy news. He said that Wigginton Creed—
water boss, steel titan, power mogul, and one of the greatest purveyors
as well as consumers of redwood products—had just finished writing the
League's articles of incorporation and bylaws. Now the organization could
get to work.

36

JOHN MERRIAM, WITH INPUT FROM OTHERS IN THE NASCENT SAVE THE Redwoods League, had chosen four individuals for the Executive Committee whose allegiances would all but guarantee unfailing support for redwood lumber manufacturers and the industries that relied on redwood products. The action allowed leading industrialist and redwood timber baron Wigginton Creed to create bylaws that rendered the League's large group of councilors nearly powerless in relation to the commanding authority of the five-member Executive Committee—though the councilors, too, would almost unanimously support full exploitation of redwood forests. Creed carefully chose his words.

"The directors shall have power . . . to conduct, manage and control the affairs and business of the corporation and to make rules and regulations . . . for the guidance of the officers and management of the affairs of the corporation," read the bylaws. The Executive Committee would also "appoint and remove at pleasure all officers, agents and employees of the League, prescribe their duties, fix their compensation and require from them security for faithful service." While the councilors would meet annually, the Executive Committee would hold quarterly meetings.

The choice of Creed to provide the League's legal muscle and founding direction reflected the lightning efficiency of the Bay Area's well-oiled economic and sociopolitical machines. As with any empire, placement of loyalists in key positions was integral to success. Serving alongside Creed was another director who would dedicate himself to preventing redwood protection. Like many of his peers, Joseph Donohoe "J. D." Grant had inherited a fortune from his pioneer father, Adam Grant, and he would leverage this wealth to finance the growth of his personal empire. Unlike William

Crocker, J. D. Grant would lead the League in public, while Crocker, a League councilor until his death in 1937, did so largely behind the scenes.

J. D. Grant was born in San Francisco in 1858, the only child of Adam and Emma Grant, who'd arrived at the Golden Gate in 1850 and 1849, respectively. Adam Grant, a Scot, cofounded Murphy, Grant & Co., which became the largest dry goods business in the West. In 1864, Adam Grant joined William Ralston, Darius Ogden Mills, and William Sharon as a founding director of the Bank of California.

Even as a young man, from the time he graduated from the University of California in 1879, J. D. Grant immersed himself in the affairs of San Francisco's economic aristocracy. That year he joined San Francisco's exclusive Pacific Club. In 1882 he joined the Bohemian Club, and four years later he became a member of the Union Club. Grant was instrumental in combining the Pacific and Union clubs into one of the nation's most powerful and exclusive fraternal orders. He was also active in seeking new digs for the Bohemian Club's summer encampment. Grant is credited with locating and securing, from the Sonoma Lumber Company, the first parcels that make up the current Bohemian Grove, which the Club occupied starting in the early 1890s and purchased in 1902. Given his research and outreach, Grant likely knew and communicated with my ancestors, though I have no record of it.

During the 1890s, Grant worked as an executive in his father's dry goods firm, and from there he branched out, developing his own fortune together with a chryselephantine self-impression. Through his first wife, Lizzie Hull, the daughter of a gold miner, Grant befriended railroad baron Leland Stanford and his wife, Jane Stanford. Lizzie was so close to the Stanfords that in some circles she became known as their "adopted daughter." As a teenager Lizzie had made her debut at the couple's extravagant Nob Hill mansion in San Francisco. In November 1886, fifteen hundred people attended the Grant-Hull wedding at Trinity Church in San Francisco, a number that reflected the "popularity of both the bride and groom in a large circle of friends and the prominent and honorable position occupied by both families," the *San Francisco Examiner* reported in a society article that spanned half a page. The couple had one child, Douglas. In July 1889 Leland and Jane Stanford offered Grant a lifetime trustee's position at the new university they'd formed in honor of their late son. One month later Lizzie, at the age of twenty-seven, died unexpectedly of "heart failure," according to brief news accounts of her passing. Some of the notices didn't even use Lizzie's name, instead referring to her as "Mrs. J. D. Grant." In 1893 Leland Stanford died, and Grant replaced him on the board of the Central Pacific Railroad.

Grant constantly sought opportunities to rub shoulders with and personally gain from the West's, and the nation's, economic and political elite. In April 1900, he hosted a luncheon at the Pacific Union Club in honor of D. O. Mills, who was out West during one of his many visits to Millbrae. While the invitations may have borne Mills's name, it was Grant's debut. The gathering presented Bay Area columnists with a who's who of local and national empire builders, all of whom, in one place, would now be associated with Grant.

Most of the attendees were, or wanted to be, profiting from the US occupation of the Philippines. The subjugation and plunder of the archipelago was largely directed out of San Francisco, whose economic sovereigns rightly viewed the "adventure" as a great source of wealth and whose docks provided the closest domestic departure points for American warships and commercial vessels. Among the many commodities dispatched to the Philippines in support of the occupation were hundreds of shiploads of redwood lumber. The ships carried back to San Francisco gold, silver, foodstuffs, sugar, cotton, hemp, and other goods produced by laborers who suffered slave-like conditions.

Holding court during the Mills gathering was UC Berkeley history professor Bernard Moses, a white supremacist who'd founded the university's political science department and was instrumental in granting the Philippine occupation an intellectual gloss. Whitelaw Reid, publisher of the *New York Tribune* and husband of Mills's daughter Elizabeth, had come west for the gathering, where he enjoyed chatting with his friends Collis and Henry Huntington. Irving Scott attended J. D. Grant's gathering. Scott's Union Iron Works built battleships for the US assault on the Philippines, where he expected Americans to unearth the "untold riches of the islands." Horace G. Platt, attorney for William Crocker's Pacific Improvement Company and a leading West Coast booster for the war, was also there, as was millionaire Robert F. Morrow, owner of cable cars. Morrow was a close friend and yachting buddy of J. D. Grant. Together Grant and Morrow owned the yacht *Halcyon*, which they sold, in 1887, to an opium-smuggling cartel.

Adam Grant died in 1904, leaving J. D. a robust estate. He was now free, rich, and connected enough to build for himself an outsized legacy. Grant's launch coincided with an era denoted by an intensive corporate feeding frenzy in which small and midsize companies were bought up by larger ones, a process that continues to this day. In this arena Grant would excel. Much like Charles Hurwitz six decades later, Grant would specialize in taking over companies built by others, spiking them with investment dollars largely not his own, and liquidating their assets to accrue great personal wealth.

Like Crocker, Grant announced his independence by building an office tower, in 1908, at Sansome and Market Streets. In the early 1920s the tower would house the first San Francisco office of Save the Redwoods League. In 1910 Grant built a mansion in San Francisco's Pacific Heights district, next door to A. B. Hammond. That year Grant served as a director of seven firms. By 1913 Grant was a director of eleven companies, including a new venture for him, the California Oregon Power Company (Copco).

After purchasing the power company, Grant began raising money to finish construction of two dams begun by Copco in 1911, on the Klamath River just south of the Oregon border. The dams required millions of board feet of the highest-grade redwood for the stave pipes that would take water to the turbines. In 1925 the *Medford Mail Tribune* reported that the sixteen-foot redwood pipe built for the Copco No. 2 plant was "the largest wood stave pipe in the world." The dams were completed in 1918, but by then the company was nearly $10 million in debt. A 1923 report issued by the US Department of the Interior noted that the California Oregon Power Company "had not been able to pay coupon interest on its outstanding bonds since July 1, 1915 [or] to make sinking-fund payments under the provisions of the deed of trust."

No matter. In 1922 Grant and other members of the firm hosted a gathering of nine hundred people at the power plant to celebrate its connection to a western power grid that ran from Mexico to Albany, Oregon. The plant's generator "was set in motion [by] Miss Josephine Grant, pretty daughter of Joseph D. Grant, capitalist and chairman of the directorate of the power company," reported William Randolph Hearst's *Examiner*. (Josephine was the daughter of Grant's second wife, Edith Macleay, whom he married in 1897.) That year the California Oregon Power Company operated twelve

power plants on ten rivers. The systems provided power as well as irrigation water, operations requiring millions of board feet of redwood lumber
for stave pipes. In 1926, Grant and his partners sold the California Oregon
Power Company to the H. M. Byllesby Company, a Chicago-based power
provider, for $20 million.

Today the water behind the Klamath dams is a toxic stew. The great
reservoirs expand across the landscape in a shocking lime-green tableau,
choked with an algae-like growth called cyanobacteria. Not only do the
dams block what were once some of the world's greatest salmon migrations,
but the hazardous water washes downstream to poison the areas salmon
and steelhead can still reach. In 2002 low flows and toxic water caused by
the dams killed seventy thousand migrating salmon in the lower Klamath
River, the largest fish kill ever on the West Coast of the United States.

Shortly before he died in 1942, Grant directed his pretty daughter, Josephine, "to open a cabinet and bring to him a leather-covered notebook."
The notebook contained the draft of a memoir, later titled *Redwoods and
Reminiscences*, a plodding aggrandization of self that makes no mention of
either of Grant's wives or his three children, including Douglas Grant, a
designer of the famous Pebble Beach Golf Links. Grant asked Josephine
to have it printed, which she did, but not until thirty years after his death
and just months before her own. The publisher was Save the Redwoods
League.

Even Josephine knew better than to release the book if she might have
to answer for it. The book is bombastic, self-serving, tone-deaf, and largely
specious. In one passage, thick with unintended irony, Grant writes, "Never
in history have there been displayed more splendid *uses* of money than in
modern America. With most of our millionaires, accumulation of dollars
has not been the objective, but the spending of money, in a manner benefi-
cent and wise. . . . On the planet Earth, little can be done without money. In
good people it brings out the good; in bad people, the evil." Grant laments
"the election of United States Senators by direct vote of the people [which]
has not worked out well."

That in 1973 Save the Redwoods League would release Grant's book is
extraordinary, and not just due to Grant's bluster and inaccuracies. Racist
proclamations in the book channel a virulent strain of hate.

"Civic virtue . . . cannot thrive where the breed is inferior," wrote Grant.

When we opened the floodgates and let in the alien hordes unrestricted, we
sold our birthright for a temporary acceleration of development. The human
mass which for more than a decade was pouring into this country was *expelled*,
much of it, from other lands, and it fastened upon a higher civilization with
distressing results. It has been responsible for most of the crime within our
borders. . . . One of the results of all this has been the shutting out of immigration, brought about largely through the patriotic work of Madison Grant.

League officials undoubtedly agreed to release J. D. Grant's book to maintain Josephine's favor. When she died, in 1972, shortly before publication of
the memoir, she left to the League half of Grant's nearly ten-thousand-acre
demesne, in the foothills of Mount Hamilton east of San Jose. According to
a history of the ranch prepared by the county of Santa Clara, the League and
the other inheritor of the ranch, the Menninger Foundation in Kansas, immediately listed the property for sale for "possible development into ranchettes." The county stepped in and convinced the owners otherwise. Today,
the Joseph D. Grant County Park is one of the finest wildlands anywhere
near San Jose.

Josephine included in Grant's book a series of photos, one of which aptly
summarizes her father's civic and environmental output. In the image,
J. D. stands in a meadow wearing knee boots and a mac. A trilby sets off
his high forehead, and Grant gives the camera an imperious, if not bored,
gaze. In one hand is a fly rod; the other holds a steelhead trout. He'd caught
the steelhead in the Williamson River, in 1911, the year he first viewed the
gorge where the Copco No. 1 dam was slated to be built. The Williamson
is one of the great upriver feeders to the Klamath River system. Seven years
later, upon completion of the dam, which was situated on the Klamath seventy miles downstream, all anadromous fish migration to the Williamson
ceased. Grant's trophy turned out to be one of the last steelhead ever caught
in the river.

Grant's memoir presents him as a Western titan of three industries in addition to hydroelectric power: oil, steel, and redwood protection. In 1913
Grant bought into John Barneson's General Petroleum Corporation,
among the largest oil companies in the United States. Grant was excited
about oil.

The author's ancestors, Sonoma County, 1915. L-R: David King, the author's great-grandfather, and David's brothers James, Thomas, and William. Courtesy of the King Family Collection.

Headwaters Forest, June 1987. © 2023 by Greg King.

Nina Williams and Mokai along a new road cut into Salmon Creek, Headwaters Forest 1987. ©
2023 by Greg King.

Mokai scissors between two ancient redwood trees. Owl Creek Grove 1986. © 2023 by Greg King.

Headwaters Forest in 1992. The clear-cut on the south side was completed in 1987. The illegal road, cut in 1990, can be seen entering the middle of the grove. © 2023 by Greg King.

Pacific Lumber's mill operation in Scotia, along the Eel River, 1989. © 2023 by Greg King.

Reporter Paul Nussbaum of the Philadelphia Inquirer inspects Maxxam clear-cutting in All Species Grove, 1987. © 2023 by Greg King.

Mary Beth Nearing perches 150 feet above the ground, All Species Grove 1987. © 2023 by Greg King

Pacific Lumber climber Dan Collings ascends redwood occupied by Greg King in All Species Grove, September 1987. © 2023 by Greg King.

Lumber Baron A. B. Hammond, 1885. Courtesy of Archives & Special Collections, Mansfield Library, University of Montana.

Early redwood logging, North Fork Elk River, 1872. Courtesy of Palmquist Collection, Cal Poly Humboldt Library.

Humboldt County timber baron David Evans, front-left, with trainloads of redwood logs from Freshwater Creek, headed to the Excelsior Mill, 1892. Courtesy of Ericson Collection, Cal Poly Humboldt Library.

View in the Redwoods Humboldt Co. California

Redwood logging on Lindsay Creek by Humboldt County timberman John Vance, early 1890s. Courtesy of Ericson Collection, Cal Poly Humboldt Library.

San Francisco industrialist William H. Crocker, late 1910s. Courtesy of the Library of Congress.

Front row, left to right: California Governor Ronald Reagan, Save the Redwoods League Executive Secretary Newton B. Drury, and Save the Redwoods President Ralph Chaney inspect a map of the Pepperwood Grove addition to Avenue of the Giants, 1968. Future League Executive Director John Dewitt stands in the back-right. Courtesy of Save the Redwoods League collection, Bancroft Library, UC Berkeley.

The author practicing spur climbing an ancient redwood tree in Headwaters Forest, late 1987. ©
2023 by Greg King.

Clear-cutting along Redwood Creek, Redwood National Park, 1976. Tall Tree Grove stands front-left. Courtesy of Dave Van de Mark.

Truck line owner Don Nolan Sr. strikes a demonstrator who is blockading one of his logging trucks, February 13, 1990. © 2023 by Greg King.

Tree-sitter "Raven" in All Species Grove, 1988. © 2023 by Greg King.

Larry Evans and Brian in Headwaters Forest, preparing to access Maxxam's new, illegal road into the grove. March 1, 1990. © 2023 by Greg King.

The illegal road cut into Headwaters Forest, 1990. State and elected officials called the road a "wildlife study trail." © 2023 by Greg King.

Sunrise over the East Bay hills, Earth First! occupation of the Golden Gate Bridge. April 24, 1990. © 2023 by Greg King.

Author guarded by an iron worker, occupation of the Golden Gate Bridge. April 24, 1990. Courtesy of John Green.

udi Bari speaks at a San Francisco rally for Headwaters Forest, September 26, 1996. © 2023 by
Greg King.

Nearly 10,000 people protest Maxxam's redwood liquidation. Fisher log deck, September 15,
1996. © 2023 by Greg King.

Early 1988: Earth First! activists pose in front of the 13-foot diameter redwood in All Species Grove where the author was a tree sitter in September 1987. © 2023 by Greg King.

By 1919, when Grant joined Save the Redwoods League, he was vice president of Barneson's company and one of just five members of its Executive Committee. By now Grant, like Creed, was also a director of several other companies, including Bankline Oil, Marina Oil, Coast Counties Gas & Electric, Economic Gas Company, First National Bank of San Jose, Security Savings Bank, and the Bank of California. That year General Petroleum operated 454 oil wells on 30,500 acres in the United States and sold oil throughout the world. The company also pumped oil on 17,500 acres in Mexico, where it had a refinery in the Gulf of Mexico city of Tampico. Grant notes that, during the Mexican Civil War, he and Barneson visited Tampico on Barneson's yacht, *Invader*, where they saw "gaunt figures hung from trees, with vile vultures busy about them." In his book, Grant shares a joke he'd heard about the hanged men.

In 1923, General Petroleum joined Save the Redwoods League as a "life member."

It was in partnership with Wigginton Creed that Grant became a steel magnate. By Grant's telling, he and Creed started Columbia Steel Company together "in 1908." Here again Grant was incorrect: not only did the company get founded in 1909 and start producing steel only in late 1910, but he had nothing to do with Columbia Steel until 1916. Only after the death of the clannish C. A. Hooper was Grant able to buy in. For six years, under Creed's management, the company grew steadily. In 1921 Creed and Grant began gathering a group of investors who could finance a much larger enterprise by feeding it with pig iron and coal from Utah. In June 1922 the Columbia Steel Corporation formed and purchased a coal and coke company in Carbon County, Utah. The acquisition gave Columbia access to untapped bituminous coal deposits. The company also acquired iron deposits from Iron County, Utah, and built coking ovens, blast furnaces, and smelting plants to produce raw pig iron, which was shipped to Pittsburg for manufacture into steel products. The company incorporated in Delaware to take advantage of generous tax laws and lax oversight, and its new officers included Creed as president and Grant as vice president, as well as John Drum and William W. Crocker, twenty-nine-year-old son of William H. Crocker. Creed ran the company, as well as Pacific Gas and Electric (PG&E). In 1923, Columbia Steel issued $4 million in bonds to further fuel the growth of the company.

Wigginton Creed died on August 6, 1927, shortly after returning from an inspection of the Columbia operation in Utah. He was fifty years old. Newspapers variously attributed his death to a "stomach ailment" or "stroke of apoplexy." He was quickly forgotten. Ten days later J. D. Grant assumed the presidency of Columbia Steel Corporation. Within months he began negotiations to sell Columbia to United States Steel, the nation's largest steel producer and one of the world's biggest corporations. On October 31, 1929, United States Steel announced that it had purchased Columbia Steel for $47 million.

In his memoir, Grant claimed that Columbia Steel had been founded in Pittsburg in part because "labor conditions there would be less disturbed than in San Francisco." An entire chapter of his memoir, "Combating the Tyranny of Union Labor," presents, in raw form, Grant's intolerance of fair labor practices. He calls union organizers "bolshies" who "met in cellars and hidden places underground, like moles, and now they came out into the open, blinking their weak eyes." The unionists were prone to "singing Soviet songs set to popular American negro melodies. A messy lot, pimply boys and blotchy faced girls."

In this chapter Grant extols the work of the San Francisco Law and Order Committee, which he said was "active in fostering individual freedom," or the "right to work," a corporate euphemism meaning that no laborer should be required to join a union and, more importantly, that no business owner should be required to hire union labor. Grant fails to note that the Law and Order Committee was formed in 1916 as an offshoot of the San Francisco Chamber of Commerce.

By 1916 the San Francisco Chamber, with seventy-three hundred members, was the largest and most powerful business organization in the United States. Its headquarters occupied the "great hall" on the bottom floor of the Merchants Exchange Building, where the Southern Pacific Railroad and the Hammond Lumber Company kept offices. The Law and Order Committee posed as a reform organization, but really it fronted a vigilante force "that actually kept the city in turmoil," writes Greg Gordon in *When Money Grew on Trees*. The turmoil was a smokescreen that fomented fear and convinced San Francisco voters, in November 1916, to approve an unconstitutional ballot measure that banned union picketing in the city.

The Law and Order Committee had formed in response to a suitcase bomb that exploded at a "Preparedness Day" parade on June 22, 1916, in San Francisco, killing ten people. It remains the worst terrorist attack in the city's history. San Francisco business leaders had staged the parade to demonstrate their support of the US entry into World War I. Labor opposed the war. Prior to the attack, labor activists had warned their members to watch for "agents provocateurs" who might try to mar the parade and blame it on the labor movement in order to crush unions. Two leading labor activists, Thomas Mooney and Warren Billings, were subsequently arrested and convicted of the bombings and spent twenty-three years in San Quentin before they were exonerated and released. Gordon writes that, no matter the total lack of evidence against them, members of the Law and Order Committee "pressured the district attorney to prosecute the two innocent men in what proved to be one of the nation's worst travesties of justice."

The bombing and the business community's response to it demonstrate the sort of opaque interplay between members of San Francisco's "interlocking directorate" and the public that would likewise inform creation of Save the Redwoods League. Indeed, we see some of the very same people.

As with the League, direction of the Law and Order Committee was determined by an all-powerful subcommittee, in this case called an advisory committee. In the summer of 1917, the full membership of the Law and Order Advisory Committee included Charles K. Field, editor of *Sunset* magazine and a prominent Bohemian Club member, and Jesse Lilienthal, an attorney and president of United Railroads of San Francisco. A. B. Hammond was on the Law and Order Advisory Committee, as were John Hooper, James Tyson of Northern Redwood Lumber Company, western timber baron George Pope, and redwood lumber and shipping magnate Robert Dollar—an extraordinarily top-heavy representation by the timber industry, which was notoriously anti-union. The two remaining members of the Law and Order Advisory Committee were J. D. Grant and William H. Crocker. One year later the close collaboration of Crocker and J. D. Grant with leaders of the timber industry to crush organized labor would segue to an inward movement to spare industrial leaders the pain of redwood preservation.

37

IN ITS FIRST YEAR OF OPERATION, SAVE THE REDWOODS LEAGUE UNDER-
went a shakeup of leadership. On July 7, 1920, J. D. Grant wrote to Merriam recommending that League councilor J. C. Sperry be moved up to the
League's Executive Committee to take the place of Ray Lyman Wilbur, who
was apparently too taxed as a physician and president of Stanford University to continue his volunteer role. Sperry was a natural choice, and he too
would work as a volunteer. Although Grant added that Sperry ought to also
be named "manager" of the League, Sperry had already been at the post for
three months, writing and signing letters with his signature above the word
"manager" and signing checks in John C. Merriam's absence.

J. C. Sperry traveled in business circles with the name, but none of the
gravitas, of his cousins, who ran the nationwide Sperry Flour Company,
though he undoubtedly owned shares. Instead, straight out of college,
Sperry began fronting for William H. Crocker, who was married to Sperry's
cousin, Ethel. J. C. Sperry represented William Crocker's many oil investments in Southern California, working under Crocker oil partner George T.
Cameron, whose father-in-law, Michael de Young, owned the *San Francisco
Chronicle*. Compared with his peers, Sperry managed a modest portfolio.

In his history of the League, Joseph Engbeck introduces J. C. Sperry as
"a successful businessman in his own right [who] served the league in many
ways, donating time, energy, and practical good judgment as its unpaid general manager." On June 2, 1920, Sperry wielded his practical good judgment,
if not surprising authority, when, in a lengthy letter, he asked Wigginton
Creed to write the League's bylaws and articles of incorporation. Sperry,
who was clearly still fronting for Crocker, was well aware that Creed was
then president of the large redwood firms Big Lagoon Lumber Company,
C. A. Hooper & Co., and Excelsior Investment Company, that he remained

a major investor in Redwood Manufacturers Company, and that he was president of the redwood-consuming firms Columbia Steel Company, East Bay Water Company, South Shore Land Company, and Tempe Land and Improvement Company. Sperry also knew that Creed was just weeks away from taking over as president of Pacific Gas and Electric, among the largest of all industrial consumers of redwood products. On June 21, Creed wrote to Sperry, "I shall be pleased to arrange for drafting appropriate Articles and By-Laws."

By now John C. Merriam was on his way to Washington to run the Carnegie Institution. At a meeting held September 8 in Merriam's Berkeley office, Merriam resigned from Save the Redwoods League's Executive Committee, though he would rejoin the organization as president following the 1921 death of Franklin K. Lane. According to minutes from the meeting, after Merriam resigned, "It was moved by Mr. Creed, seconded by Mr. [Charles F.] Stern, and unanimously carried that Mr. J. D. Grant be elected Chairman of the Executive Committee . . . and that J. C. Sperry be added to the Committee to fill the vacancy caused by the resignation of Mr. Merriam."

The first acquisitions of old-growth timber for preservation in the northern belt were made not by Save the Redwoods League but by the county of Humboldt. By the end of 1919 the county had purchased 340 acres of virgin redwood and some cutover land along the new Redwood Highway, fronting the South Fork Eel River, as the beginning of a redwood park meant to attract tourists. Funding for the purchases included two donations of $15,000, from William Kent, a wealthy congressman from Marin County who served as an early League councilor, and Stephen Mather.

Mather is a seminal figure in western conservation lore. In 1917, he became the first director of the National Park Service, having invented the position. He served until January 1929, one year before he died at the age of sixty-two, after suffering a stroke. While at the Department of the Interior in 1916, Mather proposed a "great Park to Park Highway." The new road system would be thirty-five hundred miles in length and link national parks in ten western states. For Mather, the highway idea had been brewing for a couple of years. Now, at Interior, he could make what would become the most significant contribution to date to the growing Good Roads

Movement, an allegedly grassroots campaign that was actually designed and promulgated by the petroleum and automobile industries.

During the 1910s, the oil industry was awash in excess product, primarily due to overproduction in California. By then both steamships and trains had largely been converted to oil-burning engines, but they didn't consume nearly enough to soak up the glut. Appearing as an angel was the automobile, the nascent king of petroleum consumption. In 1916 *San Francisco Chronicle* readers were urged to pass a $15 million bond initiative to finance road construction throughout the state. The Spreckels' *San Francisco Call* was likewise on board. "New markets simply *had* to be found if oil was to retain value, and the private automobile provided an ideal outlet," Gray Brechin writes in *Imperial San Francisco*.

Quickly the Good Roads Movement recognized the potential economic strength of constructing and maintaining a system of roads to and through the West's rapidly expanding network of state and national parks. By 1926 the roads and parks movements had so gelled that the National Highways Association and the National Conference on Outdoor Recreation would produce a map of the United States titled "Good Roads Everywhere," with text advocating "A Paved United States in Our Day."

In 1916 Mather said he wanted to improve park access to allow enjoyment by "everyman," or ordinary Americans, many of whom now happened to drive a car. Interior Secretary Lane, soon to be president of Save the Redwoods League, who had previously served as chair of the US Interstate Commerce Commission, supported the idea with an op-ed in *American Motorist* magazine. Lane assured industrialists that national parks and transportation systems to connect them were not frivolous ventures. He said that with Europe closed to American visitors due to the Great War, "thousands have for the first time crossed the continent and seen one or more of the national parks."

Mather was most interested in improving automobile access to the national parks. At the end of 1916 he reported that nearly 20,000 cars carrying 79,916 tourists had entered the nation's national parks, up from 12,563 cars the previous year. "The number of tourists entering the parks in private cars is astonishing when one takes into consideration the fact that they have been opened to motor traffic only a very few years," wrote Mather. "In the early future travel in private machines will overtake the increasing railroad travel and constitute the greater portion of all park travel. This makes it incumbent upon the Federal Government to prepare for the great influx of automobiles by constructing new roads and improving existing highways, [as] no policy of national-park management has yielded more thoroughly gratifying results than that which guided the admission of motor-driven vehicles." Two years later Mather decreed, "Automobiles and motor cycles will be permitted in all of the parks, in fact, the parks will be kept accessible by any means practicable."

The San Francisco Chamber of Commerce, which was largely controlled by the Southern Pacific Railroad, Standard Oil, and large oil investors such as J. D. Grant and William Crocker, proclaimed its enthusiastic support for Mather's "parkway." A Chamber newsletter announced that the parkway "will join all National Parks in the Rocky Mountain Regions and along the Pacific Coast with one good Highway."

It's no coincidence that Save the Redwoods League was founded just as cars were beginning to dominate the American landscape. Toward the end of World War I, as the use of private automobiles grew and construction of the Redwood Highway through Humboldt and Del Norte counties neared completion, Mather, the automobile and oil industries, and western industrialists understood that protecting standing redwoods alongside the new highway would provide one of the nation's greatest destinations for vacationing motorists. The trees would also screen adjacent logging that was likewise critical to their industries. By 1919 Mather was visualizing a great highway through the redwood belt that would then connect with Crater Lake in southern Oregon and to parks throughout the Pacific Northwest, as well as in Idaho, Montana, Utah, Colorado, and Arizona.

In February 1920, Save the Redwoods League hosted its first major public event in the Bay Area, a "Save the Redwoods Day" dedicated to the League at an automobile show in San Francisco. On Save the Redwoods Day, cars would be situated in what the press described as "pictorial settings, descriptive of the natural beauties of California." League officials, including Mather and Lane, attended, alongside fifteen thousand car enthusiasts. De Young's *Chronicle* ran a banner headline: "Auto Fans to Observe 'Save the Redwoods' Day at Show." Newton Drury and his brother, Aubrey—who would serve as the League's "administrative secretary" from 1920 until 1940—developed and printed tens of thousands of automobile window stickers depicting a

Packard parked in front of a single old-growth redwood tree, underscored by the words "Save the Redwoods on the Redwood Highway." The background image is of a clear-cut hillside. Such a highway, Newton Drury predicted, "is destined to become one of the most popular motor routes in the world."

By the end of the year Mather had inched closer to blazing not just his park-to-park highway but numerous highways to and through the national parks. In 1921 Mather hosted a VIP gathering in Yosemite Valley to continue marketing the idea of national parks as "natural playgrounds of the state" to be increasingly accessed by motorists. Attending the gathering were two vice presidents of the Southern Pacific, whose trains ran on fuel oil and hauled thousands of tourists each year; Charles Field, editor of *Sunset* magazine, which was largely controlled by the Southern Pacific; the president and secretary of the San Francisco Chamber of Commerce; a member of the state prison board, whose inmates built the roads; and Wigginton Creed.

Mather was also unquestionably in favor of creating national parks for the sake of preserving nature. He was an outdoorsman and an early and active member of the Sierra Club. He was also bipolar. When he fell into "depressions," he often sought succor in a Sierra wildland. As Park Service director, Mather used more than $100,000 of his own money to protect wildlands, including a donation of more than $50,000 to purchase privately held groves of giant sequoias that he then added to Sequoia National Park. National park acreage doubled during his tenure, when the Bryce, Acadia, Zion, Hawaii, Denali, and Grand Canyon national parks were added to the federal system.

Mather's job at Interior was made easier by the understanding among the nation's business interests that parklands could serve as income generators for entire regions and as shiny objects to promote the continued settlement of the West. In 1925, Mather's annual report for the National Park Service noted, "Every visitor is a potential settler and investor. . . . Hundreds of thousands in the past few years have pulled stakes in the west and invested in western ranches and fruit farms, in mines, and other industrial enterprises. In all this the national parks, as the scenic lodestones, through their attractions draw these future settlers and investors."

38

IN ITS PROMOTIONAL MATERIAL, SAVE THE REDWOODS LEAGUE WOULD, for many years, call for "acquisition of a large tract of redwood timber as a national park." Over its first decade of existence, the League would publicly identify the "large tract" as Bull Creek, which served as a beacon for fund-raising efforts. Yet League officials made clear that they were working with, rather than against, the redwood timber industry. The League's very first brochure, printed in early 1920, notes that "the California State Highway system through Humboldt County has made the magnificent redwood forests of the northern coast easily accessible to the lover of nature, to the tourist, and to the important industries dependent upon forest products." In the next paragraph we learn that the League is poised to balance "the value of the primeval redwood forests of America as natural objects of extraordinary interest as well as of economic importance." Later the brochure assures readers, "The Save the Redwoods League does not ask for any unreasonable hampering of the Redwood industry." Instead, the League sought to secure "certain areas of the most typical primitive Redwood forest known, to be preserved ultimately as a National Park, [and] particularly to protect the timber along the scenic State highway."

In private, League officials weren't so generous. As historian Susan Schrepfer noted in her 1971 PhD thesis, "The men of the league intended that no more than a small percentage of the total redwood belt should be preserved."

The League's early, in-house papers demonstrate that Save the Redwoods League sought protection only for the strip of trees along the highway through the redwood belt of Southern Humboldt County, plus a small "representative grove" of a few hundred acres at Dyerville. A few years later, as the state neared completion of the highway north of Eureka, to the Klamath

River, another beauty strip would be needed to screen from tourists' view the appalling scenes of encroaching deforestation while continuing to encourage long motor trips. Bull Creek, however, which stood two miles and across the river from Dyerville, served mostly as bait to draw the public into the League's orbit. The League never intended to save this grove.

Early in 1922, League officials circulated an internal memorandum, titled "Outline of Intention to Be Presented to the Pacific Lumber Company by the Save the Redwoods League." The confidential memo identified just how much of the company's land the League was targeting for preservation, noting that the "west bank of the South Fork of the Eel River has not been preserved and its preservation is not included in the plan submitted herewith." Bull Creek dominated the west bank and remained out of view of the traveling public. The memo notes that "Bull Creek Flat contains undoubtedly the finest Redwoods in this region and is the entrance to a very large area of timber which The Pacific Lumber Company plans to cut." The League would attempt "to save as much as possible of the finest part of Bull Creek Flat and to assure the protection of this grove when the logging further up is carried on."

"As much as possible," it turned out, wasn't very much. "At the most, it would probably be impossible for the League to save more than 250 acres of Bull Creek Flat." Still, the League had a plan. "Upon cutting over Bull Creek Flat and other areas in the region of the South Fork of the Eel River, this cut-over land shall be deeded to the Save the Redwoods League for reforestation and preservation as a park." In a 1923 letter to the US Forest Service district office in San Francisco, Newton Drury claimed that the League remained interested in some sort of preserve at Bull Creek, something much smaller than the many thousands of acres the organization was constantly touting to its membership and the public. "If it is feasible to do so at least 100 acres and probably 250 acres of this flat should be saved. . . . The problem of saving this timber however must be determined on the basis of a survey now being made by the Pacific Lumber Company."

The League's priorities for 1922 also called for residents and officials in Mendocino County to abandon efforts to preserve redwoods there, noting, "The assistance of this county might be better gained in saving one or more groves along the highway" in Humboldt County. Just two years earlier the Albion Lumber Company had purchased from the Pacific Coast Redwood

Company forty-one thousand acres of virgin redwood that stood as a single, majestic forest along the banks of the beautiful Navarro River and included numerous large flats of ancient redwoods. The company began logging the stand just before the League called for Mendocino County residents to save Humboldt's roadside trees. Unlike in Humboldt County, few great alluvial flats of ancient redwoods lined major streams in Mendocino County. The Navarro River stand was unique to the region and to the world. Yet no highway bisected the forest, so the League ignored it. If pending clear-cuts couldn't be seen from a road, the League saw no reason to save the trees.

Instead of protecting the Navarro River redwoods or even Bull Creek, the League's most pressing conservation priority that year was acquisition of 250 acres at Dyerville Flat, on the east side of the South Fork Eel River, which was bisected by the highway and the tracks of the Northwestern Pacific Railroad. Humboldt County business interests and tree lovers had long targeted Dyerville Flat for protection. The small but sumptuous grove of just over three hundred acres was situated at the confluence of the South Fork Eel River and the main stem and contained what, at the time, was thought to be the world's tallest trees.

39

O N July 8, 1919, Sonoma County congressman Clarence F. Lea introduced House Resolution 159, which would authorize the interior secretary, through Park Service director Stephen T. Mather, to "investigate and report to the House of Representatives as to the suitability, location, cost . . . and advisability of securing . . . a stand of typical redwoods [to] be set apart and dedicated as a national park." In his address to Congress, Lea waxed lyrical: "Perhaps one of the most dismal conceptions that the imagination could draw would be a treeless world. . . . The foliage of the forest has received the poisoned winds and sent them on pure. They invite the rain and turn the waters into the earth as a storage reservoir."

In a report to Interior Secretary Franklin Lane, Mather wrote that the resolution "brings the redwood problem definitely before Congress and . . . , if adopted, will result in the presentation of a comprehensive report on the redwood situation to the national legislature which may secure national aid in preserving these noble trees."

Lea's bill got immediate action from Save the Redwoods League officials, who called for a survey of redwood lands to inform the legislation. At that time the League established a Committee on Redwood National Park and a Committee on Redwoods Investigation. At the first meeting of the latter, on October 30, members agreed that "some forester or forest engineer of wide training and experience, and if possible of national reputation, [should] be hired as an employee of the Redwoods Investigation Committee" to conduct "the proposed redwood survey." The committee recommended allocating the hefty sum of $9,000 to pay the surveyor. The price tag would seem excessive, as the feds were already proposing to pay for this work themselves. The League's plan was not so much to augment federal efforts as to highjack them.

A comprehensive redwood survey conducted on behalf of the US government would appear to satisfy the League's principal objective of determining the best "representative tracts" of redwoods to save. On January 26, 1920, the League's Executive Committee determined that "such a survey is of the first importance to the League." On May 4, the House agreed to permit a federal redwood survey as the first concrete step toward Lea's proposed Redwood National Park. After the survey was completed, Congress would hold hearings. Mather was authorized to dispatch to Humboldt County a survey crew headed by Paul G. Redington, California district forester for the US Forest Service. Instead of $9,000, the League donated $400 to the effort.

On August 17, 1920, Newton Drury wrote to Mather, "I have had maps of the Humboldt redwood region prepared in Eureka and sent to Mr. Redington. We hope that it will be possible soon for him to begin the survey for the National park hearing." On October 4 the League Executive Committee met with Redington himself. The minutes note, "Mr. Mather announced that either he or Mr. Horace M. Albright of the National Park Service would conduct a hearing after facts had been gathered by the Redwood survey, in order to prepare a report to be submitted to Congress on the matter of a National Redwood Park. His suggestion was that this report might not only be printed officially but might be issued in more elaborate form with the illustrations by the Save the Redwoods League as part of their campaign literature." Albright was Mather's protégé and assistant at the National Park Service. The following week John Merriam met with League councilor Henry S. Graves, who had recently retired as chief of the US Forest Service. In a letter dated October 12, 1920, Merriam reported to J. C. Sperry, "In [Graves's] judgement such a survey is absolutely necessary to make the points which we desire to present."

But on reaching the League in November 1920, Redington's report set off alarms. It was not what they had expected. League officials did not have the report "printed officially . . . in more elaborate form" for their "campaign literature." Instead, they hastily buried it like a piece of old meat. Then they killed Lea's bill.

On October 10, 1920, Paul G. Redington gathered his crew: R. F. Hammatt, Redington's assistant district forester; M. B. Pratt, deputy California state forester; and Donald Bruce, associate professor of forestry at the

University of California. Redington stood stout and iron jawed, his angular face capped in a wide-brimmed Forest Service hat. The foursome traced a route across the Golden Gate, through the inland valleys of Sonoma and Mendocino counties, into the redwood belt of Humboldt County. They returned eleven days later. Redington did not delay in preparing his report, which Mather and League officials received in mid-November. The timeliness of the issue and the forcefulness with which Redington presented his conclusions appear to have derived from an incredible journey. The men were thrilled by what they had seen.

Redington identified five tracts of ancient redwood worthy of preservation. All were in Humboldt County. In Del Norte County, where significant redwood logging had only recently begun, the groves were considered too distant, without improved highway access or a significant population base, to generate sufficient visitation. Each of the five tracts, if allocated to a national park, would preserve an entire watershed of ancient redwoods, from ridge to ridge.

From north to south, Redington's five redwood islands were on the Klamath River, Prairie Creek, Redwood Creek, Maple Creek at Big Lagoon, and the South Fork Eel River. Redington didn't exactly pass over the League's favored tract on the Eel River, but he made the possibility of such acquisition subservient to preservation of a larger landscape, in this case along the lower Klamath River.

On the Eel, Redington's crew identified forty-four thousand unlogged acres of redwood forest growing within the South Fork watershed and surrounding its confluence with the main stem. Except for a few riverside groves of colossal trees and the six-hundred-acre flat at Bull Creek, Redington reported that, overall, the Eel River tract was "*not* a heavy redwood stand." He said that "86 percent of the total area is lightly timbered" and "inferior" to the other groves examined. Redington wrote that the Eel River forest did "not support a stand of redwood . . . typical of the redwood belt."

Those words delivered a crushing blow to the public pronouncements and aspirations of League officials, who were exclusively dedicated to preserving only a strip of trees along the Eel River and the Redwood Highway south of Eureka. "Typical," to League officials, meant museum pieces that screened clear-cuts, not whole redwood ecosystems. In June 1920 Drury wrote, "The purpose of the Save the Redwoods League is to secure preservation of adequate groves of the most representative specimans [*sic*] of redwood . . . [p]articularly along the state highway. . . . The League does not hope nor expect to save all the redwoods, but rather typical groves of sufficient extent to give the tourist and nature lover a complete idea of their beauty and grandeur." League literature and letters to supporters had promised, and would continue to promote the idea, that the Eel River held the most "typical" and "representative" groves in the redwood belt. In a few years, as the state highway expanded its reach northward, the League would revise its literature to include a beauty strip along this section as well, which then would also become "typical" and "representative."

Redington envisioned a much different redwood preserve. He didn't want postage-stamp groves along an already hard-cut river, such as the Eel. Instead, Redington recommended preserving the intact sixty-four-thousand-acre redwood expanse on the Klamath River. There is so much heart in Redington's depiction of the mighty Klamath ecosystem, which remained largely pristine along the 190-mile reach downriver of J. D. Grant's dams, that, in light of what actually happened to the redwoods of that great river, it is painful to read.

> This Klamath River Tract is untouched by the axe of the lumberman [and] has a better proportion of both bottom and slope types [of redwood] than any of the other tracts examined. . . . The timber is virgin. . . . The tract is the last unconsolidated body of redwood of its size in existence. It is far from operating concerns and will not, in the natural course of events, be logged for some little time. The Government should be able to purchase here a larger typical area, superior in every way, for less money than in any other locality. . . . The Klamath River tract excels all others examined in the excellent condition of its timber and the good representation of both slope and bottom types of redwood. It excels all others even more forcibly, however, in the attractiveness, for park and recreation purposes, of other features included within its boundaries. . . .
>
> The largest tributary to the Klamath within the tract is Blue Creek. This is a wonderfully bountiful stream and drains a big country within which is a magnificent body of virgin redwood. Blue Creek furnishes excellent trout fishing, and offers a fine chance for development. Other outstanding topographic features of this tract are the ridge composing its boundaries. They are

much more prominent—more pronounced in relation to the balance of the tract—than are the ridges on the other areas examined. . . .

The trip by boat from Requa (at its mouth) to and beyond the farther limits of the tract, is a wonderful one. The brisk down-river breeze, prevalent during the summer, roughens the water where the river spreads out behind the ocean's bar, sending sheets of spray over the bows of the small craft commonly used for the up-river trip. On the south side the redwood, in dark and solid masses, stretches from the top of the ridge to the very water's edge. . . .

Alders line the banks of a quiet stretch, their overhanging branches forming silent secluded spots, true paradises for the sentimentally inclined canoeist. Bold headlands offer, from natural openings on their summits, incomparable vistas of river and side stream, as well as glimpses, far in the distance, of the main summits of the Coast Range mountains, or in the opposite direction, of coastwise ships bound north and south. Salmon and steelhead abound. . . .

The quality of the timber, from all external appearances, leaves an extremely favorable impression. . . . The stand within the slope type everywhere it was entered, seamed clean, thrifty and in prime growing condition. In it 8, 10 and 12 foot [in diameter] are by no means the exception. . . . There is, too, a very fair representation of the river bottom type. . . . On those flats the timber is grove-like in appearance and trees 12, 14 and occasionally 16 foot in diameter occur. Ferns grow both abundantly and luxuriantly and both ferns and underbrush are much more prevalent than on the flats along the south fork of the Eel.

Redington ended his section on the Klamath River thus: "The Committee recommends that this area be acquired by the Federal Government, and created and administered as a Redwood National Park."

Redington's effusive appreciation of the Klamath redwoods radiates further when we connect the Klamath forest to the three other northern groves he examined: Redwood Creek, its large northern tributary Prairie Creek, and Maple Creek. The four watersheds connected as an unbroken ecosystem of 173,000 acres of ancient redwood, plus many thousands of additional acres along the coast. We can add to this figure a contiguous expanse, to the north in Del Norte County, of more than 100,000 acres of ancient redwood still standing not only unlogged but roadless.

That as late as 1920 a redwood domain of such vitality and size could still stand in the form of unmolested, interconnected watersheds is extraordinary. This long ribbon of low, folded mountains stood as a single organism, an aggregation of sublime hills and primordial solitude coated with enormous conifers, growing unbroken across seventy miles of California's fabled Coast Range. Here stood two hundred million years of living history, a force formidable enough to survive catastrophic shifts in climate, tectonic upheavals, and even continental drift to stand as the unlikely southern anchor of the great Pacific Northwest temperate rainforest ecosystem. Native peoples thrived in this domain for nearly ten thousand years, using redwood as needed for homes, tools, and canoes, in the process marring the forest not at all. Yet nothing could protect this world from swarms of strange and hostile bipeds brandishing tools of steel and deviant ideas about what it means to be rich.

Farther south, this great forest reserve connected with even more virgin redwood that went unmentioned in Redington's report. Adjacent to Maple Creek, the southernmost of Redington's four northern tracts, stood a contiguous band of redwoods not less than fifteen thousand acres along Little River. Hammond was logging into the headwaters of Little River, and Little River Redwood Company was cutting closer to the mouth; yet most of the watershed remained intact. The dense riverside groves included a stand of unusually large redwoods growing along a two-hundred-acre flat at the bottom of an inner gorge, at the confluence of Little River and its upper south fork. Like nearly the entirety of the redwood ecosystem, this forest was rarely seen, and now it is gone. The largest verified redwood on the flat, noted by Newton Drury in 1931, before the flat was logged, was 20 feet in diameter, stood 308 feet tall, and contained nearly 400,000 board feet of lumber.

Heading south and east from Little River, virgin redwood still grew along nearly ten thousand acres of the North Fork Mad River, though James Tyson's Northern Redwood Lumber Company would soon cut the last old-growth redwood tree from the three-thousand-acre flat at the confluence of the Mad River and its north fork. From the Mad River south, the redwood belt hugged the ridges of small watersheds that fed Humboldt Bay. Here decades of redwood logging had cut ever wider swaths into streamside groves, leaving rims of hillside redwoods intact. Some thirty thousand acres of redwood still stood along the upper reaches of Freshwater Creek and adjacent Elk River, largely held by Dolbeer & Carson and Hanify & Hooper. J. R. Hanify was a longtime partner of C. A. Hooper, as well as a Bay Area bank director and lumber shipping fleet owner. In 1911 the Hooper-Hanify partnership added an adjacent four thousand acres of Elk River redwood in a deal brokered by Eureka attorney and redwood land sharp L. F. Puter. In 1919 Puter joined Save the Redwoods League's first localized Redwood Park Committee, made up primarily of Humboldt County businessmen charged with identifying redwood tracts worthy of protection.

It was in the former Hooper-Hanify holding, sixty-seven years after Redington filed his report, that Mary Beth Nearing and I would camp for a week 130 feet into the canopy of now isolated ancient redwood trees that overlooked the South Fork Elk River, along the northernmost edge of Headwaters Forest.

Adjacent and to the south of Elk River stood some five thousand acres of ancient redwood on tiny Salmon Creek, whose abundance of fish justified the name and proved the modern adage that salmon is an old-growth-dependent species. South and east of the Humboldt Bay tributaries ran the magnificent redwood reach of Yager Creek, a tributary of the Van Duzen River that, along with its major feeder, Lawrence Creek, held twenty-two thousand acres of contiguous, unentered ancient redwood forest, which Pacific Lumber would purchase twenty years after Redington's survey. Here at the headwaters of Lawrence Creek, inside the luxurious one-thousand-acre expanse of unentered redwood at All Species Grove, Mary Beth and I would stage our second weeklong tree-sit.

The flat isthmuses of tall redwoods growing on the Van Duzen River also remained intact in 1920. The Yager and Van Duzen sections held a combined forty thousand acres of unbroken redwood that Redington's crew had overlooked. From here south, over a low ridge, ran the main branch of the Eel River and the South Fork. Although the watershed had been heavily cut by Pacific Lumber, the Eel still held some sixty thousand acres of standing redwood, Douglas fir, and hardwoods—broken by luxurious natural prairies owned by PL and several other firms in a patchwork but mostly connected expanse that extended to the Mendocino County line.

While fragmented, this combined redwood ecosystem of some 185,000 acres connected with the single block of 173,000 acres in Redington's four northern tracts and another 50,000 acres of mixed coniferous forest that included redwood and was contiguous with the greater stand. As late as 1920, after sixty years of relentless industrial logging, some 400,000 acres of Humboldt County's original expanse of 536,000 acres of ancient redwood habitat remained standing. An equivalent forest still stood in Mendocino County. Del Norte County's 100,000 acres of ancient redwood remained largely untouched. A powerful California congressman was proposing a Redwood National Park, and a federal forester had recommended preservation of the entirety of the largest single stand of primeval redwood remaining—a forest that covered the lowermost reach of one of the nation's most beautiful and dramatic rivers. An organization controlled by some of the world's richest and most powerful men had formed to save "representative areas" of this paradise. Newspapers in every American market covered the League's efforts in glowing terms. League membership grew by the thousands. Praise and donations poured in from around the globe. Americans were willing to sacrifice to protect their greatest living treasures. Here was hope. Yet, throughout the 1920s, League officials would, in the modern-day parlance of dubious publishing outlets, capture and kill this momentum.

To the industrialists who ran the League, the fantastic redwood forest on the Klamath River stood not as some arboreal "paradise" worthy of preservation but as bullion in a bank vault. It was exactly this dense inventory, the stands on the Klamath and in the other three northern units on Redington's list—each with average per-acre volumes far higher than almost anywhere along the South Fork Eel River—that American capitalists sought to preserve as a future source of industrial wealth.

On December 8, 1920, Newton B. Drury typed a memo to Merriam, who was now stationed at the Carnegie Institution in Washington, DC. Drury blithely informed Merriam that he had met with Mather to ameliorate the problem of Redington's report. Mather was in agreement with League objectives. Drury wrote, "When Mr. Mather was last here he decided that it was unnecessary for him to hold a public hearing [in Congress] on this subject at the present time. He was somewhat doubtful whether any action could be secured from the present Congress, and was not certain whether the recommendation of the survey should be embodied in a bill for congressional action during the present session." In other words, Congress should not codify Redington's strong recommendation that a Redwood National

Park be created on the Klamath River. Doing so would detract from the League's far more modest goals of creating an arboreal screen along the state highway.

Drury added, "All of this is of course strictly confidential until made public through official channels by the Secretary of the Interior." The interior secretary was now John Barton Payne, a nondescript attorney who replaced an ailing Lane to head the department during the last year of Woodrow Wilson's administration. At Interior, Mather was now the ultimate authority on national parks. Neither he nor Payne nor the League ever released Redington's report to the public, and Lea's bill died a pallid death.

Meanwhile, Drury's insistence on confidentiality appears to have remained in place at the League for decades. In the space of three brief sentences, Joseph Engbeck's 2018 book (which is dedicated to Drury) glances over the Redington report, doesn't quote from it, quickly discounts it, and misspells Redington's name. Engbeck's source was a 1972 oral history given by Newton Drury, where Redington's name is misspelled in the same way. The Redington report itself is not included in Engbeck's list of sources. It appears he never read it.

40

A T THE END OF A RAINY JANUARY IN 1921, THE NATIONAL ASSOCIA-
tion of Railroad Tie Producers met for its third annual convention at
William Crocker's Saint Francis Hotel in San Francisco. The tie convention,
which immediately followed the American Wood Preservers convention at
the hotel, would focus on developing standards for railroad ties. Paul Redington and his colleague at the US Forest Service, C. L. Hill, would give
talks on the need to conserve forests for future economic uses. Redington
warned that American industry was cutting trees "four times faster than
they're growing." The railroad reps mingled and parlayed with salesmen from
firms that sold redwood ties, many of which, even then, were hand-split by
small crews camped deep in riverside groves. However, by now mills were
also turning out ties, as they represented a dependable niche market. Four
million redwood ties were produced in 1921.

On January 29, the tie men joined a special junket on a private train ride
from Sausalito northward, through the spectacular Eel River canyon to the
working redwood tracts of Humboldt County. The *Timberman* reported that
the group of fifty railroad executives, some accompanied by wives and children, first stopped at the Pacific Lumber logging camp along Larabee Creek,
where "a splendid breakfast was served." After breakfast, PL's logging super-
intendents "took the party out in the woods to give them an idea of redwood
logging operations," after which the group moved along to "the two big sawmills" at Scotia. Pacific Lumber officials demonstrated "the various phases of
redwood production" and offered an opportunity "to see the virgin redwood
timber holdings" that would soon be leveled. The article noted that Otis
Johnson of the Union Lumber Company and W. R. McMillian of the Hammond Lumber Company had provided entertainment for the junket and that
"the 'Save the Redwoods League' [was] a host of champions."

Five weeks later, on March 1, 1921, Save the Redwoods League's Executive Committee held its first meeting of the year. At the time, redwood firms were enjoying a postwar boom in lumber sales that would continue through the decade. In 1919 redwood manufacturers milled just over 400 million board feet of product. In 1922 that number reached 557 million board feet. Historian H. Brett Melendy notes that, that year, "all the large mills were running to full capacity and huge quantities of lumber were being turned out." Most mills now ran double shifts, and timber companies were logging on ever-steeper slopes. By 1928 the Hammond Lumber Company had introduced rudimentary tractors to drag logs from hillside groves. Hammond and other companies, especially Pacific Lumber, would soon employ fleets of tractors, causing even greater scouring and compaction of hillsides. Companies also used tractors to create skid trails out of stream beds, rending delicate ecosystems with the force of industrial warfare. Subsequent winter torrents washed mountainsides of rock and slash into streams, filling once deep holes and further degrading salmon habitat.

With industrial redwood logging accelerating from south to north, toward the Klamath River, one would have thought that Paul Redington's report and Clarence Lea's proposed legislation would be hot items during the League's first meeting of 1921. Yet neither the agenda nor the minutes from that meeting contain even a hint of either. Instead, J. D. Grant was reelected as chairman, and the board agreed to pay Newton Drury $300 a month for half-time work. Drury noted that the Durant Aircraft Corporation had offered to "prepare an airplane photographic map of the Redwood region," but the board rejected the offer owing to "condition of the finances of the League." Such an aerial examination of the world's remaining redwood forest would have been unprecedented and manifestly useful, but the League already knew what it wanted, or didn't want. During the short meeting the small group focused on the last item on the agenda: the "situation along the South Fork of the Eel River," which was "explained by Mr. J. C. Sperry and Mr. Drury. . . . A minimum area which the League has decided to save was outlined."

The minutes do not identify the "minimum area" that the League had targeted for protection. League documents make clear, however, that emphasis was on the word "minimum." Susan Schrepfer notes, "Many exceptional stands—such as those of Redwood Creek and the Klamath River—were relegated to being logged. . . . The redwood parks . . . were envisioned as complementing an industrial society."

At the end of 1921, the League Executive Committee created a list of priorities for the coming year. It's a Kafkaesque document. The League's foremost objective would be to secure a "declaration of policy from Congress, as to the establishment of a Redwood National Park, including a provision for a survey by experts." After killing the possibility of not just a declaration but actual legislation from Congress for a Redwood National Park—and not just any redwood domain but likely the most stunning example of a forested river anywhere in the world—and burying the best possible redwood survey conducted by the most adept timber experts in the public sector, League officials would move forward as if operating from an alternate universe—which, in a way, they were.

Throughout the 1920s, the League continued to entice its members and the public with specious proposals for a large redwood park. Stated sizes ranged from twenty thousand acres, as noted in the League's 1924 Annual Report, to twelve thousand acres at Dyerville and along Bull Creek, which the League claimed as a primary objective in a 1926 form letter to members.

That year Drury also circulated a confidential report to League officials. Contradicting the findings of Redington, the nation's top forester, Drury told League councilors, "This Bull Creek–Dyerville area was selected after seven years of study by officials of the League because it was adjudged to be the outstanding example of typical primeval forest." Nonetheless, two years later, in a private note to Madison Grant that demonstrated the executive secretary's flexibility with facts, alongside the important objective of pacifying Grant, Drury wrote, "The Bull Creek timber is inferior in several respects to the timber in other areas that can be obtained at a much lower price."

In reviewing this incomprehensible thread of proposing, then sabotaging, then immediately again advocating for Redwood National Park legislation, I was reminded of something that Richard White wrote about why railroads may have pursued legislation. We will never know whether White's analysis is reflective of the League's subterfuge of 1920 and 1921 and several similar incidents that would occur in coming years. Yet White's conclusions are worth examining in this context.

"The goal of a public battle in Congress was not necessarily to get legislation passed," White wrote. One must "look beyond final votes . . . in Congress to understand how corporations played politics. The announced intent of a bill was not always its real purpose. . . . The goal, in short, was to produce information that could influence financial markets."

The people who controlled the League—Wigginton Creed, J. D. Grant, and especially William Crocker—enjoyed great power over western markets, which were the fastest growing in the nation and the world and wielded significant influence on Wall Street. The League's outward schizophrenia would appear to satisfy White's definition of inwardness. League actions during the 1920s undoubtedly influenced redwood investments and manipulated stock prices. Examined in sum, and as machinations in service of unstated objectives, the League's actions were not schizophrenic but rather exemplify the organization's overall objective, which was to solidify industry's control over redwood inventories and markets even in the face of growing public pressure to save the great trees.

Another important task of 1921 was the marginalization of Madison Grant, who was the driving force in creating the League in the first place. On August 26, 1918, Madison Grant wrote to his friend J. D. Grant that the "suggestion to organize the 'SAVE THE REDWOODS' LEAGUE . . . was actually started by Stephen T. Mather . . . Edward Bradley and myself in Washington, last winter and we put up the preliminary cash to carry it on, and appointed John C. Merriam secretary. Later on, Prof. [Henry Fairfield] Osborn was added to this group. It would appear that Merriam and Osborn had been doing some work during my absence but I have no doubt that I will be consulted before it will be put in proper shape."

Ed Bradley was Interior Secretary Franklin K. Lane's new assistant, hired in the spring of 1917. He also served as a director of the Federal Reserve Bank in San Francisco and as vice president and general manager of the Pacific Telephone and Telegraph Company, the giant western communications firm controlled by William Crocker, Frank Drum, and Bay Area steel pioneer Henry Scott. In 1917 Pacific Telephone notched an impressive net profit of $2.3 million. At the time, and over the coming decades, Pacific Telephone and other telephone and telegraph companies bought millions of feet of redwood for poles and for switching stations that dotted the terrain in twenty-mile intervals in all directions.

Madison Grant's concern that he would "be consulted" as the movement progressed is most instructive. Of all the glitterati associated with early League efforts, only Madison Grant expressed authentic interest in saving more than just a strip of redwoods along the highway and a small grove for camping. He had already proven himself politically and economically equipped to spearhead the preservation of hundreds of thousands of acres to protect iconic species. For this, rather than for the destructive force of his racist views, which were widely shared among his peers, Grant would find his exhortations widely ignored.

An obscure but telling representation of the effort is found buried in a letter to Stephen Mather from League manager, Executive Committee member, and Crocker proxy J. C. Sperry. Dated January 25, 1921, and sent to Mather in Washington, DC, the note reflects an ongoing conversation at the League about how to offer supporters "the exemption from income tax of donations to this League" in such a way that "it will not seem to promise too much." Sperry also wrote, "I do not think that it is necessary to bother Mr. Madison Grant with the matter as he is very busy and also a long way off."

It was an odd sentiment. In his many letters and telegrams—and in making personal appearances on the West Coast, traversing the continent and then the length of the redwood coast to strategize and attend grove dedications even as disease ravaged his body—Madison Grant insisted on being directly involved in all League activities, no matter how small. (In 1919 he would appear nearly obsessed with creating League letterhead.) In addition, Grant was a corporate attorney well versed in federal tax law and the formation and management of nonprofit organizations. Who else to bother with the question, aside from Wigginton Creed? Just a few months before, on August 31, 1920, Grant had sent a long letter to Newton Drury with his comments on Creed's proposed bylaws and articles of incorporation. He had thoroughly read the documents and provided expert input on a dozen legal points.

As for Grant being "very busy and a long way off," so were Stephen Mather and John Merriam, both in Washington, DC. Mather was running the National Park Service, and Merriam was very busy as the head of Carnegie

Institution. Yet Sperry and Drury exchanged letters with the League councilors, especially Merriam, almost daily.

Grant had been particularly excited about Redington's report and Lea's
legislation, and he let the League know it. On December 6, 1920, immediately after he'd read his copy of the report, Madison Grant wrote to J. D.
Grant, "As to the general Redwood situation in California, there are four
large sections, the Eel River Groves, south of Eureka, the Redwood Creek
Groves [including Prairie Creek], the Klamath River Groves and the Del
Norte Groves (Smith River), each and all of which are of vast importance.
Although we cannot discreetly say so publicly, it should be our ultimate aim
to save them all." Madison Grant sent a copy of the letter to Drury, adding,
"It is a mistake in my judgement to publicly abandon the effort to save any of
the groves."

It should be our ultimate aim to save them all. This from a man of great
wealth, rarified American heritage, and powerful connections who had
almost single-handedly saved the bison from extinction; who was instrumental in the creation of several national parks, including Glacier, Denali,
Olympic, and Everglades; and for whom the Alaskan porcupine caribou,
Rangifer tarandus granti, or Grant's caribou, is named. In part, the League's
early evolution into a grandiose but ineffectual coterie might be viewed as
a counterweight to the efforts and influence of Madison Grant, who had
kick-started the organization in late 1917. Now Grant was rallying behind
the Redington report to protect not hundreds, but hundreds of thousands, of
acres of virgin redwood.

Sperry also received Madison Grant's letter. He responded to Grant, "Just
how we can best accomplish this work is hard to say at this time. We agree
with you that we should not consent to the cutting of any Redwoods along
the South fork [of the Eel River]. As a practical proposition, however, I am
not sure that this will work out. . . . [I]f we have to allow some cutting to be
done . . . it is better that it should be done where it cannot be seen from the
Highway." Sperry does not mention the large and intact redwood ecosystems
north of the Eel River, as described by Redington and targeted for protection by Grant.

Correspondence between League officials and Madison Grant was semi-
regular during the 1920s, but Grant was never included in crucial decision
making. Instead, Newton Drury sought to consult with Grant "particularly

on the money-raising end," as Drury wrote to Grant in November 1925. Drury was also careful to forward to Grant the latest wisdom from American and foreign white supremacists.

"I am enclosing an article on the Nordic strain, which appeared in *Liberty*," Drury wrote in October 1927. In a follow-up, Drury wrote to Grant, "I believe you will be interested in reading the enclosed article, 'The Rising Tide of Color—Seven Years Later,' by Lothrop Stoddard, which appeared in the June 4th issue of *Liberty*." Stoddard was an American historian with a PhD from Harvard and a leading eugenicist, "the second most influential racist in the country" after Madison Grant, wrote Jonathan Spiro.

Grant was Stoddard's mentor. He wrote a long introduction to Stoddard's 1920 book, *The Rising Tide of Color*. Later Stoddard lauded the Nazi programs of sterilization and extermination, going so far as to travel to Germany in 1940 to meet with Nazi officials, including Adolf Hitler himself. That year Stoddard published a book, *Into the Darkness*, that quotes Hitler at length and praises the Third Reich: "Inside Germany, the Jewish problem is regarded as a passing phenomenon, already settled in principle and soon to be settled in fact by the physical elimination of the Jews themselves from the Third Reich."

On November 11, 1927, Grant responded to Drury, "Many thanks for sending me Stoddard's paper. As a matter of fact his prophesy about the decline of the power of the white world is remarkably accurate. The lowering of the influence of the superior races is of course a source of joy to inferior races and also to many of our so-called liberals. I hate to become bigoted, but as I grow older I find I have less and less use for radicals and sentimentalists."

41

THROUGHOUT 1921, MADISON GRANT MADE REDWOOD PROTECTION his top priority. His correspondences that year with Newton Drury, J. C. Sperry, and J. D. Grant, as well as with business leaders and policy makers who might aid redwood protection, were voluminous. Many of the letters referenced a new effort that year to influence legislation, only this time at the state level. In January a group of Humboldt County officials wrote a Redwood Preservation Bill that sought to provide $300,000 in state funding for redwood acquisitions, specifically targeting Pacific Lumber lands on the Eel River. The bill provided for redwood acquisition by condemnation if necessary. According to Susan Schrepfer, as the bill gained momentum, Save the Redwoods League stepped in. League officials took the matter straight to the timber industry.

"Drury . . . called a conference with the Pacific Lumber Company, the Eureka Chamber of Commerce, and the Sage Land and Improvement Company—a firm with large land holdings in Humboldt County," wrote Schrepfer. "Pacific Lumber . . . asked that the condemnation clause be restricted to lands in the southern portion of the county, thus excluding the holdings of Pacific Lumber." This was done, no matter that the redwood lands south of PL's holdings were sparsely forested compared with its own.

The timber companies endorsed the amended bill, as did the California Redwood Association, which represented redwood producers on the North Coast. The bill passed both houses of the state legislature, at which point the League "arranged to have the governor barraged with photographs, publications, and telegrams" in favor of the legislation, wrote Schrepfer. In June 1921 Governor William Stephens signed the bill, providing $300,000 for redwood acquisitions to be directed by the League. Two years later the League was instrumental in killing four additional bills that would have given the state the power of eminent domain to create parklands. Instead, the League sponsored scientific studies of the redwoods, hired a landscape architect to determine the best means of accommodating large numbers of visitors to the tiny redwood parklands (the number of cars traveling the Redwood highway was doubling every year), and brainstormed creation of a state parks commission that could take over both activities.

Madison Grant was the only person of authority at the League who saw the Redwood Preservation Bill as a first step toward a much broader system of condemnation and acquisition of redwood forests in Humboldt and Del Norte counties. He was also the only League official to address the yet unresolved issue of the land fraud that had placed the redwoods in private hands in the first place. A few days after Stephens signed the weakened bill, Grant wrote to John Merriam, "Now that we have our teeth into the Treasury we can bite hard on the Taxpayers, but someone should suffer for the reckless squander of public property in the past."

No such suffering would occur. At the League, Grant was alone in advocating for protection of large, intact redwood landscapes and for legal action to remedy unresolved land theft. He certainly saw the value of touting the redwoods as tourist draws to protecting them, but, he wrote in 1919, "all these are purely commercial considerations. It is scarcely necessary to dwell on the crime involved in the destruction of the oldest and tallest trees on earth."

Whereas League officials could generally be counted on to return Madison Grant's letters, J. D. Grant was not a faithful correspondent. Throughout 1921 he did not respond to Madison Grant's entreaty to save the majority of the ancient redwoods then standing, preferring instead to allow Drury and Sperry to manage Grant and keep him on the fringes of League activity. Yet, by the end of 1921, it was clear that such relative rubes could not possibly marginalize Madison Grant. Such a performance required the proven talents of J. D. Grant himself, alleged friend of Madison. On December 5, 1921, J. D. wrote an imperious and unusually long letter to Madison.

"In your last letter to me you state that you have received some very disturbing letters regarding the status of the movement to save the Redwoods," wrote J. D. (I have not found in the League archives Madison Grant's letter to J. D. or the "disturbing letters" he references.) "As a matter of fact . . . a crisis has arisen which we must recognize and meet." The "stupid" Congress, he said, had passed a new tax bill, the Revenue Act of 1921, that imposed "heavy handicaps on those with whom I have been associated in business enterprises . . . the capitalists." In doing so the government "gave way to a combination of stupidity, envy of accumulated wealth and a selfish farmers' block and enacted such an inequitable tax as to kill off the type of men who could and would always have so liberally subscribed to all big things." The new tax, J. D. warned, would dry up funding for Save the Redwoods League, "that reservoir of wealth which has aided most public causes of this sort, has endowed benificent [sic] institutions, and has tried to improve the condition of the world. . . . [It is] evident that other means to save these oldest of living things must be found. . . . Perhaps Congress or the State, should be again appealed to as representing all the people."

J. D.'s claims were deceitful. Madison Grant, a leading expert in finance, tax law, and conservation, would have read the note with incredulity. Madison Grant was well aware that League officials in San Francisco, rather than appealing to Congress, had quashed Clarence Lea's attempt to protect tens of thousands of acres of virgin redwood. In addition, J. D.'s claims about the tax law were obviously false. While the Revenue Act had modestly increased the corporate tax, from 10 to 12.5 percent, corporate profits were at an all-time high. In addition, according to the March 1922 issue of the *American Economic Review*, the Revenue Act had the "unlimited financial backing and moral support of the business interests of the nation"—a class that included J. D. as well as Madison Grant. The act also "repeals the federal excess-profits tax, the transportation taxes, some luxury and other taxes, [and] reduces slightly the maximum surtaxes upon individual incomes." Most importantly, the benefits of the act to nonprofit organizations such as the League were immense. According to the February 5, 1922, *New York Times*, "Allowances for deductions in Federal income tax returns for [charitable] contributions are more liberal under the revenue act of 1921 than under the revenue act of 1918." The new provision for charitable donations would immediately benefit the League.

Nonetheless, J. D. closed his letter in frustration.

"I am much against my will forced to the conclusion that I must now retire from all constructive activities and join my old co-workers on the golf links," writes J. D. "I am no longer of use to our League. For the League's best interests, [I] resign as chairman of the Executive Committee."

But J. D. Grant did not resign. He likely never intended to. He kept his chairmanship, and control of Save the Redwoods League, for the next nineteen years, Newton B. Drury loyally at his side. The letter was a con, and not even a good one. Why would J. D. assume that an astute Madison Grant would accept his obviously distorted claims? Whatever the case, J. D.'s offensive letter at once announced and formalized his, and the League's, exile of his old friend.

42

I N OCTOBER 1925, NEWTON DRURY PUBLISHED AN ESSAY IN THE *SPOKES-man*, a publication of the University of California. The piece put Drury's public relations genius on full display. It catered to Californians deeply concerned about redwood destruction. Drury writes, "In saving the redwoods and other forests and natural features, we are doing much more than preserving something majestic and beautiful for future generations to look and wonder at. We firmly believe that this is part of a great cause in which the very strength of civilization, as we now know it, is at stake."

An unedited draft of the same article invokes another "great cause" then dominating Save the Redwoods League priorities and does more to define the League's character than does the airy prose that found its way into print.

"We are realizing that a very large proportion of the Redwood belt must be utilized for commercial purposes," Drury wrote in the draft but excised from the final version. "A comparatively small percentage of the total stand will in any event be set aside as parks. . . . Recognizing the importance of the Redwood lumber industry to the State, the League has endeavored to appreciate and understand the problems of that industry and through co-operation and friendly negotiations to aid rather than hamper that industry's development." It was a confession.

J. D. Grant would echo the sentiment in *Redwoods and Reminiscences*. "The League was on a sound practical basis and pledged to attain its objectives in a businesslike way, respecting the lumber interest," wrote Grant. "Our League . . . proclaimed that the legitimate interests of the Redwood industry should be interfered with to the least possible extent."

By the end of 1929, Save the Redwoods League had brokered the acquisition or donation of 2,792 acres of redwood lands in Humboldt and Del Norte counties. The average price of the parcels was $160 per acre, which in most cases was at least double the land's true value. Nearly all of these scattered tracts were strung along the new state highway that now occupied the eastern bank of the South Fork Eel River. Owners of roadside timber were undoubtedly eager to sell. As Drury noted in September 1922 in a letter to Madison Grant, "The commercial bodies of the north Coast Counties have awakened to the importance of the Redwood highway from Sausalito to the Oregon line and I believe that it will be increasingly difficult for lumber companies to cut any of the trees on the highway."

Many of the riverside parcels secured by the League featured superb flats of redwoods, several of the trees nearly 20 feet in diameter and 350 feet tall. Yet much of the acquired land had already been logged or was lightly forested. One forty-acre tract was "mostly open prairie," according to the League. Eighty acres contained "5 acres of bottom land with heavy Redwoods." The League touted one eighty-acre acquisition simply for its "nice little camping spot." During the same decade the timber industry clear-cut and burned more than one hundred thousand acres of virgin redwood forest in Mendocino, Humboldt, and Del Norte counties.

I derived the figure of 2,792 acres by adding totals from a 1929 list of groves created by Newton Drury for League officers, now contained in the League archives. Nonetheless, League officials, particularly Drury, occasionally fudged the numbers. In October 1924 Drury was forced to write a letter of apology to A. E. Demaray, an assistant director of the National Park Service in charge of finance, correcting a figure he'd provided of sixty-eight hundred acres supposedly preserved in what was then called the California State Redwood Park, along the South Fork Eel River. Drury had nearly tripled the actual figure.

"Perhaps the statement we made regarding the California State Redwood Park might be somewhat misleading," wrote Drury. "Of these [acres] the original 2500 acres contained the bulk of the Redwood timber." Yet even in this landscape "there are 1300 acres . . . which are partially cut over and then there is a considerable amount of brush land surrounding it."

The finest and most pristine acquisition made by the League during the 1920s was the 1923 donation, by Zipporah Russ, of 166 acres on Prairie Creek, the northern tributary of Redwood Creek. A county road bisected the grove and would soon become the new state highway to Oregon. At the time, neither Prairie Creek nor the stream it fed, Redwood Creek, had seen

any logging. Zipporah Russ made the donation on behalf of her late husband, Joseph Russ, and the region's "early settlers." The quarter section contained a magnificent 30-acre flat of gargantuan redwoods at the confluence
of Brown Creek, in the northern, upstream reach of Prairie Creek. Did the
donation indicate some sort of familial guilt for Joseph Russ's role in stealing more than 100,000 acres of ancient redwood from the public domain?
In *Who Saved the Redwoods?* Laura and James Wasserman write that Russ's
"gift of a large redwood grove helped polish her husband's name for poster-
ity. The public and the Save the Redwoods League asserted the rule of po-
liteness. Not a word of the Russ legal issues appeared in newspaper accounts
or speeches related to the Humboldt Pioneer Redwood Grove."

On July 10, 1923, in an awkward, if not tone-deaf, missive, Newton B.
Drury sent a two-thousand-word letter to Paul Redington in response to a
request by Redington for a list of the redwood tracts then being prioritized
by the League for acquisition. Redington had gotten the memo: the forester
was now placing himself in League hands. With some of the nation's most
powerful industrialists and government officials running the League or operating in complete deference to it, there was no other place to turn to save
redwoods. The League now had a monopoly on redwood protection.

Drury writes as if Redington possessed little knowledge of redwood issues. "The Save the Redwoods League is eager to furnish whatever facts are
desired in order to help in the preserving of Redwood Tracts," wrote Drury.
He informed Redington that the League sought protection for "the timber
between Dyerville and the Scotia bridge on the California State Highway."
He noted that the League was beginning to formulate plans to create a similar beauty strip of great trees along Prairie Creek, adding to the Russ grove
and lining the newly opened state highway that connected Eureka to the
Klamath River.

Such pittances frustrated Madison Grant. Nine days after Drury wrote
to Redington, Grant wrote to Drury, "In reading over the various proposi-
tions . . . I can only emphasize, as I have done often before, the importance
of a very comprehensive scheme for preserving a maximum amount of redwood timber because anything that we do not include in the area which we
believe should be saved will be promptly butchered by the owners."

Not until 1928 could the League honestly claim it was on the road toward purchase of a large, single expanse of redwood habitat. The year marked two important, coalescing events.

The first was the overwhelming two-to-one passage of a $6 million state bond act dedicated to acquisition of lands for state parks. The act required that public monies for acquisition be matched by private funding. Clearly the people of California were willing to tax themselves to ensure access to and protection of the state's unique and picturesque landscapes as the natural world around them diminished by the day. Save the Redwoods League was a principal proponent of the initiative and was uniquely situated to take advantage of the bond. By September 1927, the League had generated $1.1 million in funding for future redwood acquisition, including $1 million from John D. Rockefeller Jr., heir to the oil fortune, and a $50,000 gift from New York oil magnate Edward S. Harkness. In his 1972 oral history, Newton Drury noted, "Mr. Rockefeller had given us a million dollars" as early as 1924, at which point the money "was deposited in the Crocker National Bank in San Francisco."

Madison Grant had secured the Rockefeller donation. Grant was a close friend of Rockefeller's personal attorney, Raymond Fosdick. The Rockefellers, Sr. and Jr., also shared Grant's zeal for eugenics. Edwin Black notes that the Rockefellers and the Rockefeller Foundation funneled hundreds of thousands of dollars into eugenics research in the United States and Germany for nearly three decades, until 1939.

In December 1923, Madison Grant met with Fosdick in New York, after which Rockefeller agreed to the donation. Grant continued to communicate with Fosdick through the 1920s, until 1929, when Fosdick notified Grant that Rockefeller would donate another $1 million—money that also would circulate through Crocker Bank.

Throughout the 1920s, according to *Walker's Manual of California Securities*, Crocker Bank's annual cash balances fluctuated between $4 million and $11 million. Large donations to Save the Redwoods League represented a significant percentage of Crocker's cash on hand and augmented the bank's ability to leverage new holdings and investments. This was especially true for the 1924 Rockefeller contribution of $1 million, which would fatten the bank's bottom line for seven years.

The second coalescing event of 1928 was a sudden drop in redwood lumber orders. The downturn signaled to the timber companies and investors that something was amiss. The year might be compared with events of 2006, when an 11 percent decline in home sales and a 28 percent drop in new housing permits foreshadowed the subprime mortgage crisis that most people wouldn't notice until the following year.

"By 1928 the redwood operators definitely knew that something was wrong with the world's economic picture," writes H. Brett Melendy. "In May, the mills were forced to curtail their operations. . . . By the end of 1929 and early 1930, the market for redwood lumber had thoroughly collapsed." By 1931 nearly two dozen redwood mills had shuttered in Del Norte, Humboldt, and Mendocino counties, leaving only four mills operating in Humboldt County (Dolbeer & Carson, Hammond, Pacific Lumber, and Northern Redwood Lumber Company; Northern Redwood would cease operations in 1933), one in Mendocino (Union Lumber Company), and none in Del Norte. Many owners of redwood tracts were brokers and speculators who borrowed on the groves to finance other ventures, then sold the timber at a profit when mills needed new inventories. Tanking production sent redwood investments into a tailspin.

In addition, mill owners large and small, especially Pacific Lumber, were very much in debt. The firm's "very expensive plant," as noted by Redington, was heavily leveraged. In 1913 Pacific Lumber floated a heavy mortgage with the Continental Trust & Savings Bank in Chicago and the Michigan Trust Company. Pacific Lumber obtained the mortgage after the banner production year of 1912, during which, according to *American Lumberman*, the company milled more than one hundred million board feet of product, "the largest [output] ever produced by any single redwood lumber manufacturing concern." The new PL mortgage was backed by "45,584 acres of timber, sawmills, and equipment for collateral," writes Melendy. Fifteen years later the debt had hardly diminished.

Bankruptcy loomed even for the largest producers. In 1931 Hammond and the Little River Redwood Company merged to avoid the wrecking of both operations. The two firms consolidated by closing the Little River mill at Crannell and laying off hundreds of workers. A few years later Hammond took control of both companies.

By dint of economic free fall, the newly approved state bond measure, and Rockefeller's millions, Save the Redwoods League could now make good on its promise to preserve the great flat of redwoods still standing alongside Bull Creek. "During the Depression, the economic crisis opened up a buyer's market," historian Jared Farmer writes in *Trees in Paradise*. Farmer notes that, prior to the Depression, the League's objective was "to create a wooded parkway." Executives at Pacific Lumber were undoubtedly ecstatic. By then the company was cratering, and creditors were knocking. Had the League not stepped in to rescue Pacific Lumber, the company likely would have declared bankruptcy.

By 1930 Pacific Lumber had clear-cut more than twenty-five thousand acres along the Eel River south of Scotia, including most of the great redwood flat along the river, and four miles up Larabee Creek. The clear-cuts ran from ridge to ridge and included the entire twenty-square-mile expanse of the river's northeastern slope and about one-third of the fifteen-thousand-acre stand that coated the southwestern reach of the river. In 1919, when Madison Grant had written his first major essay demanding redwood protection, the southwestern flats and slopes of the Eel River remained pristine. That year Grant wrote that on this "left bank there is a magnificent stand of trees extending from the water's edge to the crest of the main slope. . . . It should be preserved." It was not.

By April 1931, the League, Pacific Lumber, and the California State Park Commission (then controlled by League councilors William Colby, Arthur Connick, and Los Angeles corporate attorney Henry O'Melveny) had hammered out a purchase agreement. Total cost was $3.2 million for nine thousand acres of contiguous, uncut redwood land in the Bull Creek watershed, including most of the small, steep redwood drainages of Cabin Creek and Decker Creek, as well as Dyerville Flat. Rockefeller contributed $2 million, and the state paid the rest. The grove would now be called Rockefeller Forest, which John Jr. later said was named for his mother. The cash not only allowed Pacific Lumber to dodge bankruptcy but contributed to the company's 1940 purchase of the twenty-two-thousand-acre Yager-Lawrence Creek forest from the Dessert Redwood Company (a Wisconsin timber holding firm), the Hicks-Vaughan Redwood Company (a Michigan timber holding firm), and the Hammond Redwood Company.

The virgin redwood expanse in Yager Creek was more than twice the size of that acquired by the League and the state at Bull Creek. With the exception of the combined eight hundred acres of alluvial forest at Bull Creek and Dyerville, the Yager stand also contained far higher volumes of redwood timber per acre. In November 1940 the *Sacramento Bee* announced that Pacific Lumber was "already [building] more than four miles of new railroad" into the heart of majestic Yager Creek. Thirty-six years later, the Environmental Protection Information Center and Earth First! would attempt to save the last uncut remnants of this forest.

The price of $357 per acre for the Bull Creek tract would have been extraordinarily high even during the banner year of 1927, when redwood producers milled 569 million board feet of lumber and standing redwood was in high demand and sold at peak prices. In 1931, when redwood mills turned out just 210 million board feet—and just before the well-anticipated lumber apocalypse of 1932, when production dropped to 135 million board feet, the lowest volume in four decades—the price was at least four times greater than the timber's true market value. As part of the deal, Pacific Lumber agreed to provide the commission with one year's notice before logging any tracts along three miles of the state highway north of Dyerville, so that Save the Redwoods League could complete its Avenue of the Giants beauty strip. The provision amounted to an allowance for Pacific Lumber to ransom the roadside groves—now seen and tramped by tens of thousands of tourists, whose presence amounted to a de facto prohibition on logging the tall trees—whenever the company needed cash.

The League's 1931 annual report to members hailed the Bull Creek acquisition. Commendations were also ladled for the many individuals and organizations who contributed to the effort. A paragraph dedicated to League officials lists William Crocker, John Merriam, J. D. Grant, Robert G. Sproul (League councilor and president of the University of California), League councilor Duncan McDuffie, J. C. Sperry, and Newton Drury. The name Madison Grant appears nowhere in the lengthy brochure.

43

THE DEPRESSION CREATED A BUYER'S MARKET IN THE REDWOODS. IT also solidified Save the Redwoods League's position as the nation's sole conservation broker of redwood properties. Between 1930 and 1933, the League and the state acquired 2,816 acres of redwood north of the Klamath River for Del Norte Coast Redwoods State Park. The price was $400,000, or $142 an acre. The bulk of the land, nineteen hundred acres, had belonged to the foundering Hobbs, Wall & Co. and was acquired during 1930 and 1931. The trees were relatively small, and some of the acreage had been logged. The forest ran from the top of a high ridge along a sheer slope to the Pacific, and a strip of redwoods lined the state highway for five miles. From the ridgetop a steep and wonderful trail plummeted toward Damnation Creek to a lovely small beach secreted along an exceptionally wild ten-mile reach of the California coast.

A more consequential Depression-era acquisition occurred to the south, at Prairie Creek, the Redwood Creek tributary. In his 1920 report, Paul Redington had recommended the entire thirty-five-thousand-acre Prairie Creek watershed "as second choice for [National] Park purposes." A county road—soon the state highway—already bisected the stand, which, Redington said, was "undoubtedly a beautiful body of timber and . . . fairly typical of both the slope and the bottom types."

To its members, Save the Redwoods League consistently claimed that it was dedicated to preserving a large redwood stand at Prairie Creek. Internally, the messaging was much different. In 1926 Newton Drury prepared a report for League councilors that identified the Prairie Creek project as "a *strip* about 15 miles long. . . . [A]pproximately 3000 acres will be included in this park, which will extend far enough back from the Highway to keep the *beauty* of the primitive forest unimpaired" (emphasis added). Drury had attached a map that depicted, in pink, the long, narrow polygon that would encompass the highway, running between an eighth- and a quarter-mile wide. That year the League envisioned paying timber companies—in this case Hammond and Sage, which owned the bulk of the redwood along the road—$1.8 million, or an astounding $600 per acre, to screen the tens of thousands of acres of logging that would soon ravage Prairie Creek and, over the ridge to the east, the Klamath River.

Three years later the county of Humboldt purchased from Albert D. Roberts, a federal court clerk in Eureka, 160 acres of heavy redwood timber along Prairie Creek. The tract was bisected by the highway and cost $40,000, or $250 an acre. The Roberts property and the Russ grove, which was a half mile south, now protected 360 acres of ancient redwood forest along Prairie Creek.

In 1930, with Wall Street crumbling around them, William Crocker met in New York with Edward Harkness. As a philanthropist, Harkness, like John D. Rockefeller Jr., was earnest and generous. Harkness had inherited untold millions from his father, Stephen V. Harkness, a founder, along with John D. Rockefeller Sr., of Standard Oil and a lifelong director of the company. Harkness told Crocker he was interested in protecting redwoods. A short time later Harkness donated $500,000 toward the $1 million purchase of just under six thousand acres at Prairie Creek, an acquisition completed in 1932.

At the end of 1931, Save the Redwoods League received yet another offer it seemingly couldn't refuse. On December 8, Harold Lee Ward, representing extensive redwood tracts owned by his family on the Klamath River, wrote to the League to proclaim the family a willing seller of its entire holding on the river, including the spectacular lowermost three miles of Blue Creek. As a first installment, Ward offered to donate nine thousand acres of redwood, then sell another seventeen thousand acres "at bargain prices." At the time, the Ward family owned only eleven thousand acres along the river, so Harold Ward was likely also representing the bulk of nineteen thousand acres of redwood owned by the W. J. Hotchkiss Redwood Company, most of it adjacent to the Ward lands and found along four small Klamath tributaries north of the river's mouth. In 1931 Hotchkiss defaulted on a $1 million bond, held by Dean Witter, that was backed by the property.

Eight of the ten full-page photos featured with Madison Grant's *National Geographic* article—which ran in June 1920, five months before Redington issued his report—depict the Ward redwoods on the Klamath. In one photo, taken from a ridgetop, the wide Klamath wends through a luxurious stand of redwoods. The caption reads, "The trees shown in this illustration represent more than one billion board feet of lumber—an irresistible temptation to commerce if title to the forest is not obtained by the National Government as a reservation."

Eleven years later the great Klamath redwood forest was still intact. Ward was offering the League another outstanding opportunity to create a Redwood National Park by acquiring the holding that Redington had identified as most suitable for such a preserve. Nine thousand acres of redwood would immediately become a park, at no cost to the League or the state, thereby all but guaranteeing public support for completing the acquisition from Hotchkiss, at which point an additional seventeen thousand acres could be got on the cheap. But "the project was too big and too expensive," writes Engbeck. Neither claim was true. "Other possibilities had to be given priority."

In 1933, in a lengthy brochure that the League sent to its members, Drury listed among the organization's "other priorities" the importance of supporting the production of redwood products.

"The League recognizes the necessity of a 'balanced program,' whereby a large proportion of the Redwood forests must be devoted to economic uses," said the brochure. It went on, perhaps with unintended truthfulness, "The lumber industry has worked in harmony with the League's objectives since the beginning. Much support has come from lumbermen." The pronouncement was placed in a long caption to a photograph that described "a fallen giant" in Mendocino County. Five men stand atop an eighteen-foot-diameter redwood, now horizontal, that the caption noted would "be used in the construction of the Golden Gate Bridge, in San Francisco." Millions of board feet of redwood went into building the "unbuildable" bridge, much of it to construct scaffolding and catwalks. Two of the catwalks enabled construction of the pair of giant steel cables that would provide the bridge its famous suspension. Each catwalk was fourteen feet wide and 1.5 miles long.

Another Depression-era opportunity arose in 1935. That year Crocker National Bank foreclosed on twelve thousand acres of densely forested redwood land in Mendocino County. The property was owned by the foundering Mendocino Redwood Company, a subsidiary of the Union Lumber Company, whose San Francisco headquarters was in the Crocker Building. William Crocker's bank held a $72,000 note against the virgin redwood tract, which encompassed nearly all of Usal Creek, in what is now the Sinkyone Wilderness. The entire redwood forest of Usal Creek remained intact, from headwaters to mouth—one of the largest complete-watershed stands of ancient redwood left in Mendocino County. While narrow, Usal Creek held large redwoods throughout the watershed, including on the slopes and ridgetops. Several small, streamside flats lined the creek in a fashion "typical" of the redwood domain, as the League would say. Shortly after foreclosing, Crocker Bank paid another $13,000 and took title to the entire Usal forest.

It was a watershed moment. The bank owned by William H. Crocker— one of the country's wealthiest and most powerful individuals and a founding, if not controlling, member of Save the Redwoods League—had just purchased one of the last great coastal stands of ancient redwood remaining in Mendocino County, for the near giveaway price of just $7 an acre. At the time a mere fifty-two acres of old-growth redwood had been preserved in the county. Certainly now Mendocino County would finally get its large redwood park.

It was not to be. Crocker made no effort to protect the forest, and it remained a bank holding when he died on September 25, 1937. Five years later the bank sold the acreage to the Sage Land and Improvement Company. In 1956 the "Usal tract," as the property became known, sold to the Simpson Timber Company, along with the entirety of the Sage Company's remaining seventy thousand acres in Humboldt and Mendocino counties. That year Simpson also bought out the Northern Redwood Lumber Company, on the Mad River. Within months company choppers would level one of the largest trees left on the Mad River, a twenty-foot-diameter redwood that grew along the river's north fork. The Usal property was partially logged, then sold to the Georgia-Pacific Corporation, which cut the rest before selling the property to the state.

William Crocker's philanthropic priorities resided elsewhere. For instance, in 1932 Robert Gordon Sproul approached Crocker for a donation on behalf of Ernest Orlando Lawrence, a nuclear physicist engaged in building ever-larger cyclotrons at the University of California. Lawrence, previously a professor at Yale, arrived at the UC in 1928, at the age of twenty-seven. Although Sproul had recently retired after two decades as president of the University of California, he remained engaged. Sproul and Crocker were friends as well as League councilors. They were also fellow Bohemians. Sproul, whose camp was Pleasant Isle of Aves, had sponsored Lawrence's membership in the club.

In 1932 Sproul approached Crocker about funding a bigger, more impactful cyclotron at the college, for "medical research." Crocker had served as a UC regent since 1908, and he was president of the Board of Regents from 1926 until he died in 1937. Crocker asked Sproul how much was needed for a new cyclotron.

In his foreword to David Ryder's biography of Crocker, Sproul writes, "I told Mr. Crocker I believed $75,000 would cover it, and thirty minutes later I was back on the ferryboat . . . with his check for that amount in my pocket." Today that $75,000 would be worth $1.5 million. The name of the cyclotron facility was quickly changed to the William H. Crocker Radiation Laboratory. (The Usal tract remained the Usal tract.)

Lawrence kept working, eventually creating a product that Crocker could be proud of. On September 15, 1942, the Uranium Committee (codenamed "S-1") of the US Office of Scientific Research and Development met at Bernard Maybeck's well-secured Bohemian Grove clubhouse. Lawrence was a member of the committee, alongside five other scientists, including including physicist J. Robert Oppenheimer; Eger V. Murphree, a chemical engineer with the Standard Oil Company; chemist James B. Conant, at the time the president of Harvard University and formerly a developer of poison gases for the US Army during the First World War; and Harold C. Urey, who earned his chemistry PhD at Berkeley and in 1934 won the Nobel Prize for chemistry. During their meeting the Uranium Committee launched the Manhattan Project and its progeny, the world's first nuclear weapons.

44

THE LAST MAJOR REDWOOD ACQUISITION OF THE DEPRESSION ERA OCcurred in 1939, when Save the Redwoods League and the state purchased a tract at the confluence of Mill Creek and the Smith River, in Del Norte County. By now the forest was renowned. Virtually all of the twenty-thousand-acre Mill Creek watershed was coated in dense groves of superlative redwoods. The stream ran from south to north, parallel to and just a few miles inland from the coast. At the confluence, the Smith River ran a dazzling turquoise green, clear as glass to depths of thirty feet. The floor of the dark redwood expanse of Mill Creek was perennially wet, evergreen in ferns and oxalis and sending forth densely clustered redwoods, many wider than twenty feet across.

The League's first opportunity to preserve the Mill Creek forest occurred in 1930. That year the Del Norte Lumber Company offered to sell to Save the Redwoods League the entirety of its 18,380-acre redwood holding on Mill Creek for $2.75 million, or $149 an acre. The company was so destitute that it had recently dismantled and sold its mill and even its railroad. Throughout the previous decade the League claimed to be devising means of protecting the redwoods of Mill Creek. The offer from Del Norte Lumber was a gift. Just five years before, in 1925, the League's thirty-eight-page annual report listed two priorities: "(1) The preservation of the scenic beauty of the famous Redwood Highway by saving timber along it clear to the northern limit of the redwood belt near the Oregon line; (2) the establishment of a large redwood national park of at least 20,000 acres." By 1926 the League had identified three thousand acres worthy of preservation at Mill Creek, with an estimated cost of $2 million. Yet the League rejected the offer from Del Norte Lumber. In 1932 Del Norte Lumber reduced the price by nearly 80 percent, to $1 million, or $54 per acre—just 15 percent of what the League and the state, the previous year, had paid Pacific Lumber for the more sparsely forested tract along the Eel River, which was also half the size of the Mill Creek forest. The League rejected the second offer as well.

In 1937 the US National Park Service, now headed by Nebraskan Arno B. Cammerer, recommended that the federal government purchase eighteen thousand acres of redwood along Mill Creek from the Del Norte Lumber Company for a national park. Rather than rejoice over the new federal effort to save the redwoods of Mill Creek, officials at Save the Redwoods League voted to oppose the measure. On March 22, 1938, the League's Executive Committee passed a resolution stating that "consideration of the acquisition of these lands for either a National Forest or a National Park be deferred; and that the government agencies concerned be informed of this action." Instead, "Save the Redwoods League feels that full opportunity should be given the State to include the Mill Creek Redwoods in the system of State Redwood parks." Once he was so "informed," Cammerer was pliable, which is not surprising. In 1923 Cammerer declared that the choice of location for a Redwood National Park should be "largely governed by the recommendations of the 'Save the Redwoods League.'" Cammerer was then echoing Stephen Mather's doctrine at National Parks, a deference to the League that had led Mather to kill Clarence Lea's Redwood National Park bill and bury Paul Redington's report. In 1938, once again deferring to the League, the National Park Service dropped its Mill Creek proposal. In 1939 Cammerer became a councilor of Save the Redwoods League.

By then the League had been advocating for creation of a Redwood National Park for two decades—an objective so compelling that it was included in the League's original articles of incorporation. Why would the organization now object to a viable federal proposal to purchase a tract of forest that, as early as the mid-1920s, the League had consistently identified as a top priority for preservation? The League's opposition to a Redwood National Park on Mill Creekmade no sense.

A deeper look dissolves the apparent incongruities. By 1937, the $6 million raised by the state for park purchases, through a 1927 bond act, had been largely depleted. The state would need to find another means of purchasing parklands. That year the League was among the leading advocates for passage of what would become known as the State Lands Act, a provision of which would allow petroleum companies to drill on state-owned coastal tidelands. The state would charge oil companies a relatively small royalty—less than 20 percent of revenues—half of which would be allocated to purchase more land for state parks. The California State Park Commission was a near subsidiary of Save the Redwoods League—Newton Drury was the commission's "investigating officer for acquisitions." The commission also backed the bill, no matter that State Senator Culbert L. Olson was insisting that the measure "would enrich the Standard Oil company and its affiliates at the expense of one of the state's greatest natural resources." One of those affiliates was the General Petroleum Corporation, whose former director, League chairman J. D. Grant, was now a major shareholder of Standard Oil.

On March 24, 1938, two days after the League rejected attempts by the feds to purchase Mill Creek for a Redwood National Park, California governor Frank Merriam—elected in 1934 in a narrow defeat of Upton Sinclair—signed the State Lands Act of 1938. League officials had successfully enriched oil companies at taxpayers' expense and preserved timber inventories for future use by industry.

Late in 1938 the Del Norte Lumber Company again tried to sell its entire Mill Creek holding for a national park, this time directly to the US Interior Department. On November 10, 1938, Newton Drury recommended that League directors oppose the measure, which they did once more. Interior never pursued the opportunity. Six months later the League received $225,000 in state oil royalties resulting from the State Lands Act, which it would match with private contributions to purchase redwoods. On July 15, 1939, Drury announced that the League would pay Pacific Lumber an extraordinary $217,000 for four hundred acres of redwood standing along the beauty strip in Humboldt County, now called Avenue of the Giants. The price of $542 per acre was the highest ever paid, by anyone at any time, for a Humboldt County redwood tract, and it was at least three times the land's Depression-era value. When Newton B. Drury wrote that the League's objective was to "aid rather than hamper [the timber] industry's development," he clearly meant it. The League had been created by, and existed to serve, industry—including as a brokerage that would provide timber companies with overly generous cash outlays of taxpayer money.

Four months later, and by sheer luck, the League was able to apply surplus funds from its oil money to acquire sixty-four hundred acres of redwood on Mill Creek. The acreage encompassed the lower third of the watershed and included its confluence with the Smith River. Even the League couldn't pass up this deal. The land was practically free. The price of $80,000—$12.50 an acre—was the amount that the Del Norte Lumber Company owed the county in back taxes. For that the League and the state set aside one of the densest stands of trees on the planet.

Mill Creek was the League's last major purchase of ancient redwood. From then on, with the exception of a few donations of small parcels, most acquisitions would involve tiny old-growth groves obtained at inflated prices or, more often, swaths of cutover land also bought at inflated prices. In this fashion, as a brokerage that bought up ravaged lands, the League provided lumber firms with the ability to liquidate their timber inventories without suffering public scorn or immediate economic consequences—though local communities and watersheds would be consistently, and predictably, gutted.

As expected, the onset of World War II recharged the American economy after the doldrums of the 1930s. In 2001, historian Doris Kearns Goodwin wrote in *The American Prospect*, "America's response to World War II was the most extraordinary mobilization of an idle economy in the history of the world. During the war 17 million new civilian jobs were created, industrial productivity increased by 96 percent, and corporate profits after taxes doubled."

The war dividend increased redwood lumber production from 344 million board feet in 1939 to 455 million feet in 1941. That figure remained almost static throughout the war, dropped to 243 million board feet during the postwar economic dip and labor unrest of 1946, then immediately surged to unprecedented heights. In 1948 redwood manufacturers turned out 800 million board feet of lumber. Two years later they reached the seemingly impossible, devastating milestone of 1 billion board feet produced in a single year.

By the mid-1940s, many of the dense streamside groves of great trees growing on alluvial flats had been leveled. Cutting now occurred largely along hillside stands, where a volume of two hundred thousand board feet per acre was considered excellent. An annual volume of one billion board feet in 1950 would have required cutting nearly twice the acreage of three decades before. Every two years during the 1950s and 1960s, redwood companies would level an expanse of ancient redwood—approximately forty-five thousand acres—equivalent to the acreage protected in state parks.

After the war, developers discovered that Douglas fir made sturdy and widely available lumber well suited for developing the suburbs that were then metastasizing across the nation—the greatest housing boom in human history. Fir forests, once largely overlooked in the redwood range, were now rapidly exploited.

By 1952 nearly four hundred mills operated in Humboldt, Del Norte, and Mendocino counties, some of them running 24/7 and "establishing a record [of production] never before dreamed of in all the history of American lumber manufacture," the *Humboldt Times* reported that year. "We have billions of feet of Douglas fir which we are just beginning to tap."

Smoke from the burning of mill waste was interminable and choked residents of dozens of small towns and cities along the Coast Range who otherwise would have enjoyed the world's best air quality. In 1951, Del Norte County, once Humboldt's sleepy step-sibling in the redwood trade, saw lumber production jump to two hundred million board feet of redwood and Douglas fir. "There were five lumber mills in the county in 1945, 15 in 1946, 26 in 1947, 31 in 1950 and close to 50 mills now in 1952," reported the *Humboldt Times*.

Once an idyllic wonderland of forest, rivers, mountains, and sea, nearly the whole of Northern California was being overrun by loggers, tractors, roads, and clear-cuts. Worlds of fragile, complex, and irreplaceable biotic life were now rapidly disappearing under the weight of human consumption.

In 1940 Newton Drury left Save the Redwoods League to become director of the US National Park Service, where he would remain until 1951. Drury maintained a direct line to League leadership. His brother and public relations partner, Aubrey Drury, took over Newton's job. Yet, even while head of the Park Service, Newton Drury never attempted to establish a Redwood National Park. Drury's legacy at National Parks instead reinforced his career-long reluctance to add lands to the national park system.

League letterhead still listed Newton Drury as its "secretary," who was "on leave." Aubrey Drury's title was "administrative secretary." In 1942, following the death that year of J. D. Grant, Duncan McDuffie became chairman of the board. McDuffie had been one of Wigginton Creed's closest friends and fraternity brothers at the University of California. He was also among the Bay Area's biggest housing developers during the first half of the twentieth century. McDuffie's companies developed several luxury subdivisions in the East Bay Area and in San Francisco, consuming millions of board feet of redwood lumber. McDuffie partnered with Creed, Louis Titus, and a wealthy developer named John Hopkins Spring at the North Berkeley Land Company and the Berkeley Development Company. McDuffie was also president of the Mason-McDuffie Company, the Westgate Park Company, the Garden Homes Company, and the St. Francis Home Building Company.

To ensure that his refined and elegant subdivisions housed only the correct demographic, McDuffie invented racist "red line" municipal codes that served to exclude nonwhite homeowners from purchasing homes or living in his developments. The codes would serve as templates for racist developers throughout the country.

After the death of John Merriam, in 1945, McDuffie was elected president of Save the Redwoods League. Longtime League councilor Arthur Connick became the League's vice president. Connick was born in Humboldt County, where he'd served as president of the First National Bank of Eureka, an institution founded by A. B. Hammond. He had also served as secretary of the giant Zipporah Russ & Sons land company. Robert Sproul became treasurer. After nearly three decades of operation, League leadership remained remarkably constant. (Connick would become president of the League in 1951.)

Aubrey Drury was an adept fund-raiser and a freewheeling public relations hack. Under Drury and McDuffie, the League consistently, and almost exclusively, touted to its members and the media the importance of completing the Avenue of the Giants project and protecting the remaining twelve thousand acres of redwood in Mill Creek. For decades the League would project these forests as their "highest priority." Aubrey Drury's annual letter to members, mailed at the beginning of 1942, was typical of League talking points at the time.

"A substantial start has been made on the preservation of 'The Avenue of the Giants,' and the Mill Creek Redwoods State Park will be rounded out with the addition of successive units over a number of years," wrote Drury. Included with the letter was a ten-year-old reprint of a *Saturday Evening Post* editorial that praised the League. The League's more recent rejections of several opportunities to save the entire Mill Creek tract went unmentioned.

In 1940 League membership stood at five thousand individuals. Seven years later it had doubled. Typical results of the Drury PR muscle included a May 1942 editorial in the *Santa Rosa Press Democrat*, which made "a strong plea for preservation of the . . . ancient forest called Avenue of the Giants." That year the *Los Angeles Times* ran a similar editorial, urging readers to "heed the renewed warnings of the Save-the-Redwoods League that two of the noblest, most accessible and most cherished Northern California forests of coastal tree giants—the 'Avenue of the Giants,' in Humboldt County and the Mill Creek Grove in Del Norte County—are threatened with destruction by lumbering interests." Exactly one year later, as if observing an annual rite, the *Times* reiterated "the importance of rescuing the famous Avenue of the Giants before it is too late."

In 1948 the *San Francisco Examiner*, still controlled by William Randolph Hearst, reported that "still to be saved" by the League was more of the "Avenue of the Giants forest," as well as "the remaining units of the Smith River Mill Creek redwoods." Apparently parroting the same League press release, that year the *Press Democrat* also provided readers with the reminder that "still without protection are the Avenue of Giants . . . and the remaining trees in the Smith River–Mill Creek forest." The continuous dangling of these forests as objects to be saved allowed Save the Redwoods League to become one of the world's best-funded environmental organizations. Simultaneously, League efforts convinced the public, despite all evidence, that redwood protection was in good hands—even while more than twenty thousand acres of virgin redwood fell every year.

45

D URING THE SUMMER OF 2021, THE CALIFORNIA STATE PARK SERVICE removed a memorial that had been placed in honor of Madison Grant at the entrance to Prairie Creek Redwoods State Park. In 1948, Save the Redwoods League had created the memorial in response to a gift of $61,000 raised by Grant's brother, DeForest Grant. The donation allowed DeForest Grant to name sixteen hundred acres of prairie and redwoods that were already protected at Prairie Creek and to install a plaque affixed to a ten-ton boulder alongside the lush grassland. The plaque read, "Madison Grant Forest and Elk Refuge Dedicated to the Memory of Madison Grant, 1865–1937. Conservationist. Author. Anthropologist. A Founder of the Save-the-Redwoods League." The plaque noted that the dedication was owed to the generosity of DeForest Grant, John D. Rockefeller Jr., and Archer M. Huntington, son of Collis and Arabella Huntington.

In taking down the memorial plaque, the Park Service was responding to a request by University of California, Santa Barbara, historians Paul Spickard and David McIntosh, who represented more than two hundred scholars and historians who'd signed a letter to State Parks seeking its removal. News stories at the time quoted State Parks interpretive program manager Marnin Robbins, who said that Grant was not a "conservationist" but "a socialite, a wealthy individual who had some powerful friends." State Parks planned to erect a new sign in place of the boulder: "Because [Grant] thought redwoods were the 'apex species' of tree, he equated saving them with preserving white supremacy."

No matter the importance of exposing and condemning Grant's hateful and ultimately destructive views, the claim that he was not a "conservationist" is inaccurate. Indeed, among the relatively few individuals who maintained prominence at the League throughout most of the organization's existence, no one more than Grant sought to preserve very large tracts of ancient redwood. No one.

In 2020, in the wake of the Black Lives Matter movement, the League's board of councilors, led by League president and CEO Sam Hodder, issued a statement that "denounced our founders' association with eugenics." This was an appropriate and important action. Yet many early League officials and major supporters other than Grant, Henry Fairfield Osborn, and John Merriam were white supremacists who favored eugenics research and extreme measures to maintain the preeminence of the white race.

Ralph Chaney, who became Save the Redwoods League president in 1961, was a vocal and unreconstructed white supremacist until he died in 1971. Chaney had been John Merriam's student at Berkeley. In 1920, Chaney, then thirty years old, joined Merriam as a research associate at the Carnegie Institution. He later joined the staff at Berkeley as one of the world's leading paleobotanists.

Chaney's research, which built on Merriam's, led to the discovery that redwoods had stood on earth for more than one hundred million years in places such as present-day China, Europe, Russia, and Asia. Building on the findings of Henry Fairfield Osborn and Alfred Wegener, Chaney concluded that redwoods had made their way to North America fifty million years ago on a land bridge that once connected the continent with Asia but disappeared due to continental drift. He was also among the first group of Western scientists to explore the Sichuan district of China, in 1948, to examine the 1946 discovery, by Chinese scientist Hsen Hsu Hu, of a living grove of dawn redwoods (*Metasequoia glyptostroboides*), an oddly deciduous conifer and redwood predecessor previously thought to have disappeared from the planet twenty million years ago.

Chaney's expedition to China occurred in classic colonial style. "A guide, numerous armed guards, [and] about 12 locals" carted "cots, sleeping bags, blankets, cooking equipment, sacks of rice, a case of bourbon, DDT powder, medical supplies, chemicals for preserving botanic samples, and collecting equipment," according to a 2021 history by Fred Nadis and posted on the League's website. They also carried Chaney, who made the three-day trek seated in a sedan chair attached to two long poles and carried by Chinese porters.

In 1970, while still League president, Chaney joined the board of the Foundation for Research and Education on Eugenics and Dysgenics, headed by Stanford professor and white nationalist William Shockley. In 1956 Shockley won a Nobel Prize in physics for his co-invention of the transistor, which would benefit future computer manufacturers as well as the communications capacities of the US military. Shockley's second passion was expanding on the work of his eugenics predecessors. Among other startling proclamations, Shockley once claimed that "the US negro is inherently less intelligent than the US white. . . . Nature has color-coded groups of individuals so that statistically reliable predictions of their adaptability to intellectually rewarding and effective lives can easily be made." In the late 2010s, the Southern Poverty Law Center characterized Shockley's legacy as one of

> an ardent eugenicist whose theories of black racial inferiority eventually made him an academic pariah. . . . Despite having no training whatsoever in genetics, biology or psychology, Shockley devoted the last decades of his life to a quixotic struggle to prove that black Americans were suffering from "dysgenesis," or "retrogressive evolution," and advocated replacing the welfare system with a "Voluntary Sterilization Bonus Plan," which, as its name suggests, would pay low-IQ women to undergo sterilization.

The League also enjoyed nearly five decades of support from another prominent American racist, Charles M. Goethe. Goethe was born in Sacramento in 1875. By 1920 he'd made a fortune in real estate and banking. That year he owned twenty-two major subdivisions in the Sacramento area, and he loaned money for home building. Goethe, like his friend and mentor Madison Grant, was an early environmentalist of prominence. He was a leader of the Sierra Club and served as president of the California Nature Study League. Goethe had supported Save the Redwoods League since 1919. In 1920, the League invited Goethe to speak at the Save the Redwoods Day automobile show (he declined due to ill health), and in 1921 Newton Drury suggested that the League and the California Nature Study League collaborate.

Goethe, Madison Grant, and Henry Fairfield Osborn were mutual friends who shared and collaborated on eugenics research. Jonathan Spiro writes, "Goethe's obsession with personal purity was paralleled by a mania for racial purity, and he always testified to the 'profound influence' of Madison Grant on his 'philosophy of life.'" Goethe, wrote Spiro, referred to

Mexicans as "disease carriers" and "superstitious savages," Puerto Ricans as "largely moronic" and possessing "a jungle fecundity," and Filipinos as "living museums of intestinal parasites."

Goethe relished Grant's *The Passing of the Great Race*. He hosted monthly readings of the book during a "Madison Grant Hour" in his home library. Goethe maintained a lively correspondence with League officials from 1919 until his death in 1966, filling several folders in the League archive. Writing to Drury in 1965, Goethe recalled Grant on his deathbed, thwarted by perceived censors. Grant, wrote Goethe, "grasped my hand the last time [and said], 'Charlie, I have only you to carry on.' I've tried."

In 2005, Anthony Platt, an emeritus professor of social work at Sacramento State University, wrote in the journal *Social Justice*, "Goethe was an influential member of the most important eugenics associations and invested at least one million dollars of his own money in writing about and promoting tracts on eugenics, conservation, race, and immigration. . . . Through the 1930s, Goethe remained a firm and steadfast supporter of Nazi eugenics." He also remained a firm and steadfast supporter of Save the Redwoods League.

From the 1920s into the 1960s, Goethe contributed more than $2 million to the League. In that time Goethe established four memorial groves, one of which, created in 1948 in Prairie Creek Redwoods State Park, Goethe named for Newton and Aubrey Drury. In 1943 Goethe and his wife Mary paid to dedicate a grove, on Avenue of the Giants, to Mary's mother, Lizzie H. Glide. Mary Goethe died in 1948. That year Goethe paid to dedicate a grove to her in Prairie Creek Redwoods State Park, near the Joseph and Zipporah Russ Grove. The Mary Glide Goethe Grove holds the fourteenth-largest coast redwood tree, by volume, in the world, the Newton B. Drury Tree. In 1949 Goethe's contribution allowed him to name a grove in Mill Creek Redwoods State Park for explorer Jedediah Smith, who in 1828 was the first white man to traverse the northwesternmost corner of what was to become California and for whom the Smith River is named. The following year the state changed the name of the preserve to Jedediah Smith Redwoods State Park. (All of the "dedicated groves" were already protected in state parks. The program primarily served to raise funding for the League.)

During these years Goethe continued his work as California's most notorious eugenics activist. In 1933, shortly after Adolf Hitler took power in Germany, he founded the Eugenics Society of Northern California. Over

a period of four decades his efforts largely contributed to the forced sterilization of more than twenty thousand people in California, more than in
any other state. "California's eugenicists . . . led the nation in sterilization
and provided the most scientific support for Hitler's regime," Edwin Black
writes in *War Against the Weak*. Among Goethe's closest collaborators was
David Starr Jordan, the first president of Stanford University and a supporter
of Save the Redwoods League until he died in 1931. Goethe and Jordan
served together on the advisory board of the eugenics group the Human
Betterment Foundation. Jordan was also chairman of the American Eugenics Commission.

In 1934 Goethe made a "fact-finding" mission to Germany, where the
Nazis were then sterilizing five thousand people every month. At the time
Goethe was president of the Eugenics Research Association, a violently rac-
ist organization that in 1913 grew out of the Eugenics Record Office in Cold
Spring Harbor, New York. Members of the Eugenics Research Association
included Madison Grant as well as Corrado Gini, science adviser to Benito
Mussolini, and "several Nazi eugenicists such as Eugen Fisher and Ernest
Rüdin," writes Spiro. In 1936, Goethe publicly declared that Nazi forced
sterilizations were "administered wisely, and without racial cruelty."

Black reports that in 1936 Goethe wrote, "The last twenty years witnessed
two stupendous forward movements, one in our United States, the other in
Germany. California had led all the world in sterilization operations. Today,
even California's quarter century record has, in two years, been outdistanced
by Germany." The following year, writes Black, Goethe contacted Dr. Otmar
Freiherr von Verschuer, a "racial hygienist" in Germany since the early 1920s
who would become "crucial to the work at Auschwitz." In his fawning letter
Goethe lauded Verschuer's "marvelous work," in which he was "leading all
mankind." Goethe maintained close ties to Nazi officials throughout the war.

In *Bloodlines*, Platt writes, "What surprised me as I researched the background of the Nuremberg Laws was the extent of reciprocity between German and American researchers, and how actively the California eugenics
circle boosted the glories of Nazi 'racial science.'" In 1934 Goethe wrote to
Harry Laughlin, the Princeton-trained director of the Eugenics Record Office, excitedly embracing Germany's approach to race science, "the modern
world's first eugenic program having behind it the tremendously powerful
force of sixty two millions welded into an efficient unit under a dictatorship."

Platt's book features a photo of Goethe as a young man, at the turn of the century. The image is gothic and ostentatious, combining Goethe's preferences for opulence and severity. A pressed white shirt and high starched collar are framed by what appears to be a silk tailcoat. Clean shaven and attractive in a menacing way, Goethe stares resolutely at the camera. The chair is hand carved, ornate, likely walnut or mahogany, and of European make. A high back sprouts rosettes, and from each arm juts a growling lion's head. Goethe has the look of a man who might have ruled Germany had the Nazis won the war. He grew up speaking German. Above the photo Platt quotes Goethe, from his diary in 1902: "I am a true American and yet I am false to the land of my birth when I feel a thrill of emotion and there is an intensely German feeling comes over me when I sing in the tongue of the Fatherland the old war songs."

In 1944, with the world now fully aware of just how far Germany had taken "race science" at the death camps of Chełmno, Belzec, Sobibor, Treblinka, and Auschwitz, Goethe became a councilor of Save the Redwoods League. As Platt notes, Goethe, more than any other American racist, "kept his colleagues well informed about eugenic accomplishments in Nazi Germany." It's inconceivable that his fellow councilors were unfamiliar with the Goethe ethos and its contributions to Nazi atrocities. In the main, however, many of them likely approved of dividing humanity into a hierarchy of races, with "Nordic" Anglo-Saxons at the very top and the chips of "human residuum" left to fall where they may.

After the war, Goethe, Ralph Chaney, William Shockley, and Lothrop Stoddard emerged among a handful of Americans who would openly embrace the same virulent strain of white supremacy that had informed the Third Reich. In 1949 Goethe published the book *Seeking to Serve*, lauding the American eugenics movement and apologizing for nothing. Goethe offers appreciation for fellow eugenics pioneers Charles Davenport and Harry Laughlin. He quotes Davenport: "The laws of heredity for plants enable us to understand those of human genetics. What we do here with Jimson-weed, future generations will do for men."

Goethe writes (in all caps), "Davenport, Laughlin, Huntington, all fine old British-Nordic names. The remarkable race that can produce such intellects will remain strong as long as it keeps that strain pure. It must exercise, however, the same care required to produce our best sheep, best sweetpeas."

Goethe ponders what to do with the lesser sheep and sweet peas, writing, "One sometimes wonders whether, eugenically, the moron should have the same number of votes as one with an I.Q. of, say, 140." He praises the Californians' prewar eugenics work, which "concentrated on Negative Eugenics. It participated in campaigns in securing sterilization legislation in many of the states which have added such legislation to their statutes. . . . We-two founded Eugenics Society of Northern California. Our end of our native state was a great reservoir of Gold Rush Pioneer stock. It seemed this was our sector of the battleline of Eugenic conservation of humans."

Goethe mailed thousands of copies of his book throughout the country and presumably overseas. The copy I read Goethe had personally presented to the University of Virginia. According to League records, Aubrey Drury received his copy in June 1949.

Aubrey Drury worked as Goethe's personal publicist for the other book Goethe released that year, *What's in a Name*, an examination of old California place-names. While Goethe was pouring millions of dollars into League coffers to name groves already preserved, he also paid the Drury brothers' public relations firm at least $500 to pump his books. Aubrey sent his publicity pitch for the book on League letterhead, noting that Goethe was a League councilor. He mailed the pitch and the book to scores of reviewers at newspapers and organizations throughout the West. Reviews were generally mixed, though the most compelling analysis came in the form of a private letter to Aubrey Drury from Joseph Henry Jackson, a beloved writer for the *San Francisco Chronicle*.

"I don't think I'd better do anything about your friend Goethe's book," wrote Jackson. "I'll bet you a bang-up dinner that without going to a single reference book of any kind I can sit down and in your presence mark up . . . not 100 but 250 errors of fact, including misspellings, in this volume. . . . [I]t might be kinder all around not to do anything about Mr. G. or his book [though] I'd be doing the public a favor. . . . [I]t's disgraceful that his book should be on library shelves and some day mislead students."

In a 1964 interview with Amelia Fry, of UC Berkeley, Newton Drury notes, "My brother Aubrey . . . was very close to Mr. Goethe." He adds, "I don't think you can minimize the importance of C. M. Goethe in this whole program of nature conservation. There's no question that he had a great effect on Stephen Mather and Madison Grant and some of the pioneers, both in the formation of the National Park Service and of the Save-the-Redwoods League."

By 1949, Chaney and Goethe did not stand alone among committed racists who served Save the Redwoods League as councilors. While it would be unfair and inaccurate to lump all sixty councilors into the same racist category, many shared white supremacist views. In addition to Goethe, racist councilors who served the League at mid-century included

- David Prescott Barrows, who led the American reeducation efforts after the conquering of the Philippines.
- Harold C. Bryant, among Goethe's lifelong friends and an early member of Goethe's Eugenics Society of Northern California.
- Frederic A. Delano, a railroad magnate and Franklin Delano Roosevelt's uncle, who supported eugenics research at the Carnegie Institution.
- Red-line code pioneer Duncan McDuffie.
- Henry Graves, the Yale forester and provost who was a leading East Coast eugenics booster.
- Gilbert Grosvenor, publisher of *National Geographic* and a prominent eugenicist.
- J. W. Mailliard, who wanted to bar Asians from entering the United States. At the time of his death in 1986, Mailliard was married to Charlotte Mailliard, who went on to marry George Shultz and preside over the League's 2018 centennial celebration.
- J. D. Grant's attorney Herman Phleger, a supporter of eugenics.
- Nicholas Roosevelt, second cousin to Teddy Roosevelt and associate editor of the *New York Times*, where he advocated for US domination of the Philippines.
- Ray Lyman Wilbur, Stanford president and interior secretary. Wilbur is worthy of special mention, as he was among the nation's leading eugenicists. Wilber's positions of power lent undue influence to his odious beliefs. He was a prominent member of the American Eugenics Society and the Eugenics Research Association. Spiro writes that the Third Reich's 1933 Law for the Prevention of Hereditarily Diseased Offspring (the Sterilization Law) "was quite consciously based on the model sterilization law of Harry H. Laughlin and the American Eugenics Society." In 1913, three years before he became president of Stanford, Wilbur, in

a chilling passage, wrote that "products of the marriage of the weak and the unfit, of the criminal, of the syphilis and of the alcohol that fill many of our most splendid governmental buildings must largely disappear."

During the postwar years, the Drury brothers' notes to Goethe, which most often centered on conservation, contained asides thanking him for continuing to send the volumes of eugenics information for which he would become infamous. Even after the slaughter of six million Jews, Goethe continued to focus on "race suicide" and the "survival of the unfittest." On November 7, 1950, Newton Drury wrote to Goethe, "Thank you very much for Eugenics Pamphlet No. 67, containing the interesting information on Java and the Javanese." (Though Drury's letter is in Save the Redwoods League's archive, the pamphlet is not.) Eugenics Pamphlets Nos. 65 and 63 were also of great interest to Drury.

It's not clear whether Drury had also read Goethe's Eugenics Pamphlet No. 12, from the mid-1930s and dug up by Platt for his book. That tract happily reported, "Germany has cross-card-indexed her people until she has located all her probable weaklings. . . . Her plan is: Eliminate all low-powers to make room for high-powers. And thereby also save taxes."

Drury was too smart, too much the public relations whiz, to publicly proclaim allegiance with his colleagues' racist vitriol. Yet, given the virulent thread of white supremacy that ran throughout League leadership during the organization's first several decades of operation, even as late as the 1960s—a leadership well populated with "a great reservoir of Gold Rush Pioneer stock"—and the strong sympathies that Drury privately expressed for his colleagues' hateful racism, he was clearly on board.

"Newton Drury . . . endorsed eugenically driven immigration restriction and the dreams of Aryan and Nordic supremacy that crested to popularity in the 1920s," writes Alexandra Minna Stern, professor of history, American culture, and women's and gender studies at the University of Michigan, in her 2015 book *Eugenic Nation*.

At the time, the League never attempted to distance itself from Goethe or, of course, from Ralph Chaney. In its spring newsletter of 1965, the League announced that on March 28, Ralph Chaney and Newton Drury had been "principal speakers at the . . . C. M. Goethe National Recognition Day [and] testimonial dinner in Sacramento." In accepting his invitation to speak, Drury wrote to the event organizers, "I have spent a lifetime in this sort of thing, but I take *this* assignment most seriously." On February 8, Drury wrote to Chaney to inform him that he had recommended to John Michael, supervisor of interpretation at the California Division of Beaches and Parks and an organizer of the Goethe birthday event, that Chaney also speak at the party. "I mentioned your closeness to Mr. Goethe, and your knowledge of his fields other than the Redwoods," wrote Drury.

That same day Goethe had written to Drury to thank him for agreeing to speak at the event. "It is good of you to take the time to do this. . . . My memory goes back to the talks we-2 had in New York with both Madison Grant and Henry Fairfield Osborn about that campfire in the Redwoods, which really witnessed the birth of your League." In a postscript that was longer than the actual letter, Goethe unleashed. "There is apparently a highly organized opposition that desires to devaluate the spiritual assets of the National Park System. It links up very satisfactorily with the plans of the enemy to bid for the suffrages of near-moron voters. It parallels a certain group of scheming politician's [*sic*] work to scrap the Quota Immigration Act to gain approval of certain foreign groups. These want admission for a horde of 'cousins' from cheap labor areas."

Noting also that Drury was to be the "key speaker" at his birthday event, Goethe offered advice for capturing the crowd: "We-2 studied massenpsychologie under the Kaiser, then Mussolini, finally Hitler, and I think I understand the strategy of building public opinion."

In 1976, ten years after Goethe died, Save the Redwoods League honored him by creating the C. M. Goethe Memorial Grove, a lovely, and ironically diverse, forty-acre stand of trees atop a ridge on the west side of Prairie Creek Redwoods State Park. A quarter mile removed from the noisy Newton B. Drury Scenic Parkway that rudely bisects the ancient forest, the Goethe Grove would seem to be at peace.

46

In 1951, Newton Drury left the National Park Service to preside as chief of the California Division of Beaches and Parks. At the same time, Drury also largely ran Save the Redwoods League.

"One would be hard-pressed to differentiate between the two postings," observed Jonathan Spiro. During that decade, the League and the state would pay fortunes for small ancient redwood groves and large swaths of cutover land. The windfalls allowed the state's timber industry to remain solvent even as destructive logging practices eliminated standing timber inventories. In 1956 Drury's melded organizations spent $1.2 million to set aside three hundred acres of redwood that bordered two miles of the Avenue of the Giants. The thin strip of tall trees ran from a stony outcropping called High Rock, just north of Rockefeller Forest, northward to the small community of Englewood. National media eagerly covered the tiny acquisition.

That same year the state moved forward with plans to build a freeway through Humboldt Redwoods State Park, starting at Englewood and slicing southward for five miles through protected ancient redwoods. Nearly as many trees would be cut for the freeway as the League had just saved. The freeway plan required approval from Drury's California Division of Beaches and Parks. Freeway advocates got more than just Drury's approval. Half of the $5.25 million required to build the freeway came from the Division of Beaches and Parks.

Drury was sanguine about the freeway because, as he told the *San Francisco Examiner*, the plan for a four-lane thoroughfare, in places hundreds of feet wide, cutting through a protected grove of ancient redwoods was "happily approaching satisfactory solution through the fine cooperation of the Division of Highways." That solution was to relegate most of the freeway to the east side of the South Fork Eel River, avoiding Bull Creek and the heart of Rockefeller Forest. Yet nearly all of the new thoroughfare bisected dense, protected stands of ancient redwood, including the great flats alongside the western portion of Founders Grove and the California Federation of Women's Clubs Grove. At the 1958 dedication of the freeway, Drury was one of the featured speakers. Soon the freeway extended southward, cutting through old-growth redwoods in the Sage Grove and the Mather Grove, among many others.

In April 1959, at the age of seventy, Newton Drury retired from the Division of Beaches and Parks. Five months later his brother, Aubrey Drury, died of a heart attack. Newspaper accounts characterized Aubrey Drury as a "nationally-known author and conservationist."

A few months after Aubrey Drury died, Newton Drury returned to his post as executive secretary of Save the Redwoods League. During the critical years of the 1960s, calls to save "the last redwoods" were ringing out across the nation. At that time the skills and contacts Drury had accrued over five decades and his near-authoritarian control over redwood protection efforts could have been poured into joining the Sierra Club's emerging campaign to preserve Redwood Creek as a Redwood National Park, in addition to finally preserving the remnant stand of old growth on Mill Creek that the League had long claimed to covet. But Drury and the League had other plans and different bedfellows.

In 1966 the state, the League, and the US Interior Department paid Pacific Lumber $2.5 million for the final seven-mile stretch of Avenue of the Giants. Tourists had been driving the section of the state highway, along the main branch of the Eel River between Pepperwood and Stafford, for nearly five decades. Any attempt to cut the stand during the 1960s would have met with protest by even Humboldt County's most conservative timber boosters. Half of the 1,620-acre acquisition had been previously logged. Yet an editorial in the *Humboldt Times* praised Pacific Lumber for having "voluntarily preserved the magnificent stand of redwoods for many years in the public interest" and for abiding "by the unwritten laws of gentlemanly conduct." By now the long, wormlike grove was bordered by the state highway on one side and the four-lane federal freeway on the other. In places the roads were just three hundred feet apart. The "peaceful forest" was replete with highway noise. Road impacts have so damaged the roots and hydrology of hundreds of old-growth redwoods that many are dying from the top down, leaving a long line of ghoulish spike tops to limn the drive. Locals refer to the beauty strip as "avenue of the snags." Inside the grove many of the giant redwoods are stunning; laser-straight trees erupt out of carpets of oxalis. A trail is dedicated to Newton Drury and Ralph Chaney. Today an interpretive sign greets visitors to the trail with the headline "Logged for Progress, Replanted for the Future." The text commends Save the Redwoods League and notes that John Steinbeck once wrote that "from [redwoods] comes silence and awe."

Pacific Lumber praised itself for the deal. In an advertisement placed in the *Humboldt Times*, the company alerted readers, "[With the] new freeway . . . completed . . . motorists can see both a protected strip of giant redwoods and a new forest in the making, the product of a modern industrial forestry program. . . . [T]here is something fresh and beautiful in a vigorous stand of young trees. We are proud of what you will soon be seeing along the new Redwood Highway."

In December that year, the League facilitated a long-promised addition to Jedediah Smith Redwoods State Park. The deal required that the League pay Simpson Timber $700,000 for 830 acres of redwood adjacent to the park that lined four miles of US Highway 199. The state contributed by handing Simpson 1,500 acres of publicly owned old-growth redwood on the Smith River, downstream of the park. California governor Edmund G. Brown lauded the deal, saying, "This will give the park one of the finest stands of virgin redwoods in the entire north coast county."

In a press release issued January 5, 1967, the League celebrated the acquisition, calling the stand "some of the finest virgin Redwood forest in existence." The press release noted that the state of California had contributed $50,000 to the purchase and that Simpson had donated ten acres of the land. There was no mention that the people of California had, unwittingly, traded away fifteen hundred acres of old-growth forest to complete the deal.

Economically, Simpson did well in the League-brokered deal. Yet the company was also seeking another sort of dividend. Simpson was logging heavily on Redwood Creek, then in the public crosshairs for a national park. The Smith River timber swap would allow the company and other redwood firms to proclaim, with predictable regularity, "The redwoods *are* saved." From here out the mantra would pop up on signs in front of clear-cuts and log decks, in ads, and in public proclamations made by timber executives. Now, with under three hundred thousand acres of virgin redwood remaining uncut, and as a viable movement was emerging to protect the very last pristine redwood watershed, timber industry officials would stand atop a false legacy of preservation built by the League over five decades and wield their proclamation like a cudgel against those who would seek to set aside any more redwoods. And Save the Redwoods League would help them do it.

47

Edgar Wayburn was an avid outdoorsman who'd joined the Sierra Club in 1939, when it was still a regional hiking group. In 1947 Wayburn accepted his first post at the Club, on the executive committee of the organization's San Francisco Bay Area chapter. By then Wayburn had been in living in San Francisco for fourteen years. He'd grown up in Georgia, where he attended the University of Georgia before moving on to Harvard Medical School. He was an honors graduate of both institutions. In San Francisco, Wayburn worked as a physician, and he and his wife, Peggy, had four children. They presented a dashing, attractive couple of means. The postwar boom years ushered in the most rapid wealth-generating era in the history of the country, if not the world. The Wayburns could have lived as effete dilatants, mingling with the Bay Area elite and taking glamorous vacations. Instead, they dedicated their lives to protecting the West's disappearing wildlands.

Edgar Wayburn arrived in California in 1933, in time to watch the state and the Bay Area grow with unnerving speed. That year Wayburn would catch a ferry to reach favorite hiking destinations in Marin County. Four years later he could drive there on the Golden Gate Bridge. By the 1950s, industrial expansion was altering and forever damaging the West's remaining landscapes of coastal ecosystems, wild rivers, and untamed lands. "Suddenly there was more of everything: more houses, more people, more cars, more freeways," Wayburn writes in his memoir, *Your Land and Mine*, published in 2004, when he was ninety-seven years old. (Wayburn died in 2010, at the age of 103.) "The flip side of this was, of course, less open space, less forest, less wilderness." Through the efforts of the Wayburns, Martin Litton, Sierra Club executive directors David Brower and Michael McCloskey, and other far-thinking Club officials—local as well as national—the Club over three decades would lead efforts to protect millions of acres of the western landscape. It was the single greatest contribution to environmental protection in American history.

Wayburn moved quickly up the ranks of Sierra Club leadership until 1961, when he was elected president of the organization. He is credited with designing and creating the eighty-five-thousand-acre Golden Gate National Recreation Area, among the world's largest urban parklands, and with preserving (against the wishes of Newton Drury) Marin County's sixty-seven-hundred-acre Mount Tamalpais State Park, whose boundaries range from the top of the iconic peak to the ocean. Up the coast, in 1962 Wayburn and the Club, along with the Point Reyes Foundation, convinced Congress to approve acquisition of fifty-eight thousand acres in West Marin County for the Point Reyes National Seashore (now seventy-one thousand acres). Today, Marin County boasts the highest concentration of public lands and open space of any urban county in the world.

In 1964, Wayburn and the Club facilitated passage of the 1964 Wilderness Act (first proposed and written, in 1955, by Howard Zahniser of the Wilderness Society), which has since protected 111 million acres of pristine American landscape. Four years later the Club led efforts to pass the Wild and Scenic Rivers Act, which now affords heightened levels of protection for 12,709 miles of US rivers and creeks. Also in 1968, the Sierra Club under Wayburn was instrumental in creating the 700,000-acre North Cascades National Park and the Redwood National Park. In 1980, a thirteen-year Sierra Club campaign, led by the Wayburns, protected nearly one-fourth of Alaska, saving "103 million acres of parks, refuges and wilderness areas, such as Denali, Glacier Bay and Katmai," wrote *San Francisco Examiner* reporter Jane Kay in 2006, commemorating Wayburn's one hundredth birthday. In 1999, President Bill Clinton awarded Wayburn the Presidential Medal of Freedom.

Wayburn did his Sierra Club work as a volunteer, even while he maintained a practice in internal medicine at San Francisco General Hospital and at the University of California, San Francisco. (He also served as president of the San Francisco Medical Society.) Peggy Wayburn, who had worked as an editor at *Vogue* magazine and at the J. Walter Thompson advertising agency, also volunteered long hours with the Club. The couple were a force.

The catastrophic California floods of 1955 jarred the Wayburns. That year heavy rains saturated hundreds of square miles of recently denuded and heavily scarred timberlands, scouring whole watersheds virtually everywhere on the North Coast. Along Bull Creek, biblical flooding dislodged thousands of stumps, discarded trees, incalculable tonnages of soil and rock, and the entire town and milling infrastructure of Bull Creek, sending it all downstream into Rockefeller Forest. The deluge carved and widened the fragile stream zone and toppled hundreds of ancient redwoods, some of them among the tallest trees in the world.

The disaster of Bull Creek was preventable and predicted. Nonetheless, since 1931 Save the Redwoods League had made no effort to acquire the unlogged timberlands that stood upstream of Rockefeller Forest. Instead, the League allowed these tracts to be clear-cut and then purchased the lands for inflated prices.

"Like others, I assumed that because many redwoods were on protected land and under the eye of such a notable conservation group as the Save-the-Redwoods League, the trees were well guarded," Edgar Wayburn writes in his memoir. In January 1956, with flood waters hardly receded, Peggy Wayburn published an article in the *Sierra Club Bulletin* titled "The Tragedy of Bull Creek," which focused largely on acquisitions of picturesque islands and strips of ancient redwood at the expense of protecting whole watersheds. The Wayburns began traveling north whenever possible, often camping at Prairie Creek, where "the redwoods surrounded us, immersed us in their existence," Edgar Wayburn wrote. Through travel and wildland adventures, both Peggy and Edgar Wayburn derived an understanding that natural beauty is a good thing, but most important to planetary life and human existence was protecting whole ecosystems. At the Sierra Club they came to represent an evolving vanguard that would translate these understandings into legislative action on behalf of wilderness values.

Edgar Wayburn writes that, shortly after Peggy published her Bull Creek article, he "convinced the Sierra Club's board of directors to make the establishment of a redwood national park one of its five priority campaigns." Wayburn advocated an ecosystem approach to redwood preservation. He was wary, if not disdainful, of the League's dedication to purchasing small, isolated groves that primarily served to screen logging.

"I realized the potential trickery of such tree-lined corridors," Wayburn wrote. "They provided verdant facades for automobile tourists, but what lay beyond? I have never advocated the establishment of scenic corridors. While affording a pretty roadside view, such facades too often are shielding the public's view of destructive cuts going on behind them. . . . [T]he roadside stands—intended to prove the industry's benevolence—were nothing more than green facades camouflaging the brutal clear-cuts beyond."

In an oral history interview conducted between 1976 and 1981 by Ann Lage, an affiliate scholar at the Oral History Center of the Bancroft Library, and historian Susan Schrepfer, Wayburn said, "We wanted not just to find groves, as the Save-the-Redwoods League and the state of California wanted; we were looking for a redwood forest which could be preserved in perpetuity. We were looking for a forest to preserve from ridge to ridge; from the coast to the inland limits of the redwoods." Shortly thereafter, Martin Litton found just what they were looking for at Redwood Creek. The Sierra Club set out to save the watershed.

In early 1961, Peggy Wayburn organized the Sierra Club's seventh biennial Wilderness Conference, held in April at the Palace Hotel in San Francisco. Times were heady. Wilderness advocates anticipated a new era of conscious environmentalism at the highest levels of government. John F. Kennedy had just been elected president of the United States, and his campaign had promised to protect American wildlands. Kennedy picked progressive Arizona congressman Stewart Udall to serve as his secretary of the interior, further fanning excitement at the Sierra Club.

Edgar Wayburn, by now a known figure in Washington, DC, had gotten several dignitaries to speak at the conference, including Udall, California governor Edmund G. Brown, and US Supreme Court justice William O. Douglas. Douglas himself was a powerful advocate of environmental protection. He was so impressed by the conference that he agreed to join the Sierra Club's national board of directors, though he would resign the following year to avoid the need to recuse himself on environmental cases that he rightly anticipated would reach the Supreme Court.

At the conference dinner, Peggy Wayburn sat next to Udall, "by design," she told Lage in a 1990 oral history. She said to Udall, "I think your first park should be a redwood national park. He said, 'What are you talking about?' It was a whole new idea to him. He didn't even know what a redwood tree was." She handed him a booklet on the trees of the Bay Area, "and that was his introduction to the redwoods."

In his oral history, Edgar Wayburn said, "Udall was extremely interested. We tried to get him to come out and look at the redwoods with us. He didn't, but he sent John Carver, who was then assistant secretary for Parks, Fish and Wildlife, and we made a trip up there. The area that we looked at particularly was the Klamath River, which was once one of the great redwood areas. We drove up the Klamath to Blue Creek—at that time Blue Creek was still not logged, and parts of the Klamath weren't logged." Yet Udall balked, telling Wayburn that "this was too much—that there was too much of a fight involved. . . . But at the same time Udall did get interested. I think it was he who got the National Geographic interested in their studies."

Udall first publicly acknowledged the Kennedy administration's interest in creating a Redwood National Park during an April 1963 press conference in San Francisco. The press conference mainly addressed ongoing federal acquisitions at Point Reyes. According to a report in the *Marin Independent Journal*, Udall also alluded to the president's "interest in a possible redwoods national park. . . . No area has been decided on, but he thought it should be large, with an entire watershed to protect it." This was the Sierra Club talking.

On May 8 the *New York Times* codified the administration's "interest" by running an editorial titled "A Redwood National Park." "Secretary of the Interior Stewart L. Udall is backing a Redwood National Park, to cover a large area of Coast redwoods in northern California," wrote the *Times* editorial board. "Now Federal assistance is essential if adequate protection is to be achieved to round out the preserved redwood groves. The redwoods are a national treasure, and deserve treatment as such." A few weeks later Litton brought the National Geographic Society team to what would become known as the Tall Trees Grove.

In November 1963, the Sierra Club released a large-format book, *The Last Redwoods*, by the photographer Philip Hyde and writer Francois Leydet, with a foreword by Stewart Udall. A who's who of conservation made up the Sierra Club's Publications Committee, including David Brower, Martin Litton, Edgar Wayburn, longtime Sierra Club director and former president Francis Farquhar, and famed photographer Ansel Adams, who served as a Sierra Club director for thirty-seven years.

The celebrated American writer Wallace Stegner, a Sierra Club director, also served on the Publications Committee. In 1961, Udall invited Stegner to be his assistant at the Interior Department, and in 1962 Udall appointed Stegner to the National Parks Advisory Board—a tribute to the lucid power of Stegner's visionary pleas to protect North America's remaining wild-lands. Stegner's books later earned him both a Pulitzer Prize and a National Book Award.

Through Leydet's poetic language and the dramatic, large-format photos by Hyde, Litton, and other photographers, *The Last Redwoods* first ushers readers through the graceful, secretive world of the pristine redwood forest. Suddenly the book brutalizes the senses with full-sized images of the clear-cutting then expanding throughout the realm of the last redwoods. One memorable image shows a wasteland of stumps, debris, and bleeding earth. A woman stands near a redwood stump that bears the Orwellian designation "FOREST RENEWAL EXHIBIT. ARCATA REDWOOD COMPANY." A brochure available at the site informed visitors, "The ground does get scuffed. . . . It presents a ruffled picture"—as if the company were describing a garden path. The terrain resembled a war zone.

48

O N September 15, 1964, the US National Park Service released a report based on the National Geographic Society's studies of unprotected redwood watersheds on the North Coast. Although the Park Service was then managed by its new director, George B. Hartzog, he worked "in the subordinate role to [Stewart] Udall," who held all power at the Interior Department, Edgar Wayburn later said. It appeared that Udall was fully on board with the Club's plan for a Redwood National Park.

The Park Service document, much like Paul Redington's report of forty-four years earlier, appears to have been constructed from a heartfelt appreciation of the need to protect a large stand of redwoods. Bill Devall called the writing "almost lyrical." The writers noted the importance of acting quickly to establish a large Redwood National Park distant from roads. There was no place left to achieve such a preserve other than at Redwood Creek.

The writers repudiated Save the Redwoods League's claim that Mill Creek was the best location for a Redwood National Park. "Much of [Mill Creek] has already been cut," said the report. Rather than acquire the Mill Creek stand, the report recommended a "cooperative coordinated management plan" to allow the timber company, Miller Redwood, to continue operations under an authenticated sustained-yield basis. In contrast to Mill Creek, "the Redwood Creek and Lost Man Creek drainages contain what is apparently the largest uncut block of virgin growth not preserved—certainly the most significant large block in terms of park values. . . . Lower Redwood Creek from ridge to ridge is essentially uncut. It presents an outstanding redwood valley picture, fortunately set to one side of the main highway and much of it still inaccessible." Not incidentally, Redwood Creek was now also known as home of "the world's tallest known tree." (Lost Man Creek was a large tributary to lower Prairie Creek that shared a ridge with, and was contiguous to, the Redwood Creek forest.)

Finally, the report listed three potential plans for a Redwood National Park, all of which centered on Redwood Creek. The first option, called Plan 1, proposed creation of a Redwood National Park of 53,600 acres, including 15,220 acres of newly protected old-growth redwood on Redwood Creek and 5,870 acres of adjacent old growth on Lost Man Creek. It would incorporate Prairie Creek Redwoods State Park and add 1,490 acres of old growth that surrounded it. The plan also included ocean frontage and would absorb almost 25,000 acres of cutover lands. *New York Times* columnist Brooks Atkinson, writing in October, said, "Plan 1 is the minimum to which the public is entitled."

"To add bits and pieces here and there will not do the job," said the National Parks report. "A major addition is required, and one preferably which would add not merely size, but high quality redwood groves and forests in a situation where, so far as possible, they can be preserved, interpreted, and made available to the public as outstanding examples in an outstanding manner. Far too easily the natural heritage we 'preserve' may end up as a watered down experience seen hastily and superficially from a fast moving car."

Club officials latched on to these and many other elements of the report. Wayburn was pleased that the authors had recommended Redwood Creek as a site for a Redwood National Park, which reflected the Sierra Club's vision. (The report did note that the large Pacific Lumber holding to the south, on Yager and Lawrence Creeks, home to All Species Grove, held "significant park value.") Acknowledgment that Redwood Creek, and not Mill Creek, was the only remaining viable site for a Redwood National Park promised to make the Club's campaign in Washington, DC, infinitely easier.

Yet Wayburn and the Club were disappointed that the report did not contain the Sierra Club's ultimate plan for a 90,000-acre park. The Club blueprint would have taken the entire lower half of the 180,000-acre Redwood Creek watershed from ridge to ridge for twenty-two miles, protecting nearly 40,000 acres of old-growth redwood. The plan also incorporated 10,000 acres then held in Prairie Creek Redwoods State Park, cutover private lands in lower Prairie Creek, and coastal terrain. The Club's plan adhered to the growing ethos of the day, which viewed protection of whole ecosystems as a critical component of restoring the planet's biotic health and integrity.

In his oral history, Wayburn laid out the Club's concerns about the federal recommendation.

> The National Park Service published a report called "The Redwoods"—they had in there four alternatives, but only three plans. I went to them and said, "You left something out." They said, "Oh, no, we've got everything in there." I said, "No, you've left out what your optimum plan is. It's perfectly obvious as you identify the resource, that there had to be a plan that is bigger than any of the three which you offer." And after a while they admitted to me that that was true. The ninety thousand-acre plan that we offered had been in their private report, but they were told that they could not offer it publicly.

Club officials consoled themselves with the understanding that Interior's report was only a recommendation and they could still use the department's strong findings to bring even stronger legislation to Capitol Hill. And they already had congressional lawmakers lined up to do just that. Clearly the Sierra Club had built a formidable political and organizational phalanx with which to attack anticipated impediments to creating a whole-watershed Redwood National Park on Redwood Creek. Most of the impediments were known and planned for. Yet a serious, unforeseen obstacle arose and catalyzed an unfolding series of disasters. Newton B. Drury had returned to Save the Redwoods League just in time to join the fight.

49

DURING THE WEEK OF MAY 24, 1965, PRESIDENT LYNDON B. JOHNSON and his wife, Lady Bird Johnson, hosted the first annual White House Conference on Natural Beauty. In addition to being an independent and outspoken First Lady, an articulate public speaker, and a successful entrepreneur, Lady Bird Johnson was an effective advocate for diminishment of visual blight and protection of "natural beauty." At the conference, she said, "Our peace of mind, our emotions, our spirit—even our souls—are conditioned by what our eyes see."

Philanthropist and policy gadfly Laurance S. Rockefeller, son of John D. Rockefeller Jr., chaired the committee that organized the conference. This was not Rockefeller's first rodeo with the Texan president and his wife. He was Johnson's closest adviser on the environment, and his input was increasingly important to the president as conservation issues heated up through the decade. Rockefeller was a holdover from the John F. Kennedy years, when he'd worked closely with Stewart Udall and served as the chair of the Congressional Outdoor Recreation Resources Review Commission. Rockefeller donated millions of dollars to conservation efforts and was a singular influence in Washington, DC, and in state capitals. His input was rarely contradicted by those in power.

Edgar Wayburn had been communicating with Rockefeller about Redwood National Park since 1962. They enjoyed a cordial rapport. Wayburn had arranged to meet with Rockefeller prior to the 1965 conference, rightly anticipating that Rockefeller was poised to support a significant Redwood National Park proposal. Rockefeller granted Wayburn thirty minutes prior to the opening of the conference to make his pitch. Wayburn's version of the encounter, as told to Ann Lage, is compelling.

I went into the room where the conference was being planned and spread out my maps on the redwoods. Rockefeller seemed most interested. Instead of a half hour, we had well over an hour and would have had longer if Fred Smith, one of his assistants . . . hadn't been pulling him away to attend to the business of the conference. . . . At the end of my exposition, I turned to Mr. Rockefeller, and said, "What do you think, Mr. Rockefeller?" He said, "How much would it cost?" I answered, "A hundred and fifty million dollars," thinking that would throw him back. He said, "That shouldn't be difficult. We could put in fifty million. We'd get the Ford Foundation to put in fifty million, and the Old Dominion Foundation to add another fifty million." By this time my heart was floating on the ceiling, along with all the rest of me, in fantasy. I then said, "Mr. Rockefeller, anything I can do, I'm ready to. What do we do next?" Rockefeller answered, "I have taken no public position. When I do, I will be guided by my longstanding advisors, Newton Drury and Horace Albright." At that point, something dropped on the floor. It was my heart.

By now Wayburn's opinion of Newton Drury bordered on disdain. During the 1950s, when Drury ran the California Division of Beaches and Parks, Wayburn had to overcome Drury's fealty to industry to achieve conservation. He was well aware that Drury and Save the Redwoods League shared a bed with the timber industry.

Horace Albright had been Stephen Mather's legal adviser at the National Park Service, and he briefly took the helm as director from 1929 until 1933. By 1965, Albright had been a League councilor for more than thirty years. He had long supported Drury's version of redwood protection.

Over the July Fourth weekend of 1965, Edgar and Peggy Wayburn drove north to visit the redwoods. In Orick they stayed at Hagood Motel, owned by a longtime Humboldt County family that supported creation of Redwood National Park, even in the face of increasing local vitriol. The Hagoods loved the ancient redwood forest that stretched so regally into the hills behind their home. They believed that preserving the forest would bring greater long-term economic benefits to the region than would liquidating the redwoods in a relatively short time. When the Wayburns arrived, Jean Hagood greeted them, as she had many times in the past. She said, "Oh, you just missed Laurance Rockefeller. Are you following him around?" The Wayburns said they'd had no idea Rockefeller was in the area. "Laurance and Newton Drury were here last night," said Hagood. They were "looking at all the redwood parks."

"By this time," said Wayburn, "I was quite convinced that Laurance was not our man, and I knew that Newton was not our man. As I learned later in the summer—although I'd suspected very strongly before—Stewart Udall was no longer our man."

According to Susan Schrepfer, Drury had brought Rockefeller and his family adviser, Maurice Fred Smith—who had pulled Rockefeller away from his meeting with Wayburn—to the northern redwoods to pitch Mill Creek as the best site for a Redwood National Park. Smith had made the journey the previous year as well, "at the request and expense of Bernie Orell of the Weyerhaeuser Company," wrote Schrepfer. The Weyerhaeuser family owned the Arcata Redwood Company, which held twenty-two thousand acres of contiguous virgin redwood forest on Redwood Creek and Lost Man Creek, including the entire redwood expanse on the northeastern slope of Redwood Creek, where no cutting had yet occurred and where the Tall Trees Grove was located. It was the last of the virgin redwood inventory acquired by the Weyerhaeusers when the family bought in with A. B. Hammond in 1908. It was also the last large block of redwood left standing of the 124,000 acres stolen by the Russ gang and the Scots during the land-fraud era of the late nineteenth century.

Drury guided Rockefeller and Smith as though Redwood Creek hardly existed. The men spent a day touring Jedediah Smith Redwoods State Park, then journeyed to a beautiful high spot overlooking the lustrous redwoods of Mill Creek, most of which were already protected. They made a cursory side trip to the Bald Hills for a glimpse of Redwood Creek, then left the county. They had skipped over the nearly intact stand on Redwood Creek, a place that *National Geographic* had reported held, in a small area, "more than a hundred giants ten feet or more in diameter—most of them at least 300 feet high," including four of the ten tallest trees in the world. Similar trees grew for miles downstream, representing "one of the few remaining redwood wildernesses . . . in the world." Nonetheless, in an extraordinary deception, Drury had justified omitting Redwood Creek from the tour by telling Smith that the great conifers growing there were "scraggly."

Shortly after his tour with Drury and Smith, Rockefeller wrote to President Johnson in terms that could have been written by Newton Drury. "We believe that a national park might be created at this time with a minimum of opposition and perhaps even with considerable local support if a reasonable plan is prepared and put forward in an intelligent and constructive way," wrote Rockefeller. "The two extremes in this controversy are the Sierra Club and the Industry. It is doubtful whether the Sierra Club will actively support any but an extremely far-reaching plan."

According to Schrepfer, "Rockefeller had followed . . . Save-the-Redwoods League [and] recommended to President Johnson that the park be on Mill Creek. Guided in significant part by this advice, Johnson had defied the direction of his own party in Congress, backed the northern site, and played probably the pivotal role in forcing Interior to abandon its earlier plans."

In 1978, Wayburn told Ann Lage that, previous to this moment, Stewart Udall "couldn't have been more enthusiastic or cooperative . . . until one day in 1965 he just stopped answering my telephone calls. . . . I finally got through to him, and he said to me, 'Ed, I'm sorry, but the Save-the-Redwoods League doesn't want this, and I'm afraid I can't support it anymore.'"

Nearly fifty years after Drury and the League had thwarted the promise of a groundbreaking federal report that called for creation of a large, intact Redwood National Park and derailed promising momentum in Congress to pass park legislation, they had done it again.

50

A T THE TIME THAT NEWTON DRURY WAS GUIDING ROCKEFELLER AWAY
from Redwood Creek, timber industry officials and their business allies that relied on redwood lumber, along with friends in Washington, DC,
and Sacramento, were coalescing into a hydra of opposition to a Redwood
National Park. Some of the efforts were almost comic. Over the summer of
1965 a Redwood Park and Recreation Committee formed to present what
the *Humboldt Standard* described as "a second proposal for a national redwoods park for this area." Committee members included representatives
from Simpson Timber Company, Miller Redwood Company, Arcata Redwood Company, Pacific Lumber Company, Georgia-Pacific, and the Eureka
Chamber of Commerce. The men called their "second proposal" the Redwood Park and Recreation Plan. In exchange for environmentalists giving
up their campaigns for an actual Redwood National Park, the timber owners
would follow through on long-promised sales of small old-growth redwood
tracts (the 1,620-acre Pepperwood purchase and the 830-acre addition to
Jedediah Smith Redwoods State Park) and open up 300,000 acres of cutover
land for regulated entry by the public.

Predictably, Ronald Reagan, then a candidate for California governor,
endorsed the industry plan, saying it would protect jobs. "I don't believe that
tourism will be able to support the area tomorrow," said Reagan.

Reagan wasn't the only fan of the industry's plan. Newton Drury and
Save the Redwoods League issued a statement: "You are to be congratulated
upon the Redwood Park and Recreation Plan, indicating the desire of the
redwood industry to cooperate in presenting for public enjoyment the fine
examples of virgin forest outlined therein."

Drury also appeared in a second industry tract aimed at forestalling a
Redwood National Park. The Redwoods-to-the-Sea proposal of 1966

appeared in support of the Redwood Park and Recreation Plan. C. Robert Barnum was chairman of the Redwoods-to-the-Sea Citizens' Committee. He was also the great-grandson of Gorham Barnum, who had made bank the previous century by loaning a back room of his Eureka saloon for the signing of fraudulent deeds. C. Robert Barnum was a graduate of the University of California, Berkeley's School of Forestry and a major timberland owner in Humboldt County. In 1972, California governor Ronald Reagan appointed Barnum, a lifelong Republican, to the California State Board of Forestry, where he wrote logging rules after passage of the state's 1973 Forest Practice Act.

Barnum opened his group's expensive Redwoods-to-the-Sea tract with a quote from a 1941 statement by Newton B. Drury, issued when he was head of the US National Park Service, to explain his aversion to creating a Redwood National Park. "The best and most representative of the coast redwood forests are now in the California state parks," said Drury.

The brochure also noted that, as always, redwood remained an important contributor to American industrial might. It featured a compelling photo of a modern chemical processing facility, the foreground dominated by a newly built redwood stave pipe at least twelve feet in diameter. Seven decades after C. A. Hooper had perfected the technology, redwood remained the material of choice even for industrial uses.

The Sierra Club's Redwood National Park campaign of 1965 focused on building momentum for the 1966 legislative session. Already, in September, Congressman Jeffrey Cohelan of Berkeley had submitted legislation, largely written by the Club, to authorize implementation of the Club's ninety-thousand-acre Redwood National Park plan, centered on Redwood Creek. In the Senate, Lee Metcalf of Montana submitted the companion bill. The lawmakers knew there would be no time at the end of the 1965 session to get their bills to a vote, but they wanted to be first in line in 1966. To aid the effort, the Sierra Club spoke directly to the American people.

Today, the full-page political advertisement is a known quantity. But on December 17, 1965, when millions of readers of the *New York Times*, *Washington Post*, *Los Angeles Times*, *San Francisco Chronicle*, and *Sacramento Bee* picked up their morning papers, they encountered something very new in the political conversation. Brandishing photographs of the Tall Trees Grove contrasted with a redwood clear-cut, the Sierra Club's full-page ad announced itself as "An Open Letter to President Johnson on the last chance *really* to save the redwoods." The text was blunt.

> Dear Mr. President: The last chance for the Redwood National Park that this country needs and can still set aside is rapidly slipping away. Nothing less than boldness on your part—supported by foresighted citizens everywhere—will rescue the unique coastal redwoods it is this generation's unique obligation to save. . . . The Park Service plan (Plan 1) was a plan for a real park. We like it. So does the National Parks Association, the Wilderness Society, The National Audubon Society, Trustees for Conservation, the Citizens Committee on Natural Resources, the Federation of Western Outdoor Clubs, and—right in the heart of the redwood country—the Citizens for a Redwood National Park.

Addressing the Club's detractors, the ad said, "Others do not like it. . . . Some voices . . . are now calling for an easy, bargain-basement national park that would cost little and save little in an area no longer of national park caliber." This was clearly a dig at the League. At its April board meeting, the League had passed a resolution in support of a Redwood National Park at Mill Creek. Mill Creek held "one of the best examples of virgin redwood forest in all its majesty," read the resolution, which didn't mention Redwood Creek at all or even the Tall Trees Grove featured the previous year on the cover of *National Geographic.*

The Wayburns wrote the ad, which was edited by David Brower along with San Francisco advertising executives Howard Gossage and Jerry Mander, who worked for free. The timing of the ad was exquisite. Stewart Udall was furious. Edgar Wayburn writes that the ad "appeared the day [Udall] called a private fund-raising meeting with Newton Drury and members of the Ford and Kellogg Foundations." Drury was there to secure funding for the 1966 acquisition of 1,620 acres on the Avenue of the Giants. (The Interior Department contributed $1 million toward the $2.5 million purchase.) He was also there to push Interior to adopt Mill Creek as the best location for a Redwood National Park.

Since 1963, Drury had been hard selling the Ford Foundation's Gordon Harrison to fund the acquisition of two thousand acres of cutover land and four miles of beach owned by Pacific Lumber Company along the west side of Prairie Creek Redwoods State Park. The land included Fern Canyon, which opens onto the beach. On May 3, 1965, Drury laid out this vision in one of many letters he sent off to Harrison, now held in League archives. He also addressed the Redwood National Park controversy, writing, "The Mill Creek project is still uppermost in the minds of the National Park Service as the most desirable and realizable project for a national park. All who have studied the subject have recognized its importance. This includes the State of California, the American Forestry Association, the Sierra Club and the Save-the-Redwoods League."

Drury's claim that even the Sierra Club considered Mill Creek "the most desirable and realizable project for a national park" constitutes a bombshell lie. He also lied when he told one of his biggest funders that the National Park Service also considered Mill Creek to be the best site for a Redwood National Park. The Park Service had yet to abandon Redwood Creek. At the time that Drury wrote his letter, the Park Service was still standing behind its powerful and indisputable report that said Mill Creek was inadequate for a Redwood National Park and that only Redwood Creek was worthy of the designation. The Park Service wouldn't flip until Laurance Rockefeller, and therefore Udall, did two months later, after Drury's July field trip with Rockefeller and Smith to the northern redwoods.

Drury's inventions came to life in January 1966, when Interior Secretary Udall released the Lyndon Johnson administration's final plan for a Redwood National Park and asked Congress to authorize it. The new plan centered almost entirely on Mill Creek, no matter that the Park Service had already rejected the site for a national park. Udall's plan would create a park of 43,434 acres and include Jedediah Smith Redwoods State Park, Del Norte Coast Redwoods State Park, 18,000 acres owned by the Miller Redwood Company that ran between the parks, and 7,000 acres of other cutover lands adjacent to the state parks. Of the Miller land 12,000 acres was also cutover, the rest virgin redwood. The plan also called for protecting 1,600 acres surrounding the Tall Trees Grove, on Redwood Creek, but only if Arcata Redwood Company donated the land.

In March, Thomas Kuchel, the senior senator from California and ranking Republican on the Senate Interior Committee, submitted to Congress the Johnson administration's bill for a Redwood National Park of only 39,264 acres. The redwood region's timber-friendly Congressman Don Clausen submitted a companion bill in the House. Metcalf and Cohelan swiftly amended the Clausen legislation with their 90,000-acre Redwood Creek proposal.

That month Miller-Rellim Redwood Company began constructing additional plants on Mill Creek to augment the company's state-of-the-art lumber mill, built just three years before in the heart of the upper Mill Creek watershed, at the confluence of its two main forks and surrounded by the old-growth forest that would feed it. (Veteran timberman Harold Miller owned Miller-Rellim. "Rellim" is Miller spelled backward.) The new plants would produce plywood, veneer, and particle board, all of which generated toxic waste. Three months later Harold Miller sent bulldozers into his remaining six thousand acres on Mill Creek. He cut a road through the heart of the stand and clear-cut a wide swath of virgin forest adjacent to the state park old growth. Here Miller had pioneered the "spite cut," also known as "legislating by chainsaw," a tactic designed to decimate forests to remove their desirability as parks.

In June, when Kuchel asked Harold Miller to halt the logging, Miller refused. "That would not be feasible," he told the senator. "We can't operate that way." Nonetheless, that month Save the Redwoods League mailed to its members and the media a full-color brochure touting the now scarred Mill Creek as the only remaining choice for a Redwood National Park. To bolster its case, the League included a series of misleading testimonials, including a quote from the report issued in 1937 by Arno Cammerer's National Park Service: "The tract on Mill Creek constitutes one of the finest, if not the best dense virgin redwood forest in existence today." That statement had been made in service of the acquisition proposal that the League had actively opposed and then killed. Naturally, the brochure also noted support for the League's plan by Laurance Rockefeller, Horace Albright, and Ralph Chaney.

On June 17 and 18, 1966, the Senate Subcommittee on Parks and Recreation hosted a seminal set of field hearings at the Del Norte County High School auditorium in Crescent City. Over the two-day event, 117 witnesses appeared. Today, testimony from the hearings provides a window into this transformative time in the redwoods—the penultimate endgame, as it were.

Never before had the US government arrived to take redwoods away from timber companies. The last time government officials had so demonstrably engaged in the redwoods was eighty years before, when they had given away the forest to the Russ gang and the Scots, among others.

Lawmakers landed at the San Francisco airport and were flown to Crescent City in military helicopters, passing over the redwood groves in question. Locals packed the hearing, inside and outside the auditorium. They'd been rallied by their bosses at the mills and by an editorial in the *Humboldt Standard* that, without irony, referred to park proponents as "carpetbaggers."

Just before the hearing, Congressman Clausen withdrew his legislation and proposed an even better bill. He said Congress should adopt the industry's plan for a Redwood National Park.

> With the existing demonstration forest program and the redwood park and recreation plan of the forest products industry involved, we have the opportunity of establishing an interesting and potentially exciting new concept of coordinated conservation planning. . . . The Rellim Redwood Company has the reputation of being one of the finest land managers in the business, thereby lending validity toward acceptance of this concept. Incidentally, part of this recommendation came as a result of many discussions I held with a highly respected member of Save-the-Redwoods League.

During the hearing, Cohelan argued the opposite, insisting that preserving the forest of Redwood Creek was essential to stem the "serious danger of extinction . . . of the world's tallest trees . . . by its most persistent and deadly enemy, man himself." Cohelan warned that "time is of the essence. . . . Logging operations have been making deliberate inroads into redwood groves marked for possible preservation." He rejected the idea that Mill Creek would make a more logical site for a Redwood National Park.

"Logging roads are being pushed into every area of that last stand" on Mill Creek, said Cohelan. "Logging has in fact gone so far that there is not a single stream within Mill Creek Valley that has not been adversely affected by erosion, siltation, or choking debris resulting from the denuding of the hills."

Ralph Chaney represented the League during the hearings. Senator Alan Bible of Nevada, a Democrat and chairman of the Subcommittee on Parks and Recreation, enjoyed quizzing the famous paleobotanist. Bible asked Chaney if redwoods grew in "Wales, in England, in Australia and New Zealand?" Chaney clarified, "They are native only in California." Bible also asked if "there is a difference between old growth and second growth" redwoods. "Very much so," said Chaney.

Chaney told the lawmakers that the League preferred a Redwood National Park at Mill Creek because it "is what we might call an all-American forest," offering a diversity of trees, such as cedar and hemlock, that is found elsewhere on the West Coast. He said that the "League's objective of course is to save the most representative examples of first growth Redwood forests, to the greatest extent possible." Although the unprotected old-growth redwood expanse on Mill Creek was six times smaller than that of Redwood Creek, Chaney emphasized, "selection of a Redwood National Park should, we are convinced, be on a qualitative rather than a quantitative basis. The number of acres or of millions of board feet is not as important as the perfection and completeness of the area preserved. A Redwood National Park should be an outstanding example of nature's handiwork." Chaney included with his written testimony a map whose depiction of the forty-five-thousand-acre Mill Creek park site appeared slightly larger than the Sierra Club's ninety-thousand-acre Redwood Creek site.

Edgar Wayburn countered Chaney's claims, noting that only the broad, twenty-two-mile length of Redwood Creek could provide "the full range of the redwood native growth on a scale that allows for perpetuation of the species."

Wayburn compared the $140 million cost of the Sierra Club's Redwood National Park proposal on Redwood Creek with the $500 million expense paid by the US Air Force to produce one experimental bomber, the XB-70 "superjet." This single prototype had crashed in the Mojave Desert the previous week, killing two pilots during an "early morning sonic boom test run . . . for in-flight publicity photographs made by the General Electric Corp.," the *Oakland Tribune* reported. "We could buy this park for one-third the cost of that," said Wayburn.

By opting to protect Redwood Creek, the lawmakers would reflect the will of the American people, rather than that of timber corporations, said Wayburn. "Historically, it has been the redwood industry which ultimately has decided what kind of redwood parks there would be, or how large they would be. . . . The industry has made these redwoods available to the public strictly on its own terms. We believe it is now time for the people of the United States as a whole to decide what and where their national park should be and that that decision should be made on the peoples' terms." Alluding to the timber fraud of eighty years before, yet never remedied, Wayburn concluded, "Americans who once owned the greatest forest on earth should certainly have the best and biggest possible park, which we can get today."

As if to provide historic irony, Joseph Russ IV, great-grandson of the land grifter who'd orchestrated the theft of Redwood Creek in the first place, followed Wayburn and objected to any Redwood National Park at all. Russ did support "the Redwood Park and Recreation Plan as proposed by community and industry leaders of the Redwood Region." The man who twenty years later would join the California State Board of Forestry and school me in the terms "biological desert" and "overmature" forest sternly informed lawmakers that "there are now more redwoods than ever before [in] Humboldt County." The timber industry based this canard on a literal counting of redwood trees on logged-over lands, where a single old-growth redwood, when cut, might sprout a dozen tiny conifers.

Prior to the hearings, Rudolf Becking, a forestry professor at Humboldt State University, had received funding from the National Science Foundation to explore Redwood Creek and measure big trees. In a report, Becking claimed to have located a dozen tall trees not noted by the National Geographic Society study, including the world's tallest, a redwood that he said stood at 385 feet. Becking also claimed to have found the world's tallest Douglas fir, grand fir, and hemlock. Becking was an international leader in designing criteria for light-touch selective logging. His 1982 book *Pocket Flora of the Redwood Forest* remains the bible of plant associations in the redwood range.

Becking told the subcommittee that Georgia-Pacific's recent logging spree had taken two of the tallest trees in the world, which stood just downstream of the Tall Trees Grove on Redwood Creek. Many of Becking's findings were later found to be inaccurate, though Becking's students did confirm the cutting of the very tall trees. The 2006 discovery on Redwood Creek of the world's tallest tree (379.7 feet), a redwood growing not on a flat but on a slope and just feet from a Georgia-Pacific clear-cut, also lent some credibility to Becking's findings.

Becking's detractors, as well as his supporters, later asserted that Becking's claims betrayed a man desperate to save Redwood Creek from logging. This may have been true. He was fixed in defense of the forest—so much so that during the fight to expand Redwood National Park in the 1970s, Humboldt County loggers hung Becking in effigy. His work was also anathema to the prevailing pro-industry ethos of the Forestry Department at Humboldt State University. Becking was eventually forced out of the department, at which time he joined the school's Department of Natural Resources.

During the hearing, Humboldt County activist Lucille Vinyard bypassed technological jargon and warrens of numbers and instead appealed to lawmakers' humanity and sense of history.

> Conservationists, many times referred to as being "emotional," are certainly entitled to respond that way. They are human beings. Many are devotedly engaged in efforts to conserve portions of this Nation's natural resources: 190 million people and natural resources go hand in hand. What is one without the other? . . . [T]his generation is morally bound to take this last opportunity in creating a Redwood National Park as soon as possible. The following generation will not have the same opportunity. It must be included in recorded history that we, today, had the foresight to preserve this unique environment as a living wonder of nature.

51

G ETTING TO YES ON PARK ACQUISITION BECAME A SCRAMBLE INVOLV-
ing several competing attempts at legislation. Finally, in the spring of
1968, President Lyndon Johnson indicated that he preferred a Redwood National Park on Redwood Creek rather than Mill Creek. The Miller-Rellim
Lumber Company had so damaged the remaining Mill Creek forest that no
one outside Save the Redwoods League would continue to advocate for the
site as a national park.

The new legislation, submitted by Kuchel and Washington congressman
Henry M. Jackson, triggered another lively set of field hearings, on April 16 in
Crescent City and April 18 in Eureka. By then the League and the redwood
industry had been peppering lawmakers with claims that the trees of Redwood Creek were "comparatively small," as Gray Evans, vice president of the
Georgia-Pacific Corporation, put it. The Sierra Club responded by chartering
a helicopter and flying five key lawmakers into Redwood Creek, so they could
hike the watershed and see for themselves the streamside ancient forest. They
found a wooded paradise of colossal trees. One of the lawmakers was Senator
Morris Udall, elected when his brother joined John F. Kennedy's cabinet in
1961. After their hike, Udall told Edgar Wayburn, "You never in your life saw
five such angry congressmen when they learned how the lumber companies
had lied to us."

Martin Litton displayed grim before-and-after photographs of Lost Man
Creek, where Arcata Redwood Company was then heavily clear-cutting.
This was the "forest renewal exhibit," or "tree farm," featured in Philip Hyde
and Francois Leydet's Sierra Club book, which the industry was now touting
as "sustainable forestry." The term "tree farm," aside from reflecting a stark
contradiction in terms (no one had planted the ancient redwoods), was an
ineffectual industry effort to explain away its brutal deforestation. Here, said

Litton, after five months of logging, "not only the trees have disappeared: so has virtually every other living thing, along with the topsoil of centuries and the stream that was called the North Fork of Lost Man Creek—once a clear brook where salmon and steelhead spawned, now a streamless morass of mud and slash. . . . Please look at this picture again, and ask yourselves how an enterprise that could perpetrate anything like this was ever allowed to be in this business in the first place."

Ralph Chaney represented the League in its continued push for a Redwood National Park on Mill Creek. He told members of Congress that business interests were to be honored. When Congressman Don Clausen said to Chaney that establishment of a Redwood National Park should occur with "minimal adverse effect on the economy," Chaney concurred. "That is the position which the Save-the-Redwoods League is taking," said Chaney. "We do not subscribe to the idea that the redwood is approaching extinction. . . . The redwood is saved." Chaney added, "We are happy to see the Great White Father from Washington maybe coming to our aid."

On October 2, 1968, almost half a century after Paul Redington's crew toured the unbroken redwood wilderness of northern Humboldt County, President Lyndon Baines Johnson signed the nation's first Redwood National Park Act. The action set aside a modest stand of conifers on Redwood Creek that was far smaller than what the Sierra Club and North Coast activists had sought. In addition to absorbing the three existing state redwood parks—Prairie Creek, Del Norte Coast Redwoods, and Jedediah Smith—the act authorized acquisition of 28,101 acres of private lands, 10,876 acres of which held virgin redwood. The rest, with the exception of coastal terrain, had been clear-cut. The bulk of the purchase area was on Redwood Creek, but it also included most of the 5,625 acres acquired for a "northern unit" at Mill Creek, to buffer Jedediah Smith Redwoods State Park from Harold Miller's ongoing logging. In addition to selling approximately 4,000 acres of cutover land on Mill Creek, Miller had given up 500 acres of old-growth forest in scattered blocks. He would go on to clear-cut the rest of his 6,000 acres of virgin redwood in the watershed.

Most of the old growth in the newly created Redwood National Park stood as a single block of ancient redwood that coated both ridges of lower Redwood Creek for three miles and ran over the northern ridge into Lost

Man Creek. The park also included a narrow stream corridor of forty-two hundred acres, a quarter-mile wide on both sides of the creek, that ran for five miles from the main block of old growth along Redwood Creek to the Tall Trees Grove. Activists derisively called this slender thread of forest "the worm." Left unprotected were more than twenty thousand acres of virgin redwood, including the "Emerald Mile," considered by activists to hold the finest groves on Redwood Creek, which ran from the park boundary for fifteen miles up Redwood Creek.

A condemnation clause triggered immediate ownership by the US government of the newly acquired timberland. In a letter to members of Save the Redwoods League, dated November 22, 1968, Ralph Chaney wrote, "A *milestone* in the Save-the-Redwoods movement was reached when on October 2, the President signed . . . an act establishing a Redwood National Park. The League for fifty years has favored this and is gratified that at last the redwoods have gained the national recognition they deserve. . . . What has been accomplished is an impressive nucleus for the ultimate ideal Redwood National Park."

The total cost of the park was $198 million, twice the original estimate and at least twice the land's actual value. The price gouging reflected the timber companies' intensive lobbying and frenetic pace of logging, which generated desperate acquiescence from members of Congress who understood that they might otherwise lose the entire Redwood Creek forest. The price was also attributable to deference from lawmakers who reliably supported industry as their raison d'être, and others who took their lead for redwood protection from Save the Redwoods League.

No matter the generous compensation received by the Arcata Redwood, Georgia-Pacific, Simpson, and Miller companies, the federal government also gifted Arcata Redwood with the 14,500-acre Northern Purchase Unit. These federally owned redwood lands covered the watersheds of Hunter, Wilson, Turwar, and High Prairie Creeks—small streams that fed the lower Klamath River. Virgin redwood forest covered 8,000 acres of the purchase unit. The rest had been selectively logged, leaving half the original old-growth trees. The timber companies immediately went to work and clear-cut nearly every redwood.

The US Forest Service had acquired the purchase unit in 1940 for $500,000, from the Hotchkiss Redwood Company. It was the same land that Harold Lee Ward, in 1931, had offered Save the Redwoods League "at bargain prices," along with nine thousand acres of virgin redwood on the Klamath as a gift—a deal that the League rejected. Here again we see the full force of the League's decades-long service to industry, a result being not the saving of ancient redwoods but their preventable destruction.

The following year, on August 27, 1969, one month after Neil Armstrong and Buzz Aldrin became the first human beings to walk on the moon, the sleepy cultural island of Humboldt County awoke to the arrival of the most powerful political cadre ever to visit the region, before or since. More than ten thousand people swarmed the Arcata airport to greet the dignitaries: newly elected president Richard Nixon and his wife Pat, former president Lyndon Johnson and Lady Bird, Governor Ronald Reagan, and others. A military helicopter flew the group to Orick, and from there they made a short jaunt to dedicate the newly named Lady Bird Johnson Grove, at the entrance to the new Redwood National Park along Redwood Creek.

Seven hundred people attended the ceremony, crushing foliage in all directions. The dignitaries perched on a small grandstand set in front of a family of wide redwoods, the largest of which was thirteen feet in diameter. The trees grew not on the fecund flats of Redwood Creek but on the ridgetop far above the stream. When Drury told Rockefeller and Smith that the trees of Redwood Creek were "scraggly," he knew he was lying. Drury had built his career at the League upon a foundation of prevarication and deceit, earning a place among a small cadre of individuals most responsible for the liquidation of ancient redwoods during the twentieth century.

During a solemn moment surrounded by the great forest, Nixon sat at a makeshift redwood table and signed the dedication proclamation, flanked not by Edgar Wayburn or the lawmakers who had fought to create the park but by the presidents' wives, Interior Secretary Walter Hickel, evangelist Billy Graham, Ronald Reagan, and Congressman Clausen. As Nixon spoke and signed, there drifted up from below, within the twenty thousand acres of ancient redwoods that had been left out of the Redwood National Park legislation, the sound of several chainsaws cutting into the unprotected conifers of Redwood Creek. Thuds of giant redwoods hitting the ground punctuated the ceremony.

Nixon had never advocated for redwood protection—quite the opposite. In 1950 Nixon ran a quintessentially nasty electoral campaign against

Southern California congresswoman Helen Gahagan Douglas, among the most powerful women in the United States at the time. In 1946 Douglas had submitted legislation that would have authorized the federal government to buy back most of the redwood biome, more than two million acres, to create the Franklin D. Roosevelt Memorial National Forest. More than three hundred thousand acres of the forest, including much of the ancient redwood forest remaining at the time, would become a Redwood National Park. The first obstacle to the bill was Save the Redwoods League, which opposed the legislation. Newton Drury called it "excessive," something he'd never said about redwood logging. Douglas kept pushing the bill until Nixon defeated her in 1950. "The prospects for future action vanished when Ms. Douglas was replaced by Richard Nixon," wrote Thomas Crabtree in the journal *Environmental Law* in 1975. When the Sierra Club and other groups attempted to expand Redwood National Park during the 1970s, the Nixon administration consistently opposed it.

Today an interpretive sign commemorates the 1969 ceremony. The sign cites early redwood protection efforts—Big Basin, Muir Woods, the 1963 National Geographic Society exploration of Redwood Creek—and notes, "Save the Redwoods League was founded in 1918 to purchase redwoods and convert the land to public trust. Numerous groves were protected and redwood state parks created through the League's efforts." The sign does not mention the Sierra Club.

52

RATHER THAN PROVIDING CLOSURE, PRESIDENT LYNDON JOHNSON'S signing of the 1968 Redwood National Park Act exposed a gaping wound that would fester for the next decade. The three timber companies operating along Redwood Creek now attacked the remaining large block of forest with vicious resolve, logging at a frenetic pace in double shifts. Even as the inventory of available redwood timberland shrank by the day, lumber sales were booming.

In 1971 the Interior Department created a "master plan" for Redwood National Park that recommended a ten-thousand-acre no-cut buffer of ancient forest around the newly protected "worm" running along Redwood Creek. Already heavy logging was dumping mountainsides of sediment into Redwood Creek, creating a massive plug of debris in places fourteen feet deep, that formed in the creek bed and was slowly making its way downstream, destroying precious spawning gravels. No matter, the timber companies refused to abide by the buffer, cutting rapidly and without mercy down into the creek itself. There would be no relief for the forest of Redwood Creek until the Richard Nixon and Gerald Ford administrations were finally removed from office.

In January 1977, Jimmy Carter took the oath to become president of the United States. Almost immediately, Carter recommended to Congress a forty-eight-thousand-acre expansion of Redwood National Park. In the House of Representatives, Morris Udall, now chair of the powerful Interior Committee, supported the idea.

In March, Congressman Phil Burton introduced legislation, written by Edgar Wayburn, to expand Redwood National Park to 132,000 acres. Burton, long a champion of the Sierra Club's projects, was instrumental in passing the Wilderness Act and establishing the Golden Gate National

Recreation Area. According to Wayburn, once Burton took over as chair of the Subcommittee on National Parks and Public Lands in 1977, he declared, "Gentlemen, this committee will entertain no legislation until we first act on the expansion of Redwood National Park." Under pressure from Carter, Burton reduced his expansion request to forty-eight thousand acres. In April, the US Congress again came to Humboldt County.

The hostility that greeted park advocates at the April 13, 1977, Eureka field hearing of the Subcommittee on National Parks and Public Lands was as unexpected as it was brutish. Timber workers and employees from other Humboldt County businesses were given the day off with pay to attend the hearing. More than two thousand showed up to form a frothing mob of hostile, frightened, ill-informed locals. Three hundred logging trucks, many of them loaded with redwood boles, endlessly circled the cavernous Eureka Municipal Auditorium, as did hundreds of private vehicles. The trucks and cars honked constantly, cheered by a boisterous crowd that wielded signs and bellowed incomprehensively into the face of an uncertain future.

The North Coast's elected representatives were predictably immoderate in their opposition to park expansion. Don Clausen, a member of the subcommittee, stirred the mob by yelling at his fellow committee members, "Don't take jobs away from these people!" He called the park expansion "unwise, unnecessary, and potentially devastating to the economy of Humboldt County," something he never said to the timber companies that for a century had raced through their old-growth inventories in job-killing cycles of boom and bust and were now logging faster and heavier than ever.

Assemblyman Barry Keene adopted the tone of a schoolyard bully, no matter that in the southern reach of his district he would flourish his environmental cred. "There is no overriding national interest in park expansion," Keene said to cheers. "Jobs on the North Coast of California are just as important as jobs in San Francisco. . . . These hearings were not designed by Congressman Burton to consider the views of the people of the North Coast. They were designed to create the circus atmosphere which would make Burton look good in the national media. . . . We have been taken for a ride by the big city politicians." It was a hollow sentiment from the wealthy and well-coiffed New Jersey native who'd earned his bachelor's and law degrees at Stanford University.

The vitriol at the hearing was so consuming that few environmentalists were able to testify. Lucille Vinyard had attended all the Redwood National Park hearings as a North Coast representative of the Sierra Club and, before that, with the local Citizens for a Redwood National Park. In 2012 Vinyard told me that the 1977 hearing in Eureka "was the ugliest thing I ever went through in my life." She continued,

A bunch of us who had prepared statements—individuals or organizations— we sat up front. . . . Everybody knew who we were because we'd been in public over time. The place began to fill up with loggers, in the go-to-work outfit in the woods that's so standard, and their wives and girlfriends and mothers and whatnot, all dressed up and noisy and chattering. . . . What they did was so rude and so horrendous. . . . Next to me was a man who had already—I had seen the pocketknife that he had out at one time for one reason or another, and he just did this. [Vinyard makes a poking motion with her arm.] I could almost feel it against me. You could tell the knife was in his hand. Any time any conservationist got up and said something, then the spitballs were flying from the audience and up above—it was just full of all these men who were scared to death about their jobs, and their families, and their friends, and they're just riotous. . . . Before the recess, one of the senator's staff handed back [a note] from table to table until it reached the audience— from the stage to the tables—and then it was passed around to those of us who were definitely going to be speaking for the park. It said, "Leave quietly. Don't leave all at once. It's getting tough." It was ready to just blow up. Somebody's going to get hurt. You could feel it. There was somebody hanging from the chandeliers. I mean, it was just the rudest, riotous—close to riot. I was scared. We were all scared, those of us for the park. We did not leave all at once. Some of us, you know, like you're just going out to the restroom or something? Then a few minutes later another one of us left, and we did that until we all got out of that room, and we met out in the parking lot. And then some ugly things happened out in the parking lot, like Dave Van de Mark got punched in the chest.

Van de Mark attended the hearings as a longtime activist with Citizens for a Redwood National Park. His unnerving before-and-after images of ancient redwood groves and subsequent clear-cuts along Redwood Creek became sensations with the public and on Capitol Hill. In 2022, Van de Mark told me that, in the parking lot, a television crew was interviewing him when "five or six of these goons surrounded me, almost literally pushing the TV people away. One of them jabbed me in the chest a few times. Yeah it was scary."

The next day, more than four hundred Humboldt County residents who opposed expanding the park boarded buses in Eureka at 2 a.m. and made the six-hour journey to San Francisco's Federal Building for day two of the hearings. In addition, reported the *Eureka Times-Standard*, "a convoy of approximately 115 lumber and logging trucks, which also originated in Eureka . . ., crossed the Golden Gate Bridge and headed toward the Federal Building with horns blaring." There the truckers circled and idled for the entire day. In May, a convoy of thirty trucks, stacked with redwood logs, traveled three thousand miles from Eureka to Washington, DC, to protest the park expansion. One of the trucks carried an old-growth redwood log carved in the shape of a peanut, hung with a sign that read, "It may be peanuts to you but it's jobs to us." On arrival, the truckers demanded to see President Carter so they could present him with the peanut. Carter, offended, refused. Today the peanut, now so worn that it's just a giant piece of driftwood, lies prone in front of a decommissioned gas station in Orick.

Wisely, in September, the Senate Subcommittee on Parks and Recreation held its park expansion hearings in Washington, DC. Industry representatives would continue to provide senators with bogus laments about the "loss of jobs" that would accompany expansion, but really they were readying themselves for one of the largest windfalls in the region since the Scottish land swindles.

John Crowell, attorney for Louisiana-Pacific (spun off from Georgia-Pacific after the government's antitrust action of 1972), claimed that the addition of LP's mostly cutover lands in an expanded park would "cause an ultimate job loss to 800 to 900 people." Crowell was actually representing LP's seventy-five thousand shareholders. His assignment was not to halt park expansion but to secure taxpayer compensation far above the value of the company's land.

At the Senate hearing, John Amodio testified for the Sierra Club. A former student at Humboldt State University, Amodio was an early activist with the Emerald Creek Committee, formed to secure the park expansion.

Here Amodio appeared in his new guise as the Sierra Club's California wilderness coordinator.

"Virtually all of the [redwood] parks are what can best be described as museum pieces—grand groves fragmented out of their interdependent ecosystems and highly vulnerable to adjacent land uses," Amodio told the senators. "The park was vulnerable from the start due to a gerrymandered park boundary that conformed to political necessity but defied ecological reality."

Amodio was wise to the please-don't-throw-me-in-that-briar-patch approach of the timber industry. "What they want you to do is open the public coffers. They will be pounding at the door in 10 years anyway. They want you to do it now." Amodio warned the senators against overspending. At the time, the going rate for an acre of old-growth redwood timber was $25,000. Cutover land sold for $300 an acre. Amodio said that, with the legislation calling for acquisition of 48,500 acres from the timber companies, including slightly more than 8,500 acres of old growth, total cost to taxpayers should not exceed $225 million.

On March 27, 1978, President Carter signed the Redwood National Park expansion bill, adding forty-eight thousand acres to the park, including eighty-five hundred acres of old-growth redwood. Since 1968, timber companies had clear-cut twelve thousand acres of the Redwood Creek stand. The legislation also created the Redwood Employees Protection Program, which compensated a few hundred employees who had lost work to the new park.

The legislation required that the amount of compensation paid to timber companies be arbitrated in federal district court. After nine years of litigation, the court ordered the federal government to pay lumber firms $688 million—three times the going rate—plus interest. Small landowners were also paid off. By 1990 the total cost of Redwood National Park had reached $1.6 billion, the most expensive national park in US history, at the time or since. Tens of millions of additional taxpayer dollars have been poured into restoring the damaged watershed.

The price reflects industry's remarkable triple-dipping into the public coffers. During the nineteenth century, capitalists orchestrated the theft of these very lands from the public domain, paying pennies on the dollar. During the 1960s and 1970s, the timber industry profited from the liquidation of more than forty thousand acres of this forest, eliminating precious habitat and leaving an eviscerated landscape. Then timber companies sold the plundered land back to the federal government almost exactly a century after it had been stolen. What's so mystifying, if not enraging, is the understanding that such institutional grift and ecological destruction are not aberrations from, but instead represent the quintessence of, American commerce—a system so well-oiled and undergirded by subterfuge that it could spawn a "save the redwoods" group whose false premise of existence would go unchallenged for an entire century.

53

I N HIS ORAL HISTORY INTERVIEW, EDGAR WAYBURN REFLECTED RUE-
fully on what then appeared to be the final chapter in redwood preservation fights. He noted that timber companies operating in Redwood Creek
had been practicing an "American tradition of 'cut out and get out,' which
had followed the lumber companies all the way across the country and in
three hundred years has caused us to change a tremendous, forested country
into one that is going to be short on wood products in the future. The redwood forest is the last and the greatest. They just wanted to cut as many trees
as they could. . . . Louisiana-Pacific and Arcata [Redwood Company] played
a very dirty game. The only thing I can see behind it is greed."

Wayburn's criticism of Save the Redwoods League was only slightly
milder than his rebuke of the timber industry. Given his well-earned reputation as a "statesman," Wayburn's candor is surprising. His frustration jumps
off the page.

> As I became personally involved and worried about what was happening in
> the redwood region, I naturally went to [Newton] Drury and consulted with
> him. . . . Drury was discouraging and, as I remember it now, he felt that the
> Redwood League had done everything that was necessary for redwood pres-
> ervation. . . . [T]here's no question that the league had to be influenced one
> way or another by the lumber companies with which it was dealing. People in
> the Sierra Club felt that they had been betrayed by the failure of the league to
> go along. . . . I further feel that the league may well have a guilty conscience,
> the people in the league, because they're aware of what they did. . . . It en-
> abled the opposition to succeed. If the league had not been in the picture, if
> it weren't known that . . . some powerful members of the league were actually
> opposed to the acquisition of Redwood Creek, we would have succeeded in

getting much more land in 1968—much more virgin redwood in the basin of Redwood Creek.

When Wayburn conducted his oral history interviews with Ann Lage and Susan Schrepfer, he was still a national director of the Sierra Club, a position he held until 1996. Peggy Wayburn was less diplomatic than her husband in her assessment of Drury and the League.

"Newton Drury . . . was short-sighted in many ways, as we came to know as we became better acquainted with him," Peggy Wayburn told Ann Lage in 1990. She continued,

> He remained on very friendly terms with the logging interests. Of course, that was one of the major disappointments . . . the failure of the Save-the-Redwoods League to go along with the big park that we wanted. They wanted the Mill Creek drainage protected, and we wanted Redwood Creek *and* Mill Creek. . . . I remember this particular luncheon [in 1966], which was downtown in San Francisco . . . and I said to him, "Well, why don't we just go for both. Then we could both endorse the other's." He kind of smiled at me in a benign way as though he were sort of patting me on the head, you know. But he was unwilling to accept that idea at all. He just acted as though I were being out of order. . . . I think there had been an agreement between the Save-the-Redwoods League and the timber industry, and I think that Newton was honoring it. I can see no other reason why he should have been so weak-kneed about the whole idea. He never embraced the national park idea [in the redwoods] that fully. And when you read the history of the Save-the-Redwoods League and realize that they had actually—I would feel this might have been an agreement that was made in the twenties or in the thirties when Newton Drury was head of the Save-the-Redwoods League. Then they were acquiring land from the timber companies on the terms of the timber companies.

In 1978, when the last tractor trundled out of the watershed, Redwood Creek emerged as a violated, seemingly endless expanse of pillaged terrain, crisscrossed with skid trails and sliced by haul roads, bleeding soils into one of the last great salmon streams in California. Hardly anything green grew across thousands of acres. A long, thin, and often broken thread of ancient

forest lined the creek like the remnants of a ripped-up shirt. The denuded remains of Redwood Creek stood starkly against the words of Madison Grant,
which he wrote in 1919 after his second tour of the redwood domain: "This
Redwood Creek stand is as yet untouched and should be carefully considered
for a national park because the timber being inaccessible can be acquired at a
relatively small cost."

The staggering price of Redwood National Park cuts deeper when we
consider that all of lower Redwood Creek, including an additional twenty
thousand acres of virgin redwood, could have been purchased in 1968 for
$150 million. The catastrophically damaged Redwood Creek watershed and
the usurious levels of public treasure dedicated to purchasing and restoring it
represent the true legacy of Save the Redwoods League.

Part Four

THE EMPIRE STRIKES BACK

It was as if lost and desperate visitors to earth reduced what they wanted of its life to a thimbleful and carried it away.

—*Richard White*

There are consolations that the strongest human love is powerless to give.

—*Richard Powers*

54

I**N HINDSIGHT, IT WOULD SEEM OBVIOUS THAT** CHARLES HURWITZ AND HIS fiduciary sorcerers had studied the lessons of Redwood National Park before they would attempt a hostile takeover of the Pacific Lumber Company (PL) just seven years later. History would have told them that tractable state regulators and the "toughest logging laws in the country" would allow unfettered old-growth clear-cutting, that the North Coast's elected representatives would assist their efforts, and that Save the Redwoods League would prove a potent ally. And if clear-cutting the world's last remaining, unprotected ancient redwoods ran into legal snags, Maxxam could leverage the moment by ransoming a small reserve for an exorbitant price. All of this would happen.

Yet, as Mary Beth Nearing and I perched in the canopy of All Species Grove, I still believed that if we generated enough publicity about the logging and got the American public on our side, we could enforce state and federal laws and protect this rare and precious redwood habitat. I understood very little. Contrasted with players in Houston and Sacramento, on Capitol Hill and Wall Street, I was a babe in the woods.

After just six days of dangling from branches in All Species Grove, Mary Beth and I were done. Our rowdy logger guards had augmented their floodlights and generators with air horns, screaming chainsaws, midnight howls, and crappy country music. I called the Humboldt County Sheriff's Department and told them to come on in; we were coming down. Back at my tree I retrieved two rolls of film and taped the film canisters together. When it seemed no one was looking, I tossed them over the side. I tried to eyeball the landing.

The cops were surprisingly cordial. They allowed Mary Beth and me to ride on the tailgate of the police truck as it trundled out of the grove on the newly cut skid trail. We watched the forest disappear in a strange reverse-action tableau as we plunged into the glare of the clear-cut. The truck squeaked and pitched across a dried-up diorama of stumps, skid trails, and slash, crossed Booths Run Creek, and stopped at Kneeland Road. There we were placed without handcuffs into the backseat of a waiting sheriff's cruiser and driven to Eureka. I still wore the Swiss Army knife around my neck. We were the easiest and probably the most entertaining arrest they'd ever made.

Getting arrested on a Friday is fraught—the cops might decide to keep you in jail over the weekend. But the cells were over capacity, so we were cited and released. That evening, under a nearly full moon, Mokai and I tramped back across the clear-cut and onto the new skid trail into All Species Grove. The forest stood empty of people, full of life. Using headlamps, we found the film I had tossed from the tree.

On October 5, Mary Beth and I were arraigned in Fortuna Justice Court. An attorney for Maxxam handed us papers, indicating that we were also being sued. The company lumped us into an existing lawsuit against arrestees from the May 18 actions at All Species Grove and the Fisher log deck. We pled no contest, and the judge sentenced us to community service to be performed for a nonprofit organization. The judge also slapped us with a five-year injunction from entering Pacific Lumber property. He issued a stern warning against violating the injunction, which he said could land us in jail for a year. I would violate the injunction more than a hundred times.

That day, another alleged lawbreaker appeared in a legal setting. Charles Hurwitz himself, alongside attorneys and toadies such as Pacific Lumber director of operations John Campbell, testified before the US House Subcommittee on Oversight and Investigation to explain why Maxxam's buyout of Pacific Lumber should not be considered a violation of securities laws. Representative John Dingell, a Democrat from Michigan who had authored the Endangered Species Act, led the probe as a case study of shady mergers and acquisitions that by now were defining corporate economics during the Ronald Reagan era.

In a memorandum distributed to committee members, Dingell outlined the illicit web of stock parking and dark financing procured for Maxxam by

Ivan Boesky, Michael Milken, Boyd Jefferies, and Drexel Burnham Lambert, among other players and companies, not just in the United States but in the Netherlands and on the Spanish island of Majorca. Dingell wrote, "The annual interest payments on [Maxxam's junk] bonds—which begin in 1989—is more than Pacific's historic annual profit. . . . [Maxxam] now estimates there will be enough timber for only 20 years at the present rate of cutting. Even at this rate, in its latest 10-K annual report, the company reports that it cannot pay projected debt service and predicts increased cutting and asset sales may be necessary. Of course, this threatens to liquidate the company."

At the same time, the *Wall Street Journal* reported that, in November 1986, "Pacific Lumber was one of the 14 takeover-related stocks named by the [Securities and Exchange Commission] in subpoenas issued in connection with the Boesky insider-trading investigation. The stock also figures in the government's investigation of Drexel Burnham Lambert Inc."

By the time he was sitting in the hearing room, Hurwitz had already been legally upbraided for several securities violations in service of takeovers that had left a trail of shattered companies, ranging from the Summit Insurance Group to the Simplicity Pattern Company. Another victim was United Savings Association of Texas (USAT), which was taken over by Hurwitz in 1982 and failed in 1988, leaving a $1.6 billion debt. A Hurwitz partner in the venture was Barry Munitz, who joined Maxxam as vice president at the time of the USAT takeover and was chair of the thrift's executive committee. In 1991 California officials hired Munitz as chancellor of the California State University system.

United Savings was once the largest savings and loan in Texas. It would become one of the biggest failures of the Reagan-era savings-and-loan scandal, costing taxpayers $1.6 billion. Hurwitz had drained United Savings to purchase $1.4 billion in junk bonds issued by Michael Milken and Drexel Burnham Lambert. Milken eventually contributed $1.8 billion to fund Hurwitz's various takeover schemes. It was a tidy operation.

With surprising consistency, Maxxam's attorneys and investigators managed to evade economic and legal repercussions as Charles Hurwitz set out to achieve his life's ambition, which was to control a Fortune 500 company. To gain such a noble palm, Hurwitz would liquidate the very life of the world's last unprotected ancient redwoods.

In California, especially in Humboldt County, Hurwitz easily cultivated allies. For instance, in December 1985, Humboldt County's representative in the state assembly, Dan Hauser, had threatened Maxxam with legislative action if he noted any uptick in the company's old-growth redwood logging. In an open letter sent at the time to Charles Hurwitz, Hauser wrote, "I have asked the Office of Legislative Counsel to present me with a list of options that could be pursued should Maxxam's promises [of maintaining Pacific Lumber's low-yield forestry practices] turn out to be empty." Yet, on October 17, 1987, with Maxxam well into its tripling of the cut, Hauser sat as guest of honor at a $250-a-plate fund-raising dinner hosted by Pacific Lumber at the Scotia Inn. In announcing the dinner, PL's public relations hack, Dave Galitz, said, "Dan [Hauser] works hard for us in Sacramento, and will continue to do so."

Soon after his dinner with Maxxam, Hauser publicly ranted against any further protections of ancient redwood. "There simply is no reason to attempt to include more virgin redwood in the park system if it means the loss of hundreds or even thousands of jobs and the possible destruction of the entire town of Scotia," Hauser told the press in late 1987. In a January 1988 op-ed, I responded to Hauser:

[Pacific Lumber's] logging of old growth has at least doubled since the takeover. It probably tripled in 1986. Yet employment [at the company] rose during the same time only 20 percent. . . . Hundreds will lose their jobs after Hurwitz and his people have made millions. It is no coincidence that guaranteed wages and benefits for PALCO employees end in October this year, just a few months before Maxxam's debt payments double to $83 million annually. . . . Hauser defends his "continued friendship with executives at Pacific Lumber Co." as being "personally important to me." I have no doubt this is true, especially in an election year.

Similarly, State Senator Barry Keene and North Coast congressman Doug Bosco enjoyed "continued friendship with executives at Pacific Lumber" and therefore with Maxxam. Bosco told the press that Dingell's committee was investigating Maxxam's takeover of Pacific Lumber because the action promised "high drama" on Capitol Hill. "In my own review, I've found nothing illegal," said Bosco. "So far I have not seen any abuse of the environment that we can't resolve as we proceed." When Bosco said "we," he meant it. In 1990 Tom Lynch, who was then opposing Bosco for his congressional seat, revealed that Bosco was receiving income from the timber export business of his father-in-law, Humboldt County lumber baron Victor Guynup. (Bosco's wife, Gayle Guynup, was a Sonoma County judge.)

At the local level, Humboldt County officials, led by the district attorney's office and especially the board of supervisors, behaved largely as colonial satraps. In this way nothing had changed in nearly fourteen decades. For twenty years not a single person of authority in Humboldt County stepped up in any way to curb Maxxam's abuses, a shameful record. The only exception occurred in 2003, when the county's new district attorney, Paul Gallegos, sued Maxxam for fraudulently concocting timber yield data to justify a heavy logging regimen after conclusion of the 1999 Headwaters Forest deal. Gallegos was an outsider, a graduate of the University of Southern California who had lived in Humboldt County just nine years before being elected district attorney. Immediately the timber industry rallied to recall him. Maxxam contributed $40,000 to the signature-gathering campaign, spending $8 per signature. The company then poured $254,000 into the recall itself, an extraordinary sum in the county. Gallegos beat the recall 61 to 39 percent, a margin of victory greater than his original win. Nonetheless, in June 2005, a Humboldt County judge tossed out his lawsuit against Maxxam.

On April 13, 1988, a small core group of redwood activists staged what remains my favorite direct action in the redwoods. Ten of us were involved in planning. Five would each guide a group of protesters into All Species Grove. We would gather as many people as possible, none of whom would know where they were going until they were dropped off prior to hiking. The idea was to storm the grove from five directions, one group at a time, to shut down logging for the day.

At the appointed morning hour on April 13, more than 150 people gathered in front of my house in downtown Arcata. We were stunned. My roommates were nervous. Seventy-five people agreed to be guided wherever we would take them and to put themselves between the redwoods and the loggers and tractors. Once again the Acorn Alliance, from Southern Humboldt County, sent two dozen people, twenty of whom would be arrested. The action shut down logging all day.

On May 23, 1988, Humboldt Earth First!ers launched the second annual National Day of Direct Action against Maxxam. One of the demonstrations occurred at Dan Hauser's Eureka office. Maxxam's Houston office also was a target, as was the Manhattan office of Drexel Burnham Lambert. Four days earlier ten activists hauled gear into All Species Grove and placed three tree-sitters 120 feet into the redwood canopy. The sitters, from Santa Cruz, called themselves Rufus, Pat, and Raven. It was the first time I'd climbed trees using spurs and a lanyard to rig redwoods for tree-sitters. The sitters would be largely left alone, and they would spend ten days in the middle of All Species Grove. The tree-sit marked our thirty-sixth individual direct action against redwood liquidation in just eighteen months.

One of the May 23 actions occurred in Sacramento. Kurt Newman and Greenpeace activist Dan Zbozien climbed planted redwoods outside the capitol to protest the state's abetting of Maxxam's illegal logging. I was their ground guy. The climbers quickly reached the seventy-five-foot level and began hauling up a banner ("STOP MAXXAM"), but we were thwarted by a dozen men in suits who seemed to appear out of nowhere and were unduly agitated. One of them stomped on the banner and yelled at Zbozien to climb down. "I can't," said Dan, who looked like Clark Kent. He smiled and nodded toward his wrists, now handcuffed around the tree. I noted that the suited guys also seemed focused on their wrists—they were talking into them. One of the suits was particularly icy and looked unsettlingly like George H. W. Bush. He said to one of the other suits, a little too loudly, "Maybe we should just shoot them down." Then he turned to me and said, "If that guy puts his hand in his pocket while Jackson walks by, his mother will be sad tomorrow morning."

They were Secret Service. We'd taken to the redwoods a half hour before presidential candidate Jesse Jackson was scheduled to walk directly under them on his way to the capitol. A fire truck arrived, its extendable ladder rose to the heights, and a cop retrieved Zbozien. Kurt simply rappelled.

When we got back from Sacramento, Kurt and I climbed two more trees. These were super-tall redwoods that stood on either side of US Highway 101 in the middle of Humboldt Redwoods State Park. By now we'd gotten back most of our gear from previous tree-sits, including the giant banner that hung between Mary Beth's and my trees the previous year in All Species Grove. Kurt and I rigged the banner and a traverse line, and I zipped out onto the traverse to add drama to the banner. Cars zoomed underneath on the wide freeway that had sliced through the ancient redwoods with blessings and funding from Newton B. Drury.

55

A T THE END OF 1987, MAXXAM REPORTED THAT ITS INCOME FOR THE first nine months of that year was $153 million, half of it coming in the third quarter. The company noted that income had climbed steadily in every quarter since mid-1986 and that 75 percent of all Maxxam revenues came from Pacific Lumber. Maxxam had increased Pacific Lumber's annual lumber yield from 137 million board feet in 1986 to 248 million feet in 1987, an amount three to five times higher than in years before the takeover.

In order to deflect public outrage, in 1987 Maxxam hired the public relations firm Hill & Knowlton to advance the specious claim that in 1984 Pacific Lumber directors had "voted unanimously . . . to resume clear-cutting" and increase lumber production. Hill & Knowlton was probably also responsible for a claim made by Charles Hurwitz, in 1990, that Maxxam's liquidation of the last redwoods was "a clean, nontoxic production process that does no damage to the environment. It is renewable, provides clean air and water and wonderful wildlife habitats."

In May 1988, Pacific Lumber announced that the company had called a halt to clear-cutting virgin redwood groves and had invented a logging system called "modified selection." The pronouncement was clearly a ruse, undoubtedly cooked up by Hill & Knowlton. The "policy change" was aimed at eroding opposition to Maxxam's accelerated redwood liquidation, which was vital that year as interest payments on junk bonds came due.

Credulous reporters repeated the company line: The *Santa Rosa Press Democrat* ran the headline "Clear Cutting of Redwoods to End." The paper's timber correspondent, Mike Geniella, reported, "[John] Campbell . . . said Thursday that Pacific Lumber will continue to work closely with groups like the Save the Redwoods League."

The true purpose of the announced "change" was to provide state officials with a smokescreen to allow continued approval of Maxxam's logging. Prior to the announcement, in April 1988, a Humboldt County judge had agreed with an Environmental Protection Information Center (EPIC) lawsuit that challenged logging approval by the California Department of Forestry (CDF) of 54 acres of virgin redwood on Lawrence Creek and 641 acres of residual old-growth on Root Creek, a tributary of the Van Duzen River. A few days later the judge's ruling prompted CDF director Jerry Partain to issue an unprecedented rejection of a proposed Maxxam clear-cut of 319 acres from the heart of the Shaw Creek virgin redwood grove. As Steve Ongerth noted in *Redwood Uprising*, Partain "was by no means an environmentalist and had, in his role as director of the CDF, fast-tracked thousands of [timber harvest plans (THPs)]. He had been a P-L stockholder and cashed in handsomely when Maxxam bought the company in 1986."

Partain said that his rejection signaled "basically a moratorium," to last three months, on logging in Pacific Lumber's virgin redwood forests. He was responding not just to EPIC's court victories but to pressure from all over the state, and the country, to address Maxxam's redwood liquidation. Partain was also getting pressure from his own state attorney general's office, which was growing tired of ending up in court to defend CDF's approval of illegal timber harvest plans.

In June, shortly after Maxxam's "announcement" of its meaningless change, the California State Board of Forestry voted 8–0 to overturn Partain's denial of the Shaw Creek logging. The board was overriding not just its own forestry director but a finding from John Hummel, at the California Department of Fish and Game, that Pacific Lumber's timber harvest plans had failed to address impacts to wildlife.

Invoking the California Environmental Quality Act (CEQA), Hummel had asked CDF foresters to provide "due consideration . . . to the old growth dependent wildlife species," along with "an evaluation of the cumulative impacts of the past, present and all reasonable, foreseeable, probable future clearcut logging operations and their effect on old growth dependent wildlife species." He wanted state officials to "develop and provide a policy to ensure that sufficient populations of all old growth dependent wildlife species and the habitat necessary for their continued existence shall be maintained at optimum levels."

Hummel had listed twelve bird species "of special concern" that used Pacific Lumber's redwood groves, including the endangered peregrine falcon, spotted owl, marbled murrelet, osprey, and northern goshawk. The groves also provided habitat for fishers, a rare carnivorous species that in northwestern California is found only in old-growth forests. These species, along with the red tree vole, Olympic salamander, and tailed frog "appear to be vulnerable to extinction due to loss and fragmentation of mature and old-growth forests," wrote Hummel.

At the time I asked Hummel if his findings on the THPs pertained to any other remaining old-growth habitat on the California North Coast. "Well sure," he said. "The issue is relevant to any old growth stand. Somewhere they [CDF] have got to draw the line on the amount of acreage [that can be logged]." No California official had ever previously said such a thing.

Nonetheless, Robert Stephens and Pacific Lumber, with backing from officials at the Board of Forestry and CDF, refused to turn over wildlife information requested by Hummel and the Department of Fish and Game.

One day after Hummel issued his official findings, with its long list of species threatened by Maxxam's logging, CDF forester John Allardice repeated the old nonsense. "There should be only minimal impact on fish and may be considerable improvement in some types of wildlife habitat" after Pacific Lumber's logging, wrote Allardice, who apparently hadn't read Hummel's report. "There are no reported or known rare, threatened, or endangered species of plants or animals known to exist in this area."

To fight the Board of Forestry's approval of the logging, EPIC joined with the national Sierra Club to sue the state, Pacific Lumber, and Maxxam. It was the first action taken by a national organization to stop Maxxam's redwood liquidation.

"The Board of Forestry's decision . . . sets an intolerable precedent," said Sierra Club State Forest Practices Task Force chair Gail Lucas. "The board, in its action, has said the Department of Fish and Game—the agency designated to protect fish and wildlife and charged by law to ensure that wildlife populations in the state do not drop below self-perpetuating levels—cannot require the company that is going to log to give Fish and Game the information needed to analyze the effect of the logging on wildlife."

As soon as the Board of Forestry approved the plan, Pacific Lumber began cutting in Shaw Creek. In early July 1988, EPIC and the Sierra Club secured a state appellate court injunction to halt the logging. Plaintiffs won this case all the way to the state supreme court, which on July 21, 1994, ruled,

> We conclude that the [Board of Forestry] did abuse its discretion when it evaluated and approved the plans on the basis of a record which lacked information regarding the presence in the subject areas of some old-growth-dependent species, information which both the department and Fish and Game had determined was necessary. By approving the plans without the necessary information regarding those species the board failed to comply with the obligation imposed on it by the California Environmental Quality Act.

Once again a high court had set an important precedent. By extension, the powerful ruling also indicated that every old-growth timber harvest plan submitted by Maxxam and approved by CDF was illegal. The court concluded that when Robert Stephens refused to submit to Fish and Game requested data on wildlife that used the virgin groves, Stephens had violated CEQA.

John Hummel's courageous outspokenness in mid-1988 was threatening to end Hurwitz's gambit in the redwoods. Maxxam's entire game plan was now at risk. His findings might also force state officials to crack down on destructive logging elsewhere in the state. Yet Hummel would find himself virtually alone. In the lineage of individuals who wielded real power in California over the fate of the state's once-great forests, Hummel's voice pierced a silence rooted in collusion. He was a brave man, and his courage opened opportunities to save the last ancient redwoods that otherwise did not exist.

When the Shaw Creek THPs first landed in court, in July 1988, Charles Hurwitz and other Maxxam officials, including attorney Jared Carter, became desperately aware that the liquidation of PL's ancient redwood groves was not a given and that their economic house of cards could soon crumble. Rather than back off and regroup, the company doubled down and sought CDF approval for two more extraordinarily destructive timber harvest plans. One proposed logging 220 acres from the heart of Owl Creek Grove. The other THP would cut 230 acres from the middle of Headwaters Forest.

I spent most of July 1988 in Oregon and Washington, working with increasingly militant crews of Earth First!ers to shut down the US government's clear-cut liquidation of ancient forests on federal lands. Each day blended with another in a frenzy of direct action and protest. In eastern Washington, I and two dozen others were arrested for exercising our constitutionally guaranteed right to free speech and dissent. We had gathered with signs and chants at the Okanogan National Forest headquarters to protest Reagan-era timber giveaways in the region. We were met not with flowers but by fully militarized riot police wielding automatic weapons and snapping German shepherds. Back in Oregon's North Kalmiopsis, Kurt Newman and I aided road blockades and tree-sits.

Near the end of the month, I attended the CDF review team meetings for Maxxam's new logging plans for Headwaters Forest and Owl Creek Grove. It was largely the same old scene, apart from a minor swelling of environmental ranks. Bob Anderson attended on behalf of Mattole forest defenders, as Maxxam was continuously targeting the rare Douglas fir habitat on that river's North Fork. Also surrounding CDF that day were Cecelia Lanman, Darryl Cherney, Kurt Newman, and Lynn Ryan. Cecelia skillfully disassembled assertions by CDF officials and Pacific Lumber forester Ray Miller that somehow cutting the life out of these groves wouldn't also impact rare wildlife. She punctuated her arguments with a hand landing gently, but audibly, on the table. The velvet hammer.

Darryl noted that NASA was now "saying forcefully" that the "greenhouse effect [was] real and becoming more so every day." Tag-teaming, I added that preserving forests was perhaps the best way to "prevent or at least lessen the severity of global catastrophe."

Miller just rolled his eyes. "Aw, I don't want to even hear about that greenhouse effect," he said. "What we're talking about here is so small it don't even matter. It's the rainforest down in South America they're talking about."

After a banal exchange among themselves that reminded me of a PTA meeting, CDF officials recommended that the logging plans be approved. They'd noted that all was well because Pacific Lumber had announced it would "no longer clear-cut" in virgin redwood groves. The transparent ruse from two months before had done the trick.

John Hummel wasn't fooled. He pointed out that six species of special concern required protection from Maxxam's logging in virgin forests. He recommended that Maxxam not be allowed to log at certain times of year and that cutting be disallowed entirely in parts of the unentered groves. Even these measures wouldn't be enough to truly protect the sensitive wildlife that relied on undisturbed old-growth habitat for stability and survival. Industrial logging of a virgin redwood grove is a savage act. The disturbance and destruction of vital components of the forest are extreme and reverberate throughout the remaining stand. Partial measures were just that: partial. Yet, in the political atmosphere of the times, that was as far as Hummel could take it.

After refusing to adopt Hummel's modest recommendations, and in spite of prior court rulings against the agency, Partain and his lieutenants at CDF approved both the Owl Creek and Headwaters Forest logging plans. A short while later the state transferred Hummel to Redding, at the north end of the Sacramento Valley, a hundred miles from the nearest redwood.

Again, EPIC and the Sierra Club sued. By the end of 1988, separate decisions in Humboldt County Superior Court resulted in preliminary injunctions that disallowed logging in both Owl Creek and Headwaters Forest. Two judges had ruled that CDF officials violated their legal mandate to consider the cumulative environmental impacts that the logging would impose on the rare ancient redwood habitat.

Gail Lucas recommended that, rather than attempt to log these groves, Maxxam declare itself a "willing seller" to permanently protect them. This would indeed occur, but not for a while—not until Maxxam had logged most of its fifty-six thousand acres of residual old-growth redwood, conifers left when the "old" Pacific Lumber cut only half the trees from a virgin stand, and half of its eighty-nine thousand acres of mature second-growth redwood, a rare and precious habitat that remained largely out of the public eye. Headwaters Forest would be held hostage for years before it could be adequately exchanged for a price that would satisfy insatiable Maxxam executives.

56

IN EARLY 1988 DARRYL CHERNEY EXCITEDLY TOLD ME THAT WE HAD A
new colleague in Mendocino County. He'd met her in the office of the
Mendocino Environmental Center in Ukiah. Veteran labor and antiwar
activist Judi Bari was now talking to the county's environmental activists
about joining their movement. She understood that Louisiana-Pacific (LP)
was in the final stages of liquidating nearly three hundred thousand acres
of second-growth redwood in the county, just as Maxxam was eliminating
the last old-growth redwoods. Judi had moved to Redwood Valley, outside
Ukiah, from Sonoma County a few years before. She'd brought with her
nearly two decades of activist experience.

Darryl immediately latched on to Judi as an able companion creating
"good trouble, necessary trouble," in the words of civil rights leader and congressman John Lewis. Judi had cut her chops in Lewis's era. On May 2,
1970, when she was twenty years old and attending the University of Mary-
land (UM), Judi's name appeared on the front page of the *Baltimore Evening
Sun* after she was arrested for protesting the Vietnam War and Richard Nixon's invasion of Cambodia. At UM, Judi joined what the *Evening Sun* called
"the most destructive demonstration in the school's history." Not long after I
met her, Judi told me that she had "majored in rioting."

In Sonoma County, Judi joined Pledge of Resistance, whose members lob-
bied and demonstrated to alleviate the US government's military assaults on
Central America. In 1985 she was arrested along with eighty other protesters at the US Marine recruiting station in Santa Rosa. She spent two nights
in jail while seven months pregnant. Afterward, Judi became the Northern
California coordinator for Pledge of Resistance. That month the *New York
Times* revealed that the Ronald Reagan administration had authorized the

FBI to illegally surveil more than one hundred domestic peace groups in the United States, including Pledge of Resistance.

Judi told the *Santa Rosa Press Democrat* that she'd seen her FBI file, which seemed sparse. "I was surprised how little they knew," she said. "They had me down for a few demonstrations but they missed most of my political activity."

When I met her I immediately understood that Judi's effectiveness derived not just from her powerful lucidity and aversion to injustice. She was an infectious public speaker and earnest organizer who also worked as a carpenter. Judi would gain the trust of timber workers even as she led actions against their corporate bosses. Her wit could slay dragons.

Judi also played violin. She and Darryl formed a musical duo who wrote and performed environmental songs that were equal parts funny and reproving. Darryl also appreciated Judi's dynamism and public persona, which drew people toward whatever orbits she might inhabit.

By mid-1988 Judi was working closely with Betty and Gary Ball, founders of the Mendocino Environmental Center. She frequently challenged Louisiana-Pacific's logging and labor practices in the county, placing herself squarely in the path of LP president Harry Merlo. Merlo lorded over a sprawling timber empire. He was the ideological progeny of robber barons: he liked money, and he liked attention. In addition to the ostentatious mansion he occupied in Portland, where LP kept its headquarters, Merlo spent time on his forty-two-hundred-acre estate on the shores of Lake Sonoma. Herds of bison surrounded Merlo's tennis courts and one-hundred-acre private pond. The tower of self that Merlo built grew in reverse proportion to the forests he destroyed. Ostentation and destruction were Merlo's twin legacies. After he died, in 2016, the Portland newspaper *Willamette Week* reported, "Merlo ran the company in a swashbuckling fashion that stood out in Portland's staid corporate culture. He enjoyed the use of a 107-foot company yacht, a private jet and company-owned West Hills estate complete with a chef and helipad. Merlo favored brightly-colored sports jackets, wore a Clark Gable mustache, and spent his leisure hours with a series of beautiful women."

Merlo managed a fiefdom of timberlands, mills, and manufacturing plants in California, Oregon, Washington, Idaho, Montana, Texas, Louisiana, and Ohio. The company also owned rights to five billion board feet of publicly owned, virgin forestland in Alaska's Tongass National Forest, which was then, and today remains, the world's largest contiguous temperate rainforest. Under Merlo, Louisiana-Pacific would convert much of this spectacular forest to pulp.

"I think greed is healthy," said Charles Hurwitz's collaborator Ivan Boesky in a 1986 speech to the graduating business students at the University of California (UC), Berkeley, shortly before he was fined $100 million and shipped off to federal prison. "You can be greedy and still feel good about yourself." Harry Merlo felt good about himself—so good that in 1989 he would glibly declare to *Santa Rosa Press Democrat* reporter Mike Geniella, "You know, it always annoyed me to leave anything on the ground when I log our own lands. . . . There shouldn't be anything left on the ground. We need everything that's out there. We don't log to a 10-inch top, or an 8-inch top, or a 6-inch top. We log to infinity. Because we need it all. It's ours. It's out there, and we need it all. Now."

Merlo was crowing just three years after the US timber industry, with LP in the front row, earned $150 billion in profits ($352 billion today). That year timber companies in Humboldt and Mendocino counties produced a combined total of 1.1 billion board feet of lumber, enough to build a small city including commercial buildings. In Humboldt County, where LP owned nearly one hundred thousand acres, the company's mills operated twenty-four hours a day. In Mendocino County, LP had successfully broken the union and was paying fast-food wages for extremely dangerous jobs that involved cutting tiny trees and taking every stitch of fiber from the forest floor. Soon the company would move most of its redwood milling operation to Mexico before selling out of California entirely.

Merlo began his career hawking lumber in the small Sonoma County town of Cloverdale. He worked his way up the corporate ladder until joining Louisiana-Pacific in 1972, when the company was created out of Georgia-Pacific (GP). It was Merlo who had overseen LP's scorched-earth logging of Redwood Creek during the 1970s. In 1977 Merlo, along with Arcata Redwood Company president Jay Frank Leach and Simpson Timber Company president Gilbert L. Oswald, refused a plea from the Jimmy Carter administration to enact a six-month moratorium on logging in Redwood Creek to protect areas slated for park expansion. Instead, the companies logged in double shifts.

By the early 1980s Merlo understood that most trees from LP's second-growth timber tracts were now so small that they could not produce actual sawed lumber. So he led the pivot to fiber farms. Merlo told the *Press Democrat* that, rather than allow the forest to mature, "we've designed Louisiana-Pacific so we don't need a big tree." The new design came in the form of lumber alternately called "oriented strand board," "waferboard," "flakeboard," and "particle board," products represented by the oddly patterned stuff you see coating new housing developments nearly everywhere. The material derives from tiny trees that are chipped and pressed together with carcinogenic glues notorious for off-gassing into homes and businesses, sickening people who live and work there. When the buildings burn, they threaten the health of firefighters and neighbors. Louisiana-Pacific's waferboard products were so inferior and unhealthy that lawsuits against the company poured in like water. In Colorado, Merlo faced mounting charges of fraud and environmental violations. In 1995 LP's board of directors called Merlo in for a surprise meeting and fired him.

Yet, through the 1980s, Merlo remained one of just a handful of redwood kings, an old-school timber baron glowing in the shadow of A. B. Hammond. It's likely that over the course of Harry Merlo's career, no one had more effectively challenged his claim to redwood supremacy—the neon ego so carefully nurtured yet unspeakably fragile—than Judi Bari. She wasn't content simply to save trees. Judi stepped up to represent labor, founding a local chapter of the Industrial Workers of the World, or Wobblies, a modern resurrection of the radical labor organization founded in 1905 by Big Bill Haywood and Eugene Debs. In many ways, Judi was emerging as a potent threat to the man who ran LP.

"Bari, especially, was too dangerous, her wood worker–environmentalist union talk a chilling proposition for companies which operated effective monopolies over their workers' lives," sociologist Rik Scarce wrote in his 1990 book *Eco-Warriors*.

The environmental-labor connection was also strong in Humboldt County. Just as Maxxam was finding itself unexpectedly bogged down in the courts, Pacific Lumber's savvy and intelligent workforce was becoming agitated. They toiled long hours under increasingly dangerous conditions. Company underlings reportedly spied on and bullied workers. Employees who spoke out were harassed or simply fired. They understood that their jobs would be decimated along with the forests; it was only a matter of time. They watched Maxxam build a cogeneration power plant in the middle of Scotia, spewing smoke into the town 24/7 and consuming hardwood trees that normally would have been left standing to aid regeneration of logging sites. Maxxam also built a chipper that pulped small trees to make chips for fax paper. In 1992, with Maxxam now devouring forests at unprecedented rates, three longtime Pacific Lumber employees were shredded inside the massive chipper. The California Division of Occupational Safety and Health fined Pacific Lumber $7,500. That year Maxxam ranked 190 on the Fortune 500 list.

The workers didn't need to be told that they were getting screwed. They were well familiar with the impacts of cut-and-run logging, which had plagued North Coast communities for a century. They knew of, and had lived in, once thriving communities that were now ghost towns. Still, reporting by environmental activists presented accurate, locally sourced information about what their bosses were doing in the woods and in the board rooms. We were among timber workers' few natural allies, though few would or could admit it. I believe that's when things started to get dangerous—when we started talking directly to labor about what their bosses were doing, and when labor started listening to us, particularly to Judi, with a sympathetic ear.

57

HOW WE GOT THROUGH 1989 RELATIVELY UNSCATHED REMAINS A MYS-
tery. The pace and resolve of our actions and public outreach grew
proportionally with the timber industry's prosecution of last-gasp redwood
liquidation. Levels of violence against us—in the form of rhetoric and actual
assaults—grew as well.

We remained locked in the national spotlight. In April I guided Stone
Phillips and a film crew from the ABC News show *20/20* in a helicopter
over Maxxam's redwood clear-cuts. In the show that aired, John Campbell,
for the first time, admitted that Maxxam had tripled the cut of Pacific Lumber's ancient redwoods. Also in April, *Fortune* ran a damning exposé, "A
Raider's Ruckus in the Redwoods," on Maxxam and Charles Hurwitz. The
magazine called Hurwitz's logging "a Texas chainsaw massacre" and noted,
"Environmental extremists have declared holy war." The magazine twice ran
a "wanted" poster that offered a $1,000 reward for the "arrest and convic-
tion" of Charles Hurwitz. I'd made the poster in 1987. By now the reward
was up to $5,000.

In June, Maxxam's newest director, former Texas governor John Connally,
most famous for having taken a bullet while riding with President John F.
Kennedy in 1963, grabbed headlines when he visited Humboldt County to
strong-arm local officials who were beginning to question Maxxam's motives in the redwoods. Connally needed the work. The previous year his personal oil and real estate empire had entered bankruptcy. In August, *Time*
magazine ran "Showdown in the Treetops," and *Rolling Stone* featured Bill
McKibben's "Milken, Junk Bonds and Raping Redwoods."

On consecutive November days, I received phone calls from two CBS
News programs. One was from a producer of *Saturday Night with Connie
Chung*, who wanted our story. The second call was from producer Marley

Klaus, at *60 Minutes*. The two major CBS News shows were competing with each other for "radical environmentalist" splash. *60 Minutes* won out. In December we would take Klaus and her crew to All Species Grove. The redwoods were hot news. Even *People* magazine called.

By now, it wasn't just Maxxam but Louisiana-Pacific that had hired Hill & Knowlton. The public relations firm had a controversial history. In the 1950s and 1960s, the company cut its chops by representing big tobacco companies against growing public concerns that smoking might cause cancer—one result being the helpful forty-eight-page booklet "Smoke Without Fear."

While Hill & Knowlton was doing dirty work for big timber in Humboldt and Mendocino counties, it was simultaneously raking in millions from clients around the world, including the Bank of Credit and Commerce International (BCCI), then one of the world's largest international financial institutions. When investigators discovered that BCCI had for years laundered drug money and other ill-gotten gains from such luminaries as Saddam Hussein and Manuel Noriega, Hill & Knowlton was hired to salvage the firm's reputation. (In 1991 several governments simultaneously forced the closure of BCCI.) In his 1996 book *Green Backlash*, Andrew Rowell notes that in 1990 Hill & Knowlton, representing the government of Kuwait, "arranged for the daughter of the Kuwaiti Ambassador to the USA to appear as an ordinary Kuwaiti girl who had witnessed Iraqi soldiers taking babies out of incubators and killing them. It was a testimony that drove the USA to war. It was a testimony that was totally fictitious."

When Wigginton Creed said, "There is need of the story," this is what he'd meant.

Though at the time I knew nothing about Hill & Knowlton and very little about the FBI, by early 1989 it was clear that our group was being targeted and surveilled by outside forces. Darryl Cherney liked to make fun of my insistence on keeping information secure and being careful when we traveled alone (or even together), but his New York bravado was alarming me.

Judi Bari was a more seasoned activist than either Darryl or I. She believed that it would be unusual, if not unprecedented, for the FBI *not* to be infiltrating and manipulating Earth First!, especially the North Coast group, the highest-profile Earth First! faction in the nation. Each month we generated ever-greater public outrage against some of the nation's biggest corporations, our relationships with labor were growing, and we were setting a national example of what a few people could do against implacable forces.

Darryl stopped teasing me after May 31, 1989. That day, in a defining moment, three FBI agents broke into the home of Earth First! founder Dave Foreman and woke him at 5 a.m. with .357 magnum revolvers pointed at his face. The day before, fifty FBI agents had descended on three Arizona activists—Peg Millett, Mark Davis, and Marc Baker—who were attempting to cut down power lines. Millett managed to elude the million-dollar dragnet by escaping across sixteen miles of desert on foot, at night, chased by dozens of militarized agents wearing night-vision goggles and aided by Black Hawk helicopters with floodlights. The next morning Millett turned up at work, at Planned Parenthood in Prescott, as scheduled and on time, where she was arrested. Explaining her ability to escape, Millett said, "I did not have an adversarial relationship with the natural world and all of the people who were chasing me did."

Dave Foreman had made two donations to the small core group, totaling less than $700. He said he didn't know they were plotting sabotage. The FBI agents on the case understood that Foreman's claim of ignorance was probably true. One of them, Michael Fain, employing the nom de guerre Mike Tate, had infiltrated the Arizona Earth First! group in 1988, during the national Earth First! Rendezvous in Washington State. He posed as a barely literate recovering alcoholic and Vietnam vet. By then, according to FBI documents subsequently released in discovery, Fain had been leading the infiltration of Earth First! for two years. As an "activist," he was a rowdy demonstrator at the Okanogan National Forest headquarters where two dozen of us were arrested.

Naturally Fain wore a wire when he talked with the Arizonans. The FBI also bugged homes and phones and even recorded conversations from a circling airplane. After one conversation with Foreman, Fain and two other FBI agents had lunch at Burger King. Fain had forgotten to turn off his recorder, and the tape was later played for a jury. On the tape Fain said that Foreman "isn't really the guy we need to pop, I mean in terms of actual perpetrator. This is the guy we need to pop [arrest] to send a message. And that's all we're really doing."

I found the revelation startling. I too had received funding from Foreman. In June 1987 Foreman sent me a check for $250, along with a personal note. He wrote, "You are doing an outstanding job! I personally think the national Maxxam demos were the best coordinated & most effective action EF! has done anywhere. I know many people are responsible for that good work but it was obvious that you were absolutely crucial." Michael Fain apparently agreed. Years later, during a deposition, Fain suggested that I might have been under investigation by the FBI for my work with Earth First! If this was true, the action would have constituted a clear violation of my constitutional right to free speech through nonviolent, civil disobedience protest, a violation the federal government has never remedied or apologized for. On the scale of what was to come, however, what happened to me was mild.

58

On June 15, 1989, Judi Bari joined a large group of Mendocino County activists for a demonstration at a new Louisiana-Pacific mill in the tiny town of Calpella. As the first major public action of the summer against LP, Georgia-Pacific, and Maxxam, events at Calpella launched a freewheeling slate of road blockades, public demonstrations, logging occupations, tree-sits, public outreach, and media saturation that would prevail unabated for the next year.

One of the speakers at Calpella announced that planning had recently begun for the Humboldt and Mendocino Earth First! groups to join a co-ordinated Earth First! National Tree Sit. In early August I would travel to Colorado to lead a tree-climbing workshop for the national action, which launched two weeks later. Tree-sits eventually occurred in eight states, three of them on the California North Coast. The most prominent of the redwood tree-sits was an all-woman action in immature trees slated for logging by Louisiana-Pacific in Mendocino County.

Louisiana-Pacific had designed its Calpella plant to turn tiny trees and even branches to wood chips for its glue-and-fiber lumber products. At the demonstration, Judi Bari, joyous in battle, pointed and said, "The log deck over there is stacked with all kinds of little treetops and hardwoods. All kinds of stuff that's got no business on a log deck. It ought to be in the forest." She added, "We are not here to protest against either the loggers or the millworkers or anyone who is an employee of Louisiana-Pacific. They don't have any more control over these logging practices than we do. . . . So the person we're here to protest is not the logger, not the millworker. It's the president of Louisiana-Pacific, a man named Harry Merlo."

At this point Judi launched a provocative rhetorical flourish: "Harry Merlo is the ultimate tree Nazi," she said with considerable relish. "He wants to cut every last tree and implement the final solution of waferboard in our county."

Judi read Merlo's "we log to infinity" screed, then said,

> This maniac is actually in charge of most of the forestland in Mendocino County. . . . There's no benefit to this strip logging except to the greedy millionaire, Harry Merlo. Harry is practicing the economics of extinction. Well we have a surprise for him in Mendocino County. He's about to run into the politics of resistance. . . . We are not going to let Harry Merlo chip our county to satiate his greed. This is not the last demonstration Harry, this is the first. The next one will be at your office, and the next one will be at your house.

At that moment a young man wielding a diesel pickup and a jutting middle finger accelerated at high speed past demonstrators, who were forced to scatter. He ran the truck back and forth a few times, stopped fifty feet up the road, grabbed an enormous chainsaw from the back of the pickup, fired it up, and revved it. He'd let it idle to yell insults, epithets, and threats, then hit the throttle. A large phalanx of Mendocino sheriff's deputies surrounded the demonstration. Three cops stood directly across the street from the unhinged young man. Arms crossed, shoulder to shoulder, the cops seemed almost pleased with his reckless driving and menacing delivery with the chainsaw.

I sauntered over to the logger. Here was an opportunity to engage. The chainsaw continued to idle on the open tailgate. It was a big Stihl with a four-foot bar. The logger stood tall and lean, slightly slouched, sandy blond hair. Up close his face was taut. I could see his cheeks flushing in and out, like a chipmunk. His eyes were wide and bloodshot, with dark circles underneath. He talked as if he had marbles in his mouth. I asked the logger why he was protesting us and not LP's overcutting and general liquidation, which was far more of a threat to his job than we ever could be.

"Aw, bullshit," he said. "You guys are communists. You want to stop everything."

"Communists? I don't know the first thing about communism."

From the lowered tailgate he picked up the chainsaw, looked at it quizzically, held it up, and gunned it. When the tool quieted, I wisely pointed out, "You know, that bar is too big for LP's woods. They've cut all the old growth. Now you're logging baby trees, right?"

He shot me a look I didn't like. "Get out of here," he said, "before I slap you."

"You're not going to hit me," I said as he started to turn away.

As I picked myself up off the ground, I realized what had happened. He'd wheeled and sucker punched me. One of the demonstrators, a woman in her mid-thirties, stood nearby screaming at the logger. She had dressed up as a tree by affixing redwood shoots to her hair. In her left hand she held a wide, six-foot redwood branch. The three cops looked on, bemused. My Guerneville instinct kicked in, and the nonviolent code evaporated under a scorching, unexpected rage. I grabbed the woman's branch and smacked the logger across the chest. His eyes grew wider still—he couldn't believe that an activist would hit back. I might have kept pummeling him—one never knows in these situations—but then he saw, rising up behind me, two dozen ferocious protesters heading his way. He ran across the street, straight into a bar.

By now the angry crowd had surrounded the cops. After much cajoling, they begrudgingly allowed me to write out a complaint. Nothing came of it.

The following year, a discovery action uncovered a trove of internal memos from Pacific Lumber executives to each other and to Charles Hurwitz. In one of the memos, PL public relations manager Dave Galitz crowed, "Enclosed is an article on King and [Darryl] Cherney's latest stunt. As soon as we find the home of the fine fellow that decked Greg King, he has a dinner invitation waiting at the Galitz residence."

Shortly after Calpella, a man whom we knew as "Riverhouse Bill" contacted Darryl to complain of a rogue logging operation trashing the forest and shredding soils near his home on the upper Mattole River, upstream of Whitethorn. The loggers careened down the public dirt road in overloaded logging trucks, cut trees at night, filled streams with slash and mud, and in their spare time fired guns, also at night. The land straddled the Lost River, an important spawning tributary of the upper Mattole. The Douglas fir and redwoods had already been logged off. Now the stand was being mowed for the remaining hardwood trees, which would be pulped. Darryl thought it would be a good idea to confront them. I was game. So were Judi and thirty other activists.

In the early morning of August 16, we gathered on the public road in front of a gate that allowed access to the logging site. When a loaded logging truck trundled out of the private land, we blockaded it. A young man named David Lancaster emerged from a pickup. He wasn't quite sure what he was seeing. This had never happened to his operation. The Lancasters were among several middle-tier timber families on the North Coast that specialized in locating and logging small tracts of remaining forestland. They'd promise landowners big profits for the privilege of cutting their trees. The Lancasters butchered forests. The family's terrestrial shitshows left landscapes barren and streams clogged with debris and sediment.

At first David Lancaster seemed oddly sanguine about the blockade, as if he was more curious than upset. He leaned against the pickup and drank beer, a dirty white T-shirt dangling off his lean frame onto grease-stained blue jeans. He wore a backward CAT ball cap and large, teardrop glasses.

David's father, Doyle Lancaster, seemed more agitated. Both of Doyle Lancaster's parents were on-site. Three generations of Lancasters ran the business. Soon arrived Doyle's father-in-law, a grizzled codger whom we knew as Logger Larry. The old man charged his pickup directly into demonstrators, scattering us. He emerged from the truck and, no matter his bent frame and advanced age, hobbled toward the crowd waving a baseball bat. His dynamic entrance drew howls from the crowd. Riverhouse Bill pounded the truck with his fist. When an elderly Bay Area activist, Hal Carlstadt, snapped Logger Larry's picture, his sister, Doyle's mom, grabbed Hal's camera. After a weird geriatric tussle, I watched the Nikon fly in slow motion out of Hal's hands over the crowd and onto the ground.

Then the whole family got into the act. Doyle's wife and Judi Bari exchanged jabs. Chaos erupted. David Lancaster waded into the crowd, throwing punches and howling about his mother like Dick Shawn in *It's a Mad, Mad, Mad, Mad World*. Everyone and everything seemed to move at great speed with the exception of Logger Larry. To my right, from the corner of my eye, I watched the old man amble patiently over to Hal's Nikon, pick it up, dodder to the tailgate of his truck, draw out an axe, and smash the camera to pieces.

David Lancaster continued working the crowd, arms flying, pushing and screaming incomprehensibly. He jabbed a fist directly into the face of Mem Hill, now fifty years old, the same woman whose arm had been broken by a Georgia-Pacific logger six years earlier. Blood spouted from Mem's nose, as it was broken in two places. She had simply been standing there, on a public road. Lancaster retreated to his truck and emerged with a .12-gauge shotgun. He screamed, "You fucking commie hippies, I'll kill you all!"

Only then did Doyle Lancaster intervene. He grabbed the gun and pushed it into his son's chest. The old man was strong. Doyle took the shotgun and tossed it back into the truck. David Lancaster returned to his work, ranting and pushing protesters until he briefly stilled, surrounded by a seething crowd. At first I thought he'd come to his senses. Instead, he'd finally noticed that I was taking pictures. He jammed both arms into my chest and knocked me down. My camera bounced off the ground. Without even knowing what I was doing, I launched myself out of the dust and into a roundhouse of my own, crushing the side of David's face and sending him to the ground. I was as stunned as he was. The crowd charged in, like the sled dogs that finished off Spitz in *The Call of the Wild*. But David's brother, all of eighteen, grabbed the shotgun and twice fired it into the air. Everyone scattered. End of demo.

A local resident drove to the Whitethorn pay phone and called the Mendocino County Sheriff's Department, but law enforcement was already on the way. No fewer than ten police cruisers—Humboldt County sheriffs, Mendocino County sheriffs, and California Highway Patrol officers—raced straight into the scene. The Lancasters gave statements, but the Mendocino deputies, who had jurisdiction, refused to talk with us. When we protested, they stared blankly and told us we'd have to file complaints at the sheriff's substation in Willits, a three-hour drive.

I told the lead officer that David Lancaster had threatened us with a loaded shotgun, and his brother had fired it. David Lancaster had assaulted several people and appeared to have broken a woman's nose. Shouldn't the cops arrest him?

"We know where he is and where to find him," said the cop.

"What if meanwhile this crazy guy who threatened to kill all of us while brandishing a loaded shotgun then lives up to his promise and decides to come after me?"

"I can't predict the future," he said.

"So I should just buy a gun?"

"That's your constitutional right."

We filed statements in Willits. No Lancaster was ever arrested or even cited for an obvious set of felony assaults. Mendocino County district attorney Susan Massini, adhering to a pattern she would maintain for years in office, refused to file charges. She said, "There was insufficient evidence to determine who broke this woman's nose. There was no way to determine who did what to whom, and when." With the exception of thirty eyewitness accounts and several photos of an unhinged David Lancaster running amok and even wielding a shotgun, I guess she was right. In January, twenty Earth First!ers stormed Massini's bunkered office in the basement of the county building in Ukiah to demand charges against Lancaster, but she wouldn't budge. The following year Mem Hill won a $26,000 judgment against the county for refusing to adequately prosecute the assault against her.

By June 1990, the Lancasters' Lost River logging site was so heavily damaged that the North Coast Regional Water Quality Control Board ordered the company back onto the land to stabilize soils, which were draining into and fouling the important fishery. That year just two hundred salmon returned to the Mattole River, an extinction event along a stream that once supported annual runs of hundreds of thousands of fish. The empty river ran as symptom and symbol of industrial logging on the North Coast.

On August 19, 1989, three days after the Whitethorn riot, a log truck driver named Donald Blake rear-ended his giant rig into Judi Bari's small Subaru in the tiny outpost of Philo, along the Navarro River in Mendocino County. Blake had apparently accelerated to forty-five miles per hour in a twenty-five mph zone. Darryl was in the car, along with Santa Rosa activist Pam Davis, two of Pam's children, and two of Judi's young children. The smashed Subaru careened off the road and into a parked car, which leapt the curb and crashed into the side of a restaurant. No one was in the parked car, the owner of which, a state Fish and Game biologist, was in the restaurant with a Georgia-Pacific employee, having breakfast before leaving for GP lands to call for spotted owls, which were now listed as endangered. Later Judi said, "It's the whole struggle in a nutshell."

After hitting Judi's car, Blake emerged from the truck. "The kids!" he cried, upset. "I didn't see the kids!"

Judi recognized the truck. It was one that she and fifty other demonstrators had blockaded just the day before, as it tried to leave a Louisiana-Pacific logging operation on the Navarro River. Again, Massini refused to press charges or even to investigate. Again, the result was a successful lawsuit, in which a jury awarded Judi, Darryl, and Pam Davis $34,000. The money wasn't the point. There had to be some way to address and dilute the impunity with which attackers could harm nonviolent activists. Turns out there wasn't any. For 140 years the people and terrain of the California North Coast had remained firmly under the thumb of powerful outside forces. In that time, little had changed except the names and the faces.

59

Throughout 1989 and into 1990, Judi Bari, Darryl Cherney, and I were barraged with death threats. Late in the year, when asked about the threats, Judi said she "stopped counting after the first thirty." Some threats were copied and sent to all three of us. In April 1990 the "Stompers" greeted us with a hand-drawn image of spiked cork boots over text sent to "the following *lowlife*: Darryl Cherney, Greg King, Judi Bari." The threat promised, "Our justice will be swift and very real. We know who you are and where you live. If you want to be a Martyr, we will be happy to oblige." Another was a poster-sized "welcome" of "dirt first" to Humboldt and Mendocino counties. The words surrounded a hangman's noose. Some of the threats landed on my answering machine. (I always screened calls.) One of them, a guy doing his best Luca Brasi, typified the sentiment: "Greg King will die in the forest. This is a dirt bike fanatic that's looking for him right now. We caught him, we know where he is. He's history."

On April 29, 1990, Rob Morse, a columnist for the *San Francisco Examiner*, reported that he'd received an odd press kit from Hill & Knowlton, on behalf of Pacific Lumber. "Donald Segretti is alive and well in the North Woods," Morse reported. (Segretti had run Richard Nixon's "dirty tricks" campaign against Democrats during the 1972 election.)

> A press kit arrived from the PR firm of Hill & Knowlton. . . . The kit included a press release on the Earth First! letterhead, but not written in the usual careful, sweet style of Earth First! It read like a bad Hollywood version of what radicals talk like. . . . At the bottom of this ridiculous flyer was the name of Earth First! leader Darryl Cherney, with his first name misspelled. . . . [I]t's hard to tell who made it up but it's easy to see it's a fake.

Things are getting pretty weird up there. Not only are trees being clear-cut, but dirty tricksters are turning them into fake press releases.

Darryl forwarded every threat to the Humboldt County Sheriff's Department. One day he called to see if the cops were investigating. The sergeant chuckled and said no, there would be no investigation. In April, Darryl presented evidence of threats to the Eureka field office of the FBI, where a special agent simply shrugged, claimed no knowledge of Earth First! activities, and said he should contact the Sheriff's Department.

Not once did local police authorities investigate or arrest anyone for scores of threats and numerous attacks against us. When Judi Bari brought all her death threats to Mendocino County sheriff's sergeant Steve Satterwhite, he told her, "We don't have the manpower to investigate. If you turn up dead, then we'll investigate." She then took the threats and the sheriff's insouciance to the Mendocino County Board of Supervisors, but the board refused to take action. "You brought it on yourself, Judi," said Supervisor Marilyn Butcher.

In late 1989 Judi Bari looked back on our year and said to me, "We're in the crosshairs." In early May 1990, Judi found herself literally in the crosshairs when she received a death threat that included a graphic of a rifle scope superimposed on a photograph of her face. The photo was the same one featured in the *Ukiah Daily Journal* the month before, when Judi had appeared before the Mendocino County Board of Supervisors flanked by several Louisiana-Pacific mill workers. Judi and the mill workers had come in response to an announcement by Louisiana-Pacific, in March, that the company would soon close two more mills, one in Covelo, Mendocino County, and the other in Oroville, in the Central Valley, and eliminate a shift in Ukiah in order to send the jobs to Mexico. The company blamed environmentalists. Governor George Deukmejian lauded the move. "I believe the strength of our overall state economy depends on active participation in international markets," said Deukmejian. Instead, said Judi and the mill workers, the county should seize all of LP's nearly three hundred thousand acres and its mills through eminent domain in order to keep jobs in the county. She charged that the move was "just a way for Harry Merlo to make money."

Delivery of the rifle-scope death threat was made by way of stapling it, at night, to the door of the Mendocino Environmental Center, along with a yellow ribbon, a symbol of timber worker solidarity concocted by corporate management. Below the threat, on the stoop, was a pile of excrement.

Later Judi told me that she had immediately recognized the rifle-scope symbol as that of the Secret Army Organization (SAO), a violent right-wing paramilitary group founded and funded by the FBI in Southern California in 1971 to antagonize and even kill student antiwar activists and leftist professors. In 1975 the American Civil Liberties Union provided the Senate Select Committee on Intelligence with a five-thousand-word report that exposed the SAO as an FBI front. At that time the Senate was investigating widespread civil rights violations conducted by the FBI and the CIA for more than a decade. In its coverage of the Senate investigation, the *New York Times* reported that, to create the SAO, "the Federal Bureau of Investigation recruited a band of right-wing terrorists and supplied them with money and weapons to attack young anti-war demonstrators . . . particularly campus leaders of the New Left protesting the war in Southeast Asia. . . . The group's acts of terrorism . . . range from espionage, vandalism and mail theft to bombings, assassination plots and shootings."

The violent, rogue operation was an element of the FBI's Counterintelligence Program (COINTELPRO), created in 1956 by FBI director J. Edgar Hoover to "disrupt, misdirect, isolate and neutralize" pretty much anyone of the agency's choosing. COINTELPRO targets included but were not limited to perceived Communists, the Black Panthers, the American Indian Movement, the Puerto Rico independence movement, antiwar demonstrators and assorted student radicals, and just about any other group or individual whose ideologies and actions might threaten smoothly functioning markets or a robust American war machine. COINTELPRO tactics included fake press releases and forged documents, infiltration, harassment, psychological warfare, and assassination.

60

On August 20, 1989, I met with activists in San Francisco to plan anti-Maxxam actions in the Bay Area. Driving out of the city, I exited at the north end of the Golden Gate Bridge, turned into the vista view parking lot, and hiked onto the bridge walkway. Tourists packed the path. They were taking pictures of each other and the view. I photographed the structure. The Golden Gate Bridge stands as one of the world's most recognizable symbols of majestic suspension and rapid economic expansion. Eleven men died building the bridge. Nineteen more—the "halfway-to-hell club"—were saved by a net that ran under construction.

I noted the two gigantic cables that ran ninety feet apart, on either side of the road, and swooped downward from the tops of two magnificent towers that stood nearly a mile apart. The big cables had a pebbled, nonslip texture to secure iron workers who walked up and down the span no matter the weather. Two smaller cables, about the width of my wrist, ran parallel to and a few feet above each of the big cables. I paid close attention to the cyclone fence that blocked any ambler's attempt to scale the big cable and scurry upward toward the sky. A gate allowed ingress for iron workers, and a hefty padlock secured the gate. Not a problem.

I had taken this walk before. Since mid-1987 I had wanted to banner the Golden Gate Bridge. I envisioned our demands for redwood protection emblazoned across this most potent international projection of industrial power. But as I stood staring at the bridge, in the late summer of 1989, I also knew I was ready to leave the Earth First! movement. The harassment, the threats, the arrests, the assaults, the poverty, and the risks we took had to be set against the timber companies' essentially uninterrupted pogroms of forest liquidation. There was also the need to differentiate myself from people who advocated property destruction. I thought it was perhaps time to check out, find some arable land with water, grow food with like-minded souls, and establish one of the many cells of ecological restoration and harmonious human relations with the land that I believed would become increasingly necessary for humanity to withstand what was coming. But first I had some unfinished business.

A few days after my bridge stroll, I made some calls. I asked my contact at Patagonia if he could hook me up with a small trove of Chouinard climbing equipment. We needed six nine-millimeter static climb lines of 150 feet, 200 feet of six-millimeter prusik line, 100 feet of one-inch tubular webbing, and 50 feet of half-inch webbing, mechanical ascenders, climbing harnesses, and 100 carabiners.

"Yeah, we can probably do that," he said.

"Also," I asked, "can Patagonia spare a bolt of rip-stop nylon?"

"What color?"

I had to think about that. What color might best stand out against the bridge's International Orange?

"How about blue?" He sent periwinkle, plus a small bit of red that we would need.

Finally, I asked him if he might be able to connect me with a company that manufactured climbing hammocks. "Something strong and light but with big holes." A banner hung at the Golden Gate would need to withstand high winds. I got a number and called it. When the owner of the company learned what it was for, he donated the single piece of hammock netting, thirty by one hundred feet.

By September we had all the pieces. Under the direction of Mickey Dulas, the Arcata core group cut letters from the periwinkle nylon. They were variously eight feet and six feet tall. Sporadically over the course of months we sewed the letters onto the hammock netting. We carted the nascent banner everywhere with us, sewing whenever we had a break and a large floor to work on.

61

BY NOVEMBER 1989 THE TIMBER INDUSTRY WAS IN A STATE OF TURMOIL over a pair of environmental ballot initiatives that had been announced the previous month. One of the measures, called "Big Green," was led by California state assemblyman Tom Hayden, the former 1960s radical, and backed by California attorney general John Van de Kamp. In a hearing, Hayden said, "I want to thank the protestors in the north woods for their opposition to cutting. I want to thank them for bringing this to the attention of the public. They have been marginalized, abused, arrested. It has been for them a very long struggle."

Big Green, or Proposition 128, proposed the establishment of a $200 million fund to purchase ancient forests in the state and called for a one-year moratorium on clear-cutting old-growth forests, a restriction on pesticide use, and a ban on offshore oil drilling.

The other initiative directly threatened the timber industry's carte blanche in the California woods. The Environmental Protection Information Center's Robert Sutherland—the Man Who Walks in the Woods—had written most of what would become known as the Forests Forever initiative. If successful, the measure would, for the first time, provide binding legal provisions to actually curtail some of the timber industry's worst abuses in California. The industry would go to extraordinary lengths to block its passage. Never had any authentic logging restrictions been implemented.

Forests Forever, or Proposition 130, proposed creation of a fund of $710 million to purchase ancient forests for preservation. Top priority was acquisition of Headwaters Forest, whose sale to the state would be mandated at fair market value rather than at Maxxam's extortionary price. The measure would also ban clear-cutting and limit logging to 60 percent of a tract's board foot volume—essentially making selective logging the law of the land. Not even Pacific Lumber was selectively logging anymore.

Under Forests Forever, Dave Galitz told one newspaper, "life on the North Coast as we know and enjoy it would never be the same," as if nothing had changed over the past few years. "Placing these trees off limits will change our entire operations, and goddammit we have responsibilities to our people here," said Galitz, dabbing his eyes.

The timber industry responded to the Forests Forever initiative by floating a ballot measure of its own. Called the Reforestation, Wildlife and Timber Management Act of 1990, the measure—which detractors called "Big Stump"—did nothing to protect standing forests. Rather, it adhered to the model perfected by Save the Redwoods League by providing $300 million of taxpayer money to reforest savaged corporate timberlands. More importantly, if voters passed both Forests Forever and the industry measure and Big Stump got more votes, it would nullify Forests Forever.

One week after proponents announced the Forests Forever initiative, Maxxam retaliated by submitting to the California Department of Forestry two timber harvest plans that again targeted Headwaters Forest. The THPs proposed cutting hundreds of acres from the middle of the grove. The largest THP would log 399 acres of virgin redwood on Salmon Creek, in the northwest quadrant of the stand. Over the ridge, to the east, the second plan proposed cutting 165 acres on Little South Fork Elk River, the delicate, diminutive tributary that defined the very heart of Headwaters Forest. Little South Fork ran northward for two miles through the middle of Headwaters Forest, flowing gently in a state of aquatic perfection, banked by stately trees and glowing in neon arrays of ferns, oxalis, and the wide brushstrokes of blue-green lichens that typically grow on the north sides of redwood trees.

Road building and heavy tractor use would gouge both Salmon Creek and Little South Fork. Thousands of redwoods, many of them greater than ten feet in diameter and possibly two thousand years old, would be converted to cash.

When I drew these plans onto my topographic map, I saw baleful Rorschach blots, a darkness of the human heart. The plan that straddled Little South Fork was a quarter-mile wide throughout and ran as a solid band northward in a slight, upward arc, alongside the stream. At the bottom of this long tubelike drawing were two connected but separate loops pointed southwesterly. It looked like a penis in the act of penetrating the womblike heart of Headwaters Forest. Whether intentional or not, the drawing stood as a perfect metaphor.

Maxxam's new THPs would be delayed for months. The California Department of Fish and Game, having found its feet under John Hummel and a series of environmental court victories, continued to require adequate wildlife protections. In reviewing the THPs, Ken Moore, the wildlife biologist who had replaced Hummel, demanded that Pacific Lumber provide more data on the presence of protected wildlife. After fielding several legal objections to the plans, Len Theiss, the resource manager at Republican CDF, delayed approval of the THPs. Theiss was even backed by California's governor-elect Pete Wilson, who said the THPs "raise[d] serious issues regarding assuring ecologically sound protection of our rare or threatened wildlife species." A subsequent study determined that the endangered marbled murrelet might face extinction in California if Headwaters Forest were logged. At the time under two thousand murrelets survived in California— one-quarter of them nested in Headwaters Forest.

In December 1990, Harold Walt, the new CDF director, denied approval of the THPs, based on potential impacts to wildlife. Pacific Lumber appealed the decision to the state Board of Forestry, no doubt expecting a quick reversal. Yet by then the pressure and momentum to save Headwaters Forest was too great. On January 9, 1991, in front of three hundred cheering spectators, the board voted 5–3 to uphold CDF's denial. Joseph Russ IV led the minority dissent.

By now it was clear that Maxxam could never log in Headwaters. Board of Forestry member Mike Anderson, who owned a small logging company in Mendocino County, told the press, "I am absolutely certain logging will never be permitted in the Headwaters area."

Maxxam apparently had not done its homework and failed to anticipate the opposition that would grow in the face of the company's remorseless liquidation of the last redwoods. All estimates now placed the true market value of Headwaters Forest at about $50 million. Even John B. Dewitt, executive director at Save the Redwoods League, said the grove was worth just $80 million, giving credence to the lower figure. But Charles Hurwitz, whose company continued to log at will throughout the rest of PL's two hundred thousand acres, had a few more cards to play, a few more allies to squeeze.

62

ON MONDAY, FEBRUARY 12, 1990, MORE THAN A HUNDRED PROTESTERS marched through Eureka to the North Coast offices of Congressman Doug Bosco, State Senator Barry Keene, and Assemblyman Dan Hauser. We'd arrived to protest a private "timber summit" that the three lawmakers had held with Charles Hurwitz of Maxxam and Harry Merlo of Louisiana-Pacific. The series of meetings had ended on February 8 and resulted in a number of "concessions" from the timber chiefs devised to pretend that timber reform was on the march.

In the negotiations, Maxxam had "conceded" that it would undergo an "independent review" of how much timber was being cut (the state already had this information), vowed to support a ban on clear-cutting in old-growth forests (but without imposition of an actual ban), and agreed to a prohibition on exporting raw logs. (Maxxam didn't export raw logs anyway, but the company would be allowed to continue selling raw logs to the eight other independent mills that were now suddenly flooded with high-grade redwood.) The most egregious "concession" was a two-year moratorium on logging in Headwaters Forest, a restriction that the state Board of Forestry, backed by the governor and the courts, had essentially just imposed, the only difference being that it appeared to be permanent. (Louisiana-Pacific's "concessions" were equally vacuous.)

The Eureka protests were augmented by a large Earth First! contingent from the Bay Area, including Mike Roselle and Karen Pickett, and longtime activists Daniel Barron, Helen Matthews, and Brian Gaffney. Protesters marched through the city dressed as animals, chanting and toting signs ("NO TIME FOR SLIME," with a photo of Hurwitz encircled by a red crossed-out symbol). At Hauser's office a few activists, finding the doors locked, simply removed the door from its hinges and waltzed right in.

Bosco's office was deep inside the Eureka Inn, a beautiful one-hundred-room Elizabethan Tudor hotel built in 1922 to accommodate motorists traveling the new Redwood Highway. Here protesters attempted to storm the building but were turned back by private security and Eureka police. One of the private guards politely addressed the rowdy but friendly crowd, announcing, "Mr. Bosco is not here at the moment." He added, to guffaws, "And all of his aides are out to lunch."

That night we regrouped for a large meeting at the Arcata Action Center, a downtown building whose owner had donated the space. Overnight three inches of snow had covered the small city, a rare event. Fifty people attended the free-flowing meeting. We designed an action to take over the Pacific Lumber office in Scotia, with the specific intent of confronting John Campbell. But the planning meetings were too open, with people wandering in off the street, wide-eyed. That night a local TV reporter told Darryl Cherney that she'd been talking with her boss, who told her to make sure to be in Scotia for the big Earth First! demonstration at Campbell's office.

A few of us designed a new plan. A college kid with a big white van offered to drive. He didn't know the plan until we'd piled into his car. On February 13, ten of us rolled south on Highway 101 to the intersection with State Highway 36. Today that intersection has a freeway offramp, but in 1990 travelers entering 101 from Highway 36 had to do so from a stop sign. The young driver took a left onto 36 and drove east, toward the Fisher log deck. We were looking for a log truck. We'd only gone a couple of miles down the road when a Freightliner passed in the opposite direction. It was loaded with three enormous redwood boles.

I knew the college kid as a soft-spoken young man who didn't like controversy and avoided trouble. But when that log truck passed, he veered straight into a gravel turnout, cranked the wheel hard, and spun a U-turn in the middle of the highway. He floored it and quickly caught up to the truck.

"This is great," I said from the passenger seat, "but we need to be in front of the truck."

We banked a tight curve and entered a short straightaway. No cars traveled toward us. I knew what the kid was going to do, and I didn't have the heart to stop him. Everyone waved to the bug-eyed driver as we passed his truck at an appalling speed. At the freeway stop sign we all piled out, the kid drove away, and we sat down in front of the log truck. Almost instantly four or five more cars appeared, followed by several others. Swarms of people surrounded the big rig and climbed onto the logs. Five people chained and locked themselves to the truck. Traffic backed up for five miles. Across the uppermost log, protesters unfurled a banner—"SAVE THE ANCIENT FORESTS"—and the truck was ours. Judi Bari and Darryl Cherney belted out songs. A celebratory chorus of wolf howls marked the moment. I heard the truck driver groan, "Oh, *man*."

The Freightliner was owned by Don Nolan Sr., whose trucking empire was making bank under Maxxam's limitless demand. When Nolan himself showed up at the blockade, he climbed onto the running board of the truck and demanded that the driver move forward, onto the freeway, and down to the mill—even if the people in front of the truck didn't move. The spooked driver actually inched the truck forward, but a cop quickly stopped him. Then Nolan turned and took a swing at an observer, smashing a camera into her face. The attack was distressing enough, but worse, it had been witnessed, from two feet away, by a Humboldt County sheriff's deputy who refused to take action. I was standing directly behind Nolan and the deputy when Nolan struck the photographer. I got a clear photograph of the assault with the deputy looking on. I sent a copy of the photo to Humboldt County district attorney Terry Farmer, who declined to press charges against Nolan for an assault that was not only captured on film but witnessed by several people, including one of his deputies. Here was more evidence that activists in Humboldt County would enjoy no legal or constitutional protections under the county's rogue government commissaries.

By 1990 Farmer had held his post for eight years. He would remain the county's district attorney until his upset loss in 2002 to Paul Gallegos. By then, Humboldt County voters were looking for a change. They'd seen how, in 1997, Farmer had failed to prosecute at least four incidents when Humboldt County sheriff's deputies had used cotton swabs to smear pepper spray directly into the eyes of nonviolent protesters, an action that Amnesty International condemned as "torture." The activists won a lawsuit against the county.

Farmer also refused to press charges in 1998, when a hostile Pacific Lumber logger felled a tree onto David "Gypsy" Chain, crushing his skull. Chain was twenty-four when he died. The logger who killed Chain,

A. E. Ammons, had previously been recorded on video threatening to fell a tree directly at protesters and to return the next day with his gun.

"You fuckin' cock suckers!" Ammons screamed. "Get the fuck out of here! You've got me hot enough now to fuck! . . . Get outta here! Otherwise I'll fuckin', I'll make sure I got a tree comin' this way! Ohhhhh, fuck! I wish I had my fuckin' pistol! I guess I'm gonna just start packin' that motherfucker in here. 'Cause I can only be nice so fuckin' long. Go get my saw, I'm gonna start fallin' into this fuckin' draw!" The draw was a steep, heavily forested ravine where quick movement was virtually impossible. One of the other protesters described what happened.

> When we had arrived on the scene earlier the loggers had been falling trees downhill but this tree had been purposely fallen in our direction, side hill. . . . I looked up just in time to see a huge Douglas fir coming down nearly on top of me. The main trunk came within 10 feet of me and if I hadn't been under the small trees the Douglas fir's branches would have hit me. . . . Almost instantly the protesters and the logger congregated on the scene. Someone was shouting at him that he could have killed us. It was then that I heard someone frantically calling out "Gypsy, Gypsy, where's Gypsy? He was right behind me." I shouted out for him but there was no answer. It was then that his body was found by the logger. . . . [H]e had massive head trauma. . . . Gypsy died doing CDF's job.

Despite the evidence, Farmer told the press, "There was no criminal conduct that could be proven. He [Ammons] just didn't know that they were there."

Although violence resided in the hearts of some loggers, and while Ammons himself bears direct responsibility for Chain's death, some responsibility lies with executives at Maxxam and Pacific Lumber and with county officials who at best would seem aloof about violence directed against activists. The toxicity that these institutions had injected into Humboldt County communities, and into the forest, was now pervasive.

63

IN LATE FEBRUARY 1990, I JOINED LARRY EVANS AND A FRIEND OF HIS
from work, Brian, on a journey through Headwaters Forest. Larry was
enrolled in the forestry program at Humboldt State University, where he'd
learned how to cruise timber. Cruising determines the amount of board feet
of lumber in a given stand, an essential precursor to collecting, consolidat-
ing, owning, leveraging, logging, and selling timber. We figured that the
information might be useful in future negotiations to purchase the grove,
but really the cruise was an excuse to spend some days in Headwaters Forest
and to inspect logging operations in the region.

At 4 a.m. on February 28, a driver dropped us off, and we tramped a dirt
lane four miles along the South Fork Elk River until veering onto an old
haul road south toward the northwest corner of the grove. As expected, the
easy traveling gave out early, and we struggled across a mile of dense underbrush and tightly woven small trees. Atop a ridge we found a small tin tag
wired to a tree. The tag contained a faint "x" that denoted our location on a
topographic map.

"This should be old growth," I said.

We rested and wondered how long it would be before we'd reach the big
trees. As I sat studying the map and taking bearings, Larry and Brian wandered off. After a short while Larry called over. "Hey Greg, come here!" I
told him to hold on, as I was studying the map. He laughed. "Old growth!"
he yelled.

In the heart of the redwoods, we camped along a semiflat. I found a
soft dry spot under a large fallen redwood that was perched five feet above
the ground. As dusk fell, we ate and chatted about the value of Headwaters Forest. We knew that if the company couldn't log, then the land was
worth no more than $50 million. Yet Maxxam had already announced that

Headwaters Forest was worth $750 million, nearly as much as the firm had paid for the entire Pacific Lumber Company just a few years before. Clearly greed knew no bounds, an illness ameliorated only by a constant IV drip of money.

On March 1 our trio sat secreted into the west bank of Little South Fork Elk River. For three days we had slowly made our way from the lowermost reach of the old growth, weaving in and out of countless tiny tributaries, and in this fashion traced a route up toward the south end of the grove. From there we would hoof a private logging road down to Fortuna and use the radio phone to call for a pickup.

Only now we sat in the forest in stunned silence—at least, *we* were silent. From across Little South Fork came the sickening scream of chainsaws and a D8 tractor. At that moment a timber crew was carving an illegal road straight into the heart of Headwaters Forest.

We were outraged. Not only was there no legal means for Maxxam to blaze a road into the grove, but hadn't our fair elected representatives just gained the "concession" of a two-year moratorium on logging in Headwaters Forest?

I called Judi Bari, who, when she wasn't blockading or chiding timber companies through a bullhorn, was almost always at her desk.

"Oh, hey, Greg," she said, delighted as always. "You sound like you're in a tree? Where are you?"

I told her. I asked Judi to call the offices of Doug Bosco, Barry Keene, and Dan Hauser to let them know the result of their heralded "handshake" agreement. I also asked her to call the California Department of Forestry, for whatever good it might do.

We had to assume that these radio phone calls could be overheard by anyone with a decent radio system, compromising our secrecy. This was something that Larry and I, still under injunction, had to consider. As always, Larry contemplated the matter carefully before determining a good next step.

"Fuck 'em," he said.

A short while after the saws and dozers quieted, we tramped eastward into and across Little South Fork Elk River. Apparently, road cutting had been ongoing even during past rains, as the stream ran a deadly brown. I'd been in Headwaters Forest after five inches of rain had fallen in twenty-four hours; yet even that deluge had not impaired water quality. Now, according to Larry's measurement, Little South Fork Elk River was filled with forty centimeters of silt.

We continued along the southeastern flank of Little South Fork and crawled up a steep, muddy escarpment to access the new road. In places the road was two hundred feet wide and studded with stumps, many of them massive. We followed the muddy laceration downstream, toward its terminus, where Maxxam hadn't even bothered to build a road but instead simply clear-cut the trees. Along the way we found stumps that were eight feet across and some that were ten feet in diameter or wider. That day I wrote in my journal, "Some timber summit."

We made it back to town without incident. I made some calls. Judi had somehow spoken directly to John Campbell, who claimed that the road—or, really, the linear clear-cut that knifed into the heart of the world's largest unprotected ancient redwood grove—was a "wildlife study trail." The dozer had been "clearing brush," said Campbell, so that the company's and the state's wildlife biologists could conduct required "wildlife surveys." Campbell ladled the same lies to the press.

So did the state Department of Forestry. On Saturday, March 3, *Press Democrat* reporter Steve Hart wrote that Joe Fassler, a CDF forester in Fortuna, told him, "I went and looked at it this morning. It's a single wildlife access trail eight to 10 feet wide." Hart wrote that Campbell "accused the environmentalists of trying to inflame the public. 'We have an agreement not to cut for two years,' Campbell said."

The following Monday I called Len Theiss at CDF's Coast District headquarters in Santa Rosa. Theiss was apparently caught flat-footed.

"I haven't talked with anybody up there," Theiss told me. "The only thing I know is what I read in the paper. The *Press Democrat* indicated that there were no violations of the rules, that the road was in fact a trail so that they could get the biologists in there to do the necessary surveys in the Headwaters. That's about the extent that I know." I was dismayed to learn that the *Press Democrat* was now regulating logging in the state.

Next I called Keene's office in Sacramento and got his aide, Andrea Tuttle. I asked if the senator was planning any legal sanctions against Maxxam for having violated the so-called agreement by carving an illegal road into the heart of the grove that, less than one month before, Charles Hurwitz himself had promised to save.

"Well, we don't interpret it that way," said Tuttle. "I called and was told by the company what the road was and then we had that confirmed by both Fish and Game and the department of Forestry and we feel the matter is closed."

I protested. "No Andrea, it was a *road*, with a giant clear-cut at the end. I *saw* it. I'll have the photos at your office in a week." Again, she demurred.

"It was a clearing through the brush," said Tuttle, who held a doctorate in environmental planning from the University of California, Berkeley. "It is indeed a road, but it is through brush; there were no trees cut to create access so that the negotiated wildlife studies could be conducted."

"Hundreds if not thousands of trees were cut, Andrea."

"According to Fish and Game and Forestry, it was an approved, agreed-upon cutting of a road, brushing out of an area. There were agreements that the area was too dense for anyone to physically get in there to do the studies. It's difficult to physically get across."

"I've been getting across that terrain for years. I've crossed it *at night*. In any case, it's not a 'wildlife study trail'; it's a horrendous, illegal clear-cut gouging straight into the middle of the last ancient redwood grove still standing outside of parks. I expect some sort of action on this from Barry Keene."

No such action was forthcoming. Tuttle had apparently done her job well. In March 1999, two weeks after the state and federal governments purchased Headwaters Forest for $480 million, California Republican governor Gray Davis appointed Andrea Tuttle as director of CDF. During her tenure, Pacific Lumber would continue its heavy logging of whatever was left of its two hundred thousand acres of forestland—leaving Headwaters Forest a forsaken island of critical biodiversity surrounded by ecological ruin.

64

O NE OF THE MOST REMARKABLE EVENTS OF THE LATE 1980s WAS ONE
that didn't happen. Save the Redwoods League never sought protection for the very last ancient redwood groves still standing outside parks. It
wasn't just that the League had preferred to remain quiet in public to more
effectively negotiate in private with Maxxam. Internal League documents
show no discernible attempt by the organization to bring Charles Hurwitz
to the negotiating table during the crucial first five years of Maxxam's logging spree in the redwoods—or ever. After seventy years of operation, it
seemed as if the League was no longer dangerous, just irrelevant. Yet even
this summation would turn out to be generous.

My first contact with the League occurred early in 1986, when I implored
the organization to step up to protect LP's Sonoma County redwoods and
the last ancient redwoods now being clear-cut by Maxxam. My entreat-
ies went nowhere. I did speak a couple of times with Bradlee Welton, the
League's assistant to Executive Director John Dewitt. Welton was unhelpful
and clipped, as if he couldn't be bothered about Maxxam's inconvenient in-
trusion into the serenity that now appeared to guide the League.

I figured that if I could simply provide the League with needed information regarding the size and whereabouts of the groves now held by Maxxam,
the organization would act. It never occurred to me that the League would
be content to sit out the last great redwood fight. I kept the League up-
dated on Maxxam's ongoing logging and forwarded documents I'd obtained
through the California Department of Forestry. Three decades later, when I
scoured the League's voluminous and newly curated archive housed at UC
Berkeley's Bancroft Library, I discovered that the League had tracked the
Maxxam takeover of Pacific Lumber since day one; it had stuffed files with
news clippings, and with my missives, yet had taken no action.

A couple of documents in the archive demonstrated the League's lofty in-
difference. One was a copy of the first of just two letters that I would receive
from John Dewitt himself. On January 21, 1987, after a year of my hound-
ing, Dewitt wrote, "Of necessity, the League has focused its efforts on completing each of the Redwood parks over the years since there is never enough
money to buy all the trees." The League was not interested in saving Pacific
Lumber's redwoods because lands to be acquired "should adjoin the existing
parks in the Eel River District. . . . We appreciate that you have obtained a
good photographic record. You might consider lobbying the Director of the
Department of Forestry."

I was baffled that Dewitt could suggest that I rely on CDF. Didn't he
know? At the time, the League was raising millions of dollars annually to
"save the redwoods"; yet what redwoods could be more important than the
very last of the ancient trees?

I'd kept Dewitt's letter. What I didn't have was Dewitt's copy of a letter that I'd received from Richard J. Ernest, chief of CDF's Coast Forest
District, which I'd forwarded to him. The twelve-hundred-word letter,
dated November 24, 1986, responded to a number of questions I had about
Maxxam's forest destruction. It provided acreage figures I'd asked for and
suggested that I contact Robert Stephens for more information. The letter
curtly addressed what I charged were the agency's violations of state laws.

When I found this letter in the League archive, someone had highlighted
seven sentences, but not the one from Ernest that confirmed Maxxam had
logged nearly ten thousand acres of old-growth redwood in a single year.

"To date, the Department has found no significant impacts to the various biological or environmental resources as a result of The Pacific Lumber
Company timber harvesting," wrote Ernest in the League-highlighted text.
"Tourism should not be affected by The Pacific Lumber Company's harvesting. Their lands are not open to the general public. Those that are generally visible have been operated on to achieve asthetic [sic] enjoyment. . . .
Whether it be clearcutting or selection, this harvesting has been ongoing
since the turn of the century. Hopefully, it will continue on indefinitely into
the future. The actions by The Pacific Lumber Company are not expected to
deter that prospect." It was a stirring justification for the League to do nothing, which is what the organization conspicuously did.

The League archive contains a series of hopeful letters, articles, and phone messages from me to League officials, alerting them to our protests and asking for support. All of them I delivered in the naive belief that we shared a common objective. My letters rarely received a reply, and they certainly never moved the League to oppose Maxxam's ongoing destruction of the last ancient redwoods.

After 1987 I stopped trying to sway the League. I no longer saw purpose in it. I would not send John Dewitt another note until 1993, this one with some of my recent newspaper articles that examined Maxxam's ongoing redwood logging and a plea for the League to get involved to save Headwaters Forest before it was gone.

On November 3, 1993, Dewitt wrote back. "We all hope the trees can be ransomed without paying Maxxam or Mr. Hurwitz 'obscene profits,'" he wrote, without offering to help out. "All your good work to save the Redwoods is appreciated." Three years later, Dewitt died after what his family said was "a long illness." He was fifty-nine years old.

Between the time I wrote to Dewitt, in 1993, and he wrote back, Dewitt and the League had made another important contribution to the history of redwood preservation. That year I provided information and language for a bill, submitted by freshman North Coast congressman Dan Hamburg, that sought preservation of the three-thousand-acre Headwaters Forest, as well as the six-hundred-acre remainder of Elk Head Springs Grove, all of the remaining smaller ancient redwood groves, and forty-one thousand acres of surrounding timberland held by Maxxam. The smaller islands comprised twenty-three hundred acres of old growth in the headwaters of Lawrence Creek. The legislation would allow light-touch logging of second-growth trees in the forest that surrounded the virgin groves to maintain a timber economy while allowing the landscape to heal and provide habitat connectivity. Hamburg's staff had largely based the legislation on a January 1988 proposal created by the Arcata Earth First! group.

Our Headwaters Forest Wilderness Complex recommended a preserve of ninety-eight thousand acres. We'd designed it to protect all of Pacific Lumber's remaining virgin redwood groves inside protected wildlife corridors that would run to the coast. The proposal so outraged Maxxam officials that they took out a full-page ad against it in the *Eureka Times-Standard*. The proposal embraced a "whole ecosystem" approach to allow rare and sensitive species to recover and thrive within a diverse and fully functioning ecological region. We recommended that the PL lands be protected through acquisition and the rest through conservation easements, with some logging and other resource industries allowed. For an Earth First! proposal, ours was mainstream. It would go nowhere until Hamburg mined it for his legislation.

Under Hamburg's bill, the acquired redwood lands would become the property of the US Forest Service, with the virgin forests and connecting buffers protected through a newly created Headwaters Forest Wilderness. "The ecosystem approach is the heart of this bill," Hamburg said in 1993. "The idea is we're not creating museums, we're protecting an ecosystem, and to me that is the bill. . . . We're not just protecting a few groves, we're trying to protect the wildlife values, and all the values, that are attendant to an ancient forest."

Although he was a new congressman, Hamburg and the measure's co-sponsor, Bay Area representative Pete Stark, skillfully guided the legislation through the House. The Sierra Club and the National Audubon Society backed the bill, which quickly garnered eighty-six cosponsors. Hamburg's friend, singer Bonnie Raitt, testified in favor of the legislation on Capitol Hill. On October 13, 1993, James Lyons, assistant secretary for the US Department of Agriculture's Office of Natural Resources and the Environment, told the House Subcommittee on Specialty Crops and Natural Resources that the Bill Clinton administration was offering its "strong support for the goals and objectives of this legislation . . . the Headwaters Forest Act. . . . The Administration stands committed to enter into aggressive negotiations with involved parties" after the legislation's passage.

Yet Hamburg's bill would face an unexpected threat. In October, Save the Redwoods League came out against it. The League's action left Hamburg blindsided, mystified, and outraged. Just two weeks earlier the League had celebrated its seventy-fifth anniversary, hosting twelve hundred League members for a ceremony at Founders Grove. At the time, the organization remained much loved and extremely powerful, with fifty thousand members and a board of councilors made up of wealthy and well-connected professionals. Yet, once more, the League would actually undermine, rather than support, protection of primeval redwoods—and not just any ancient redwoods but the very last virgin stands outside parks.

Dewitt publicly opposed Hamburg's legislation, calling it "fatally flawed." He told the *Press Democrat* that the fight to save Headwaters was trivial and compared it to "debating the value of the last few gold bars to come out of Fort Knox." The dissembling pronouncement was on par with a pamphlet written and published by Dewitt and the League in 1985, which claimed, "The two-stage creation of the Redwood National Park represents a milestone for Save-the-Redwoods League which had supported establishment of a Redwood National Park for more than 60 years."

Joining Dewitt in opposing Hamburg's legislation was former North Coast congressman Doug Bosco, who by then was employed by Maxxam as a lobbyist. In an October 17, 1993, op-ed in the *Press Democrat*, Bosco (who would soon buy a controlling share of the paper) echoed Dewitt, calling Hamburg's legislation "fatally flawed." By then Bosco had been joined at Maxxam by Vernon Jordan, chairman of President Clinton's 1992 presidential transition team, and Stuart Eizenstat, a former adviser to both Clinton and former president Jimmy Carter. The trio had a much different deal in mind.

The timing of Hamburg's bill was critical. In June 1992, Maxxam had illegally leveled twenty acres of Owl Creek Grove without providing required marbled murrelet surveys. State officials were forced to halt the logging. Not coincidentally, that year the federal government had finally afforded marbled murrelets protection under the Endangered Species Act. Owl Creek Grove was home to the second-highest concentration of murrelets on PL land, after Headwaters Forest. Hurwitz would exercise his control over what now constituted one of the world's most important remaining murrelet habitats by setting out to destroy it.

Five months later, over the long Thanksgiving weekend, Maxxam again sent several crews of bulldozers and fallers into Owl Creek Grove in violation of court orders and state and federal laws. The company's loggers cut ten to twenty trees per hour in double shifts. Bulldozers scoured the delicate stand. In just a few days Maxxam cut a wide swath directly into the center of the grove.

Thirty Humboldt County activists stormed the forest to save it. Not surprisingly, Pacific Lumber had already arranged for several deputies from the cash-strapped Humboldt County Sheriff's Department to be on hand to arrest citizens who were essentially doing the sheriff's job. The protesters saved dozens of ancient redwoods by shutting down logging for most of a day.

"Them going to work this soon was kind of a surprise to us," said Ross Johnson at CDF. James Steele, the environmental services supervisor at the state Department of Fish and Game, said that his agency had secured a "word-of-mouth type" agreement with Pacific Lumber that logging would not commence in Owl Creek Grove until all the required wildlife surveys and court motions had concluded. Steele said Pacific Lumber officials had promised "that they wouldn't harvest until we had all this business behind us. We were unaware that this harvesting was going to go on."

Steele may have been caught off guard because there was no legal means permitting Maxxam to log in Owl Creek Grove. Cutting of the stand had been stayed in 1989 by the California Supreme Court. The Environmental Protection Information Center was forced to again petition the court to stop the logging, which it did on November 30, the Monday after Thanksgiving. In just a week Maxxam had succeeded in cutting the very heart out of Owl Creek Grove, destroying the best habitat within the stand for marbled murrelets as well as for endangered spotted owls. EPIC attorney Rod Jones charged that, by Thanksgiving Day, state and federal officials knew full well that Maxxam was rampaging through Owl Creek Grove, but "they sat on their hands while the grove was being destroyed by corporate barbarians in direct violation of the Endangered Species Act."

65

O N September 21, 1994, Dan Hamburg's Headwaters Forest Act passed overwhelmingly in the House, by a vote of 288–133. California senator Barbara Boxer had submitted a companion bill in the Senate, but she did not champion it. Boxer's inertia was likely due to opposing efforts by California's other Bay Area senator, Dianne Feinstein.

Feinstein and her wealthy husband, Richard Blum, were a San Francisco power couple who enjoyed close ties with several councilors of Save the Redwoods League. In the Senate, Feinstein was consistently helpful to the League. In 2001, Feinstein passed legislation that provided the League with half the $10.3 million purchase price for the Dillonwood Grove, comprising 1,540 acres of forestland in the Sierra Nevada mountains. The purchase was lauded as an important acquisition of one of the last privately held groves of giant sequoias. Yet the grove had been logged for more than a century and contained just one hundred giant sequoia trees. In 2002 Feinstein led the congressional campaign to secure funding for the League's $60 million purchase of 25,000 acres of denuded timberland on Mill Creek and Rock Creek, adjacent to Jedediah Smith Redwoods State Park and Del Norte Coast Redwoods State Park, "completing" the League's long held "vision" for the parks.

In October 1994, Feinstein killed Boxer's Headwaters Forest companion bill by insisting that it not be heard until her own Desert Lands Act passed the Senate. On the last day, at nearly the last minute, of the Senate session, the 6.6-million-acre desert wilderness bill passed, but now there was no time to hear the Headwaters Forest Act, a fatal delay. That year, Hamburg lost his congressional seat, and the Headwaters Forest Act passed into memory.

In 1996, Feinstein announced that an "accord" had been reached between Maxxam and the state and federal governments to buy Headwaters Forest.

Between 1996 and 1999 Feinstein would lead the federal negotiating team in talks with Maxxam. Owing to restrictions imposed by the Endangered Species Act, Charles Hurwitz would need serious help to achieve a purchase price higher than $50 million. He would get that help from Dianne Feinstein.

"Hurwitz has done it again," Kathy Bailey, the Sierra Club's forestry chair, said in 1996, when Feinstein and Maxxam announced their "accord." She said Headwaters Forest was being held "hostage. . . . For the past 10 years, Hurwitz has been in control here and he has done nothing but destroy the forest."

In an exposé on the Headwaters deal in *CounterPunch*, investigative journalists Alexander Cockburn and Jeffrey St. Clair alleged that Feinstein was integral to the scheme to achieve a purchase price for Headwaters that would turn out to be ten times higher than the grove was worth. They wrote,

> From December of 1995 through February of 1996, the [Bill Clinton] administration regarded the support of the mainstream enviro groups as of crucial importance in the 1996 [presidential] race. . . . On Dec. 15, 1995 two corporate executives who sit on the board of the Wilderness Society sipped coffee with Clinton. One of them was real estate baron Richard Blum—husband of Dianne Feinstein—who is also a longtime friend and sometime business partner of Charles Hurwitz, the corporate raider from Houston who wanted the government to purchase from him at an exorbitant price the Headwaters Redwood Forest in Northern California. The other attendee was David Bonderman, a financier and chairman of Continental Airlines. Bonderman is based in Houston and is also a pal of Hurwitz. Six months after this session, Sen. Dianne Feinstein brokered a Headwaters deal for the administration that was highly favorable to Hurwitz. The Wilderness Society was the only national environmental group to praise the bailout.

The Wilderness Society was one of the largest and oldest conservation organizations in the United States. It was also the primary driver of the Desert Lands Act. At the time, Maxxam and Charles Hurwitz were under enormous economic pressure. The Clinton coffee klatch had occurred less than one month after the federal Office of Thrift Supervision announced that it would file a lawsuit against Maxxam and Hurwitz to recover the $1.6 billion lost in the looting of United Savings Association of Texas. The government filed its suit on December 26, 1995.

The "accord" to preserve Headwaters Forest bulldozed forward into the face of fierce opposition from critics who demanded that, instead of providing Hurwitz with hundreds of millions of dollars, state and federal officials must enforce the Endangered Species Act. Enforcement of the act would have not only continued to afford Headwaters Forest full protection but substantially lowered the cost to taxpayers of preserving the grove while disallowing an end around that would threaten to weaken the act throughout the country.

In September 1996, shortly after the deal was announced, a crowd of five hundred people rallied at the Arcata Plaza to protest the bailout of Maxxam and the government's rewarding of the company for its destructive practices. "This doesn't even come close to what we want," said Cecelia Lanman of the Environmental Protection Information Center. "Tear up that contract today." Lanman called for a sixty-thousand-acre preserve. Kurt Newman called the agreement a "slimy, unmitigated sellout."

Yet, in 1999, the ad hoc coalition that included Dianne Feinstein, the Clinton administration, the Wilderness Society, California Republican governor Pete Wilson, Save the Redwoods League, and Maxxam presented Charles Hurwitz with $480 million in taxpayer money for Headwaters Forest, the remainder of Elk Head Springs Grove, and a larger, heavily logged "buffer," comprising a total of 7,472 acres. The company's remaining 2,300 acres of virgin redwood standing in smaller groves—which Feinstein basely dubbed "lesser cathedrals"—were not included in the deal; nor were thousands of acres of residual old-growth redwood. State Senator Byron Sher and the Sierra Club did manage to secure a fifty-year conservation easement that disallowed logging in the smaller groves. At this writing, that time span is half over with no movement from any party to fully protect these groves.

Cynthia Elkins, then EPIC's executive director, said at the time, "The deal in essence didn't really protect any areas. It put them into public ownership, but those areas that were purchased were already off-limits to logging because of EPIC's murrelet case. . . . So we lost ground through the Headwaters deal, and we paid them a lot of money for it."

The lawsuit referenced by Elkins was *Marbled Murrelet and EPIC v. Pacific Lumber Company*. Filed in 1993, the suit catalyzed the Headwaters deal. It was the first federal lawsuit in the United States, brought by the public, that successfully enforced the Endangered Species Act on private timberlands. The Clinton-Bonderman-Blum confab occurred in anticipation of Maxxam's losing this important federal action, which occurred in May 1996.

Naturally, Charles Hurwitz loved the Headwaters agreement. He told the press, "It's a very good deal. It shows we can preserve old trees and continue to log in an environmentally sound manner."

Feinstein agreed. "There always has to be some compromise," she said. "It may not have all the stars, the moon and the sun in it for everyone . . . but did we save Headwaters? Yes. Do we have a scientific process in place for logging of the rest of the land in an environmentally sound way? Yes. . . . To those who care about the trees, this is the best we can get right now."

California resources secretary Douglas Wheeler noted, "The outstanding leadership of Save-the-Redwoods League also deserves recognition. Save the Redwoods, which—since 1918—has done more than any other group to protect redwoods in California, supports the Headwaters agreement and is working with us to assure its implementation."

Mary Angle was the League's executive director at the close of the Headwaters deal. She was the only environmental representative who attended Governor Pete Wilson's signing ceremony, on September 19, 1998, which authorized a state allocation of $242 million toward the final purchase price of $480 million. In 2022 Angle told me, "If the grove had not been purchased for permanent protection, it would always be vulnerable to logging and would eventually [have been] destroyed."

I don't agree with Angle. By the mid-1990s, Maxxam's ability to cut Headwaters Forest had been effectively neutered by lawsuits, the Board of Forestry, and public opinion. Even the California Department of Forestry was sick of Pacific Lumber. Between 1995 and 1998 the agency issued more than three hundred citations against the company for violating the Forest Practice Act. In 1998, the state revoked PL's logging license, meaning the company now had to find licensed contractors to log its own land. Maxxam was desperate to sell.

From my remove, it was clear that powerful members of the League's board of directors, flexing their close ties with Feinstein, had helped to usher in this deal. I do agree with Angle that it was better to throw money at Maxxam than to allow Headwaters Forest to be logged. But virtually everyone who knew the political landscape at the time understood that paying such a ransom was unnecessary to save the grove.

Angle was a neophyte. Before joining the League, she'd worked as a park ranger. The League board brought her in as an assistant to John Dewitt, and when Dewitt died, the board elevated her to executive director. Shortly after the Headwaters deal closed, Dianne Feinstein gave Angle an official US Senate "Certificate of Commendation" for her "steadfast support of the Headwaters agreement." Then the League fired her.

No matter her relatively brief tenure at the League, Angle was instrumental in steering the organization toward a greater involvement in scientific research, which has proven to be a positive transition for the organization. Angle commissioned the book *The Redwood Forest*, which was edited by renowned biologist Reed Noss. Published in 2000, *The Redwood Forest* stands as a definitive scientific analysis of redwood biology and the species' ecological history, and it examines environmental conditions and challenges within the redwood biome. Since then the League has provided millions of dollars in funding for myriad scientific studies, some of which, such as those parsing the impacts of climate change and wildfires on redwoods, have contributed to a greater understanding of how best to protect the species under quickly changing conditions. During the new millennium the League has also added acreage to existing redwood parks and preserved one small residual old-growth grove in Sonoma County.

"We serve as the transaction function to acquire and protect land," Sam Hodder, the League president and CEO, told me in 2022. "The more people who experience the redwoods, the better off the world is going to be." Hodder said that his acquisition objective as chief of the League is to "get the [redwood] property out of harm's way."

In contrast, Feinstein's reference to the "science" of the Headwaters deal was simply galling. In order to swing the transaction, Pacific Lumber was compelled to create a Habitat Conservation Plan (HCP), as well as a sustained yield plan, for the rest of its two hundred thousand acres of forestland. The plans would supposedly guide the company's continued logging in a way that would meet the requirements of the federal Endangered Species Act. In granting the HCP, the US Fish and Wildlife Service issued Pacific Lumber an "incidental take permit" that allowed the company to kill marbled murrelets.

Yet both plans were based on inputs of data so fraudulent that they later triggered a lawsuit from Richard Wilson, the California Department of Forestry director who had signed off on them. For a former CDF chief to take such an action was extraordinary. In the end it was futile. During the second week of trial, Wilson and his coplaintiff, state forester Chris Maranto, who had blown the whistle on the fraud, settled the suit for $4 million, which went to the state and federal governments and to attorneys. Maxxam was able to keep logging "to infinity," to use Harry Merlo's pithy phrase.

No matter the bonanza of taxpayer money that Maxxam received for Headwaters Forest, the deal did not require the company to pay down the debt with which it had saddled Pacific Lumber or to repay taxpayers for Maxxam's $1.6 billion plunder of United Savings Association of Texas, though the case was then in the courts. In 2002 Hurwitz and Maxxam agreed to pay the federal government $206,000 to settle the United Savings suit brought by the Office of Thrift Supervision.

After the Headwaters deal closed in 1999, *Texas Monthly* reported that Charles Hurwitz kept on his desk a framed pencil drawing of an owl done by Dianne Feinstein, given to him as a memento of their successful Headwaters deal. The magazine noted that Hurwitz referred to Feinstein as "'the glue' who kept the [Headwaters] accord moving forward despite intense political pressure from some environmental groups in her state."

As if on cue, in January 2007, Maxxam, after liquidating nearly all of Pacific Lumber's assets—valued at between $3 billion and $4 billion—placed the timber company into Chapter 11 bankruptcy. Pacific Lumber still owed bondholders $714 million, virtually the same debt incurred at the time of the takeover in late 1985. In 2008, the California Supreme Court invalidated both the habitat conservation plan and the sustained yield plan, ruling that the documents violated state laws designed to protect habitat. By then both fraudulent documents had well served their intended purpose. Maxxam, thanks to profits realized in its liquidation of Pacific Lumber, had made the Fortune 500 list eight times between 1989 and 1998.

Charles Hurwitz and his cronies had gotten exactly what they'd wanted out of the life of the last virgin redwoods. They'd built their wealth through numerous violations of state and federal statutes and collaboration with shady financiers who would later be convicted of felonies. They enjoyed the blind support of rogue public officials, and they could count on silence, then support, from a "redwoods league" that for 80 years had served industry. Maxxam's destruction of the last redwoods perfectly symbolized and brought to a close the 150-year history of ancient redwood liquidation.

66

O N Tuesday, December 5, 1989, I received an eerie phone call from a reporter named Bill Israel. Israel had got his start at the *Eureka Times-Standard* and now worked as a North Coast stringer for Bay Area newspapers. I had spoken with Israel several times. He often covered our actions. I liked Bill. He was friendly, if skittish. As the redwood wars heated up, he became increasingly off-putting and nervous, sometimes visibly sweating. Today his call was not for an interview but to relay a *feeling* he had.

"I'm worried about you," he said. "I want you to be very careful in the coming days. I haven't heard anything, it's just a feeling, a gut feeling, nothing based on anyone I've talked with. I'm very concerned that you take it easy. There's a potential for injury or worse."

"Is that it?" I asked.

"That's it." Then he hung up.

At the time I understood that Israel was constantly talking with timber representatives. Had he actually heard something that he didn't feel he could disclose? Perhaps most extraordinary about Bill's call is that I never bothered to follow up with him. Thirty years later, when I found a transcript of the call in my notes, I scoured the pages looking for more. Nothing. It's as if the call had synced seamlessly with the rest of the lunacy ongoing at the time, and I'd just shrugged it off.

The year 1989 had ended with the total timber haul, for Mendocino County alone, coming in at four hundred million board feet, the highest figure in twelve years. Judi Bari wanted a commensurate response. She began organizing a "Mississippi Summer in the Redwoods," which would soon be called Redwood Summer. The idea, as the title implies, was to emulate the 1964 "Freedom Summer" voter-registration drives in the South by coaxing thousands of outsiders to travel to the California North Coast and challenge the end-stage logging then ongoing. Since 1986, Darryl Cherney and I had discussed the need for just such a mass action in the redwoods. I wondered if Judi's Redwood Summer campaign would delay my plan to leave the movement once we'd bannered the Golden Gate Bridge.

By March 1990, Judi and several other activists had contacted more than twelve hundred student organizations throughout the country to participate in the Redwood Summer protests. They wanted several thousand people to descend on Humboldt and Mendocino counties over the summer, sending timber country into chaos and shining the national spotlight on the extreme deforestation. The demonstrations would also support the Forests Forever and Big Green voter initiatives that would be on the ballot in November.

Tensions ran high. County sheriffs charged that they hadn't the manpower to address the coming hordes, and trucker Don Nolan called for police to preemptively round up Redwood Summer organizers and charge them with "conspiracy."

The *Press Democrat* ran a long story in which Dave Galitz trivialized the intent of Redwood Summer organizers, saying the movement amounted to "let's have fun on our summer vacation." Galitz added, "When their activities reach the point that it seems to threaten our way of life, our very lifestyle, then let me tell you these folks up there are going to feel very threatened."

We already felt, and were being, threatened, and we had been physically attacked, as Galitz well knew. Judi told the paper, "I fear we're reaching the vigilante violence stage on the North Coast. I think it's very dangerous out there."

On December 18, 1989, a five-member New York news crew from *60 Minutes* dropped into Humboldt County. They lodged at the Eureka Inn, which is where we met them at 4 a.m. the next morning. The idea was to interview Larry Evans, Darryl, and me in All Species Grove, whatever happened to be left of it. I hadn't been there in more than a year, plenty of time for Maxxam's cash machine to have ravaged ancient history. We guided their rented van to the jump-off at Booths Run Creek.

Now into a third year of drought, the creek crossing was easy. Two miles up the old skid trail, we moved through the 1986–1987 clear-cut and into the tiny All Species Creek watershed. Maxxam had wreaked destruction. We entered a tableau of churned earth pimpled by blackened stumps. All Species Creek was a muddy, ripped-open vein. Hardly a shred of green remained.

We found the stump of my tree, where I'd spent a week in the canopy. The width of the stump was more than double my height. I have never returned.

We made our way to a small remnant grove of mixed redwood, Douglas fir, and some hardwoods. The producer, Marley Klaus, said she would interview Larry first, then me, then Darryl. Klaus was attractive, savvy, and game. She interviewed me standing atop a stump, and later Larry said, "You did great." He said it was the best interview he'd heard out of me. I had hoped to seize the opportunity to bring truth to national TV. But *60 Minutes* used none of it. Larry didn't make the cut either.

During his interview Darryl was, as always, insightful and clever, delivering razor-sharp bon mots and gutsy New York irony. After a while I sensed that Klaus was massaging his ego and that a fall was coming. For Darryl, appearing on *60 Minutes* was a personal holy grail. He happily called himself a "media slut." He lived for moments like this, and it made him vulnerable.

Darryl had apparently been too charmed to know where he was being led, but we heard it coming. By now Darryl was well versed in the art of repeating a reporter's question in his answer. So when Klaus asked him if, upon learning he had a terminal disease, he would strap bombs to his body and take out an industry, Darryl took the bait.

"If I knew I had a fatal disease," said Darryl, "I would definitely do something like strap dynamite to myself and take out Glen Canyon Dam, or maybe the Maxxam building in Los Angeles, after it's closed up for the night."

Larry and I locked eyes, then rolled them. Darryl had just uttered what turned out to be the only statement from us that would make it into the broadcast. When we parted up on Kneeland Road, Marley Klaus gave us all hugs and kisses. She spent the evening at a Eureka bar, buying "incalculable quantities of liquor" for Mike Roselle.

The next day Darryl asked Klaus if he could retract his statement, which we were already referring to as the "body bomb." She was noncommittal.

"We'll see," I said to Darryl. "They like that stuff."

I spoke with Klaus on January 17, as she and her editing crew were wrapping up the segment. I tried to talk her out of using Darryl's quote.

"He would never do that," I said. "You would be hard-pressed to find a less violent person in the movement, and anyway he has no mechanical skills whatsoever." I recalled a time after a demonstration when someone had slashed one of Judi Bari's tires. Darryl sat in the car while Judi changed the tire.

I asked Klaus if my interview had made it in.

"I'm trying any way I can to get that in," she said.

"Trying? Aren't you the producer?"

When *60 Minutes* aired, on March 4, 1990, the nation's jaw dropped. Here were these loony, universally bearded, and obviously violent vigilante types poised to take over the country by destroying the machinery of decent, law-abiding mom-and-pop businesses—and, in Darryl's case, promising worse. Of course, many Earth First!ers were fish in a barrel, rhetorically easy pickings. Yet the segment that aired wasn't news. It was a specifically crafted and expertly executed political noose.

When I watched it, I understood that Marley Klaus had interviewed Larry and me as a diversion. She'd had no intention of using the tape unless she could have gotten us to utter something ludicrous. Darryl, with his scruffy beard and wild hair spewing from the side of his head—more than one person would comment on his unfortunate resemblance to Charles Manson—was caught on tape threatening to use a bomb while smirking and squirming delightedly with himself. I wouldn't have wanted him anywhere near my children.

Maxxam's destruction of the last redwoods, the hottest environmental story in the nation at the time, was mentioned in one line of the segment. Louisiana-Pacific, Georgia-Pacific, Ford, Exxon, Dow, Dupont, Drexel Burnham Lambert, Hill & Knowlton, Bank of Credit and Commerce International, and Wall Street—the confederacy of planetary destruction that had given rise to Earth First! in the first place—were not mentioned at all.

Stuffing airtime with a pack of wild-eyed monkey wrenchers was low-hanging fruit for an outfit like *60 Minutes*. Yet I had been very clear with Klaus that not all the Earth First! groups advocated monkey wrenching. The Humboldt and Mendocino County factions, among others, had foresworn the tactic, I said, which was a growing trend within the movement. A movement dedicated to nonviolent civil disobedience, which had rejected violence and property destruction, would have presented in the eyes of most viewers a far more potent, transformative, and acceptable social force than just some rabid band of eco-anarchists. An accurate portrayal by *60 Minutes* would have grown our ranks and strengthened the cause. Instead, the segment added powder to the charge aimed at us.

Two days after CBS aired *60 Minutes*, I visited my parents in Guerneville. At the time my mother, Jessie, was attempting to fight off cancer. My parents offered to send me to graduate school, all expenses paid, at the college of my choice. I had recently lectured at Sonoma State University, in the environmental studies class of Professor Erv Peterson. Dad attended the lecture, as he would for many years afterward as my appearances in Peterson's class became an annual rite.

"You're missing your calling, Greg." He'd meant it; the lecture was decent. But what my father wasn't saying was that watching *60 Minutes* had only deepened my parents' concerns for my safety. My family was not wealthy—the offer was earnest, but it would have been a financial burden. Still, I would have taken them up on it, but I had one more thing to do.

67

On Sunday, April 22, 1990, I rented two rooms in a skeevy motel on Lombard Street in San Francisco. I'd raised enough money to keep the room for several nights, as the action would be weather dependent. Papers the previous day had predicted mostly clear skies in the Bay Area, which we'd need to pull off a visible occupation high above the Golden Gate, one of the foggiest places in the world. The papers also ran lead stories on Michael Milken's plea bargain down to six felonies and a $600 million fine "to settle the massive criminal case against him," as the *San Francisco Examiner* reported. Milken had faced ninety-eight counts of racketeering and securities fraud. By the end of the year one of Milken's most loyal clients, Charles Hurwitz, would celebrate Maxxam's best annual return to date. In 1990, Maxxam reached 184 on the Fortune 500 list, with $2.4 billion in revenue and $161.9 million in profit, derived in large part from the life of the last ancient redwoods.

The gathered activists made me think twice about quitting the movement. I was steadfast in my decision, but still I admired the troops. Most were from the Bay Area, anchored by Karen Pickett, whose solidity was and remains esteemed in Bay Area environmental circles.

Twenty people crammed into one room for our first meeting. I knew or had heard of the exploits of almost everyone. In addition to the North Coast crew of Larry Evans, Mickey Dulas, Mikal Jakubal, and Darryl Cherney, the group included Bay Area activists Pickett, John Green, Brian Gaffney, Jennifer Grant, Mark Heitchue, Christine Batycki, and Tracy Katelman. A couple of new faces concerned me. By now there was no question that the FBI and possibly private security had us under surveillance. If you're going to climb the Golden Gate Bridge, it's nice to be able to trust your partners.

We strategized on how best to take the bridge. We would necessarily be operating in the middle of the night, on a freeway, one that happened to be among the state's most dangerous thoroughfares. During the meeting I said we'd need to block off a wide section in the middle two lanes so we could park and get people and gear to either side. "We'll need a bunch of orange cones," I said. An hour later someone returned with twenty cones, stolen from a construction site.

In the corner of a room sat the banner. It weighed fifty pounds and was carefully folded into a military gunny sack equipped with backpack straps. It could be pulled from the top end, attached at the corners to one of the traverse lines, and carefully lowered to occupy the middle reach of the bridge. The banner—30 feet wide and 100 feet long, with the bottom end 150 feet above the road—would greet morning commuters with messages that, unfortunately, are even more pertinent today.

At the banner's top were eight-foot letters:

SAVE

THIS

PLANET

Underneath, in six-foot lettering, were the admonitions:

1) DEFEND

ANCIENT

FORESTS

2) FOSSIL

FUELS

3) EARTH

FIRST!

In Eureka I'd bought the biggest pair of bolt cutters I could find. These would snap the gate locks so we could access the big cables. During one of the planning meetings, I scanned the group and said, "We'll need someone strong enough who can cut the east lock and then run across the freeway and cut the other lock, then toss the bolt cutters into the water." I saw the face of Mikal Jakubal light up like a neon sign. "Oh, yeah," he said, rubbing his hands together. He was as tightly wound as a golf ball.

An even dicier task would be running a piece of paracord seventy feet across the freeway to connect both sides of the span and allow climbers to pull the traverse lines from one end to the other. The paracord would have to make it across the road and at least twenty feet above the span before any vehicles, especially semis, roared past.

Eight people would take the span. From our high point on the big cables, two climbers would descend the vertical cables and attach the lower guy ropes to anchor the banner. Two people would go out on the traverse, over the roadway, drawing out and anchoring the top of the banner. And two people would descend vertical ropes affixed to the traverse lines, hovering over the road and stopping at the bottom corners of the banner. This bit of derring-do would allow a human to anchor the bottom corners of the banner in case bridge security was somehow able to cut the lower ropes. It would also look really cool.

Additional climbers would remain on the big cables to guard the traverse lines. These were the "Bettys"—a term I'd learned from a woman in Humboldt County, a surfer. While she surfed the rugged, lonely beaches of the wild Humboldt coast, I sat on the sand, watching as a backup in case she got into trouble. "You can be my Betty," she said wryly, employing a term she'd picked up in Malibu.

Longtime Bay Area activist John Green would be a Betty on the west side, flanked by Mark Heitchue. Both activists were calm and strong. Larry Evans would be an east side Betty, and he would also haul up the banner. Larry had brought in a young friend, who called himself Jesse, who had rock-climbing experience. Jesse would draw the banner out of the big sack and shimmy across the traverse toward the west side, where I would meet him on the traverse, grab the top corner of the banner, drag it over, and anchor it to the horizontal rope. For extra security Jesse and I would each have two traverse lines, four total, that would span 90 feet from one side of the bridge to the other, 250 feet above the road, 470 feet above the water.

I'd prepared notes for the meeting. At the very top I'd written, "CAN'T DROP ANYTHING—#1 CONSIDERATION." At that height an errant carabiner could do serious damage to a pedestrian or a driver. I also wrote, "Speed with calm," "cut locks," "run paracord," "each person gets # at fence for order of ascent," "recon 1-2 a.m.," "all gear in Greg's name," and "jail solidarity."

We were likely to be spotted early. We needed to buy time. Two people would kryptonite-lock themselves to the bottom gates to keep security from accessing the cables. The other way to get at us would be from the elevators that ran inside the towers, allowing access to the tops of the cables. Big iron doors closed in the elevators, and they had locks. Someone said, "Superglue."

Two counties, San Francisco and Marin, share a border in the middle of the Golden Gate Bridge. We would ascend on the Marin County side to greet morning commuters. A crowd would inevitably form, and they would be leafleted by six activists. Karen Pickett and Darryl Cherney would head up media outreach, manning the pay phone at the vista view parking lot.

On the night of April 22, a gorgeous plume of fog wafted across the Golden Gate and engulfed Lombard Street. The next night was better. Someone regularly walked outside to check the night sky through the bright streetlights that infect nearly all human communities. "Stars!" was the common report.

At 1 a.m. we loaded the cars. A reconnaissance crew returned and gave the all clear. They also exulted, "The middle two lanes are blocked off!" I'd driven the bridge countless times at night but had forgotten that, every night, bridge authorities closed two lanes of traffic to prevent head-on collisions. There was no barrier, just orange tubes. The traffic cones were superfluous. (Later someone returned them to the construction site.)

We waited for barfly bitter-enders to clear off the roads. Then, just before 3 a.m., we drove. We pulled three cars into the generously provided center lanes and unloaded. Traffic was light. Jakubal grabbed the heavy bolt cutters, ran east, and leapt the small barrier to the walkway. We heard a loud metallic *clank*. Then, hoisting the bolt cutters over his head like a lance taken in battle, he sprinted gleefully across six lanes, clanked the second lock, ran south along the walkway until he was above water, and chucked the tool into San Francisco Bay.

Larry toted the heavy banner while the rest of us carried the six ropes, carabiners, and assorted gear. We also had supplies of food and water, and I carried a radio phone and a camera. By 3:30 a.m. we were scaling the cables.

Such a climb, even in a group, is a solo experience. No one talked. The mild hiss of traffic ebbed with ascension, and the sparkly skyscrapers of San Francisco seemed to shorten as we gained height. For safeties we used prusik loops that extended from our harnesses to the guy cables that ran parallel to the big cables at waist level. The prusik loops ran around the small cables and locked back onto the harness. Every twenty feet we would stop to negotiate the safeties around the vertical posts that anchored the small cables. In this fashion we quickly gained an exceptional height.

Even while huffing up the wide cable, I was awed by the scene. Only the slightest breeze blew, a condition almost unheard of at the Golden Gate. At the appointed height we stopped and quickly began pulling static lines with the paracord. Just after 5 a.m. we were set. Jesse eased himself onto the traverse, the banner in tow, and edged out onto the line, dangling hundreds of feet above the roadway. I ran two safety loops to each of my traverse lines—four safeties total—checked my gear (water, food, radio phone, camera), and turned to give Mark Heitchue the thumbs-up when I noticed several silhouetted human figures swiftly descending the cables toward us.

"Shit!" We'd counted on more time than this. When the bridge's iron workers got to the elevator doors and found the locks superglued, they'd simply melted the glue with a torch.

I yelled across to Larry and Jesse, "Dump the banner! Dump the banner!" There was no time to pull it out carefully. The whole thing would have to be launched, at which point Jesse and I could untangle it and hang it from the traverse, where we'd be untouchable. But those iron workers were quick. They fairly trotted down the cables, shouting epithets. Later we learned that we'd angered them. The iron workers who maintain the Golden Gate Bridge are possessive of their span. No one else—not tourists, not activists, not cops—ascends the bridge. We'd breached their domain—seized their gates and glued their locks—and they were not happy.

The Bettys tried to block the iron workers. On Larry's side the workers reached over and removed his safeties and tried to push him down the cable. Not good. When Larry reattached his prusik line an iron worker made to cut it with wire cutters. Unaware of what was happening, I kept yelling at Larry to toss the banner, but he was continuing to hold off the most vicious of the iron workers. "He was dangerous," Larry later said. Embracing his inner bouncer, Larry wrapped his giant arms around the iron worker, who was neither small nor weak, and gripped the man so tightly he could hardly breathe. Now realizing the risk at hand, overpowered by this huge man in a frenzied struggle nearly five hundred feet above San Francisco Bay, the iron worker calmed.

On our side, iron workers also assailed Mark Heitchue. I readied for what seemed like a fight, though it never developed. Everything stopped. We all stilled at once in a state of impasse.

Then a blood-orange sunrise eased over the East Bay hills. The bridge, the bay, everything exploded in an effusion of color so lustrous that everyone, even the iron workers, seemed to take notice. The apricot blaze appeared as a sign of the life force we'd come to protect; it illuminated, yet also somehow trumped, our thousand industrial cuts—perhaps as a reminder, as the Earth First! bumper sticker promised, that "NATURE BATS LAST."

Shortly after sunrise I was on the radio phone, live on the air, with a reporter from KCBS, the big San Francisco news radio station. I told the host that we'd taken the bridge. "What we're trying to do is indicate the severity of the crisis the planet faces." At that moment an iron worker pushed past Mark Heitchue and grabbed the phone's antenna. I jerked it from him, bade the reporter to hold on, and gave the iron worker a look he could not ignore. We all knew where we stood. He backed off, and I continued with the most surreal interview I'd ever given.

After the call I stopped talking to the press and just enjoyed the view. The Golden Gate stands among the world's most dramatic natural features, a magnificent crack in a long reach of otherwise impenetrable coastline. I could see the entire bay, 550 square miles, more than ten times larger than the city of San Francisco. Two fabled river ecosystems, the Sacramento and the San Joaquin, feed the bay.

For five thousand years the Ohlone and the Coast Miwok peoples lived rich lives in the Bay Area. These communities thrived alongside wildlife and within fully functioning ecosystems. We are warned against idealizing the lives of Native peoples. Yet the original human inhabitants of California did lead largely ideal lives "in a land of unbelievable plenty," Malcolm Margolin writes in *The Ohlone Way*.

> There is no record of starvation anywhere in Central California. Even the myths of this area have no reference to starvation. . . . [F]or century after century the people went about their daily life secure in the knowledge that they lived in a generous land, a land that would always support them. . . . San Francisco Bay rimmed with vast saltwater marshes, rivers that flowed throughout the year, springs that bubbled out of the hillsides, natural lakes, ponds, and innumerable creeks. Water was everywhere, and everywhere it was teeming with life.

Then arrived the Hoopers, the Huntingtons, the Crockers, the Creeds, the Grants, the Stanfords, the Drums, and the Hammonds. These ruthless men and their forebears carried to this bountiful but fragile world a severe imbalance, insecurities so deeply wrought that they would learn to justify, indeed celebrate, the wreckage left in the wake of their rapid industrial expansion. From some deep and malign well they embraced riches and power, status and admiration, somehow unable to see or to care about the cataclysms and suffering they caused. They revered false idols of success achieved through violence and theft and cloaked their misdeeds in a fictitious benevolence. Their worlds coalesced as an inexorable heat that within a single generation would despoil the San Francisco Bay region. These men had many equals around the country and throughout the world. Today we face an abyss of their making, a juggernaut full-steam ahead and professionally managed by their ideological progeny, who remain dedicated to the cause, whatever that may be. Yet somehow we were the terrorists.

By now hundreds of people had gathered on the ground below the bridge and in the vista view parking area—the entire tableau bathed in golden light. Traffic backed up for several miles to and through the rainbow-painted Waldo tunnels (now renamed for actor Robin Williams). I was sad we hadn't gotten the banner out; it would have been epic. But there we were, alive and fighting. The clean ocean air felt good in my lungs. It was a beautiful day.

Two hours later we ambled down the bridge into the arms of California Highway Patrol (CHP) officers, who were professional and polite. Nonetheless, those of us on the bridge were arrested on suspicion of "resisting a police officer" and "assaulting a police officer," potential felonies. We retained several lawyers, including famed San Francisco civil rights attorney Tony Serra, who quickly brought the Marin County district attorney down to earth. In the end we received two misdemeanor trespassing charges.

In the tank at Marin County jail, we were surprised to see Darryl Cherney and two other male members of the ground support crew. Karen Pickett and another woman from ground support were on the women's side. The ground crew had somehow been picked out of the packed crowd and arrested, no matter that they were breaking no laws. We soon learned that they'd been arrested not by Marin County sheriffs, nor by CHP, but by Oakland Police, whose jurisdiction was twenty miles away, across the bay. It would have been impossible for those cops to have picked out our ground crew unless an infiltrator had breached our action group. The mystery of why Oakland cops were making arrests in Marin County would become clear exactly one month later.

Darryl didn't say much. He was embarrassed because the cops had also impounded his car, which he'd driven from Humboldt County with virtually his entire set of office files in the back, "in case I needed them," he said sheepishly. Included were the names and addresses of all donors to Darryl's Earth First! group over the past three years, all of his contacts, notes, flyers, the works.

A cop approached the tank and brought us back to the processing area, one by one. At first I thought we were to be released. But in the fluorescent room I heard, "More fingerprints." A female officer appeared. I hadn't seen her before. She pressed my inky fingertips onto a small white card containing ten spaces. This was my sixth arrest. I'd never seen a card like this. I said, "I thought we already did this."

"Not this," she said.

"What are these?"

"FBI," she said.

National and overseas media generously covered the bridge action. Newspaper articles often included an iconic photo, shot from the Marin Headlands, of activists being escorted off the cables, with the San Francisco skyline hovering as backdrop. But no banner. It would have been beautiful. After our case settled and we'd performed community service, I got all of our climbing gear back—everything except the banner. For the next month I tried to retrieve the banner, but I only got runaround. Then everything changed, and I no longer cared.

I spent much of May in the Bay Area and at my parents' house, dealing with the legal repercussions of trying to hang a banner on a bridge, but mostly spending time with my mother. Jessie's life was waning; yet she gripped tightly. She now had two young grandchildren. It pained her to think of leaving.

In mid-May, a producer from a San Francisco television station invited me to attend one of the weekly roundtables hosted by a group of Bay Area TV and radio journalists. She said that each week they discussed current issues. Would I like to address their lunch meeting on May 24, a Thursday, and provide input on what, perhaps, they should cover? I prepared a short discourse on Maxxam's ongoing redwood liquidation, but I emphasized the need for media to pay greater attention to "the ongoing and often illegal harassment, incarceration, and violence wielded by the state, in partnership with private companies, against activists who are exercising their constitutionally protected rights of free speech such as demonstrations and direct action."

After the meeting I returned from the Bay Area to a quiet home. My father, Tom, was at work. Jessie hobbled from the bedroom and told me I had a phone message from a friend in Humboldt County. In her shaky hand mom had written a note on the chalkboard by the phone.

"Darryl and Judi in car accident."

I called my friend.

"They got into a wreck?" I asked.

"No," she said. Her voice broke. "It was a bomb."

68

THE PIPE BOMB EXPLODED DIRECTLY UNDER JUDI BARI'S DRIVER'S SEAT just before noon on Thursday, May 24, 1990. The sophisticated anti-personnel device was wrapped in finishing nails, for shrapnel, and detonated while Judi was driving along Park Boulevard, near Oakland High School, in the East Bay Area. When Judi hit the brakes a ball bearing broke out of a small slot and rolled into a groove where it connected two points and ignited the bomb. The explosion blew a wide hole through the floorboard beneath Judi's seat and blasted the roof of the Subaru wagon into a dome. Nails from the bomb entered the seat back but miraculously missed Judi. Also miraculously, the gas-oil mixture included with the bomb did not ignite. Still, the seat spring impaled Judi's butt, and her pelvis and coccyx were both shattered. Nerve damage was severe, and surgeons initially told Judi she would never walk again. But Judi was a fighter. After six months she could walk a hundred feet until the pain forced her to sit.

Darryl Cherney was also in the car. The pair were headed to Santa Cruz to perform a benefit concert for Redwood Summer. Darryl had intended to ride with someone else. At the last minute, he'd caught a ride with Judi. The bomb scratched one of Darryl's corneas and blew an ear drum, but otherwise he was all right.

The bomb was meant to kill Judi. And it would have, except the full force of the blast shot downward instead of up. Had it worked perfectly, Judi would have been blown to pieces, and both she and Darryl would have been immolated.

In her 1994 book *Timber Wars*, Judi wrote,

I knew it was a bomb the second it exploded. I felt it rip through me with a force more powerful and terrible than anything I could imagine. It blew right through my car seat, shattering my pelvis, crushing my lower backbone, and leaving me instantly paralyzed. I couldn't feel my legs, but desperate pain filled my body. I didn't know such pain existed. I could feel the life force draining from me, and I knew I was dying. I tried to think of my children's faces to find a reason to stay alive, but the pain was too great, and I couldn't picture them. I wanted to die. I begged the paramedics to put me out.

As she was being wheeled into surgery, an Oakland Police officer asked Judi, "Who did this to you?"

"Timber," said Judi.

The following year, when a reporter asked Judi what she wanted the FBI to do about the bombing, she said, "Find the bomber and fire him."

Both answers were undoubtedly correct. In 1991, Judi and Darryl filed a lawsuit against the FBI and Oakland Police for conducting a "sham investigation, bogus investigation of the bombing," which was but one element of "an intelligence gathering operation . . . political spying operation about the Earth First movement and about the environmental movement in Northern California," famed civil rights lawyer and lead attorney in the case Dennis Cunningham said in his opening remarks during Judi and Darryl's trial against the FBI and Oakland Police, in 2002. "The mechanism of this was in classic terms a frame-up, a frame-up that was concocted by the FBI and Oakland Police."

Within hours of the bombing, as she lay in a hospital bed, Oakland Police placed Judi Bari under arrest for "transporting an explosive device." For days a police officer hovered outside her door, as if she were somehow a flight risk. Darryl was also arrested and thrown into the Alameda County jail, where he used his one phone call to ring up Humboldt County's progressive KMUD radio station. "Someone's trying to kill us," he said. "We are demanding, demanding that the Oakland Police Department and the FBI seek out this assassin and bring him to justice immediately." To this day, no such search has occurred.

The first FBI agent to show up at the bomb scene was Special Agent Timothy McKinley. He'd arrived less than twenty minutes after the bomb detonated. Later, in a report, McKinley wrote that the next FBI officer on the scene had told him, "Judy Beri [*sic*] and Darryl Cherney are the subjects of an FBI investigation in the terrorist field." This agent was Frank Doyle, a bomb expert with the FBI. Later court testimony revealed that exactly one month before the Oakland bombing—on the same day that we were trying to banner the Golden Gate Bridge—Doyle had "run what he called 'bomb school' anti-terrorism courses on Louisiana-Pacific land" in Humboldt County, reported the *Los Angeles Times*.

Doyle arrived on scene shortly after McKinley. Later he told the court he just happened to be "driving around the East Bay" in his Suburban. Special Agent John Conway, who had worked under Doyle to orchestrate the Arizona Earth First! bust the previous year, showed up next, followed by a dozen other agents from what the FBI called its Terrorist Squad. Later Judi quipped that the FBI had arrived so quickly, it was as if agents had been "standing around the corner with their fingers in their ears."

Doyle immediately took over the investigation. One of the FBI agents videotaped the scene. Later Judi and Darryl obtained the tape, whose visuals were "suspiciously damaged," said their attorney, but the audio was clear. The assembled agents were jocular, laughing as they examined the bombed-out car.

During a briefing on the evening of the bombing, FBI agent John Reikes told Oakland Police officers that he was "in charge of the FBI terrorist investigation unit and that these people [Judi and Darryl] in fact qualified as terrorists, and that there was an FBI investigation going on other incidents where these individuals were suspects," Oakland Police sergeant Michael Sitterud later declared in a sworn deposition. At the time of the bombing, Reikes was in a meeting with Soviet security agents to formulate a safety plan for an upcoming visit by Mikhail Gorbachev, then the president of an unraveling Soviet Union. Yet, when the call came, Reikes left the important meeting. At the bomb site he told the assembled cops and G-men that Judi and Darryl had been headed to Santa Cruz County to bomb the Moss Landing power plant and that the pair were "known terrorists." In court, both statements would be revealed as false.

The FBI moved with remarkable speed to link Judi and Darryl with the bomb. Dennis Cunningham said, "They cooked [an affidavit] up and presented it to a judge at 2:00 in the morning, got a search warrant, searched the homes of Darryl and Judi overnight. The next day, the news was there. It was all on the news. They took several of [Judi and Darryl's] friends into custody, and then they went ahead with this case."

FBI agents traveled by helicopter two hundred miles to Judi's and Darryl's homes. The FBI didn't just search Judi's house; they tore it apart and terrorized her young children, who were there with Judi's ex-husband. They confiscated hundreds of common household items—a red marker, duct tape, Elmer's glue—that they said were bomb-making materials. Agents ripped apart windowsills in search of nails, which they would later claim matched those that were strapped to the bomb. It was a transparent fabrication, but from coast to coast the press covered the "discovery" as fact. Even after the FBI's own top crime lab analyst, David R. Williams, based in Washington, DC, examined the nails and determined that they were nowhere near a match—nor could they possibly be, since nails are produced in batches of many millions—the FBI insisted that indeed they were. In his affidavit, Sitterud, the Oakland Police sergeant, even reported that Williams had told him that the "'bomb fragmentation nails' and the two identical nails from the box in Ms. Bari's residence were manufactured by the same machine within a batch of two hundred to one thousand nails." In a later deposition, Williams testified that he had said no such thing.

FBI agents also ravaged Darryl's home. By then Darryl had left the Bridgewood Motel and was living in a tiny dome-like structure in the Salmon Creek watershed, fifteen miles north of Garberville. His home was almost impossible to find. It was secreted toward the back of a friend's large property, reached by miles of dirt road, including a series of gated, private lanes. FBI agents drove right to it. Darryl's neighbors lived on beautiful homesteads that dotted the scenic watershed. They constituted a collective of artists, back-to-the-landers, intellectuals, renegades, and pot growers. When the FBI showed up to search Darryl's dome, so did the neighbors. They surrounded the agents and escorted them across the compound. The neighbors knew that neither Darryl nor Judi was capable of bombing anyone. Still, when an FBI agent sauntered up to Darryl's front door and made to go in, a canny neighbor said, "You're not going to just open that, are you?" The agent hesitated an instant, then waltzed right in. Everyone, including and especially the FBI, understood the fallacy of the charges against Judi and Darryl.

The pipe bomb had clearly been placed under Judi's seat, where police and paramedics found a gaping two-foot-by-four-foot hole. Later a paramedic would testify that he had actually stood in the hole under the driver's seat to extract Judi from the car. Yet, within an hour of the bombing and forever afterward, the FBI and the Oakland Police would insist that the bomb had been on the floor of the backseat, no matter that the backseat was virtually undamaged. Therefore, they said, Judi and Darryl must have seen the device and were "knowingly carrying their own bomb."

In 1999, investigative reporter Nicholas Wilson published a retrospective article on the bombing in the *Albion Monitor*, based in Mendocino County. Wilson was one of the few reporters to follow the bombing story in real time and throughout the 1990s. By 1999 Wilson had access to troves of material made public through Judi and Darryl's lawsuit.

Wilson wrote that, two months after the bombing, "the Alameda County District Attorney refused to file any charges for lack of evidence. There is evidence, though, from the FBI's own files, that agents falsified evidence against Bari and Cherney, suppressed exonerating evidence, and conspired with Oakland [Police] to try to frame them. . . . There is . . . good reason to believe the FBI was actively (or passively) involved in the bombing."

Wilson continued,

> Within an hour of the Oakland explosion, none other than Special Agent Doyle, the bomb school instructor, was taking charge of the bomb scene in-vestigation. Since he was the FBI's top Bay Area bomb expert, the other FBI and Oakland bomb investigators first at the scene, some of whom had been his students, deferred to his assertions about the evidence.
>
> It was Doyle who allegedly overruled the Oakland sergeant on the scene who said the bomb was under the driver's seat and that he could see the pave-ment under the car through the hole in the seat. It was Doyle who falsely said the bomb was on the floor behind the driver's seat where it would have been easily seen. It was also Doyle who falsely claimed that two bags of nails found in the back of Judi's car matched nails taped to the bomb for shrapnel effect, when in fact they were not even the same type, and were clearly different to the naked eye.
>
> Other officers on the scene testified that Doyle argued with them, and quoted him saying, "I've been looking at bomb scenes for 20 years, and I'm looking at this one, and I'm telling you you can rely on it. This bomb was vis-ible to the people who loaded the back seat of this car."

Was it an honest mistake? Not likely, the judge ruled in denying Doyle immunity from the lawsuit. Dennis Cunningham argued in a court brief,

"In sum, there was no way such an experienced bomb technician as Frank Doyle . . . or the other investigators—or Ray Charles or Stevie Wonder— would not have known that the bomb was under the seat when it blew up."

Cunningham went on to argue that "the investigation that [the FBI] conducted was in fact really a sham. There was not a serious or good faith attempt to solve the bombing either. . . . And within the cover of that . . . they did a lot of work investigating Earth First."

The bombing was big news. Later Judi said, "It was the only time we made the front page of the *New York Times*." The *Times* article ran on May 26. In the first sentence, reporter Katherine Bishop wrote, "Their supporters were quick to blame opponents of a protest aimed at stopping the logging of redwoods in northern California." In the seventh paragraph the article noted, "Friends of the two people . . . denounce[d] the charges as ridiculous, asserting that the timber industry interests or Government officials were responsible for the bombing."

From the day of the explosion, the FBI and Oakland Police fed state and national media with streams of lies and false leads to further discredit Earth First! and convict Judi and Darryl in the press. In 1990 the FBI's media outreach about the bombing was so regular and ubiquitous that in July, when Mickey Dulas arrived in New York to appear on the *Donahue* daytime TV show, her cab driver, learning that she was there to represent Judi and Darryl, said, "You mean the people who bombed themselves?" On the Sunday after the bombing, *60 Minutes* reran its Earth First! "exposé."

Everything got weirder one week after the bombing. On May 30, *Press Democrat* reporter Mike Geniella received a letter from the "Lord's Avenger" taking credit for making and placing the bomb. The letter provided such exact details about the bomb construction that the FBI accepted it as authentic. The Lord's Avenger had supposedly attacked Judi because she and Darryl had recently appeared at an antiabortion demonstration in Willits, Mendocino County, where they waged a pro-choice counteroffensive. Mostly they sang outrageous satirical songs, including the crowd pleaser "Will the Fetus Be Aborted." Sung to the tune of "Will the Circle Be Unbroken," the song includes the verse "Brigit had two kids already / And an abortion is what she chose / Christian showed her a bloody fetus / She said, 'That's fine, I'll have one of those!'"

"I built with these Hands the bomb that I placed in the car of Judi Bari," began the Lord's Avenger letter. The writer claimed to have planted the bomb in Ukiah; yet that was impossible. The motion detector would have detonated the bomb somewhere in Mendocino County. But that didn't matter to the people who wrote the letter, the most obvious purpose of which was to deflect attention away from the FBI and the timber industry as the prime suspects in the bombing, now that virtually no one in a position of authority believed that Judi and Darryl had bombed themselves.

"The one group of people who would know every single detail in that letter is the FBI," Darryl Cherney said at the time.

The Lord's Avenger scribed with a deft hand.

This woman is possessed of the Devil. The Lord cleared my vision and revealed this unto me outside the Baby-Killing Clinic when Judi Bari smote with Satan's words the humble and Faithful servants of the Lord who had come there to make witness against Abortion. This possessed demon Judi Bari spread her Poison to tell the Multitude that trees were not God's gift to Man but that trees were themselves gods and it was a Sin to cut them. I felt the Power of the Lord stir within my Heart and I knew I had been Chosen to strike down this Demon.

To activists, the Lord's Avenger letter came to represent FBI jitters over the strong and widespread support that emerged for Judi and Darryl across the country. The Bureau quickly announced that one of Judi's confederates had written the letter. They used it to justify further attacks against Judi that included a second destructive search of her Mendocino County home.

69

I SPENT THE FIRST THREE DAYS FOLLOWING THE BOMBING IN MY PARENTS' kitchen, on the phone. I spoke with dozens of people, including activists and reporters. I even tried calling FBI officials in San Francisco and Washington, DC, and the Oakland Police. No law enforcement official or agent ever called me back.

On the afternoon of the bombing, I got through to Karen Pickett, who had immediately stepped in to respond to the mayhem that the bombing and the FBI had now loosed upon activist communities in the United States and upon the imaginations of the American public. Karen quickly admonished me, "I think you'd better lay low, Greg." After we hung up, Karen proved the point when she attempted to visit Judi Bari in the hospital, where she was arrested.

I watched the TV news. "It's hard to say who the victim is here," reported the local CBS affiliate, KPIX Channel 5. "One of the victims has previously said he'd strap dynamite to himself." Images of Judi's bombed-out Subaru shocked my father. At the time, I happened to be reading Brian Glick's 1989 book *War at Home: Covert Action Against U.S. Activists and What We Can Do About It*. My dad lifted the book from the dining room table, walked outside, and began reading.

Well before the bombing, I understood that our group had been under FBI surveillance for at least a couple of years and definitely since the Golden Gate Bridge action, when the agency took our fingerprints. I didn't yet know, however, that the FBI chief snitch for its Arizona Earth First! investigation, Michael Fain—the guy who, working under Frank Doyle, had passed himself off as a recovering alcoholic and Vietnam veteran—may have been investigating *me* for some time before the bombing. This bit of information came out during Fain's deposition in Judi and Darryl's ensuing lawsuit.

Dennis Cunningham took Fain's deposition in Washington, DC, on August 21, 2001. FBI attorney Joseph Sher represented Fain. Most of the ninety-nine-page deposition focused on Fain's work to set up the Arizona activists. But Cunningham, ever wily, steered the discussion until he'd got Fain to talk about the FBI's presence in California. Fain consistently denied knowing anyone in the San Francisco FBI office. He'd never seen an FBI film of the Golden Gate Bridge action; he hadn't even seen pictures of the action, no matter that photos had run in dozens of daily newspapers in the United States. He had never been asked to identify any of the people arrested during the bridge action. He had never looked at Redwood Summer or talked about the bombing case with anyone at the FBI. He didn't know a thing about California activists—until he got to me.

"Mr. Fain," asked Cunningham, "is it your testimony that you never were assigned to investigate and you never did investigate Judi Bari, Darryl Cherney, Redwood Summer, is that right?"

"That is correct," Fain answered.

"Greg King, Karen Pickett?

"What about them?"

"That you were never assigned to investigate them and you never did investigate them?"

"I investigated whatever illegal activity I became aware of," said Fain.

"Did you become aware of any illegal activity on the part of Greg King or Karen Pickett?" asked Cunningham.

"I think Greg King has been involved in a lot of illegal activity."

"That came to your attention? Illegal activity of the type that the FBI has jurisdiction over or just civil disobedience?"

"I think it's more than civil disobedience," said Fain, though he was wrong.

"And did you investigate it yourself?" asked Cunningham.

At that point Sher stepped in and halted the deposition. "I think that's about as far as we're going to go down the line of casting aspersions on people who are not parties to this case."

Cunningham kept on.

"Greg King, regardless of the fact that he's not a party to the case, is a person who is known for a long and complicated association with the plaintiffs and the events that are part of the facts of the background of the case. Our witness refers to some knowledge of Greg King and alleged criminal activities by him. I want to know what he knows about Greg King or what source of information he's had about Greg King or what activities he's engaged in to acquire that information."

Sher replied, "You're going to have to get Judge Larsen to approve that." At that point the deposition ended. Judge Larsen approved nothing of the sort.

In June I drove to my office in Humboldt County. The small, stand-alone building sat on a lovely hillside outside Garberville. I needed to gather files and whatever else I could cram into my small car before returning to Sonoma County. I hadn't been to the office in weeks. All was in order until I went to my secret cache, where I'd hidden my passport and $300 in cash. Gone. The tape on the phone machine was full. I hit play. I stopped listening after the third message, in which a man's voice said, "I hear you like pipe bombs. In your summer actions we are going to impact you with several pipe bombs and plastic explosives to give you a dose of your own medicine. Good-bye."

Two weeks later I visited Judi in a Santa Rosa rehabilitation hospital. It was the first time I'd seen her since the bombing. She looked better than I'd expected, though the dark circles under her eyes were pronounced, and she still could not walk. But her smile remained infectious, her wit keen. Judi said the *New York Times* might accept an op-ed from her exposing the Oakland attack as a resurgence of the FBI's illegal Counterintelligence Program operation. The article ran on August 23. Judi called the bombing an act of "unspeakable terrorism." She warned, "If [the FBI] can succeed in framing and discrediting us, then domestic dissent is not safe from Government sabotage. The right to advocate social change without fear of harassment is the cornerstone of a free society."

On July 17, 1990, Alameda County assistant district attorney Chris Carpenter announced that his office would not prosecute Bari and Cherney due to lack of evidence. By then, most people in possession of even a cursory understanding of American politics—and everyone who knew Judi and Darryl—understood that the case against the pair had been made up.

"The D.A. didn't want to go down with the ship that the FBI and the Oakland Police were sinking in," Darryl told the press after the district attorney's announcement. He added, "There's little joy in vindication when there's still a mad bomber on the loose."

The DA's action may have also been hastened by a letter sent on July 16 by East Bay congressman Ron Dellums to the US and California attorneys general and three congressional committees. The letter called for an investigation of police tactics in the case.

"We are very concerned by reports that the Oakland police and the FBI seemed to have prematurely ruled out or discounted the possibility that the bomb was planted by people wishing to kill the two key environmental leaders of 'Redwood Summer' and thereby destroy the summer campaign," said the letter, which was signed by more than fifty supporters, including David Brower, the Sierra Club, Friends of the Earth, the National Organization for Women, California assemblyman Tom Bates, the American Civil Liberties Union, the National Lawyers Guild, Greenpeace, and Agar Jaicks, an executive board member of the California Democratic Committee. Greenpeace, whose flagship *Rainbow Warrior* had been bombed and sunk by the French government in 1985, killing a crewman, also paid for a private investigator to examine the bombing and police tactics in the Bari case.

Judi told the *Press Democrat*, "I don't intend to be run out of town. I don't intend to shut up." Now, she said, "We're going to sue their asses."

70

As Judi, Darryl, and their legal team prepared strategies and gathered evidence with the hope of actually getting to the trial phase of their lawsuit against the FBI, they would make sure to develop legal arguments that explored not just who had set them up and how, but why. In his 1999 report, the *Albion Monitor*'s Nicholas Wilson explored the questions in the context of the anticipated election of November 1990, which would include Proposition 130, the "Forests Forever" initiative that promised to slow the timber industry's rapid pace of logging.

> The FBI stubbornly refused to do a genuine investigation of the bombing, and failed to pursue real evidence and leads turned over to them. Why would they refuse to investigate solid clues, like identifying fingerprints they found? Was it a cover-up of FBI complicity in the bombing? Was it because they already knew it would show involvement by the timber industry? And if someone wanted to get rid of her, why was Judi Bari bombed when a bullet would have been easier? A new analysis suggests that the key to unraveling the mystery is a timber industry public relations strategy to defeat a logging reform initiative in the fall election. . . . With an enormous financial motive to defeat the initiative, [timber companies] hired public relations firms including Hill & Knowlton to manage a multimillion-dollar PR campaign to turn public opinion against the initiative. . . . [T]hey quickly labeled Prop. 130 "the Earth First! initiative," and said it was "too extreme."

Although initially Forests Forever and Redwood Summer had evolved independently of each other, the timing was serendipitous. By early May 1990, Judi was promoting Redwood Summer as a means for concerned citizens from throughout the United States to show up in Humboldt and Mendocino counties to hold off as much logging as possible until the initiative could pass. That month polls showed a large majority of California voters in favor of the measure, which would eventually be endorsed by more than two hundred mainstream organizations.

Wilson wrote, "It seems far more rational than paranoid to believe there was an FBI and corporate timber connection to the bombing of Judi Bari. Both corporate timber and the FBI had ample motives, history, means and opportunity to bomb Judi. . . . She was the redwood timber industry's most outspoken, brilliant, and effective opponent. . . . [M]illions, even billions of dollars were at stake."

On August 1, 1990, the *Redding Record-Searchlight*, the daily paper serving Shasta County, California, ran a representative editorial that began, "The environmental terrorist group Earth First! is inexorably linked to the Forests Forever initiative." The editorial ran in support of a lawsuit, filed against the state by the Timber Association of California, that sought inclusion of its own language with the pro and con arguments presented in the Proposition 130 ballot pamphlet. The association won its lawsuit, inserting into the pamphlet a series of falsehoods, topped by the baseline lie that the initiative was principally the work of Earth First!, when in fact no one in the movement was actually working on it. The ballot argument read,

> Not surprisingly, Proposition 130 is supported by persons associated with the radical environmental group Earth First!, notorious for driving spikes into trees, vandalizing logging equipment, and harassing timber workers and families. And their antics don't stop there. On the national TV program *60 Minutes* Earth First! leader Darryl Cherney advocated terminally ill people should strap bombs to themselves and blow up dams, power plants, and other structures they believe harm the environment. In fact, several members are currently under arrest for blowing up a power plant, and under federal indictment for conspiring to sabotage power lines. We must take steps to protect our forests. But not the drastic steps proposed by Proposition 130.

Among the leaders of the Timber Association's campaign was "Earth First!" argument author Jerry Partain, the former head of the California

Department of Forestry. Timber companies pumped nearly $6 million into defeating the measure, including $1 million from Sierra Pacific Industries, California's largest private landowner, with a timber holding of 1.5 million acres. Although the day before the election Proposition 130 was polling to win, the measure lost by 3 percent of the vote.

71

J UDI BARI AND DARRYL CHERNEY FILED THEIR LAWSUIT AGAINST THE
FBI on Tuesday, May 21, 1991. Three days later, on the first anniversary
of the bombing, Judi addressed two hundred supporters gathered outside the
federal building in San Francisco. In her trenchant fashion, Judi laid out the
basis of her suit.

"I was targeted for assassination by the timber corporations, backed by the
full power of the police state," said Bari. "No serious investigation has taken
place. I've been blamed for the crime like a rape victim."

In addition to highlighting the FBI's history of repression, the
Bari-Cherney lawsuit would expose the Oakland Police Department's long
collaboration with the FBI to disrupt and destroy political movements. In a
deposition, Kevin Griswold, the "intelligence division" chief of the Oakland
Police Department, admitted that his office had monitored Earth First! activities since 1984, including through the efforts of at least one informant
who had infiltrated West Coast Earth First! groups. He noted that his department kept files on more than three hundred political groups and individuals in the San Francisco Bay Area. That's why Oakland Police made
arrests at the Golden Gate Bridge action—they were fronting for the FBI.

In a 1997 brief, Dennis Cunningham told the court,

What can be found . . . is overwhelming evidence that the FBI engaged in a
plot to "neutralize" Earth First! by fomenting the arrest of Judi and Darryl,
after they were bombed, by willing co-conspirators in the Oakland Police
Department. Both groups lied about the evidence in order to smear Judi and
Darryl in the headlines, then lied again and again to keep the sensational
case going, when it was clear there was no evidence to connect the two to the
bombing in any way. And they're lying now to cover-up the lies they told in

1990 & 1991. . . . [T]he major lying and political foul play by the FBI which
occurred in this case qualify it as a major scandal in its own right. . . . A Special Prosecutor should be appointed to look into the lying and falsifying that
has occurred, and is still going on.

There would be no such special prosecutor. But after eleven years and
many attempts by the FBI to quash the suit, the case would go to court.
Plaintiffs' attorneys in the suit—Dennis Cunningham, Tony Serra, William
Simpich, and Robert Bloom, joined by William Goodman and Michael
Deutsch at the Center for Constitutional Rights in New York—emphasized
that the bombing of Judi and Darryl was not an isolated case but a symptom
and manifestation of an internal US government program of repression that
had existed throughout the twentieth century.

"As plaintiffs have constantly tried to get the Court to see, and accept,
the gravamen of their case is that defendants' plot against them, the uncon-
scionable and illegal acts and omissions by defendants, and the blatant lies
told and now to be told again in furtherance of it, was born of the unholy,
anti-constitutional mission of political repression set for the FBI by J. Edgar
Hoover, maintained by his successors, and carried on by various chains of
command and legions of field agents throughout its history," the attorneys
wrote on page two of the Bari trial brief, filed on April 8, 2002. "The essence
of the conspirators' secret efforts to smear Earth First!, and 'otherwise neutralize' plaintiffs and Redwood Summer, was to manipulate the investigation of the Oakland bombing in such a way as to generate sensational news
stories, proclaiming that these environmental activists had been engaged in
an effort to carry out a terrorist attack of some sort."

Leading up to the trial, plaintiffs' attorneys conducted more than fifty
depositions of FBI agents, Oakland Police officers, activists, and others. The
FBI and Oakland Police conducted no depositions, an astonishing derelic-
tion that mirrored the agency's refusal, to this day, to carry out an actual
investigation. During the two-month trial, which ran from April into June
2002, plaintiffs called forty-one witnesses. The defendants called none.

The FBI went so far as to attempt to disallow Judi Bari from providing
her own deposition in her own case. In 1996 Judi was diagnosed with breast
cancer, which had spread to her liver. Rather than undergo chemotherapy
treatments that were unlikely to work and would further debilitate her and

disallow pursuit of the lawsuit, Judi set herself to organizing into a set of binders a complete record of more than fourteen thousand pages of documents and three hundred photos for the legal team to utilize in her absence. The team would also need Judi's testimony, which she was unlikely to be alive to provide. When Judi's attorneys asked that she be allowed to give her deposition, Justice Department attorney Joseph Sher managed to block the action for more than a month, accusing Judi of "faking cancer."

The court finally allowed Judi to give her deposition on January 30 and 31, 1997, providing testimony while reclining on a couch. Attorneys for the FBI and Oakland Police asked not a single question. Judi Bari died on March 2, 1997. Her estate and Darryl Cherney continued to prosecute their case. Judi's filmed deposition anchors Darryl's 2012 documentary *Who Bombed Judi Bari?*, which is available on YouTube. In the documentary, Judi is shown examining FBI crime scene photos of her car that clearly show a gaping hole directly under the driver's seat and an intact backseat. "They released to us these incredible photos that absolutely, without a doubt, show that the FBI and the Oakland Police lied and they knew they were lying," said Judi. "Any idiot would have known that the bomb was under the front seat and meant to kill. . . . My observation of these photos is that the evidence was unambiguous, and so the arrest, based on the claim that they thought the bomb was in the backseat, must have been deliberate rather than a mistake." The photos were taken by Michelle Gribi of the Oakland Police, who was also the first police officer on scene. In her report, Gribi writes that she "took photos showing the damage under the driver's seat."

In the film, an elderly David Brower says, "We've seen, in the operation of our own government, all sorts of acts that make it almost impossible to believe our government. As they can fund death squads in El Salvador, they can fund death squads in the United States."

During the trial, in his opening statement, Cunningham said that, whereas the Oakland Police were willing participants in a fabricated effort to harm Judi and Darryl, "particulars of the frame-up were pretty much all—not all, but mostly generated by the FBI agents." He continued,

> The FBI had a major role. They took possession of all the evidence. . . . They were really the driving force behind the case [which was] instigated by the FBI because of a preexisting desire to harm Earth First in the First Amendment

context, harm this group to disrupt its work . . . to smear the group in the public mind, and this was a golden opportunity for that and the people in the car who had been bombed to be represented as bombers. And the headlines could reflect that fact, and the world would be told that Earth First had bombers in it and these environmentalists were dangerous and had to be feared. . . . [W]hen the FBI came on the scene . . . the FBI agents there spoke to the [Oakland] police officers . . . Sergeant [Michael] Sitterud in particular, [and said] that the FBI was familiar with these people already as terrorist suspects, as people who in his words, the kind of people who would be carrying a bomb. And that was told to the police officers within the first hour after the explosion. . . . But you'll see that the Oakland officers in no sense were duped. . . . [T]hey were willing coparticipants. They jumped right in. They thought it was a fine idea, and they made their own contributions. And they took on the burden of making the arrests themselves, and putting the case into their system instead of the federal system so that they were operating at the front for the case, for the false case, and the FBI was in the background.

On June 11, 2002, the federal jury agreed. They found six of the seven FBI and Oakland Police defendants liable for violating Judi's and Darryl's First Amendment right of free speech and for violating the Fourth Amendment through false arrest and illegal search and seizure. A predominantly conservative jury awarded Judi's estate and Darryl Cherney $4.4 million in compensatory and punitive damages. Darryl Cherney told the press, "The American public needs to understand that the FBI can't be trusted. Ten jurors got a good, hard look at the FBI and they didn't like what they saw."

In 2017, the Environmental Protection Information Center posthumously honored Judi Bari with its annual Sempervirens Lifetime Achievement Award. Several people spoke in her honor, sang environmental songs, and gathered with three hundred revelers at the Mateel Community Center in Redway, Southern Humboldt County. One of the speakers was Dennis Cunningham.

Cunningham was well known for representing prisoners who had been involved in the 1971 riot at Attica State Prison in New York, which left forty-three people dead after guards opened fire on prisoners and hostages alike. He was also a leading attorney in the lawsuit that exposed the

FBI–Chicago Police conspiracy to assassinate Black Panther leader Fred Hampton, a case Cunningham pursued for thirteen years. In 1983, plaintiffs won a $1.8 million settlement in the suit, the largest damage result against the FBI until the Bari case. Cunningham and attorney Mark Harris also represented plaintiffs in the pepper spray lawsuit against the Humboldt County Sheriff's Department. He arrived at the Mateel a folk hero.

On stage, Cunningham honored Judi Bari's acumen and courage. But he also said something that, because it came from the lead attorney in the case, surprised me. Cunningham said, without equivocation, that he believed the FBI must have been directly involved in planting the pipe bomb in Judi's car. Cunningham told an attentive crowd,

Judi was someone, as events proved, who was dangerous to the state. She was like some of the Panthers and some of the other organizers who were really special targets of the FBI in the sixties and seventies that had something that they could recognize was powerful, that she could generate herself out of her own personality, her own experience, her own understanding of the politics that she was involved in. It was only because she holds that kind of danger that they took the risk of striking at her the way they did. I don't think after the case that we were ever in too much doubt that they [the FBI] were in on the bombing before it happened. It was the only way to explain how they dealt with it and how they managed to persuade the Oakland cops to arrest her immediately, and how they were able then to put out all the poison in the press and to generate this sense that Earth First! was a closet terrorist group, and it worked for them. It worked for the people that they were working with, which was timber, and it worked in the sense of defeating the Forests Forever initiative, which clearly was gonna win and then clearly lost because it was possible for the timber industry to associate it with the bombing. It took a lot of years—I mean, that bombing happened in 1990, the trial took place in 2002. And then, only then, was it possible to establish that that was all a lie, that the whole case against Judi and Darryl was a lie. Judi and Darryl worked all those years and kept that movement alive to fight back against that terrific and horrendous strike at her, at them, that the bombing represented.

72

DURING THE LAST YEARS OF HER LIFE, JUDI BARI WAS AMONG THE most visible advocates for preserving Headwaters Forest. In September 1996, Judi appeared at a large rally for Headwaters in San Francisco, alongside former (and future) California governor Jerry Brown, state assemblyman and future San Francisco mayor Willie Brown, and Bob Weir of the Grateful Dead—all of whom called for a sixty-thousand-acre redwood protection package to include Headwaters Forest, the remaining smaller groves, and fifty-five thousand acres of surrounding forestland. This was two weeks after a public rally at Pacific Lumber's Fisher log deck on September 15, 1996— the same forest morgue I'd forded while exiting company land during my first long solo hike through Headwaters Forest in March 1987. On this day nearly ten thousand people crammed onto the narrow public road in front of the log deck, and more than one thousand were arrested, including Cecelia Lanman and celebrities such as Don Henley, of the Eagles, and Bonnie Raitt. It remains the largest single-day arrest for an environmental protest in US history.

The most luminous speaker that day was Judi. She was also arrested. By now Judi understood that cancer would kill her, as it did six months later. Still, when she stepped onto that elevated stage, overlooking a long and tightly packed community of human beings who had dedicated themselves, for a day or a lifetime, to defending the environment, Judi exalted in the moment. She wore a black T-shirt with a big Earth First! fist. Her bodyguard, Larry Evans, escorted Judi to the stage. Fire and heart carried her words.

"This is the largest forest rally in the history of the US forest protection movement," Judi began. She implored the crowd to get involved, even to get arrested if it could help to forestall another human-caused cataclysm. "The system does not respond to us when we politely ask them," she said. "As we are walking over that line [to be arrested], they hear us when we're taking that kind of action."

Judi spoke in the warm afternoon sunlight beneath a deep blue sky. Small, white puffs of cloud glided gently overhead. She was just five feet tall, but her presence was large. Judi stood poised at the microphone, wearing a big smile, candescent. She spoke with warmth and irony and hit high notes of joyful imperative. She loved her work. The crowd cheered her, celebrating the moment and their collective power. Everyone was smiling, fists pumping. When Judi hit her meter, she could become almost hypnotic. She was indisputable, which is why she was so dangerous. By the time she'd finished, several people were cheering through their tears.

We've done everything we can to work within their system. We've changed their laws. We've put the "best forestry laws in the country" on the books. We've done everything that we could to enforce those laws and they still take every tree in the forest. That's why we're going to make this statement in the only way that they seem to be able to hear. This statement is not just being made for Headwaters. We're here for Headwaters because Headwaters is in danger today, and Headwaters is the last best thing left. But this is not just for Headwaters. This is for all of the trees that we've been fighting so hard to save all these years. This is for Albion Enchanted Meadow. This is for Osprey Grove. This is for China Left. This for Sugar Loaf. This is for Enola Hill. This is for Rocky Brook, the Olympic Peninsula. This is for Cove Mallard. This is for Mount Graham and Shawnee and Breitenbush and Millennium Grove, and all of the trees that they have taken despite every effort we've ever made. This is where we make our stand. And when you go home, you're going to take this spirit with you, and take it back to the forest where you live or whatever issue you work on. Because this is all one issue. This is all one system, the same corrupt system that rewards Charles Hurwitz while they take welfare checks away from needy mothers. That's what we're here for. We're here to stop the destruction of the Earth. We're making our stand. So we're going to start taking our stroll down Fisher Road, and we'll see you down at that gate. Let's get out there. Watch out, Charles Hurwitz. We're coming, and you can't stop us.

Part Five

HOME

There is always a certain hour of the day and of the night when a man's courage is at its lowest ebb, and it was that hour only that he feared.
—*Albert Camus*

He was a newcomer in the land . . . and this was his first winter.
—*Jack London*

73

M Y MOTHER, JESSIE KING, DIED ON AUGUST 4, 1990, THREE WEEKS
shy of her fifty-fifth birthday. I'd been at our family home in
Guerneville since the bombing in May, spending time with Jessie, finding
safety in the embrace of family. Three hundred people, many of them Jessie's
former students from Guerneville Elementary School, attended her funeral
at the old redwood Presbyterian chapel next door to the school. The school
and the church occupy the heart of the Big Bottom, not far from my grandparents' ranch.

The day after the funeral, our family, now just the four of us, moped
around our old home on a hillside surrounded by apple trees. Dad's garden
brimmed with food; baseball was on TV. As we sat on the redwood deck,
Dad emerged from the house and offered each of his children a letter. The
letters were from our mother; she'd written them more than twenty years
earlier, in January 1968, a few weeks after doctors had first diagnosed her
with terminal breast cancer and given her six months to live. I was just six
years old. When I was little, I'd had a notion that Mom was very sick, but it
always remained vague; we never spoke of it.

The letters didn't say good-bye. They offered analysis, succor, and some
motherly advice from a woman who loathed the idea of leaving her children. But Jessie was a fighter, and she would live another twenty-two years.
During these years I often heard her fiery resolve railing against injustice.
But Jessie was also warm, thoughtful. She possessed a unique capacity to
see deeply into the individual, even her six-year-old son. In a way, this book
exists to honor people like Jessie and my father, Tom, as well as Judi Bari,
herself a strong and faithful woman and mother and a foe of injustice. It is
to honor all the activists who have dedicated themselves, across this country
and around the world, now and through history, to alleviating suffering, to

405

protecting ecosystems and human communities. I could not have written
this book without their examples.

Jessie's letter illustrates the old maxim "Love is attention." Jessie paid
attention—to her family and to the world around her. Her penmanship was
perfect, her thoughts as elegant and fluent as her script. I still read her letter
whenever I need guidance, or a salve.

Dear Greg,

*Truly, this should begin, Thomas Gregory. You carry a fine name, Tom
King. You won't meet many men in your life with the heritage your father and
grandfather have given you. It was I who insisted we call you by your middle
name on the grounds that so many Toms in the family would be confusing.
Truthfully, it was a small rebellion on my part against being told how my son
would be named before you were even in the world. And yet, I have always
been as proud as the Kings of the privilege of a family tradition like "the first
born son of each generation shall be named Tom King." Some day you must
travel to North Ireland to "Castle Blaney" from whence came your ancestors
and your name.*

*It would be my hope that you will always pursue the avenues of experi-
mentation and explore all the routes of your inclination. In whatever areas
of knowledge you feel most comfortable, never allow yourself to become too
comfortable, too satisfied with your accomplishments. Originality, the creative
spirit, cannot flourish in a stifled atmosphere which too often follows on the
heels of comfort. Always feel free to explore, Gregor, even in the face of failure
and grave disappointment. . . . Be not hesitant, then, after the rigors of at-
taining knowledge through the collective knowledge of man that is provided
through schools, to strike out with directness and freely on your own experi-
mentations. The specifics of your choice of special interests is important only if
it is here you be the most free and creative.*

*So, you have perceived by now, Gregor, it is your mind and the freedom of
your spirit with which I am so concerned. The kind of man you are depends on
the direction of these two aspects of your person. . . . You have always had an
open and friendly manner and I hope this warm quality has stayed with you.
For your own sake, always remain an open person, ready to give love and
friendship to others. As in a painting, Gregor, it is the contrasts that give the
composition strength, so in our growth as persons, our strength grows from the*

contrasts in our lives. Even as a little boy, your laughter has been a joy to all your family, that ability of yours to hear the joke when it missed others. That quality you have for finding the "fun" in life I hope will sustain you through times that may seem too dark for even a smile.

As you stride through life, Gregor, do so with confidence tempered with kindness and love. Look for the extra and the exciting, but keep your eyes open to the small and detailed in life. It is the contrasts that make this world and the mortal life worth whatever struggle may be ahead. You have been and are now deeply loved, my son, and such an important person to the entire family. They look to you for great things and I know your potential is of the highest measure. Your soul is truly beautiful, Gregor, and I love you, always.

your Mother

ACKNOWLEDGMENTS

The Ghost Forest is at once a universal exploration and a deeply personal accounting of the dismantling of California's ancient redwood ecosystem. For forty years I have pivoted between journalism and activism and between the historical and the contemporary. *The Ghost Forest* reflects these dualities. My effort is to tell the redwood story whole, from the timberland privatization schemes of the nineteenth century to the junk-bond-fueled last redwood roundup of the late twentieth century. Such an accounting has never before been presented in a single volume.

At this writing I have lived my entire sixty-one years surrounded by what was once the greatest expanse of trees ever to have grown upon the planet. Yet, when I look around at my North Coast homeland, I understand that the rapid and near-total elimination of the original redwood ecosystem was meticulously planned, demonstrably destructive in real time, and achieved largely through criminal acts and subterfuge. *The Ghost Forest* attempts to preserve this record and to honor the countless individuals who, for more than a century, have dedicated their lives to protecting redwoods.

I set out to write a book that was fair to the actions and memories of all parties. Yet fairness need not wear kid gloves. Many of the characters who prosecuted liquidation of the redwoods, and even some who created and managed a prominent organization that was allegedly designed to "save" the great conifers, have rendered my account inhospitable to their memory. An early reader of *The Ghost Forest* called the book "an indictment." That wasn't my intention. At times it reads that way because a full accounting of what's been done to the California redwoods necessarily paints a grim, often criminal picture of the men, and a very few women, who conspired to liquidate the life of this remarkable forest.

I am immensely grateful to Clive Priddle and PublicAffairs Books for providing me with an opportunity to tell this story. This is not an easy account to stuff into a single book. Clive slashed my distracting tangents and held me on course, keeping the book readable and, one hopes, entertaining. Deft editing by Jen Kelland tightened the manuscript. Production editor Katie Carruthers-Busser expertly managed the long road toward publication. My deepest thanks to the outstanding staff of PublicAffairs for their devotion to the creation and distribution of this book.

I am forever thankful for my agent, Elise Capron at Sandra Dijkstra Literary Agency, who knew just where to go with *The Ghost Forest*. Elise's support has remained constant throughout the long process of bringing this book to life.

Several historians and academics not only provided me with hours of their time for regular questions and to vet some of my conclusions but turned over troves of documentation that they had collected for their own books, essays, and studies. Staff at libraries and historical societies were universally patient and astute. Interviewees were candid as they generously fielded my questions. Readers checked my sometimes wordy prose, made excellent inquiries, and caught gaffes. All of these contributions and more have buoyed this book. That said, the charges and conclusions contained herein, as well as any mistakes, are entirely my own.

The Bancroft Library at the University of California (UC), Berkeley, stands as a premier example of the benefits of publicly funded higher education. Over several years I spent hundreds of hours examining collections at Bancroft, where Collections Manager Lorna Kirwan oversees operations. Susan McElrath, head of Bancroft Public Services, patiently walked me through the processes and collections of the library and answered my many questions, always in a timely fashion. Chief among those collections was that of Save the Redwoods League, which contains hundreds of thousands of pages, of which I copied nearly ten thousand. This work would hardly have been possible until the 2010s, when Theresa Salazar, Bancroft's curator of Western Americana, expertly organized and curated this massive tranche. These women exemplify Bancroft's skilled and dedicated staff, who were always courteous and helpful. I am also grateful for timely research assistance from Maria Brandt.

Special Collections at Cal Poly Humboldt (formerly Humboldt State University), in Arcata, is also a treasure. Special collections librarian Carly Marino was consistently helpful, as was her predecessor, archivist Edie Butler. From 1997 through 2012, Edie Butler curated several important collections of primary source material. I relied on many other institutions for material and direction. These include the Humboldt County Historical Society, the Mendocino County Historical Society, the Mendocino County Museum, the Sonoma County Historical Society, the Sonoma County Library, and the Del Norte County Historical Society.

Humboldt County historian Jerry Rohde is a historical society in his own right. Jerry, a research associate at Cal Poly Humboldt, generously provided me with property maps, articles, and even unpublished chapters from his own forthcoming book. He answered my many questions with good cheer and timeliness. Jerry's contributions to the collective knowledge of Humboldt County history are unmatched. I am deeply grateful for his assistance.

The late Susie Van Kirk was an important North Coast historian. She dedicated much of her life to uncovering and analyzing primary documents relating to North Coast history. For several years, until her untimely death in 2016, Susie contributed to my research, personally as well as in the trove of impeccable documentation she created. Susie was excited about the prospect of this book coming to life. I am saddened that she is not here to read it.

My investigations of the massive land grant thefts that occurred in Humboldt County during the late nineteenth century were greatly augmented by historian Marvin Shepherd, who wrote *A Scottish Syndicate in the Redwoods*. When I asked Marvin if he had any information he could share about the land thefts, he sent two boxes of primary source documents that would have taken me months to compile. To retrieve some of the material, Marvin had traveled to Scotland.

Greg Gordon, author of *When Money Grew on Trees: A. B. Hammond and the Age of the Timber Baron*, was also generous with his time and knowledge. Understanding the granular detail that I sought, Greg, a professor of environmental studies at Gonzaga University, sent me hundreds of pages of scans he'd made from hard-to-get journals, newspapers, and historic trade magazines, along with volumes of notes he'd made in his research.

Insights and documents provided by Bay Area historian Gray Brechin, a historical geographer at UC Berkeley and author of *Imperial San Francisco*, became integral to my understanding of Gilded Age accumulation of capital and resources in the Bay Area. Similarly, Stanford University history professor and author Richard White generously provided important insights and leads. Richard's grasp of the inner workings of western industries is unparalleled, as he well demonstrated in his book *Railroaded*, a finalist for the Pulitzer Prize.

Jonathan Spiro, the History Department chair and now interim president of Castleton University, was a faithful correspondent. His book, *Defending the Master Race: Conservation, Eugenics, and the Legacy of Madison Grant*, is the definitive account of the life of the cofounder of Save the Redwoods League. Paul Rhode, a professor of economics at the University of Michigan, generously shared his deep understanding of the economic history of the American West. Paul always responded to my many questions, adding significantly to my grasp of economics during the Gilded and Progressive eras.

John Hooper, the great-grandson of the redwood timber baron of the same name and an environmental activist in his own right, provided documents and background about his family's history. In Sonoma County, the publications of historian John Schubert, and my personal correspondence with him, added detail about redwood history in the area. Sonoma County historian and newspaper columnist Gaye LeBaron also led me to key bits of information, including an important set of property maps that for the first time allowed me to chart the King family's redwood holdings along the Russian River.

For more than thirty years I have been blessed by a single, unbroken conversation with my great friend Ken Miller. Through his keen insights and passionate humor, Ken has inspired and encouraged my work. His careful and generous analyses helped to refine several difficult elements of this book. Ken, a physician and activist, has spent decades examining and attempting to remedy abusive logging and other environmental threats on the California North Coast. His work has transformed the region's politics and significantly informed ongoing environmental debates.

Like Ken Miller, our mutual friends Jen Card and Howard Russell read early drafts of this book and offered important input. Jen did so with edits on nearly every page, improving several sections. (Jen Card, aka Remedy, also holds the distinction of spending a full year tree-sitting in an ancient redwood grove to keep it from being cut down.) For many years Ken, Howard, and Jen worked together to organize community groups and legal actions aimed at ameliorating the localized impacts to watersheds as they unraveled under the pressures of industrial forestry.

I am also grateful to Bruce Cockburn, Susan Faludi, Yvon and Malinda Chouinard, Norman and Robin Coates, Frank Green, Ali Freedlund, and many others who have supported my work through the years. Hats off to the Humboldt County office of the federal Bureau of Land Management for protecting the old-growth habitat of Headwaters Forest and restoring the cutover land within the reserve.

As a redwood activist, I worked with dozens of remarkable individuals who, as activists themselves, attorneys, or local residents, were as outraged as I was over Maxxam Corporation's savage liquidation of the last redwood wilderness. Some struggled for years; others pitched in for a few weeks. Many risked arrest and even their lives without ever receiving or expecting praise or commendation. Every contribution counted. Would that I could name them all here. Today a few thousand acres of redwood still stand because of their efforts. I am forever grateful.

The Ghost Forest is rooted in family. I share this history with my sisters, Anna Heidinger and Laura Mattos. We remain very close siblings, best of friends. When we redwood activists found our worlds crashing in around us, in 1990, both Anna and Laura picked me up and supported me.

My parents, Tom and Jessie King, to whom this book is dedicated, raised their three children to uphold themselves by the twin pillars of exploration and integrity. For two weeks each year, in mid-September, Tom and Jessie took their kids out of school to camp in the northern redwoods. There, and always, they gave us freedom to find our place in life. We also spent countless days exploring the small ancient redwood wonderland of Armstrong Woods, in our hometown of Guerneville. When we went to the redwoods, that was my place. I would wander alone among the great trees, a precocious child immersed in a fairy world of living history. When, as an adult, I moved north to defend the last of these magic realms, it was as if I'd been called to rescue family.

This book might not exist if I hadn't married Joanne Rand. By the time we wed, in 1997, Joanne and I had been friends for a decade. We met at a radio station. I was giving an interview. Joanne, a virtuoso songwriter and musician, was performing. Joanne patiently allowed me to read her chapters of this book. Among her contributions was a checking of my bombast. Joanne and I connect through love of place—the California Northwest—and through shared ideologies that exalt family, land, and community. In 2019, as I was deep into writing this book, Joanne doubled down on her contributions to my life by literally saving it. Her collaborator in the task was our daughter, Georgia King. Like her mom, Georgia sets a high bar for integrity and for loyalty to the people and places she loves. She understands the challenges ahead, the need for humans to reduce consumption and to restore rather than attack our delicate biosphere. I see in Georgia and her generation a clarity of courage and the loyalty necessary to keep our planet whole and beautiful.

APPENDIX

UNIVERSITY OF CALIFORNIA REGENTS OF 1917

In 1917, most regents of the University of California (UC) operated within a tightly woven web of corporate relationships. In *The Goose-Step: Study of American Education*, Upton Sinclair writes, "Arriving in San Francisco we shall be welcomed by the interlocking directorate in charge of railroads, telegraphs, telephones, electricity, land, water, gas—and education." In 1917, it would be this "interlocking directorate" of finance and industrial fortune, rather than torchbearers of Progressive-era reforms, that would assemble and run Save the Redwoods League.

Regents are appointed by the California governor, who also serves as their ex officio president. In 1917 the governor was William Dennison Stephens. Previously Stephens had served three terms in the US House of Representatives, representing the Central Valley east of the Bay Area. Stephens served just one full term as governor, distinguishing himself by attempting to bar Japanese immigration to California. He believed in a strong combination of population growth (among whites) and industrial expansion for California.

In his history of Save the Redwoods League, Joseph Engbeck briefly identifies just four UC regents. He notes that Board of Regents comptroller Ralph Palmer Merritt was the "titular captain of the Pleasant Isle of Aves," where Save the Redwoods League allegedly came to life. As comptroller Merritt oversaw all donations to the university. In 1920, Merritt ran the California campaign for Herbert Hoover's presidential run, and the following year he became president of the California Rice Growers Association. Rice production in the state would consume rivers' worth of water, which reached crops in redwood stave pipes. In 1923, Merritt would move from comptroller to official regent just as he was accepting the position as president and managing director of the giant Sun-Maid Raisin Growers company, another

415

extremely thirsty industry requiring miles of redwood stave pipes and enormous redwood water tanks. Through the rice and raisin industries, Merritt frequently traveled to Asia, developing what he said at the time was "an interest in the Japanese people." In 1942 Merritt's "interest" grew more acute as he took the director's position at Manzanar, the Japanese concentration camp built by the US government in California's Inyo Valley. Merritt held the position until the end of the war, after which he parceled out and sold the Manzanar property to white ranchers.

The remaining regents who in 1917 served UC president Benjamin Ide Wheeler included

- William H. Crocker, who during his lifetime was president of several firms, including the Crocker Estate Company, the Pacific Improvement Company, Crocker National Bank, the Crocker Investment Company, the Crocker-Huffman Land and Water Company, the Crocker Realty Company, the Curlew Ranch Company, the Mortgage & Loan Corporation, and the Provident Securities Company. Crocker served as a director of two dozen other firms, and he owned asphalt plants that served much of California.
- Isaias William Hellman, a Bavarian national who'd immigrated to the United States in 1859, at the age of seventeen. Hellman joined the regents in 1881, replacing San Francisco banker Darius Ogden Mills after Mills returned to the East Coast to apply his western riches to the legerdemain of Wall Street. Hellman was an early developer of Los Angeles, where he'd founded a bank in 1871. In 1890 he moved to the Bay Area and there took over the Nevada National Bank of San Francisco. He later purchased the Wells Fargo Bank and merged it with Nevada National, creating the Wells Fargo Nevada National Bank. By the time Hellman died in 1920, Wells Fargo held more than $80 million in assets.
- Phoebe Hearst, widow of wealthy San Francisco gold and silver miner George Hearst and mother of the famous publisher, William Randolph Hearst. Phoebe Hearst, a close friend of Benjamin Ide Wheeler, was one of the few women to serve on the Board of Regents prior to World War II. The regent's seat was another major acquisition for the Hearst dynasty. Beginning in 1897, Hearst made regular contributions to the

college that eventually totaled $4 million, much of it donated to the College of Mining. By 1902 nearly 20 percent of Berkeley students attended the College of Mining, which was the largest of its kind in the world. Hearst was canny and independent, and no one's toady. From 1916 to 1917, Berkeley mining students practiced their art by dynamiting a nine-hundred-foot horizontal mine shaft under the college, directly through the Hayward fault. The shaft is still there, and most of the original redwood timbers that hold it up remain sound. The Hearst estate was managed by Phoebe's cousin, Edwin H. Clark, and included several major mines around the world, all of which imported shiploads of redwood for railroads, stave pipes, housing, and mine shafts.

- Charles Stetson Wheeler was a corporate attorney who managed the interests of his close friend, Phoebe Hearst. Wheeler and another friend, Benjamin Ide Wheeler (no relation), frequently hunted together at Charles Wheeler's Bend Ranch on the McCloud River, southeast of Mount Shasta in Northern California. A Bohemian since 1903, Charles Wheeler represented numerous corporations that at the time were expanding across the West. Wheeler was a leading California Republican who often represented the state at the Republican National Convention.

- Guy Chaffee Earl served in the California State Senate. He was president and general counsel of the Great Western Power Co., a director of PG&E, and vice president of two other power companies—all major consumers of redwood products. Earl's law partner was Charles Wheeler. One of Earl's most coveted clients was James Irvine of the Southern California real estate empire. The Irvine family once owned one-third (more than 100,000 acres) of Orange County. The Irvines also owned redwood timberland. In 1944 James Irvine donated to the state 160 acres of redwood on Mill Creek in Del Norte County as an addition to Jedediah Smith Redwoods State Park. The James Irvine Trail, in Prairie Creek Redwoods State Park, is named for him.

- Regent Arthur William Foster was an Irishman born in 1850 who had immigrated to San Francisco at the age of fifteen. He'd been a regent since 1900 and a Bohemian Club member since 1889. Foster was noteworthy as the former owner of the San Francisco and North Pacific Railway. Foster's line extended to Guerneville, where he logged redwoods and developed the Mirabel Park subdivision on the Russian

River, a few miles upstream of my childhood home. Later Foster incorporated the California Northwestern Railroad, which reached Willits
in 1902 and which he leased to the San Francisco and North Pacific
Railway. The following year Foster sold the line to the Southern Pacific
Railroad, which, with the Santa Fe Railroad, built the Northwestern
Pacific line to Humboldt County. Foster was a director of the powerful
Anglo & London Paris National Bank of San Francisco, which advertised itself as "Inseparably Identified with Western Development." As a
regent, Foster was credited with endowing the University of California
satellite campus at Davis with funding that allowed it to grow as a paragon of industrial agriculture, whose successful expansion in the West
rested in large part on the ability to move great flows of water through
giant redwood stave pipes.

- UC regents treasurer Mortimer Fleishhacker was also a director of the
Anglo & London Paris National Bank. Fleishhacker was vice president of the bank; his brother, Herbert, was president. Both brothers
were born in San Francisco during the 1860s, and together they formed
something of their own social register of San Francisco's business elite.
By 1917 they were serving as directors of a combined thirty corporations. Twelve of the companies were controlled by both brothers, most
often in the president and vice president positions. These included
banks, agricultural conglomerates, several electric companies, pulp and
paper firms, chemical companies, realty companies, sugar producers,
and timber firms. The Fleishhackers were also major investors in several hydroelectric power companies, and they were among the richest
Californians of their day. Nonetheless, neither brother would appear in
the actual San Francisco Social Register of 1917. They were Jewish. Nor
could they belong to the Pacific Union Club or the Bohemian Club. The
elite coterie of UC regents who gathered that year at the hardly bohemian Pleasant Isle of Aves would have to do without the Fleishhacker
brothers.

- Philip Ernest Bowles was a native not of San Francisco but of Humboldt County. He was born in 1858 on a plateau near Arcata now
known as "Bowles's Prairie." In 1853 his father, Elliott Bowles, settled
in Arcata, then a Wild West outpost, where he established the general
store Bowles & Coddington. In 1883, at the age of twenty-five, Philip

Bowles, now living in San Francisco, purchased 1,318 acres of virgin redwood forest and prime agricultural land one mile east of Arcata. Later the forest would be clear-cut and the open land farmed. Much of the Bowles property is now owned by the city of Arcata as part of its nearly three thousand acres of forested open space adjacent to the city. Bowles long served as president of Reward Oil Co. of Kern County, which was headquartered in San Francisco and by 1917 was owned by the Southern Pacific Railroad. The California Historical Society called Bowles "one of the foremost figures in California finance." In 1900 Bowles became president of the First National Bank of Oakland. In 1902 he bought American National Bank and developed it until it had more than twenty branches throughout the state. Fellow directors at the bank included C. H. Crocker and Henry J. Crocker, son and cousin of William H. Crocker, respectively. Bowles was also a director of the powerful East Bay Water Company, alongside John Drum and Wigginton Creed.

• John Alexander Britton was a San Francisco attorney who designed and built Oakland's first electric plant. By 1902 he was president of the newly formed California Gas & Electric Corporation. He joined the Bohemian Club the following year. In 1905 Britton cofounded Pacific Gas & Electric and served as company president until 1908. He would remain vice president and general manager of the company for the next fifteen years, securing troves of redwood lumber and, in 1920, ushering in Save the Redwoods League founding director Wigginton Creed as president of the power company. Britton also served as a director of Bowles's American National Bank.

• James Kennedy Moffitt was born in San Francisco in 1855. His father, James Moffitt, was a native of Enniskillen, a small village on the River Erne, in what is now Northern Ireland, some forty miles from my ancestors' homeland in the village of Castleblayney. The elder Moffitt arrived in California in 1849, at the age of twenty-two, in search of gold. He ended up forming a partnership, Blake, Moffitt & Towne, a paper company that would eventually print thirteen daily San Francisco newspapers. By 1917 James Moffitt Jr. had been a Bohemian Club member for twenty years. That year he served as vice president of the Mutual Savings Bank alongside fellow director and redwood baron

John Hooper. Moffitt also served as vice president, director, and cashier of the First National Bank of San Francisco, controlled by John Hooper alongside bank president Rudolph Spreckels.

- Rudolph Julius Taussig was a wholesale liquor dealer and treasurer of the California Academy of Sciences.
- Chester Harvey Rowell was editor and publisher of the *Fresno Republican*, and he made his own news as a member of the US Shipping Board and the powerful California Railroad Commission. During the 1930s Rowell took over as editor of the *San Francisco Chronicle*.
- James Mills was a Southern California attorney and a founder of Riverside, California, where he owned the James Mills Orchard Corporation. Mills grew nine thousand acres of oranges, peaches, pears, olives, apricots, and almonds, and he owned the second-largest lemon grove in the world. His companies consumed vast quantities of redwood lumber.
- Edward Augustus Dickson was a prominent California Republican who owned and edited the *Los Angeles Evening Express*. Dickson served as director of the Biltmore Hotel Company, and he was a commissioner of the redwood-consuming Los Angeles Department of Water and Power. Dickson was the first Southern Californian on the UC Board of Regents, and he was instrumental in founding the University of California, Los Angeles.
- James Wilfred McKinley was a Southern California attorney and superior court judge, and he served as city attorney of Los Angeles from 1884 until 1888. He also represented the Southern Pacific Railroad and the Pacific Electric Railway.
- Charles Adolph Ramm was a prominent Catholic priest in San Francisco, where he served as rector of Saint Mary's Cathedral.
- Garrett William McEnerney was the personal attorney of James Leary Flood. Flood was born in San Francisco in 1857, another Bay Area inheritance prince with fortunes tied to the Comstock Lode. His father, James Clair Flood, was among the richest Americans when he died in 1889, leaving his fortune and the famous Flood mansion, in San Francisco's Pacific Heights, to his only son. Nearly every transaction made by James Leary Flood went through McEnerney. McEnerney was a member of the Pacific Union Club, and he had been a Bohemian since

1911. As an attorney he represented, for fifty years, the Roman Catholic bishop of California, as well as numerous titans of the Bay Area superrich. He also represented parties in disputes over bountiful estates, such as that of mining banker William Sharon and Humboldt County redwood lumberman John Dolbeer.

BIBLIOGRAPHY

Archival Collections

Baker, Susie. Collection. Special Collections. Cal Poly Humboldt, Arcata.

Becking, Rudolf. Papers. Special Collections. Cal Poly Humboldt, Arcata.

Clar, C. Raymond. Papers. Bancroft Library, University of California, Berkeley.

Clausen, Don. Papers. Special Collections. Cal Poly Humboldt, Arcata.

Department of Forestry Records. California State Board of Forestry. California State Archives, Sacramento.

Hammond Lumber Company. Records. Special Collections. Cal Poly Humboldt, Arcata.

Miller, Ken. Papers. Special Collections. Cal Poly Humboldt, Arcata.

Save the Redwoods League. Collection. Bancroft Library, University of California, Berkeley.

Van Kirk, Susie. Collection. Special Collections. Cal Poly Humboldt, Arcata.

Vinyard, Lucille. Papers. Special Collections. Cal Poly Humboldt, Arcata.

Interviews (Background and on the Record, by Greg King)

Angle, Mary. Save the Redwoods League.

Cunningham, Dennis. Attorney.

Gordon, Greg. Professor. Gonzaga University.

Lebaron, Gaye. Historian.

Litton, Martin. Sierra Club.

Miller, Ken. Humboldt Watershed Council.

Rhode, Paul. University of Michigan.

Rohde, Jerry. Historian.

Shepherd, Marvin. Historian.

Spiro, Jonathan. Professor. Castleton University.

Vinyard, Lucille. Redwood National Park advocate.

Legal and Public Documents Including Testimony

"Abstract of Title to the Lands of C. A. Hooper & Co. Made for W. E. Creed." Contra Costa Abstract & Title Company, 1912.

Amodio, John. Testimony. Redwood National Park Hearing. US Senate Subcommittee on Parks and Recreation, September 6, 1977.

Armstrong, Andrew. "Wood-Using Industries of California." California State Board of Forestry, 1912.

423

Bearss, Edwin. "Redwood National Park: History Basic Data." National Park Service, September 1, 1969.

Becking, Rudolf. Testimony. Redwood National Park Hearing. US Senate Subcommittee on Parks and Recreation, June 17, 1966.

Becking, Rudolf. Testimony. Redwood National Park Hearing. US Senate Subcommittee on Parks and Recreation, April 17, 1967.

Becking, Rudolf. Testimony. Redwood National Park Hearing. US Senate Subcommittee on Parks and Recreation, September 6, 1977.

California Division of Beaches and Parks. "A Report of Erosion Within the Rockefeller Forest." 1959.

California Redwood Company, Inc. Articles of Incorporation, 1883.

California State Board of Forestry. *Biennial Report*, 1885–1886.

California State Board of Forestry. *Biennial Report*, 1889–1890.

Chaney, Ralph. Testimony. Redwood National Park Hearing. US House Subcommittee on National Parks and Recreation, April 16, 1968.

Chaney, Ralph. Testimony. Redwood National Park Hearing. US Senate Subcommittee on Parks and Recreation, June 17, 1966.

Chaney, Ralph. Testimony. Redwood National Park Hearing. US Senate Subcommittee on Parks and Recreation, April 17, 1967.

Civil Liberties Monitoring Project. "Pattern of Violence Against Headwaters Activists Specific to Incidents Involving Pacific Lumber Employees in Humboldt County, California." 1999.

Clausen, Don. Testimony. Redwood National Park Hearing. US Senate Subcommittee on Parks and Recreation, June 17, 1966.

Cohelan, Jeffery. Testimony. Redwood National Park Hearing. US Senate Subcommittee on Parks and Recreation, June 17, 1966.

Committee on the Public Lands, House of Representatives. "Construction of Roads, etc., in National Parks and Monuments," February 7, 1924.

Congressional Quarterly Almanac, 1968.

Congressional Record, 1913.

Congressional Record, 1919.

Congressional Record, 1920.

Congressional Record, 1967.

County of Santa Clara Parks and Recreation Department. "Historic Structures Report: Joseph D. Grant County Park," November 7, 2012.

Cunningham, Dennis. Opening Statement. *Judi Bari v. United States*, April 9, 2002.

Cunningham, Dennis, et al. Plaintiffs' Trial Brief. *Judi Bari v. United States*. US District Court. Northern District of California, April 8, 2002.

Dewitt, John. Testimony. Redwood National Park Hearing. US House Subcommittee on National Parks and Recreation, April 16, 1968.

Emerald Creek Committee. "Emerald Creek: Redwood National Park's Last Chance for a Virgin Watershed." 1975.

Environmental Protection Information Center v. Department of Forestry and Fire Protection, California State Board of Forestry, et al.

Environmental Protection Information Center v. Pacific Lumber Company (1-6).

EPIC v. CalFire; Pacific Lumber Company; et al.

EPIC v. Johnson I.

EPIC v. Johnson II.

Evans, Gray. Testimony. Redwood National Park Hearing. US Senate Subcommittee on Parks and Recreation, June 17, 1966.

Fain, Michael. Deposition. *Judi Bari v. United States*, August 21, 2001.

Fairbank, C. W. "A Review of Redwood Harvesting." California Division of Forestry, 1972.

Fisher, Richard, et al. "The Redwood." US Department of Agriculture Bureau of Forestry, 1903.

Fowler, Frederick. "Hydroelectric Power Systems of California and Their Extensions into Oregon and Nevada." US Geological Survey, 1923.

Greene, Daniel. *Public Land Statutes of the United States*. US Department of the Interior, 1931.

Greene, Linda. "Historical Overview of the Redwood Creek Basin and Bald Hills Regions of Redwood National Park, California." US National Park Service, 1980.

House Subcommittee on Specialty Crops and Natural Resources. Hearing. "Headwaters Forest Act," October 13, 1993.

Humboldt County Chamber of Commerce. *Annual Reports of Officers*, 1918.

Lisle, Thomas. "The Eel River, Northwestern California: High Sediment Yields from a Dynamic Landscape." *Surface Water Hydrology*. Geological Society of America, 1990.

Litton, Martin. Testimony. Redwood National Park Hearing. House Subcommittee on National Parks and Recreation, April 16, 1968.

Marbled Murrelet and EPIC v. Pacific Lumber Company.

Mather, Stephen. "Report of the Director of the National Park Service to the Secretary of the Interior." Fiscal year ending June 30, 1919.

May, Richard. "A Century of Lumber Production in California and Nevada." US Forest Service, 1951.

McCloskey, Michael. Testimony. Redwood National Park Hearing. US Senate Subcommittee on Parks and Recreation, June 17, 1966.

McCollum, Larry. Testimony. Redwood National Park Hearing. US Senate Subcommittee on Parks and Recreation, June 17, 1966.

Monroe, Gary. "Natural Resources of the Eel River Delta." California Department of Fish and Game, November 1974.

Moore, Eli, et al. "Roots, Race, Place: A History of Racially Exclusionary Housing in the San Francisco Bay Area." University of California, Berkeley, Haas Institute for a Fair and Inclusive Society, 2017.

North Coast California Earth First!. "Headwaters Forest Wilderness Complex." January 1988.

People v. Pacific Lumber.

Proceedings of the American Water Works Association. Boston, 1906.

Public Law 90-545. Redwood National Park Act, 1968.

Redington, Paul. "Report on Investigation for Proposed Redwood National Park." US House of Representatives, October 1920.

Redwood National Park. "Middle Fork Lost Man Creek Second-Growth Forest Restoration Environmental Assessment." May 2014.

"The Redwoods: A National Opportunity for Conservation and Alternatives for Action." US National Park Service, September 15, 1964.

"Report of the Conservation Commission." State of California, January 1, 1913.

Rohde, Jerry. "Historic Profile of the McKay Tract: Logging, Ranching, and Railroads." Humboldt County Department of Public Works, 2014.

Russ, Joseph. Testimony. Redwood National Park Hearing. US Senate Subcommittee on Parks and Recreation, June 17, 1966.

Schurman, Rachel. "Public Policy, Oil Production, and Energy Consumption in Twentieth-Century California." US Department of the Interior Minerals Management Service, October 2003.

Scobey, Frederick. "The Flow of Water in Wood-Stave Pipe." US Department of Agriculture Bulletin No. 376, November 25, 1916.

Sierra Club v. Pacific Lumber Company. Court of Appeal, First District, Division 5, California. Decision, December 29, 1993.

Spence, Mark David. "Watershed Park: Administrative History, Redwood National and State Parks." National Park Service, 2011.

Stone and Associates. "Redwood National Park: An Analysis of the Buffers and the Watershed Management Required to Preserve the Redwood Forest and Associated Streams in the Redwood National Park." 1969.

Valachovic, Yana, and Richard Standiford. "Changes in the Redwood Region from 1996–2016." *Proceedings of the Coast Redwood Science Symposium,* 2016.

Van de Mark, David. Testimony. Redwood National Park Hearing. US House Subcommittee on National Parks and Recreation, April 16, 1968.

Van Kirk, Susie. "Historic Resources Study." Redwood National Park, 1999.

Van Kirk, Susie. "Historical Information on Redwood Creek." Redwood National Park, 1994.

Van Kirk, Susie. "Klamath River References." US Fish and Wildlife Service, 2005, 2015.

Van Kirk, Susie. "Korbel Sawmill Report." Humboldt Digital Commons, November 2015.

Van Kirk, Susie. "Land Uses on Humboldt Bay Tributaries." KRISWeb. www .krisweb.com/krishumboldtbay/krisdb/html/krisweb/humbay_historic/bayfish2 .htm.

Van Kirk, Susie. "Lost Man and Little Lost Man Watersheds." Redwood National Park, 1999.

Van Kirk, Susie. "Lower Prairie Creek Project: Redwood National Park 'Forest Owners.'" Humboldt Digital Commons, December 2016.

Van Kirk, Susie. "Lower Prairie Creek Project: Scottish Syndicate." Humboldt Digital Commons, Summer 2015.

Van Kirk, Susie. "Prairie Creek Redwoods State Park A History." California State Parks, September 2015.

Van Kirk, Susie. "Redwood Creek Notes." Redwood National Park, 2011.

Van Kirk, Susie. "Redwood Highway/Save the Redwoods Movement." California State Parks, 2015.

Van Kirk, Susie. "References on Logging, Mills, and the Industry 1939–1960s Research Notes." Special Collections. Cal Poly Humboldt, April 2008.

Van Kirk, Susie. "Russ Family Research Notes." Humboldt Digital Commons, 2013.

Vilas, William. "Report of the Secretary of the Interior Relative to Alleged Frauds upon the Government by the California Redwood Company." April 27, 1888.

Vinyard, Lucille. Testimony. Redwood National Park Hearing. US Senate Subcommittee on Parks and Recreation, June 17, 1966.

Wayburn, Edgar. Testimony. Redwood National Park Hearing. US Senate Subcommittee on Parks and Recreation, June 17, 1966.

Wayburn, Peggy. Testimony. Redwood National Park Hearing. US Senate Subcommittee on Parks and Recreation, June 17, 1966.
Yard, Robert Sterling. "Glimpses of Our National Parks." US Department of the Interior, 1920.

Newspapers

I culled thousands of articles from more than one hundred newspapers, dates ranging from the 1860s to the present. Following are frequently utilized newspapers:

Alameda Daily Argus	*New York Times*
Albion Monitor	*North Coast Journal*
Arcata Union	*Oakland Tribune*
Berkeley Gazette	*Sacramento Bee*
Blue Lake Advocate	*San Francisco Call*
Country Activist	*San Francisco Chronicle*
Daily Californian	*San Francisco Examiner*
Del Norte Record	*San Francisco Bay Guardian*
Del Norte Triplicate	*San Francisco Recorder*
Earth First! Journal	*San Jose Mercury News*
Econews	*Santa Rosa Democrat*
East Bay Express	*Santa Rosa Press Democrat*
Ferndale Enterprise	*Sebastopol Times*
Fort Bragg Advocate	*The Paper*
Humboldt Beacon	*Ukiah Daily Journal*
Humboldt Standard	*Ukiah Dispatch-Democrat*
Humboldt Times	*Wall Street Journal*
Humboldt Times-Standard	*Washington Post*
Los Angeles Times	*Willits News*
Mendocino Beacon	

Oral Histories

Drury, Newton B., and Enoch French. "Cruising and Protecting the Redwoods of Humboldt." By Amelia Fry. Regional Oral History Office. Bancroft Library. University of California, Berkeley, 1963.
Drury, Newton Bishop. By Amelia Roberts Fry and Susan Schrepfer. Regional Oral History Office. Bancroft Library. University of California, Berkeley, 1972.
Fritz, Emanuel. By Elwood R. Maunder and Amelia Fry. Regional Oral History Office. Bancroft Library. University of California, Berkeley, 1972.
Howard, Bruce S. President. Save the Redwoods League. By Ann Lage. Regional Oral History Office. Bancroft Library. University of California, Berkeley, 2003.
McCloskey, Michael. Executive director, Sierra Club. By Susan Schrepfer. Regional Oral History Office. Bancroft Library. University of California, Berkeley, 1981.
Sproul, Robert. Councilor, Save the Redwoods League; president, University of California. By Suzanne B. Rice. Regional Oral History Office. Bancroft Library. University of California, Berkeley, 1984–1985.

Wayburn, Edgar. President, Sierra Club. By Ann Lage and Susan Schrepfer. Regional Oral History Office. Bancroft Library. University of California, Berkeley, 1976–1981.
Wayburn, Peggy. Sierra Club. By Ann Lage. Regional Oral History Office. Bancroft Library. University of California, Berkeley, 1990.

Periodicals and Trade Publications

American Lumberman
Moody's Manual of Railroad and Corporation Securities
Northwestern Lumberman
Pacific Coast Wood and Iron
Pacific Municipalities and Counties
Poor's Publishing Company
Russian River Historical Society Newsletter
Sierra Club Bulletin
The Humboldt Historian Humboldt County Historical Society
The Wasp
Timberman
Walker's Manual of California Securities and Directory of Directors
Who's Who in Finance and Banking

Published Sources

Abbey, Edward. *The Monkey Wrench Gang*. J. B. Lippincott, 1975.
Abramson, Pam. "Razing the Giant Redwoods." *Newsweek*, July 6, 1987.
Allen, Garland. "'Culling the Herd': Eugenics and the Conservation Movement in the United States, 1900–1940." *Journal of the History of Biology* (spring 2013).
Anderson, Dewey. "A Program for the Redwoods." *Annals of the American Academy of Political and Social Science* (May 1952).
Andrews, Ralph. *Redwood Classic*. Bonanza Books, 1958.
"The Annual Meeting of the Board of Trustees of the American Museum of Natural History." *Science*, February 20, 1920.
Arendt, Hannah. "Truth and Politics." *New Yorker*, February 25, 1967.
Arvola, T. F. "The Maturing of California State Forestry, 1943–47." *Journal of Forest History* (January 1985).
Bari, Judi. *Timber Wars*. Common Courage Press, 1994.
Barnett, Gabrielle. "Drive-by Viewing: Visual Consciousness and Forest Preservation in the Automobile Age." *Technology and Culture* (January 2004).
Beach, Patrick. *A Good Forest for Dying: The Tragic Death of a Young Man on the Front Lines of the Environmental Wars*. Doubleday, 2003.
Becking, Rudolf. *Pocket Flora of the Redwood Forest*. Island Press, 1982.
Bevington, Douglas. *The Rebirth of Environmentalism: Grassroots Activism from the Spotted Owl to the Polar Bear*. Island Press, 2009.
Black, Edwin. *War Against the Weak: Eugenics and America's Campaign to Create a Master Race*. Dialog Press, 2003.
Blakey, Roy. "The Revenue Act of 1921." *American Economic Review* (March 1922).
Bledsoe, A. J. *History of Del Norte County, California*. Wyman & Co., 1881.
Bohakel, Charles. "Los Medanos Rancho History Complicated." *East Bay Times*, May 21, 2008.
Bohemian Club. "Members of the Club." 1914.

Bonner, W. G. *The Redwoods of California: A Glimpse at the Wonder Land of the Golden West.* California Redwood Company, 1884.

Brechin, Gray. "Conserving the Race: Natural Aristocracies, Eugenics, and the U.S. Conservation Movement." *Antipode* (July 1996).

Brechin, Gray. *Imperial San Francisco: Urban Power, Earthly Ruin.* University of California Press, 2006.

Brechin, Gray. "Pecuniary Emulation: The Role of Tycoons in Imperial City-Building." *Reclaiming San Francisco: History, Politics, Culture.* City Lights, 1998.

Brower, David. *For the Earth's Sake: The Life and Times of David Brower.* Gibbs-Smith, 1990.

Brown, Alan, and Frank Stanger. "October 9, 1769: Discovery of the Redwoods." *Forest History Newsletter* (October 1969).

Burgess, Sherwood. "The Forgotten Redwoods of the East Bay." *California Historical Society Quarterly* (March 1951).

Burgess, Sherwood. "Lumbering in Hispanic California." *California Historical Society Quarterly* (September 1962).

"California Redwood." Pacific Lumber Company (brochure), 1915.

"California Redwood: Nature's Lumber Masterpiece." California Redwood Association (brochure), 1916.

"California Redwood for Tanks and Pipes." *Mining and Oil Bulletin* (June 1917).

"California Redwood for the Engineer." California Redwood Association (brochure), 1917.

"California Redwood on the Farm." California Redwood Association (brochure), 1916.

"Californian Redwood as a Substitute for Steel." *American Architect and Building News*, October 3, 1903.

Cargill, Hazel. "The Fieldbrook Story." *Humboldt Historian* (March-April 1971).

Carpenter, Aurelius. *History of Mendocino and Lake Counties, California.* Historic Record Company, 1914.

Carranco, Lynwood. *The Redwood Country: History, Language, Folklore.* Kendall/Hunt Publishing Company, 1971.

Carranco, Lynwood. *Redwood Lumber Industry.* Golden West Books, 1982.

Carranco, Lynwood, and John Labbe. *Logging the Redwoods.* Caxton Printers, 1975.

Carranco, Lynwood, and Henry Sorensen. *Steam in the Redwoods.* Caxton Printers, 1988.

Carroll, Allyson, et al. "Millennium-Scale Crossdating and Inter-annual Climate Sensitivities of Standing California Redwoods." *Plos One* (July 2014).

Case, Alexander. *The Annals of the Bohemian Club, 1907–1972.* Bohemian Club, 1972.

Chaney, Ralph. "Bearing of Forests on the Theory of Continental Drift." *Scientific Monthly* (December 1940).

Chase, Alston. *In a Dark Wood: The Fight over Forests and the Rising Tyranny of Ecology.* Houghton Mifflin, 1995.

Chew, Sing. *Logs for Capital: The Timber Industry and Capitalist Enterprise in the Nineteenth Century.* Greenwood Press, 1992.

Christen, Arthur. "My Yager Valley: Life in a Pioneer Setting." *Humboldt Historian* (January-February 1980).

Clar, C. Raymond. *Brief History of the California Division of Forestry.* State of California, 1957.

Clar, C. Raymond. *Government and Forestry: From Spanish Days Until the Creation of the Department of Natural Resources in 1927.* State of California, 1959.

Clar, C. Raymond. *Out of the River Mist*, 1973.

Coman, Edwin. "Sidelights on the Investment Policies of Stanford, Huntington, Hopkins, and Crocker." *Bulletin of the Business Historical Society* (November 1942).

Cornford, Daniel. *Workers and Dissent in the Redwood Empire.* Temple University Press, 1987.

Coy, Owen. *The Humboldt Bay Region, 1850–1875.* California State Historical Association, 1929.

Creed, Wigginton. Safeguarding the Future of Private Business. Houghton Mifflin Company and the UC Board of Regents, 1923.

Cronise, Titus. *The Natural Wealth of California.* H. H. Bancroft & Company, 1868.

Dangerfield, Cody, et al. "Long-Term Impacts of Road Disturbance on Old-Growth Coast Redwood Forests." *Forest Ecology and Management* (November 2021).

"Darien Ogden Mills." *Overland Monthly* (January 1917).

Devall, William. "David Brower." *Environmental Review* (autumn 1985).

Devall, William. "Redwood National Park: The Clearcutting of a Dream." *Humboldt Journal of Social Relations* (fall/winter 1974).

DeVoto, Bernard. "The Sturdy Corporate Homesteader." *Harper's* (May 1953).

Dewitt, John. *California Redwood Parks and Preserves.* Save the Redwoods League (pamphlet), 1985.

Dick, Everett. *The Lure of the Land: A Social History of the Public Lands from the Articles of Confederation to the New Deal.* University of Nebraska Press, 1970.

Domhoff, G. William. *The Bohemian Grove and Other Retreats.* Harper, 1974.

Downs, Winfield. *Encyclopedia of American Biography.* American Historical Company, 1944.

Drury, Aubrey. *California: An Intimate Guide.* Harper and Brothers, 1935.

Drury, Aubrey. *John A. Hooper and California's Robust Youth.* Self-published, 1952.

Drury, Aubrey. "Joseph Donohoe Grant, 1858–1942." *California Historical Society Quarterly* (March 1942).

Dunham, Harold. *Government Handout.* Self-published, 1941. Da Capo Press, 1970.

Eddy, J. M. *In the Redwood's Realm: Byways of Wild Nature and Highways of Industry.* D. S. Stanley & Co., 1893.

Engbeck, Joseph. *Saving the Redwoods.* Save the Redwoods League, 2018.

Engbeck, Joseph, and Philip Hyde. *State Parks of California from 1864 to the Present.* Graphic Arts Center Publishing, 1980.

Epstein, Jack. "Raiding the Redwoods: How Junk Bonds Are Carving Up One of Our Last Timber Empires." *California Business* (September 1987).

Etcheverry, Alfred. *Irrigation Practice and Engineering: Conveyance of Water.* McGraw-Hill, 1915.

Evarts, John, and Marjorie Popper. *Coast Redwood: A Natural and Cultural History.* Cachuma Press, 2001.

Farmer, Jared. *Trees in Paradise: A California History.* W. W. Norton, 2013.

Fischer, Duane. "The Short, Unhappy Story of the Del Norte Company." *Forest History Newsletter* (April 1967).

Forbes, B. C. "Why Creed Puts Service Above Money-Making." *Forbes,* April 28, 1923.

Foreman, Dave. *Confessions of an Eco-Warrior.* Crown Trade Paperbacks, 1991.

Foreman, Dave. *Ecodefense: A Field Guide to Monkeywrenching.* Ned Ludd Books, 1985.

Forsyth, Suzanne. "Lucille Vinyard: A Voice for Redwoods and Wilderness." *Humboldt Historian* (fall 2009).

Fritsvold, Erik. "Under the Law: Legal Consciousness and Radical Environmental Activism." *Law & Social Inquiry* (fall 2009).

Fritz, Emanuel. *California Coast Redwood: An Annotated Bibliography*. Foundation for American Resource Management, 1957.

Frontier Moments from the Humboldt Historian. Humboldt County Historical Society, 1982.

Gannett, Henry. "The Redwood Forest of the Pacific Coast." *National Geographic* (May 1899).

Gates, Jon. *Falk's Claim: The Life and Death of a Redwood Lumber Town*. Pioneer Graphics, 1983.

Gates, Paul. *The Wisconsin Pine Lands of Cornell University: A Study in Land Policy and Absentee Ownership*. State Historical Society of Wisconsin, 1943.

Gibbons, William. "The Redwood in the Oakland Hills." *Erythea* (August 1893).

Gibbs, George. *Journal of Redick McKee's Expedition in Northwestern California*, 1851.

"Good Roads to National Parks." US Chamber of Commerce, 1916.

Gordon, Greg. *When Money Grew on Trees: A. B. Hammond and the Age of the Timber Baron*. University of Oklahoma Press, 2014.

Grant, Joseph. *Redwoods and Reminiscences*. Save the Redwoods League, 1973.

Grant, Madison. *Conquest of a Continent*. Charles Scribner's Sons, 1933.

Grant, Madison. *The Passing of the Great Race*. Charles Scribner's Sons, 1916.

Grant, Madison. "Saving the Redwoods." *National Geographic* (June 1920).

Grant, Madison. "Saving the Redwoods: An Account of the Movement During 1919 to Preserve the Redwoods of California." *New York Zoological Society Bulletin*, 1919.

Grosvenor, Melville. "World's Tallest Tree Discovered." *National Geographic* (July 1964).

Haas, Jeffrey. *The Assassination of Fred Hampton: How the FBI and the Chicago Police Murdered a Black Panther*. Lawrence Hill Books, 2010.

Hager, Stan. "In the Logging Woods." *Harper's* (October 1979).

Hamm, Lillie. *History and Business Directory of Humboldt County*, 1890.

Hammett, R. F. "An Interesting Talk on California Redwood." *New York Lumber Trade Journal*, August 1, 1921.

Hanrahan, Noelle. "America's Secret Police: FBI COINTELPRO in the 1990s." Redwood Summer Justice Project, April 1998.

Hansen, Harvey, et al. *Wild Oats in Eden: Sonoma County in the 19th Century*. N.p., 1962.

Harris, David. *The Last Stand: The War Between Wall Street and Main Street over California's Ancient Redwoods*. Times Books, 1995.

Hart, Tom. "Albert Etter: Humboldt County's Horticultural Genius." *Eden: Journal of the California Garden & Landscape Society* (winter 2021).

Hildebrand, J. R. "California's Coastal Redwood Realm." *National Geographic* (February 1939).

Hipp, Rudolph. "Humboldt Bay Sawmills." *Humboldt Historian* (May-June 1971).

History of Humboldt County, California. Wallace W. Elliot Co., 1881.

The Home of the Redwood. Pacific Coast Wood and Iron, 1897.

Hoopes, Chad. *Lure of the Humboldt Bay Region*. Wm. C. Brown Book Co., 1966.

Hoopes, Chad. "Redick McKee and the Humboldt Bay Region, 1851–1852." *California Historical Society Quarterly* (September 1970).

House, Freeman. *Totem Salmon: Life Lessons from Another Species*. Beacon Press, 1999.

Humboldt County Chamber of Commerce. "Annual Reports of Officers for 1918."

Hyde, Philip, and Francois Leydet. *The Last Redwoods*. Sierra Club Books, 1963.

Illustrated Atlas of Sonoma County California. Reynolds & Proctor, 1898.

Ingersoll, Ernest. "In a Redwood Logging Camp." *Harper's* (January 1883).

"An International Congress to Improve the Race." *Literary Digest*, August 17, 1912.

Irvine, Leigh. *History of Humboldt County, California*. Historic Record Company, 1915.

Irvine, Leigh. *The Playground of the West: What Humboldt County, California, Offers the Autoist and Sportsman*. Humboldt Promotion and Development Committee, 1913.

Ise, John. *The United States Forest Policy*. Yale University Press, 1920.

Isenberg, Andrew. *Mining California*. Macmillan, 2006.

Issel, William, and Robert Cherny. *San Francisco, 1865–1932: Politics, Power, and Urban Development*. University of California Press, 1986.

Jackson, Turrentine. *The Enterprising Scot: Investors in the American West After 1873*. Edinburgh University Press, 1968.

Jensen, Derrick, and George Draffan. *Railroads and Clearcuts: The Legacy of Congress's 1864 Northern Pacific Railroad Land Grant*. Koekee Company Publishing, 1995.

Johnstone, James, et al. "Climatic Context and Ecological Implications of Summer Fog Decline in the Coast Redwood Region." *Proceedings of the National Academy of Sciences*, 2010.

Johnstone, Peter, and Peter Palmquist. *Giants in the Earth: The California Redwoods*. Heyday Books, 2001.

Jones, Kathryn. "Charles Hurwitz Is a Greedy Clear-Cutter. Charles Hurwitz Is a Caring Environmentalist." *Texas Monthly* (June 1999).

Kane, Joe. "Mother Nature's Army: Guerrilla Warfare Comes to the American Forest." *Esquire* (February 1987).

King, Greg. "Another Tragedy at Headwaters." *Santa Rosa Press Democrat*, March 24, 1999.

King, Greg. "Fish and Game Halts PALCO Logging." *Humboldt News Service*, January 8, 1988.

King, Greg. "Fish and Game Says Pacific Lumber/CDF Eliminating Wildlife." *Humboldt News Service*, May 11, 1987.

King, Greg. "The Groves of Maxxam." *Country Activist* (September 1989).

King, Greg. "Headwaters Forest." *Berkeley Ecology Center Newsletter* (February 1990).

King, Greg. "Outside Agitator: How Darryl Cherney Set Out to Save the Redwoods and Ended Up Suing the FBI (and Winning)." *The Sun* (September 2002).

King, Greg. "PL Chips Away at Headwaters." *Sonoma County Independent*, January 1, 1994.

King, Greg. "Spurning Fish and Game, CDF Approves Logging." *Humboldt News Service*, March 16, 1988.

King, Greg. "There Has Never Been a 'Timber War.'" *Humboldt Journal of Social Relations* 40 (2018).

King, Greg. "Timber Summit Charade." *Santa Rosa Press Democrat*, February 8, 1988.

King, Greg. "Unprotected Redwoods." *Siskiyou Journal* (June/July 1987).

Kneiss, Gilbert. *Redwood Railways: A Story of Redwoods, Picnics and Commuters*. Howell-North, 1956.

Koester, Frank. *Hydroelectric Developments and Engineering*. D. Van Nostrand Company, 1915.

Lemonick, Michael. "Showdown in the Treetops." *Time*, August 28, 1989.

London, Jonathan. "Common Roots and Entangled Limbs: Earth First! and the Growth of Post-Wilderness Environmentalism on California's North Coast." *Antipode*, 1998.

Lorimer, Craig, et al. "Presettlement and Modern Disturbance Regimes in Coast Redwood Forests: Implications for the Conservation of Old-Growth Stands." *Forest Ecology and Management* 258 (September 2009).

Lundmark, Thomas. "Regulation of Private Logging in California." *Ecology Law Quarterly* (September 1975).

Lyons, Kathleen, and Mary Cuneo-Lazaneo. *Plants of the Coast Redwood Region.* Looking Press, 1988.

Madley, Benjamin. *An American Genocide: The United States and the California Indian Catastrophe.* Yale University Press, 2016.

Magliari, Michael. "Masters, Apprentices, and Kidnappers: Indian Servitude and Slave Trafficking in Humboldt County, California, 1860–1863." *California History* (summer 2020).

Manes, Christopher. *Green Rage: Radical Environmentalism and the Unmaking of Civilization.* Little Brown and Company, 1990.

Margolin, Malcolm. *The Ohlone Way: Indian Life in the San Francisco–Monterey Bay Area.* Heyday Books, 1978.

Mark, Stephen. *Preserving the Living Past: John C. Merriam's Legacy in the State and National Parks.* University of California Press, 2005.

Martien, Jerry. "Burl: Lesson Plans for a Redwood Forest." *Terrain,* January 14, 2022.

McCloskey, Michael. "Wilderness Movement at the Crossroads, 1945–1970." *Pacific Historical Review* (August 1972).

McCormick, Evelyn. *Living with the Giants: A History of the Arrival of Some of the Early Northwest Coast Settlers.* Self-published, 1984.

McKibben, Bill. "Milken, Junk Bonds and Raping Redwoods." *Rolling Stone,* August 10, 1989.

McKinney, Gage. "A. B. Hammond, West Coast Lumberman." *Journal of Forest History* (October 1984).

Melendy, H. Brett. "Two Men and a Mill: John Dolbeer, William Carson, and the Redwood Lumber Industry in California." *California History* (March 1959).

Merriam, John. "Forest Windows." *Scribner's Magazine* (June 1928).

Merriam, John. *The Garment of God: Influence of Nature in Human Experience.* Charles Scribner's Sons, 1943.

Merriam, John. *The Living Past.* Charles Scribner's Sons, 1926.

Miles, John. "The Redwood Park Question." *Forest History Newsletter* (April 1967).

Mills, Amy. "Headwaters: What's the Deal?" *Mother Jones* (May 1998).

Morgan, Judith and Neil Morgan. "Redwoods, Rain, and Lots of Room." *National Geographic* (September 1977).

"Mr. Wiggington [*sic*] Creed on Public Ownership." *Pacific Municipalities and Counties* (January 1920).

Myrick, David. "Rails Around the Bohemian Grove." Bohemian Club, 1973.

Nordhoff, Charles. "Northern California." *Harper's* (December 1873).

Norman, James. "A Takeover Artist Who's Turning Redwoods into Quick Cash." *Businessweek,* February 2, 1987.

Norton, Jack. *Genocide in Northwestern California.* Indian Historian Press, 1979.

Noss, Reed. *The Redwood Forest: History, Ecology, and Conservation of the Coast Redwoods.* Island Press, 2000.

O'Hara, Susan, and Alex Service. *Mills of Humboldt County.* Arcadia Publishing, 2016.

O'Hara, Susan, and Alex Service. *Mills of Humboldt County, 1910–1945.* Arcadia Publishing, 2018.

O'Hara, Susan, and Dave Stockton. *Humboldt Redwoods State Park.* Arcadia Publishing, 2012.

Old Growth in Crisis. North Coast California Earth First! (April 1987).

Ongerth, Steve. *Redwood Uprising,* 2010. Internet published.

Onstine, Frank, and Rachel Harris. *Organize! The Great Lumber Strike of Humboldt County,* *1935.* Lychgate Press, 2019.

Orsi, Richard. *Sunset Limited: The Southern Pacific Railroad and the Development of the American West, 1850–1930.* University of California Press, 2005.

Paine, Veeder. "Our Public Land Policy." *Harper's,* September 30, 1885.

Palais, Hyman, and Earl Roberts. "The History of the Lumber Industry in Humboldt County." *Pacific Historical Review* (February 1950).

Palmquist, Peter, and Charles Goodwin Noyes. *Redwood and Lumbering in California Forests.* Book Club of California, 1983. Edgar Cherry & Co., 1884.

Parfit, Michael. "Earth First!ers Wield a Mean Monkey Wrench." *Smithsonian* (April 1990).

Parish, Will. "DiFi and Blum: A Marriage Marinated in Money." *Counterpunch,* February 26, 2010.

Parmenter, Jon. "Flipped Scrip, Flipping the Script: The Morrill Act of 1862, Cornell University, and the Legacy of Nineteenth-Century Indigenous Dispossession." Cornell University, 2020.

Partridge, J. F. "Modern Practice in Wood State Pipe Design and Suggestions for Standard Specifications." *Transactions of the American Society of Civil Engineers,* May 16, 1917.

Pearsall, Clarence, et al. *The Quest for Qual-a-wa-loo (Humboldt Bay).* Holmes Book Co., 1943.

Pearson, Byron. "Newton Drury of the National Park Service: A Reappraisal." *Pacific Historical Review* (August 1999).

Pincetl, Stephanie. *Transforming California: A Political History of Land Use and Development.* John Hopkins University Press, 1999.

Platt, Anthony. "Engaging the Past: Charles M. Goethe, American Eugenics, and Sacramento State University." *Social Justice,* 2005.

Platt, Anthony, and Cecilia O'Leary. *Bloodlines: Recovering Hitler's Nuremberg Laws, from Patton's Trophy to Public Memorial.* Paradigm Publishers, 2006.

"Popularity of Redwood." *Salt Lake Mining Review,* March 15, 1917.

Powers, Richard, *The Overstory.* W. W. Norton, 2018.

Preston, Richard. *The Wild Trees.* Random House, 2007.

Purcell, Mae Fisher. *History of Contra Costa County.* Gallick Press, 1940.

Puter, S. A. D. *Looters of the Public Domain.* Portland Printing House, 1908.

Quam-Wickham, Nancy. "'Cities Sacrificed on the Altar of Oil': Popular Opposition to Oil Development in 1920s Los Angeles." *Environmental History* (April 1998).

Raphael, Ray, and Freeman House. *Two Peoples, One Place.* Humboldt County Historical Society, 2007.

"A Record of Financial and Commercial Achievement for Year 1913." *Financial Year Book of the Daily Commercial News.* San Francisco, 1914.

"Redwood Pressure Pipe." *Engineering World* (January 1921).

Raphael, Ray. *An Everyday History of Somewhere.* Knopf, 1974.

Raphael, Ray. "Back Country Economics." *Harper's* (January 1974).

Raphael, Ray. *Little White Father: Redick McKee on the California Frontier.* Humboldt County Historical Society, 1993.

Reed, Susan "Ecowarrior Dave Foreman Will Do Whatever It Takes in His Fight to Save Mother Earth." *People,* April 16, 1990.

Regal, Brian. "Madison Grant, Maxwell Perkins, and Eugenics Publishing at Scribner's." *Princeton University Library Chronicle* (winter 2004).

Reinhardt, Richard. "The Bohemian Club." *American Heritage* (June/July 1980).

Rhode, Paul. *The Evolution of California Manufacturing.* Public Policy Institute of California, 2001.

Rickard, T. A. *The Yukon Ditch.* Mining and Scientific Press, 1909.

Rinn, Daniel. "Deep Ecology in Humboldt County: Bill Devall and a Philosophy for Direct Action." *Left in the West.* University of Nevada Press, 2018.

Rohde, Jerry. *Both Sides of the Bluff.* MountainHome Books, 2014.

Rohde, Jerry. *Humboldt Bay Shoreline, North Eureka to South Arcata: A History of Cultural Influences.* Humboldt State University Press, 2021.

Rohde, Jerry. "Mid-May Morning at the Mill: Reflecting on the Cycle of Boom and Bust." *Humboldt Historian* (fall 2009).

Rohde, Jerry, and Gisela Rohde. *Humboldt Redwoods State Park: The Complete Guide.* Miles & Miles, 1992.

Rohde, Jerry, and Gisela Rohde. "Lumbermen and Land Fraud." *Humboldt Historian* (fall 2009).

Rohde, Jerry, and Gisela Rohde. *Redwood National and State Parks: Tales, Trails, and Auto Tours.* MountainHome Books, 1994.

Rowell, Andrew. *Green Backlash: Global Subversion of the Environmental Movement.* Routledge, 1996.

Russell, Will. "The Influence of Industrial Forest Management Interests on Forest Restoration and Carbon Sequestration Policy and Practice." *International Journal of Environmental, Cultural, Economic, and Social Sustainability,* 2010.

Russell, Will, et al. *Edge Effects and the Effective Size of Old-Growth Coast Redwood Preserves.* Vol. 3. US Forest Service Proceedings, 2000.

Russo, Michael. *Environmental Management.* Sage Publications, 2008.

Ryder, David. *Great Citizen: A Biography of William H. Crocker.* Historical Publications, 1962.

Ryder, David. *Memories of the Mendocino Coast.* Self-published, 1948.

San Francisco Chamber of Commerce. *Financial Year Book 1915.*

Save the Redwoods League. *The Once and Future Forest.* Heyday Books, 2018.

Scarce, Rik. *Eco-Warriors: Understanding the Radical Environmental Movement.* Noble Press, 1990.

Schrepfer, Susan. "Conflict in Preservation: The Sierra Club, Save-the-Redwoods League and Redwood National Park." *Journal of Forest History* (April 1980).

Schrepfer, Susan. "A Conservative Reform: Saving the Redwoods, 1917 to 1940." PhD diss., 1971.

Schrepfer, Susan. *The Fight to Save the Redwoods.* University of Wisconsin Press, 1983.

Schubert, John. *Guerneville Early Days.* Chapbook Press, 2016.

Schubert, John. *Tales of the Russian River: Stumptown Stories.* History Press, 2013.

Schultz, Ellen. "A Raider's Ruckus in the Redwoods." *Fortune,* April 24, 1989.

Scott, W. A. "Kerckhoff Hydroelectric Project in California." *Engineering World* (March 1921).

Scott, W. A. "Observations Relative to Wood-Stave Pipe." *Engineering World* (February 1921).

Scott, W. A. "Water Supply for Phoenix, Ariz." *Engineering World* (May 1921).

Shantz, Jeffrey. "The Judi Bari and Darryl Cherney Lawsuit Against the FBI and Oakland Police: A Landmark Victory." *Feminist Review,* 2003.

Shepherd, Marvin. *A Scottish Syndicate in the Redwoods: Monopoly and Fraud in the California Redwoods, 1882–1892.* Georgie Press, 2015.

Shirley, James. *The Redwoods of Coast and Sierra*. University of California Press, 1936.

Simons, Eric. "The Spine of California." *Bay Nature*, March 24, 2020.

Sinclair, Upton. *The Goose-Step: Study of American Education*. N.p., 1922.

Slack, Gordy. "In the Shadow of Giants: The Redwoods of the Oakland Hills." *Bay Nature* (July-September 2004).

Smith, B. J. "Falling and Bucking Redwood Timber." *Humboldt Historian* (November-December 1971).

Smith, Esther. *The History of Del Norte County, California*. Self-published, 1953.

Social Register, San Francisco, Including Oakland, 1916.

Speece, Darren. *Defending Giants: The Redwood Wars and the Transformation of American Environmental Politics*. University of Washington Press, 2017.

Speece, Darren. "From Corporatism to Citizen Oversight: The Legal Fight over California Redwoods, 1969–1999." *Journal of the California Supreme Court Historical Society*, 2018.

Spiro, Jonathan. *Defending the Master Race: Conservation, Eugenics, and the Legacy of Madison Grant*. University of Vermont Press, 2009.

St. Clair, Jeffrey, and Alexander Cockburn. "The Clinton Files: Those White House Coffee Klatches." *Counterpunch*, December 4, 2015.

Stegner, Wallace. "Wilderness Letter." *Sound of Mountain Water*, 1969.

Stern, Alexandra. *Eugenic Nation: Faults and Frontiers of Better Breeding in Modern America*. University of California Press, 2016.

Stock, Chester. "John Campbell Merriam: 1869–1945." National Academy of Sciences, 1951.

"The Story of the Golden Gate Bridge." Bay Bridges Educational Bureau, Inc. (brochure), 1936.

Swearingen, M. Wesley. *FBI Secrets: An Agent's Exposé*. South End Press, 1995.

Thornbury, Thomas. *California's Redwood Wonderland: Humboldt County*. Sunset Press, 1923.

Truitt, Shirley. "The Railroads That Make Up the Present Northwestern Pacific R. R." *Railway and Locomotive Historical Society Bulletin* (October 1932).

"Two Births 2000 Years ago: A Story of the Oldest Living Thing in the World." California Redwood Association (brochure), 1917.

"U.S. Playgrounds Are Valuable and Undeveloped Asset." *American Motorist* (January 1916).

Vale, Thomas. "Conservation Strategies in the Redwoods." *Yearbook of the Association of Pacific Coast Geographers*, 1974.

Walker, Richard. "California's Golden Road to Riches: Natural Resources and Regional Capitalism, 1848–1940." *Annals of the Association of American Geographers*, 2001.

Wallace, David Rains. *The Klamath Knot*. Sierra Club Books, 1983.

Walters, Mark. "California Chain-Saw Massacre." *Reader's Digest* (November 1989).

Wasserman, Laura and James Wasserman. *Who Saved the Redwoods? The Unsung Heroines of the 1920s Who Fought for Our Redwood Forests*. Algora Publishing, 2019.

Wayburn, Edgar. *Your Land and Mine: Evolution of a Conservationist*. Sierra Club Books, 2004.

Weiss, Marc. "Urban Land Developers and the Origins of Zoning Laws: The Case of Berkeley." *Berkeley Planning Journal* 3 (1986).

"What Forestry Can Do for the Redwoods." *Plant World* (November 1903).

White, John. "Among the Big Trees of California." *National Geographic* (August 1934).

White, Richard. "Information, Markets, and Corruption: Transcontinental Railroads in the Gilded Age." *Journal of American History* (June 2003).

White, Richard. *Railroaded: The Transcontinentals and the Making of Modern America.* W. W. Norton, 2011.

Whitman, James. *Hitler's American Model: The United States and the Making of Nazi Race Law.* Princeton University Press, 2017.

"Why America Must Not Wait for the Redwood National Park." Sierra Club (brochure), 1965.

Widick, Richard. *Trouble in the Forest: California's Redwood Timber Wars.* University of Minnesota Press, 2009.

Wilson, Nicholas. "Judi Bari (1949–1997)." *Albion Monitor* (March 1997).

Wilson, Nicholas. "The Judi Bari Bombing Revisited: Big Timber, Public Relations and the FBI." *Albion Monitor,* May 28, 1999.

Wilson, Nicholas. "Juror Talks About the Bari vs. FBI Trial." *Albion Monitor,* July 16, 2002.

Wilson, Simone. *The Russian River.* Arcadia Publishing, 2002.

"Wooden Stave Pipe Built by Redwood Manufacturers Co." (company brochure), 1911.

Zahl, Paul. "Finding the Mt. Everest of All Living Things." *National Geographic* (July 1964).

Zakin, Susan. *Coyotes and Town Dogs: Earth First! and the Environmental Movement.* Viking, 1993.

Ziegler, Victor. *Oil Well Drilling Methods.* John Wiley & Sons, Inc., 1923.

Unpublished Theses and Papers

Buck, Joshua. "Awfully Muddy, Precariously Ledged, and Going Nowhere in Particular: The Rise and Fall of the Northwestern Pacific Railroad." Cal Poly Humboldt, Arcata, 2018.

Emenaker, Ryan. "Corporations and Resistance in the Redwood Empire: Towards a Corporate History of Humboldt County (1579–1906)." Master's thesis. Cal Poly Humboldt, 2005.

Farnsworth, Kenneth. "Gyppo Logging in Humboldt County: A Boom-Bust Cycle on the California Forest Frontier." Master's thesis. Cal Poly Humboldt, 1996.

Jager, Douglas, and Richard LaVen. "Twenty Years of Rehabilitation Work in Bull Creek, Humboldt Redwoods State Park." Cal Poly Humboldt, 1985.

Jones, Alicia. "Seeing the Forest for the Redwood Trees: Understanding the Social Impacts of a Protected Area on a Local Community." Master's thesis. Cal Poly Humboldt, 2016.

Melendy, H. Brett. "One Hundred Years of the Redwood Lumber Industry, 1850–1950." PhD diss. Stanford University, May 1952.

Mengel, Lowell S., "A History of the Samoa Division of Louisiana-Pacific Corporation and Its Predecessors, 1853–1973." Manuscript. Special Collections. Cal Poly Humboldt, Arcata.

North Coast Timber Association. "Facts and Fiction About the Redwood Forests: Responsible Citizens Should Know Which Is Which." Paper, January 10, 1972.

Phillips, Peter. "A Relative Advantage: Sociology of the San Francisco Bohemian Club." PhD diss. University of California, Davis, 1994.

Wattenburger, Ralph. "The Redwood Lumber Industry on the Northern California Coast, 1850–1900." Master's thesis. University of California, Berkeley, 1935.

Yaryan, William. "Saving the Redwoods: The Ideology and Political Economy of Nature Preservation." PhD diss. University of California, Santa Cruz, June 2002.

INDEX

Greg King is an award-winning journalist and activist credited with spearheading the movement to protect Headwaters Forest, in Humboldt County, California. King initiated the "redwood wars" following the notorious 1985 takeover of the venerable Pacific Lumber Company by the Houston energy and real estate conglomerate Maxxam. Greg King has spent decades researching redwood logging and preservation efforts. King's articles and photographs have appeared in *The Sun, Sierra, Smithsonian, Rolling Stone, Newsweek, the Portland Oregonian, the Sacramento Bee, Mother Jones,* and other publications. In 2016 the Environmental Protection Information Center presented King with its annual Sempervirens Lifetime Achievement Award. King is founder and executive director of Siskiyou Land Conservancy, a land trust that serves Humboldt, Mendocino, and Del Norte counties. He lives in Humboldt County.

PublicAffairs is a publishing house founded in 1997. It is a tribute to the standards, values, and flair of three persons who have served as mentors to countless reporters, writers, editors, and book people of all kinds, including me.

I. F. STONE, proprietor of *I. F. Stone's Weekly*, combined a commitment to the First Amendment with entrepreneurial zeal and reporting skill and became one of the great independent journalists in American history. At the age of eighty, Izzy published *The Trial of Socrates*, which was a national bestseller. He wrote the book after he taught himself ancient Greek.

BENJAMIN C. BRADLEE was for nearly thirty years the charismatic editorial leader of *The Washington Post*. It was Ben who gave the *Post* the range and courage to pursue such historic issues as Watergate. He supported his reporters with a tenacity that made them fearless and it is no accident that so many became authors of influential, best-selling books.

ROBERT L. BERNSTEIN, the chief executive of Random House for more than a quarter century, guided one of the nation's premier publishing houses. Bob was personally responsible for many books of political dissent and argument that challenged tyranny around the globe. He is also the founder and longtime chair of Human Rights Watch, one of the most respected human rights organizations in the world.

  •   •   •

For fifty years, the banner of Public Affairs Press was carried by its owner Morris B. Schnapper, who published Gandhi, Nasser, Toynbee, Truman, and about 1,500 other authors. In 1983, Schnapper was described by *The Washington Post* as "a redoubtable gadfly." His legacy will endure in the books to come.

Peter Osnos, *Founder*